T0235753

Communications
in Computer and Information Science   427

More information about this series at http://www.springer.com/series/7899

Ali Movaghar · Mansour Jamzad
Hossein Asadi (Eds.)

Artificial Intelligence and Signal Processing

International Symposium, AISP 2013
Tehran, Iran, December 25–26, 2013
Revised Selected Papers

 Springer

Editors
Ali Movaghar
Mansour Jamzad
Hossein Asadi
Department of Computer Engineering
Sharif University of Technology
Tehran
Iran

ISSN 1865-0929   ISSN 1865-0937   (electronic)
ISBN 978-3-319-10848-3   ISBN 978-3-319-10849-0   (eBook)
DOI 10.1007/978-3-319-10849-0

Library of Congress Control Number: 2014949559

Springer Cham Heidelberg New York Dordrecht London

Printed on acid-free paper

Springer is part of Springer Science+Business Media (www.springer.com)

Preface

The Computer Society of Iran (CSI) and Sharif University of Technology (SUT) are proud that the 2013 International Symposium on Artificial Intelligence and Signal Processing (AISP 2013) was held on December 25–26, 2013 in the Department of Computer Engineering at Sharif University of Technology, Tehran, Iran.

AISP 2013 is a premier artificial intelligence and signal processing event that brings together industry professionals and academics to exchange information on recent advances in the fields of artificial intelligence, signal processing, and emerging applications. Papers presented in the symposium were mainly on general topics of artificial intelligence aspects, signal processing techniques, and emerging applications.

The total number of submissions were 106 among which only 33 papers were accepted for oral presentation. The acceptance rate was near 30 %. All papers were peer reviewed by at least two expert reviewers. A booklet containing paper abstracts and conference schedule was distributed to all participants during the conference. The conference was held with the help of professional organizers and all sessions were held according to the symposium schedule.

We take this opportunity to thank all our colleagues in the scientific committee and also all reviewers whose support was one of the main factors for success in this symposium. In addition, we extend our appreciation to all members of the symposium organizing committee, scientific societies, and also to those who financially supported the symposium.

We hope more papers would be submitted to AISP 2014 and consequently more papers would be accepted for presentation in broader fields of artificial intelligence and signal processing.

December 2013

Mansour Jamzad
Ali Movaghar
Hossein Asadi

AISP 2013 Organizers

Honorary Chair

Reza Roosta-Azad   Sharif University of Technology, Iran

General Chair

Ali Movaghar   Sharif University of Technology, Iran

Program Chair

Mansour Jamzad   Sharif University of Technology, Iran

Organizing Committee Chair

Jafar Habibi   Sharif University of Technology, Iran

Registration Chair

Abbas Heydarnoori   Sharif University of Technology, Iran

Workshop and Tutorial Chairs

Mohammad Izadi   Sharif University of Technology, Iran
Maziar Goudarzi   Sharif University of Technology, Iran

Publication Chair

Hossein Asadi   Sharif University of Technology, Iran

Local Arrangement Chair

Mohammad Ali Abam   Sharif University of Technology, Iran

Internet Chair

Hamid Zarrabi-Zadeh   Sharif University of Technology, Iran

Publicity Chair

Hossein Ajorloo   Sharif University of Technology, Iran

Organizing and Technical Committee

Hamid Haghshenas   Sharif University of Technology, Iran
Mohammad Salehe   Sharif University of Technology, Iran
Hamidreza Mahyar   Sharif University of Technology, Iran
Mohammadreza Tahzibi   Sharif University of Technology, Iran
Mostafa Kishani   Sharif University of Technology, Iran

Contents

Natural Language Processing

Systems and AI Applications

Robotics

Image Processing

Kernel Grouped Multivariate Discriminant Analysis for Hyperspectral Image Classification

Mostafa Borhani[(⊠)] and Hassan Ghassemian

Faculty of Electrical and Computer Engineering, Tarbiat Modares University,
Tehran, Iran
{m.borhani,ghassemi}@modares.ac.ir

Abstract. This paper proposes a grouping based technique of multivariate analysis, and it is extended to nonlinear kernel based version for hyperspectral image classification. Grouped multivariate analysis methods are presented in the Euclidean space and dot products are replaced by kernels in Hilbert space for nonlinear dimension reduction and data visualization. We show that the proposed kernel analysis method greatly enhances the classification performance. Experiments on Classification are presented based on Indian Pine real dataset collected from the 224-dimensional AVIRIS hyperspectral sensor, and the performance of proposed approach is investigated. Results show that the Kernel Grouped Multivariate discriminant Analysis (KGMVA) method is generally efficient to improve overall accuracy.

Keywords: Kernel methods · Kernel trick · Multivariate discriminate analysis · Hyperspectral images · Hyperdimentional data analysis · Grouping methods

1 Introduction

Hyperspectral sensors simultaneously capture hundreds of narrow and contiguous spectral images from a wide range of the electromagnetic spectrum, for instance, the AVIRIS hyperspectral sensor [1] has 224 spectral bands ranging from visible light to mid-infrared areas (0.4–2.5 m). Such numerous numbers of images implicatively lead to high dimensionality data, presenting several major challenges in image classification [2–6]. The dimensionality of input space strongly affects performance of many classification methods (e.g., the Hughes phenomenon [7]). This requires the careful design of primitive algorithms that are able to handle hundreds of such spectral images at the same time minimizing the effects from the "curse of dimensionality". Nonlinear methods [8–10], are less sensitive to the data's dimensionality [11] and have already shown superior performance in many machine learning applications. Recently, kernels have a lot of attention in remote-sensed multi/hyperspectral communities [11–16]. However, the full potential of kernels—such as developing customized kernels to integrate a priori domain knowledge—has not been fully explored.

This paper extend traditional linear feature extraction and dimension reduction techniques such as Principal Component Analysis (PCA), Partial Least Squares (PLS),

© Springer International Publishing Switzerland 2014
A. Movaghar et al. (Eds.): AISP 2013, CCIS 427, pp. 3–12, 2014.
DOI: 10.1007/978-3-319-10849-0_1

Orthogonal Partial Least Squares (OPLS), Canonical Correlation Analysis (CCA), NMF (Non-Negative Matrix Factorization) and Entropy Component Analysis (ECA) to kernel nonlinear grouped version. Several extensions (linear and non-linear) to solve common problems in hyper dimensional data analysis were implemented and compared in hyperspectral image classification.

We explore and analyze the most representative MVA approaches, Grouped MVA (GMVA) methods and kernel based discriminative feature reduction manners. We additionally studied recent methods to make kernel GMVA more suitable to real world applications, for hyper dimensional data sets. In such approaches, sparse and semi-supervised learning extensions have been successfully introduced for most of the models. Actually, reduction or selection of features that facilitate classification or regression cuts to the heart of semi-supervised classification. We have completed the panorama with challenging real applications with the classification of land-cover classes.

We continue the paper with an exploring the MVA to the Grouped MVA and then extend the Grouped MVA to the Kernel based Grouped MVA algorithms. Section 3 introduces some simulation of extensions that increase the applicability of Kernel Grouped MVA methods in real applications. Finally, we conclude the paper in Sect. 4 with some discussion.

2 Kernel Grouped Multivariate Analysis

In this section, we first propose the grouping approach and then we extend the linear Canonical Correlation Analysis to kernel based grouped CCA as a sample of kernel based Grouped MVA Methods such as Kernel Grouped Principal Component Analysis (KGPCA), Kernel Grouped Partial Least Squares (KGPLS), Kernel Grouped Orthogonal Partial Least Squares (KGOPLS), and Kernel Grouped Entropy Component Analysis (KGECA). Figure 1 shows the procedure scheme of a simple grouping approach.

For a given a set of observations $\{(x_i, y_i)\}_{i=1}^{n}$ the grouping algorithm first compute the mean (1) and covariance matrix (2) of entries, where T denotes the transpose of a vector.

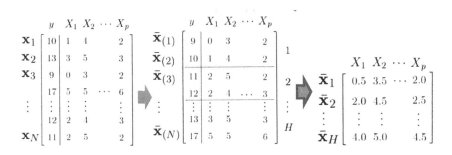

Fig. 1. Procedure scheme of a simple grouping approach

$$\bar{x} = \frac{\sum_{i=1}^{N} x_i}{N} \tag{1}$$

$$\hat{\Sigma}_x = \frac{1}{N} \sum_{i=1}^{N} (x_i - \bar{x})(x_i - \bar{x})^T \tag{2}$$

Then extended data set are sorted and collected in H groups. Then again, the procedure leads to compute the mean (3) and weighted covariance matrix (4) of grouped data when n_h is the number of elements in group h and H is the number of groups and N is the total number of elements.

$$\bar{x}_h = \frac{1}{n_h} \sum_{i=1}^{n_h} x_i \tag{3}$$

$$\hat{\Sigma}_W = \frac{n_h}{N} \sum_{h=1}^{H} (\bar{x}_h - \bar{x})(\bar{x}_h - \bar{x})^T \tag{4}$$

The last covariance is explored form the mean of groups and the total mean of elements, like Fisher discriminates analysis. The rest of algorithms are similar the conventional formulation and their extensions to nonlinear kernel based analysis. The use of unbiased covariance formula in (2) and (4) is straight forward.

Canonical Correlation Analysis is usually utilized for two underlying correlated data sets. Consider two iid sets of input data, x_1 and x_2. Classical CCA attempts to find the linear combination of the variables which maximize correlation between the collections. Let

$$y_1 = w_1 x_1 = \sum_j w_{1j} x_{1j} \tag{5}$$

$$y_2 = w_2 x_2 = \sum_j w_{2j} x_{2j} \tag{6}$$

The CCA solves problem of finding values of w_1 and w_2 which maximize the correlation between y_1 and y_2, with constrain the solutions to ensure a finite solution.

Let x_1 have mean μ_1, x_2 have mean μ_2 and $\hat{\Sigma}_{11}, \hat{\Sigma}_{22}, \hat{\Sigma}_{12}$ are denotation of autocovariance of x_1, autocovariance of x_2 and covariance of x_1 and x_2. Then the standard statistical method lies in defining (7). Grouped CCA uses the (4) for computing the covariance of grouped data and K is calculated as (8).

$$K = \hat{\Sigma}_{11}^{-\frac{1}{2}} \hat{\Sigma}_{12} \hat{\Sigma}_{22}^{-\frac{1}{2}} \tag{7}$$

$$K = \sum_{\hat{W11}}^{-\frac{1}{2}} \sum_{\hat{W12}} \sum_{\hat{W22}}^{-\frac{1}{2}} \tag{8}$$

GCCA then performs a Singular Value Decomposition of K to get

$$K = (\alpha_1, \alpha_2, \ldots, \alpha_k) D(\beta_1, \beta_2, \ldots, \beta_k)^T \tag{9}$$

where α_i and β_i are the eigenvectors of Karush–Kuhn–Tucker (KKT) conditions and Tucker-Karush (KTK) conditions respectively and D is the diagonal matrix of eigenvalues.

The first canonical correlation vectors are given by (10) and (11) and in Grouped CCA the canonical correlation vectors are derived from (12) and (13).

$$w_1 = \sum_{\hat{11}}^{-\frac{1}{2}} \alpha_1 \tag{10}$$

$$w_2 = \sum_{\hat{22}}^{-\frac{1}{2}} \beta_1 \tag{11}$$

$$w_1 = \sum_{\hat{W11}}^{-\frac{1}{2}} \alpha_1 \tag{12}$$

$$w_2 = \sum_{\hat{W22}}^{-\frac{1}{2}} \beta_1 \tag{13}$$

As an extension of Grouped CCA, the data were transformed to the feature space by nonlinear kernel methods. Kernel methods are a recent innovation predicated on the methods developed for Support Vector Machines [9, 10]. Support Vector Classification (SVC) performs a nonlinear mapping of the data set into some high dimensional feature space. The most common unsupervised kernel method to date has been Kernel Principal Component Analysis [18, 19]. Consider mapping the input data to a high dimensional (perhaps infinite dimensional) feature space. Now the covariance matrices in Feature space are defined by (14) for i = 1, 2 and covariance matrices of grouped data are by (15) where $\Phi(.)$ is the nonlinear one-to-one and onto function.

$$\sum_{\hat{\Phi ij}} = \frac{1}{N} \sum_{i=1}^{N} (\Phi(x_i) - \Phi(\bar{x}))(\Phi(x_j) - \Phi(\bar{x}))^T \tag{14}$$

$$\sum_{\hat{W\Phi ij}} = \frac{n_h}{N} \sum_{h=1}^{H} (\Phi(\bar{x}_{ih}) - \Phi(\bar{x}))(\Phi(\bar{x}_{jh}) - \Phi(\bar{x}))^T \tag{15}$$

However the kernel methods adopt a different approach. w_1 and w_2 exist in the feature space and therefore can be expressed as

$$w_1 = \sum_{i=1}^{2} \sum_{j=1}^{M} \alpha_{ij} \Phi(x_{ij}) \tag{16}$$

$$w_2 = \sum_{i=1}^{2} \sum_{j=1}^{M} \beta_{ij} \Phi(x_{ij}) \tag{17}$$

where α_i and β_i are the eigenvectors of SVD of $K = \hat{\Sigma}_{\Phi 11}^{-\frac{1}{2}} \hat{\Sigma}_{\Phi 12} \hat{\Sigma}_{\Phi 22}^{-\frac{1}{2}}$ Karush–Kuhn–Tucker conditions and Tucker-Karush conditions respectively for KCCA and α_i and β_i are the eigenvectors of SVD of $K = \hat{\Sigma}_{W\Phi 11}^{-\frac{1}{2}} \hat{\Sigma}_{W\Phi 12} \hat{\Sigma}_{W\Phi 22}^{-\frac{1}{2}}$ KKT and KTK conditions respectively for KGCCA where $K = (\alpha_1, \alpha_2, \ldots, \alpha_k) D (\beta_1, \beta_2, \ldots, \beta_k)^T$ and D is the diagonal matrix of eigenvalues. The rest of Kernel Grouped CCA procedure is similar to KCCA method.

This paper implements several MVA methods such as PCA, PLS, CCA, OPLS, MNF and ECA in linear, kernel and kernel grouped manners. Tables 1, 2 and 3 are summarizing maximization target, Constraints and number of feature of different methods for linear, kernel and kernel grouped approaches where $r(A)$ returns the rank of the matrix A.

Figure 2 shows the projections obtained in the toy problem by linear and modified kernel based MVA methods. Input data was normalized to zero mean and unit variance. Figure 2 shows the features extracted by different MVA methods [20] in an artificial

Table 1. Summary of linear MVA methods

Method	PCA	PLS	CCA	OPLS
Maximize	$u^T C_x u$	$u^T C_{xy} v$	$u^T C_{xy} v$	$u^T C_{xy} C_{xy}^T u$
Constraint	$U^T U = 1$	$U^T U = 1$	$U^T C_x U = 1$	$U^T C_x U = 1$
		$V^T V = 1$	$V^T C_y V = 1$	
# features	$r(X)$	$r(X)$	$r(C_{xy})$	$r(C_{xy})$

Table 2. Summary of kernel MVA methods

Method	KPCA	KPLS	KCCA	KOPLS
Maximize	$\alpha^T T_{\Phi x}^2 \alpha$	$\alpha^T T_{\Phi xy} Y v$	$U^T C_{\Phi xy} V$	$U^T C_{\Phi xy} C_{\Phi xy}^T U$
Constraint	$A^T T_{\Phi x}^2 A = 1$	$A^T T_{\Phi x} A = 1$	$A^T T_{\Phi x}^2 A = 1$	$A^T T_{\Phi x}^2 A = 1$
		$V^T V = 1$	$V^T C_{\Phi y} V = 1$	
# features	$r(K_{\Phi x})$	$r(K_{\Phi x})$	$r(K_x Y)$	$r(K_{\Phi x} Y)$

Table 3. Summary of kernel grouped MVA methods

Method	KGPCA	KGPLS	KGCCA	KGOPLS
Maximize	$\alpha^T T_{W\Phi x}^2 \alpha$	$\alpha^T T_{W\Phi xy} Y v$	$U^T C_{W\Phi xy} V$	$U^T C_{W\Phi xy} C_{W\Phi xy}^T U$
Constraint	$A^T T_{W\Phi x}^2 A = 1$	$A^T T_{W\Phi x} A = 1$	$A^T T_{W\Phi x}^2 A = 1$	$A^T T_{W\Phi x}^2 A = 1$
		$V^T V = 1$	$V^T C_{\Phi y} V = 1$	
# features	$r(K_{W\Phi x})$	$r(K_{W\Phi x})$	$r(K_{W\Phi x} Y)$	$r(K_{W\Phi x} Y)$

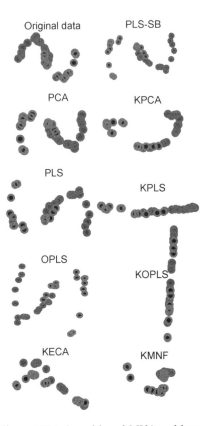

Fig. 2. Score of various linear MVA, kernel based MVA and kernel grouped MVA methods

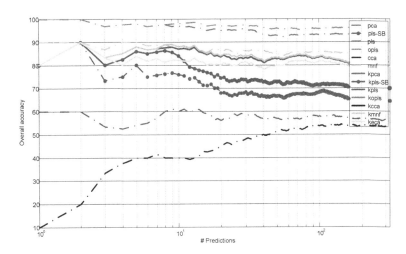

Fig. 3. Feature extraction methods: PCA, PLS, OPLS, CCA, MNF, KGPCA, KGPLS, KGOPLS, KGCCA, KGMNF and KGECA, Train Sample = 16

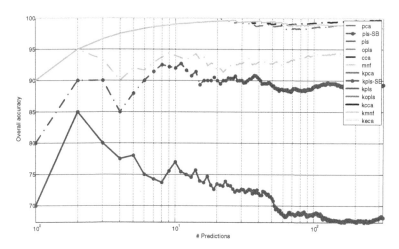

Fig. 4. Feature extraction methods: PCA, PLS, OPLS, CCA, MNF, KGPCA, KGPLS, KGOPLS, KGCCA, KGMNF and KGECA, Train Sample = 144

two-class problem using the RBF kernel. Table 1 provides a summary of the MVA methods and Tables 2 and 3 summarized the kernel MVA and KGMVA methods. For each method it is stated the objective to maximize (First row), constraints for the optimization (second row), and maximum number of features (last row).

3 Experimental Results

Following the kernel grouped dimension reduction schemes proposed in Sect. 2, the performance of the KGMVA methods is compared with a standard SVM with no feature reduction kernel, on AVIRIS dataset. False color composition of the AVIRIS Indian Pines scene and Ground truth-map containing 16 mutually exclusive land-cover classes are showed in Fig. 5.

The AVIRIS hyperspectral dataset is illustrative of the problem of hyperspectral image analysis to determine land use. However the AVIRIS sensor collects nominally 224 bands (or images) of data, four of these contain only zeros and so are discarded, leaving 220 bands in the 92AV3C dataset. At special frequencies, the spectral images are kenned to be adversely affected by atmospheric dihydrogen monoxide absorption. This affects some 20 bands. Each image is of size 145*145 pixels. The dataset was collected over a test site called Indian Pine in north-western Indiana [1]. The database is accompanied by a reference map; signify partial ground truth, whereby pixels are labeled as belonging to one of 16 classes of vegetation or other land types. Not all pixels are so labeled, presumably because they correspond to uninteresting regions or were too arduous to label. Here, we concentrate on the performance of kernel based grouped MVA methods for classification of hyperspectral images. Experimental results are showed in Figs. 3 and 4, for various numbers of train samples and for supervise and unsupervised methods. We use class 2 and 3 for data samples.

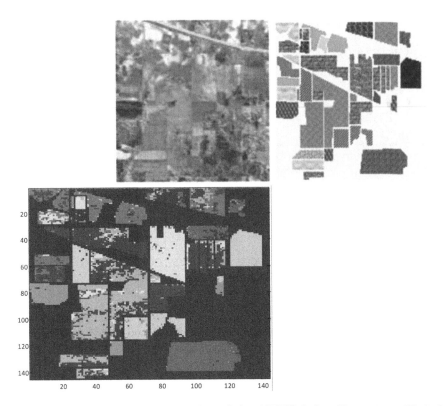

Fig. 5. (Up-Right) False color composition of the AVIRIS Indian Pines scene. (Up-Left) Ground truth-map containing 16 mutually exclusive land-cover classes, (Down-Right) standard SVM, average accuracy = 72.93 % and (Down-Left) SVM with kernel grouped MVA, average accuracy = 79.97, for 64 train samples, 10 classes.

Overall accuracy as a performance measure is depicted v.s. number of prediction for various feature extraction methods such PCA, PLS, OPLS, CCA, MNF, KGPCA, KGPLS, KGOPLS, KGCCA, KGMNF and KGECA. Simulations were repeated for 16 train samples and 144 train samples. Figure 6 shows the average accuracy of different classification approaches, Indiana dataset.

Classification among the major classes can be very difficult [21], which has made the scene a challenging benchmark to validate classification precision of hyperspectral imaging algorithms. Simulations results verified that utilizing the proposed techniques improve the overall accuracy especially kernel grouped CCA in spite of CCA.

4   Discussions and Conclusions

Feature extraction and dimensionality reduction are dominant tasks in many fields of science dealing with signal processing and analysis. This paper provides a kernel based grouped MVA methods. To illustrate the wide applicability of these methods in

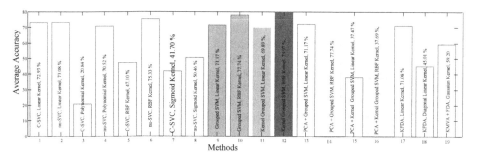

Fig. 6. Average accuracy of different classification approaches, Indiana dataset, 10 classes, 64 train samples. 1. C-SVC, Linear Kernel, 72.93 %, 2. nu-SVC, Linear Kernel, 73.08 %, 3. C-SVC, Polynomial Kernel, 20.84 %, 4. nu-SVC, Polynomial Kernel, 70.52 %, 5. C-SVC, RBF Kernel, 47.10 %, 6. nu-SVC, RBF Kernel, 75.33 %, 7. C-SVC, Sigmoid Kernel, 41.70 %, 8. nu-SVC, Sigmoid Kernel, 50.46 %, 9. Grouped SVM, Linear Kernel, 71.17 %, 10. Grouped SVM, RBF Kernel, 77.74 %, 11. Kernel Grouped SVM, Linear Kernel, 69.89 %, 12. Kernel Grouped SVM, RBF Kernel, 79.97 %, 13. PCA + Grouped SVM, Linear Kernel, 71.17 %, 14. PCA + Grouped SVM, RBF Kernel, 77.74 %, 15. PCA + Kernel Grouped SVM, Linear Kernel, 37.47 %, 16. PCA + Kernel Grouped SVM, RBF Kernel, 37.69 %, 17. KFDA, Linear Kernel, 71.08 %, 18. KFDA, Diagonal Linear Kernel, 45.01 %, 19. KMVA + FDA, Gaussian Kernel, 59.20 %

classification program, we analyze their performance in a benchmark of general available data set, and pay special attention to real applications involving hyperspectral satellite images. In this paper, we have proposed an novel dimension reduction methods for hyperspectral image utilizing kernels and grouping methods. Experimental results showed that, at least for the AVIRIS dataset, the classification performance can be improve to some extent by utilizing either kernel grouped canonical correlation analysis or kernel grouped entropy component analysis. Further work could explore the possibility of localizing grouped of analysis and exploring the algorithms on multiclass datasets. The KGMVA methods were shown to find correlations greater than could be found by linear MVA and also kernel based MVA. However the kernel grouping approach seems to offer a new means of finding such nonlinear and non-stationary correlations and one which is very promising for future research.

References

1. Airborne Visible/Infrared Imaging Spectrometer, AVIRIS. http://aviris.jpl.nasa.gov/
2. Landgrebe, D.: Hyperspectral image data analysis. IEEE Signal Process. Mag. **19**(1), 17–28 (2002). doi:10.1109/79.974718
3. Landgrebe, D.: On information extraction principles for hyperspectral data: a white paper. Technical report, School Electrical and Computer Engineering, Purdue University, West Lafayette, IN 47907-1285 (1997). https://engineering.purdue.edu/~landgreb/whitepaper.pdf
4. Yu, X., Hoff, L.E., Reed, I.S., Chen, A.M., Stotts, L.B.: Automatic target detection and recognition in multiband imagery: a unified ML detection and estimation approach. IEEE Trans. Image Process. **6**(1), 143–156 (1997). doi:10.1109/83.552103

5. Schweizer, S.M., Moura, J.M.F.: Efficient detection in hyperspectral imagery. IEEE Trans. Image Process. **10**(4), 584–597 (2001). doi:10.1109/83.913593

6. Shaw, G., Manolakis, D.: Signal processing for hyperspectral image exploitation. IEEE Signal Process. Mag. **19**(1), 12–16 (2002). doi:10.1109/79.974715

7. Hughes, G.: On the mean accuracy of statistical pattern recognizers. IEEE Trans. Inf. Theor. **14**(1), 55–63 (1968). doi:10.1109/TIT.1968.1054102

8. Boser, B.E., Guyon, I.M., Vapnik, V.N.: A training algorithm for optimal margin classifiers. In: 5th Annual Workshop on Computational Learning Theory, Pittsburgh, PA, pp. 144–152, (1992). doi:10.1.1.21.3818

9. Cortes, C., Vapnik, V.N.: Support-vector networks. Mach. Learn. **20**(3), 273–297 (1995). doi:10.1023/A:1022627411411

10. Burges, C.: A tutorial on support vector machines for pattern recognition. Data Min. Knowl. Disc. **2**(2), 121–167 (1998). doi:10.1023/A:1009715923555

11. Camps-Valls, G., Bruzzone, L.: Kernel-based methods for hyperspectral image classification. IEEE Trans. Geosci. Remote Sens. **43**(6), 1351–1362 (2005). doi:10.1109/TGRS.2005.846154

12. Gualtieri, J., Cromp, R.: Support vector machines for hyperspectral remote sensing classification. In: 27th AIPR Workshop Advances in Computer Assisted Recognition, Washington, DC, pp. 121–132 (1998). doi:10.1.1.27.838

13. Brown, M., Lewis, H.G., Gunn, S.R.: Linear spectral mixture models and support vector machines for remote sensing. IEEE Trans. Geosci. Remote Sens. **38**(5), 2346–2360 (2000). doi:10.1109/36.868891

14. Roli, F., Fumera, G., Serpico, S.B. (ed.) Support vector machines for remote-sensing image classification. In: Proceedings of SPIE Image and Signal Processing for Remote Sensing VI, vol. 4170, pp. 160–166 (2001). doi:10.1.1.11.5830

15. Lennon, M., Mercier, G., Hubert-Moy, L.: Classification of hyperspectral images with nonlinear filtering and support vector machines. In: IEEE International Geoscience and Remote Sensing Symposium 2002, IGARSS'02, 24–28 June 2002, vol. 3, pp. 1670–1672 (2002). doi:10.1109/IGARSS.2002.1026216

16. Melgani, F., Bruzzone, L.: Classification of hyperspectral remote sensing images with support vector machines. IEEE Trans. Geosci. Remote Sens. **42**(8), 1778–1790 (2004). doi:10.1109/TGRS.2004.831865

17. Mardia, K.V., Kent, J.T., Bibby, J.M.: Multivariate Analysis, 1st edn. Academic Press, New York (1980). ISBN 10: 0124712525, 13: 978-0124712522

18. Scholokopf, B., Smola, A., Muller, K.-R.: Nonlinear component analysis as a kernel eigenvalue problem. Technical report 44, Max Planck Institute fur biologische Kybernetik, December 1996. doi:10.1.1.29.1366

19. Scholokopf, B., Smola, A., Muller, K.-R.: Nonlinear component analysis as a kernel eigenvalue problem. Neural Comput. **10**, 1299–1319 (1998)

20. Arenas-Garcia, J., Petersen, K., Camps-Valls, G., Hansen, L.K.: Kernel multivariate analysis framework for supervised subspace learning: a tutorial on linear and kernel multivariate methods. IEEE Signal Process. Mag. **30**(4), 16–29 (2013). doi:10.1109/MSP.2013.2250591

21. M. Borhani, H. Ghassemian, Novel Spatial Approaches for Classification of Hyperspectral Remotely Sensed Landscapes, Symposium on Artificial Intelligence and Signal Processing, December 2013

Robust Zero Watermarking for Still and Similar Images Using a Learning Based Contour Detection

Shahryar Ehsaee and Mansour Jamzad[(✉)]

Department of Computer Engineering,
Sharif University of Technology, Tehran, Iran
Ehsaee@ce.sharif.edu, jamzad@sharif.edu

Abstract. Digital watermarking is an efficacious technique to protect the copyright and ownership of digital information. Traditional image watermarking algorithms embed a logo in the image that reduces its visual quality. A new approach in watermarking called zero watermarking doesn't need to embed a logo in the image. In this algorithm we find a feature from the main image and combine it with a logo to obtain a key. This key is securely kept by a trusted authority. In this paper we show that we can increase the robustness of digital zero watermarking by a new counter detection method in comparison to Canny Edge detection and morphological dilatation that is mostly used by related works. Experimental results demonstrate that our proposed scheme is robust against common geometric and non-geometric attacks including blurring, JPEG compression, noise addition, Sharpening, scaling, rotation, and cropping. The main advantage of the proposed method is its ability to distinguishable key for images taken from the same scene with small angular rotation and minor displacement.

Keywords: Zero-watermarking · Copyright protection · Canny edge detection · Counters detection · Hierarchical Image Segmentation

1 Introduction

Digital watermarking is an efficient technique to protect the copyright and ownership of digital information. In the traditional methods of image watermarking, the Information of original image will be distorted by means of embedding the watermark in the image. Most watermarking methods, no matter in spatial domain or frequency domain, modify the original data while embedding the watermark.

A new watermarking approach named zero watermarking is proposed to watermark the image by not actually apply any modification in the image. Zero-watermarking is different from traditional digital image watermarking, which constructs a key (secret data) from the watermark and the information extracted from the image. This key is securely saved in a trusted authority.

In Zero-watermarking a set of features expressed as binary data are extracted from the image XOR ed with the watermark (logo) and a key is produced. This key is kept in a trusted Authority (TA). Zero-watermarking can successfully solve the conflict between invisibility and robustness. In this paper we first show that we can reach higher

© Springer International Publishing Switzerland 2014
A. Movaghar et al. (Eds.): AISP 2013, CCIS 427, pp. 13–22, 2014.
DOI: 10.1007/978-3-319-10849-0_2

robustness with the new learning based counter detection method then we compare the results with Canny edge detection method. Also we show that with this learning based counter detection method we can reach good results for the image taken from different point of views.

The aim of this work is to watermark these images so that their identity could be distinguishable although they are very similar. In this paper we first show that by using new learning based contour detection method we can rich higher robustness compared with traditional Canny edge detector mostly used by related works. And also we show that with this contour detection method we can reach good results for the image taken from different point of views from the same scene.

2 Previous Works

2.1 Canny Edge Detection Method

Canny edge detection method due its high performance and flexibility is used in many applications. Its high performance in zero-watermarking has been shown in several related works. In this work we show that the new Learning based detection method that will be explained in the following has a better performance compared with Canny.

Zero watermarking with Canny edge detection has two main steps:

- **Image Registration:**
  We apply Canny edge detector to the image to obtain an edge image.

$$E_o = \text{CannyEdge} \left(\text{o}, [T_H, T_L], \sigma \right) \tag{1}$$

o is the main image and T_H and T_L are the low and high thresholds. σ is the standard derivation for Canny edge detector. It is explained in [1] to how to choose these values for results.

After applying Canny edge detection in input image morphological dilatation with radius disk of size 3 is used because the edges that are obtained from previous step are very thin.

$$E_{od} = \text{Dilation} \left(E_o, \text{disk}, 3 \right). \tag{2}$$

Then the logo is permuted and XOR ed with the E_{od} and a key is produced. Figure 1 shows the steps:
- **Verification procedure:** In this step the logo is retrieved without using the main image.
  We first get the key from the Trusted Authority. Canny edge detection is used to extracting the binary feature from the attacked image. A dilation operation with radius disk of size 3, as a structuring element is used to thicken the edge width of the binary feature. Then this image is XOR ed with the key taken from the trusted Authority(TA) to extract the logo. Finally, the verifier can visually verify the accuracy of retrieved logo and validate the ownership of the test image. Figure 2 shows the steps of verification procedure.

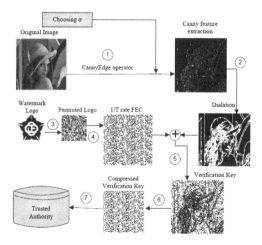

Fig. 1. Image registration steps using canny edge detector [1]

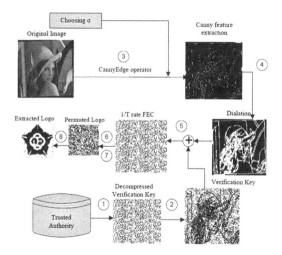

Fig. 2. Verification Procedure using canny edge detector [1]

3   Learning Based Contour Detection and Hierarchical Image Segmentation [2]

This is a unified approach to contour detection and image segmentation. Contributions include:

- A high performance contour detector, combining local and global image information.
- A method to transform any contour signal into a hierarchy of regions while preserving contour quality.

Early approaches to contour detection, through local measurements, aim at quantifying the presence of a boundary at a given image location. The Roberts, Sobel, and Prewitt operators detect edges by convolving a grayscale image with local derivative filters. Marr and Hildreth use zero crossings of the Laplacian of Gaussian operator. The Canny detector also models edges as sharp discontinuities in the brightness channel, adding non-maximum suppression and hysteresis thresholding steps [3].

3.1   Learning Based Contour Detection

As a starting point for contour detection, we consider the work of Martin et al. [4], who define a function Pb(x, y, Θ) that predicts the posterior probability of a boundary with orientation Θ at each image pixel (x; y) by measuring the difference in local image brightness, color, and texture channels. In this section, we review these cues, and then introduce the multi-scale version of the Pb detector. The basic building block of the Pb contour detector is the computation of an oriented gradient signal G(x, y, Θ) from an intensity image I. This computation proceeds by placing a circular disc at location (x, y) split into two half-discs by a diameter at angle Θ. For each half-disc, we histogram the intensity values of the pixels of I covered by it. The gradient magnitude G at location (x, y) is defined by the χ^2 distance between the two half-disc histograms g and h:

$$\chi^2(g,h) = \frac{1}{2} \sum \frac{(g(i) - h(i))^2}{(g(i) + h(i))} \tag{3}$$

We then apply second-order Savitzky-Golay filtering [5] to enhance local maxima and smooth out multiple detection peaks in the direction orthogonal to Θ. This is equivalent to fitting a cylindrical parabola, whose axis is orientated along direction Θ, to a local 2D window surrounding each pixel and replacing the response at the pixel with that estimated by the fitting a cylindrical parabola.

Figure 3 shows an example. This computation is motivated by the intuition that contours correspond to image discontinuities and a histograms provide a robust

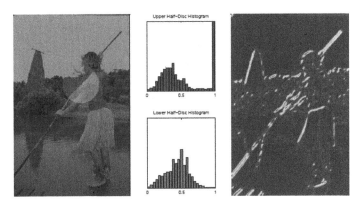

Fig. 3. Oriented gradients and their histograms

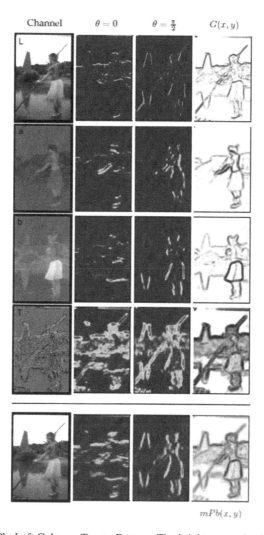

Fig. 4. Multiscale Pb. Left Column, Top to Bottom: The brightness and color a and b channels of Lab color space, Rows: Next to each channel, we display the oriented gradient of histograms

mechanism for modeling the content of an image region. A strong oriented gradient response means a pixel is likely to lie on the boundary between two distinct regions. The Pb detector combines the oriented gradient signals obtained from transforming an input image into four separate feature channels and processing each channel independently. The first three correspond to the channels of the CIE Lab colorspace, which we refer to as the brightness, color a, and color b channels. For grayscale images, the brightness channel is the image itself and no color channels are used. The fourth channel is a texture channel, which assigns each pixel a texton id. These assignments are computed by another filtering stage which occurs prior to the computation of the oriented gradient of histograms. This stage converts the input image to grayscale and convolves it with the set of 17 Gaussian derivatives and center-surround filters. Each pixel is associated with a (17-dimensional) vector of responses, containing one entry for each filter. These vectors are then clustered using K-means. The cluster centers define a set of image-specific textons and each pixel is assigned an integer id in [1; K] of the closest cluster center. Experiments show choosing K = 32 textons is sufficient. We next form an image where each pixel has an integer value in [1, K], as determined by its texton id. An example can be seen in Fig. 4 (left column, fourth panel from top). On this image, we compute differences of histograms in oriented half-discs in the same manner as for the brightness and color channels. Obtaining G(x, y, Θ) for arbitrary input I is thus the core operation on which our local cues depend.

Figure 5 compares this new contour detection with other edge and contour detection methods.

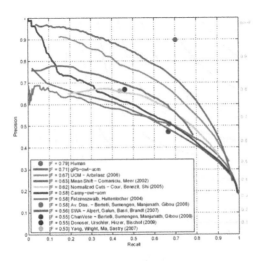

Fig. 5. Evaluation of segmentation algorithms on the BSDS300 Benchmark [2]

4   Results of Applying Canny Edge Detection and Learning Based Contour Detection Method

We should choose σ according to the complexity of the image to get the best result and we calculate the σ according to [1].

We use the same test image and binary logo as [6, 7] in our experiments for better comparison. Lena is of size 512 × 512 and the binary watermark logo is of size 64 × 64 as shown in Fig. 6.

We evaluate the quality between original image O and the attacked image $\acute{O}$ by using PSNR. We use normalized cross correlation (NC) to evaluate the correctness of an extracted watermark (Tables 1 and 2).

As we can see the new learning based contour detection method increases the robustness especially in Quarter Cropping and rotation attack.

Fig. 6. (a) Test image Lena (b) Binary watermark logo

Table 1. PSNR and NC using Canny edge detector

	Rotation	Quarter Cropping	Sharpening	JPEG	Adding noise	Blurring
Attacked image						
PSNR(db)	11	10.23	23.1	30.9	17.2	33.1
Retrieved logo						
NC	.95	.83	.94	.99	.93	.97

Table 2. PSNR and NC using learning based contour detection

	Rotation	Quarter Cropping	Sharpening	JPEG	Adding noise	Blurring
Attacked image						
PSNR(db)	11	10.23	23.1	30.9	17.2	33.1
Retrieved logo						
NC	.99	.94	.95	.99	.98	.99

5 Watermark Similar Images

Suppose that some people are taking picture from the same scene at the same time. These pictures are very similar to each other so when we zero watermark these pictures the produced key are very similar to each which might cause difficulties in ownership protection. The purpose is to find a feature that makes a key distinguishable so that the ownership can be protected.

As described in above the new learning based contour detection method has good results in images that are taken from different point of views. The purpose is to find distinct features from these images so that they could be watermarked without having problem in the ownership of the images. The feature that we used should be good enough to have different results in images that are taken from different point of view in the same scene. We want to show that the new learning based contour detection method has a much better results in these kinds of images than Canny edge detector that is mostly used for finding features in zero watermarking.

Since there is no databases for the images that are taken from different point of views we created one such database. We set a camera on a Tripod. There is a moving graded circular plate below this tripod so that we can move the plate and take picture from different angles.

Figure 7 show some images from our database. The image angles differ from each other by 5°. The first picture is at center of the plate (angle 0). Then we move the plate 5° to the right and take a picture, we move it by another 5° and take another picture, etc. We use the same procedure for the left side.

This database has 9 classes. In each class there are 5 pictures. The difference between these classes is that we move the camera set 10 cm to the left or right and then take 5 pictures at that new location as we explained above.

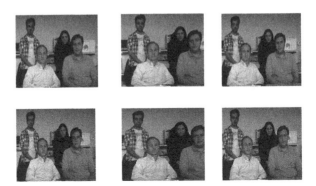

Fig. 7. Image samples from the database taken from different angle view

5.1 How It Works

At the first step we apply the learning based contour detection method to our databases. Since now we have binary features for our images that are XOR ed with a logo for each image. As a result a key produced which is compared to show how the watermarks in these images are similar to each other. We use the first image in the first class of our 9 class as a base image to compare the keys. We use the NC to estimate the numbers of bits that are the same in the keys. Less similar results are better. Because we can understand that these keys are more distinguishable.

In Tables 3 and 4 we show the results (NC value) obtained using Canny edge detector and the learning based contour detection method.

Table 3. Results (NC value) of watermarking similar images using Canny edge detector

	Image1	Image2	Image3	Image4	Image5
Class1	1000	764.2136	727.7222	737.3734	726.2726
Class2	724.9756	719.6732	766.8381	725.9140	725.5478
Class3	749.3134	738.4567	759.4910	738.9069	727.9663
Class4	736.0458	722.4731	721.8933	738.5483	723.0148
Class5	713.9587	712.1658	752.9984	697.1283	697.1283
Class6	731.6208	772.3083	726.3184	752.6398	749.7482
Class7	712.6617	734.4589	734.4589	718.5593	766.6092
Class8	709.0378	714.8819	757.3166	760.2081	747.6501
Class9	714.3097	698.6084	755.5542	733.3374	744.4916

Table 4. Results (NC value) of watermarking similar images using learning based contour detection method

	Image1	Image2	Image3	Image4	Image5
Class1	1000	432.7698	398.1400	403.2669	460.4950
Class2	397.1481	436.9812	426.3077	450.9888	459.3430
Class3	403.2593	421.0587	405.1895	395.3934	442.0547
Class4	436.0123	403.5721	411.1710	462.8143	435.9436
Class5	399.6277	404.4876	421.7987	421.7987	394.3710
Class6	402.2064	386.0931	391.6397	389.9689	390.4343
Class7	457.7713	457.7713	387.0926	409.7519	449.1882
Class8	383.2016	380.5847	384.5825	385.2158	383.7509
Class9	383.5754	409.7443	388.0386	398.6359	460.4950

As seen in above tables, the NC s in new method are decreased very high. It shows the difference between the keys indicating the difference between zero-watermarked images. This supports the ability of the proposed method for providing ownership protection to very similar images.

This new learning based contour detection method returns the edges that are very similar to that the human can see. We showed that these edges are good features for watermarking similar images. In fact the more similarity between detected images to those perceived by humans, the more accurate results we will get in zero-watermarking. In Canny edge detection method we may get the best results by tuning the parameters but in the proposed method the best results are obtained without the need for parameter tuning.

6 Conclusion

Recently a new digital watermarking method called zero-watermarking has been proposed that does not degrade the quality of the host image. In this method binary feature are extracted from the image. Then these binary features are combined with a watermark logo and a key is produced. This key is kept in a trusted authority for security and authentication. In this paper we first show that the learning based contour detection method has better results in watermark robustness compared to the traditional Canny edge detection. Then we show that the learning based contour detection method has reliable performance when zero-watermarking highly similar images (images that are taken from different angle views).

With this new algorithm we can watermark similar images. The produced keys are distinguishable enough for protecting the ownership of similar images. As we have shown, the Canny edge detection method features (that is mostly used in recent papers) are not good enough for watermarking similar images. Because the Canny method returns edges that are very similar to each other and cannot understand the overall changes of similar images.

References

1. Shakeri, M., Jamzad, M.: A robust zero-watermarking scheme using Canny edge detector. Int. J. Electron. Secur. Digit. Forensics 5(1), 25–44 (2013)
2. Arbelaez, P., Maire, M., Fowlkes, C., Malik, J.: Contour detection and hierarchical image segmentation. IEEE TPAMI 33(5), 898–916 (2011)
3. Shapiro, L.G., Stockman, G.C.: Computer Vision, Prentice Hall (2001)
4. Martin, D., Fowlkes, C., Malik, J.: Learning to detect natural image boundaries using local brightness, color and texture cues. PAMI 26(5), 530–549 (2004)
5. Savitzky, A., Golay, M.J.E.: Smoothing and differentiation of data by simplified least squares procedures. Anal. Chem. 36(8), 1627–1639 (1964)
6. Chen, T.H., Horng, G., Lee, W.B.: A publicly verifiable copyright proving scheme resistant to malicious attacks. IEEE Trans. Ind. Electron. 52(1), 327–334 (2005)
7. Abdel-Wahab, M.A., Selim, H., Sayed, U.: A novel robust watermarking scheme for copyright-proving. In: The 2009 International Conference on Computer Engineering and Systems, ICCES 2009, art. no. 5383216, pp. 482–486 (2009)

Multi-focus Image Fusion for Visual Sensor Networks in Wavelet Domain

Mehdi Nooshyar[1], Mohammad Abdipour[2(✉)], and Mehdi Khajuee[2]

[1] Faculty of Electrical and Computer Engineering,
University of Mohaghegh Ardebili, Ardebil, Iran
mnooshyar@uma.ac.ir

[2] Computers and Electrical Engineering, University of Mohaghegh Ardebili,
Ardebil, Iran
{abdipour.mohammad,khajoie.mehdi}@gmail.com

Abstract. The aim of multi-focus image fusion is to combine multiple images with different focuses for enhancing the perception of a scene. The result of image fusion is a new image which is more suitable for human and machine perception or further image-processing tasks such as segmentation, feature extraction and object recognition. Existing methods are suffering from some undesirable side effects like blurring or blocking artifacts which reduce the quality of the output image. Furthermore, some of these methods are rather complex. This paper, an efficient approach for fusion of multi-focus images based on variance calculated in wavelet domain is presented. The experimental results and comparisons show that the efficiency improvement proposed fusion model both in output quality and complexity reduction in comparison with several recent proposed techniques.

Keywords: Multi-focus · Image fusion · Segmentation · Feature extraction · Object recognition · Wavelet

1 Introduction

In sensor networks, every camera can observe scene and to be recorded either still images or video sequences. Therefore, the processing of output information is related to image processing and machine vision subjects [1]. The need for image fusion is increasing mainly due to the increased number and variety of image acquisition techniques [2].

A prominent feature of visual sensors or cameras is the great amount of generated data, thus requires more local processing resources to deliver only the useful information represented in a conceptualized level [1]. Image fusion defined is the process of combining information from several sensors or cameras using mathematical techniques in order to create smaller set of images, usually a single one, that will be more comprehensive and thus, more useful for a human operator or other computer vision tasks [2].

The cameras that are used in visual sensor networks or computer vision systems have a limited depth of field, only the objects at a particular depth or certain distance in the scene are in focus whiles objects at other distances will be blurred thus for

© Springer International Publishing Switzerland 2014
A. Movaghar et al. (Eds.): AISP 2013, CCIS 427, pp. 23–31, 2014.
DOI: 10.1007/978-3-319-10849-0_3

extending the depth of focus used multiple cameras. Therefore, the multi-focus image fusion technique is desirable to fuse a set of images.

Recently, multi-resolution analysis has become a widely adopted technique to perform image fusion [3–7]. The algorithms based on multi-scale decompositions are more popular. The key step is to perform a multi-scale transform on each source image, and then performed coefficient combination, the process of merge the coefficient in an appropriate way in order to obtain the best quality in the fused image. These methods for obtain the best quality, combine the source images by monitoring a quantity that is called the activity level measure. The activity level determines the quality of each source image [8]. The combination can be performed by choosing the coefficients with larger activity level. Examples of this approach include Laplacian, gradient, morphological pyramids, and the superior ones, discrete wavelet transform (DWT) [9] and shift invariant discrete wavelet transform (SIDWT) [10].

In [11], proposed image fusion technique in wavelet domain, that fusion performed by apply a wavelet decomposition on source image, then for detailed and approximation subbands, by proposed method in [11] combined the coefficient. Finally apply an inverse wavelet transform to obtain a fused image. The other approach that proposed in [12], to retain the visual quality and performance of the fused image with reduced computations, a discrete cosine harmonic wavelet (DCHWT)-based image fusion is proposed.

Variance value is usually assumed as a contrast measure in image processing applications. In [8], image fusion technique in DCT domain is proposed. The variance of 8×8 DCT coefficients in a block is considered as a contrast criterion to be used for activity level measure. It was shown that the calculation of the variance value in DCT domain is very easy. Then, with using a consistency verification (CV) stage increases the quality of the output image.

Tang [13] by considering the issue of complexity reduction proposed two image fusion techniques DCT + average and other, based on a contrast measure defined in the DCT domain is presented (DCT + contrast). Tang has implemented his proposed methods on 8×8 DCT blocks defined.

DCT + Average obtains the fused image by taking the average of the DCT coefficients of the input images. This method leads to some undesirable side effects including blurring.

In other methods, DCT + contrast, activity level is based on a contrast measure. The DCT block of the output image made up with highest contrast for AC coefficient and DC coefficient by averaging of DC coefficient produce.

This algorithm is also complex in calculating the contrast measure for each coefficient and suffers from some side effects including blocking artifacts.

In order to reduce the complication and enhance the quality of the output image, an image fusion technique in wavelet domain is proposed in this paper. The variance of 8×8 wavelet coefficients in a block is considered as a contrast criterion to be used for activity level measure. Then, with use a consistency verification (CV) stage increases the quality of the output image. Simulation results and comparisons show the considerable improvement in the quality of the output image and reduction in computation complexity.

This paper is organized as follows: in Sect. 2, presents our proposed method of image fusion. In Sect. 3 the simulation results are demonstrated and analyzed; and finally the main conclusion is drawn in Sect. 4.

2 Proposed Method

After dividing the source images into blocks of 8 × 8 pixels and calculating the wavelet coefficients for each block, the multi-resolution decomposition gives four bands at each level, where contain detailed information in horizontal, vertical, diagonal direction and the approximation that illustrate with H, V, D and A respectively. For 2 levels of decomposition, H_1, H_2 represent horizontal subbands, V_1, V_2 represent vertical sub-bands, D_1, D_2 represent diagonal subbands, and A_2 represent approximate subband, the fusion algorithm is performed using calculates variance of these subbands coefficients in four dimensions and two scales. Here, considered the variance values of the blocks from source images as activity level measures that computed using Eq. (1).

$$AC_I(P) = \left[\frac{1}{NM} \sum (X_I(P) - \bar{X}_I(P))^2 \right] \tag{1}$$

For simplicity the processing of just two source images, If more than two source images are observed, they are combined one by one by iteratively applying the method, so we consider two source images F and G, and the fused image Z. Generally, an image I has its MSD representation denoted as X_I and the activity level as AC_I. Thus, we have X_F, X_G, X_Z as MSD representation of source and fused images AC_F and AC_G as activity level of source images.

Let $P = (k;l)$ indicate the index corresponding to MSD coefficients, where k indicates the decomposition level, and l the frequency band of the MSD representation.

The subband of blocks that having high value of AC_I is considered clearer, consequently fused wavelet coefficients obtain by choosing maximum AC_I for each frequency bands (horizontal, vertical, diagonal and approximation) of source coefficients.

Therefore, a good integration rule, just pick the coefficient with the larger activity level and discard the other. If Z is the fused image, this can be described *as* X_Z $(p) = X_i(p)$, where $i = F$ or G depending on which source image establish Eq. (2).

$$AC_i(P) = max(AC_F(P), AC_G(P)) \tag{2}$$

Simultaneously a binary decision map is created to record the selection results based on a maximum selection rule in Eq. (2).This binary map is subject to a consistency verification that follow in Sect. 2.1.

2.1 Consistency Verification (CV)

Assume a region in a scene including several blocks that is completely in the depth of focus of image F so all the blocks in this region must be chosen from image F but due to noise or undesired effects during the selection process that can lead to erroneous selection of some blocks from image G. This defect can be solved with a consistency verification procedure [8]. The algorithm plan is demonstrated in Fig. 1.

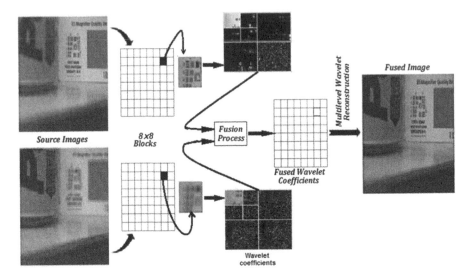

Fig. 1. Proposed image fusion method

Li [9] applied consistency verification using a majority filter. If the center block comes from source image G while the majority of the surrounding blocks come from source image F, the center sample is then changed to from image F. The fused image is finally obtained based on this modified decision map. The steps of the proposed method are elucidated as follows.

ALGORITHM

Step 1: Divide source images into 8×8 blocks.
Step 2: Compute the multilevel 2-D wavelet decomposition of 8×8 blocks.
Step 3: Calculate variance of wavelet coefficients for all subbands as activity level(AC_I).
Step 4: *if* $AC_F > AC_G$
          Then $X_F(P)$ is select for $X_z(P)$.
          Otherwise $X_z(P) = X_G(P)$.
Step 5: Repeat step 4 for all subband.
Step 6: The fused subimage is obtained by applying the inverse wavelet transform on the fused wavelet coefficient.
Step 7: Repeat above steps until all the subimages in the entire images are processed.
Step 8: Apply consistency verification using a majority filter for modification the incorrect decision map.

3 Experimental Results and Analysis

In this section, experiments are conducted to compare the performance of the proposed approach with other prominent techniques. Two of them are DCT based image fusion techniques, namely, DCT + Variance + CV in [8], DCT + Average in [13], and the other four techniques are multi-focus and multi-spectral image fusion based on pixel significance using discrete cosine harmonic wavelet transform (DCHWT) [12], adaptive multi-focus image fusion using a wavelet-based statistical sharpness measure [11] that represent with SP, standard wavelet based fusion (DWT) [9] and the shift invariant wavelet based technique (SIDWT) [10] that have been briefly described in Sect. 1.

For simulation of DWT and SIDWT, the "Image Fusion Toolbox", kindly provided by Rockinger [14] and for proposed method in [11], the code in [15], was used.

The proposed approach exploits a two-level wavelet decomposition using a Daubechies's wavelet. The experiment is to conduct image fusion using two sets of images with different focus levels: Pepsi, Clock.

On the other hand, three image quality evaluation criterions are used to provide objective performance comparison in our work. These three metrics are: (i) mutual information metric (MI) [16], (ii) Petrovic metric (Qabf) [17], which measures the relative amount of edge information that is transferred from the source images (A and B)

Table 1. Objective evaluation of the image fusion algorithms for "Pepsi" database in Fig. 2.

Method	Metric		
	Qabf	MI	FMI
DCT + average	0.6294	6.86	0.9123
DWT	0.7290	6.36	0.9204
SIDWT	0.7446	6.61	0.9200
SP	0.7283	7.31	0.9238
DCHWT	0.7527	6.85	0.9182
DCT + Variance + cv	0.7851	8.67	0.9246
Proposed method	**0.7863**	**8.84**	**0.9247**

Table 2. Objective evaluation of the image fusion algorithms for "Clock" database in Fig. 3.

Method	Metric		
	Qabf	MI	FMI
DCT + average	0.5855	6.99	0.9108
DWT	0.6366	6.21	0.9168
SIDWT	0.6933	6.67	0.9184
SP	0.6910	8.18	0.9222
DCHWT	0.6543	6.80	0.9191
DCT + Variance + cv	0.7142	8.82	0.9258
Proposed method	**0.7159**	**8.83**	**0.9262**

into the fused image (F), and (iii) the new metric feature mutual information (FMI) [18], which calculates the amount of information conducted from the source images to the fused image. The objective performance comparisons are presented in Tables 1 and 2.

The subjective test of the resultant images approves the objective measures. By carefully observing the fusion results in Fig. 2, it is concluded that the method DCT + Average results in the side effect of reduction in contrast or blurring the fused image (Fig. 2c). In addition there are some artifacts for the wavelet based methods

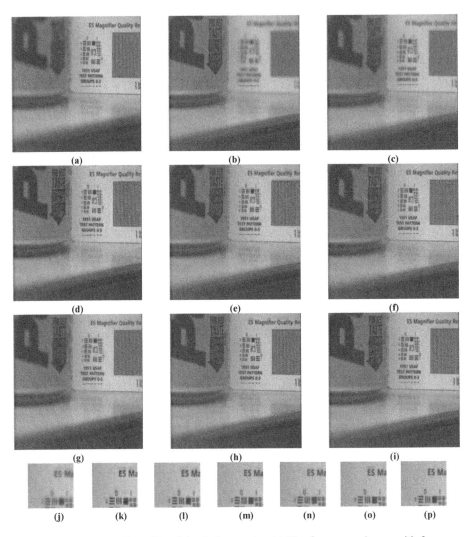

Fig. 2. Source images "pepsi" and the fusion results. (a) The first source image with focus on the right. (b) The second source image with focus on the left. (c) DCT + Average result. (d) DWT result. (e) SIDWT result. (f) SP result. (g) DCHWT result. (h) DCT + Variance + CV result. (i) Proposed method. (j), (k), (l), (m), (n),(o),(p) are the local magnified version of (c), (d), (e), (f), (g),(h) and (i) respectively

DWT, SIDWT, SP, DCHWT and DCT + Variance + CV, given in Fig. 2d–h, respectively.

As it can be seen in the magnified images corresponding to DWT, SIDWT, SP, DCHWT and DCT + Variance + CV, respectively, in Fig. 2k–o, the wavelet based algorithms suffer from a kind of ringing artifact. This ringing artifact is a common problem in wavelet based algorithms and some wavelet based methods (e.g. SIDWT) has somewhat blurring problem.

Figure 2i is the results of our proposed method. One can see that the fused images obtained using the proposed method yield better image quality than that of conventional approaches. In order to have some real application experiments, other experiments were conducted on four other well-known images "Pepsi" and "Clock" from Rockinger's database [14].

Eventually, the corresponding objective results, are given in Table 2. These quantitative evaluations prove the superiority of our proposed method.

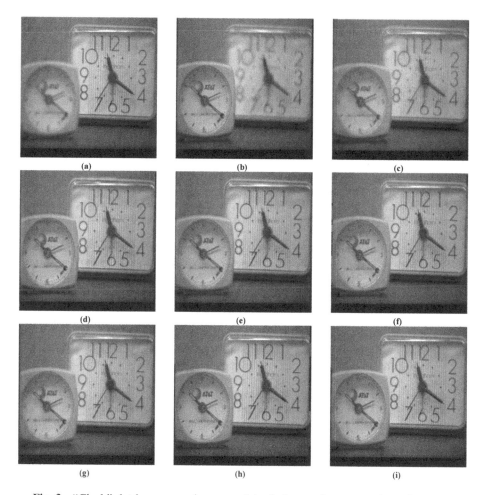

Fig. 3. "Clock" database source images and the fusion results: same order as in Fig. 2.

4 Conclusion

In this paper, a new wavelet based image fusion technique for multi-focus images was proposed. The method is based on the variance in wavelet domain. Utilization of variance in the proposed algorithm, leads to better quality of the fused image. Numerous experiments on evaluating the fusion performance were conducted and the results show that the proposed method outperforms the previous wavelet and DCT based methods both in quality and complexity reduction.

Acknowledgements. We would like to thank M.B.A. Haghighat for guidance helpful and tanks from E. Aghaei Kiasaraei for helping us to preparing template of this paper.

References

1. Castanedo, F., Garcia, J., Patricio, M.A., Molina, J.M.: Analysis of distributed fusion alternatives in coordinated vision agents. In: Proceedings of the IEEE Eleventh International Conference on Information Fusion (ICIF), pp. 1–6
2. Tania, S.: Image Fusion: Algorithms and Applications, 1st edn. Academic Press is an imprint of Elsevier, Tokyo (2008)
3. Lewis, J.J., O'Callaghan, R.J., Nikolov, S.G., Bull, D.R., Canagarajah, N.: Pixel- and region-based image fusion with complex wavelets. Inf. Fusion **8**(2), 119–130 (2007)
4. Li, S., Yang, B.: Multifocus image fusion using region segmentation and spatial frequency. Image Vis. Comput. **26**(7), 971–979 (2008)
5. Xu, L., Roux, M., Mingyi, H., Schmitt, F.: A new method of image fusion based on redundant wavelet transform. In: Proceedings of the IEEE Fifth International Conference on Visual Information Engineering, pp. 12–17
6. Zaveri, T., Zaveri, M., Shah, V., Patel, N.: A novel region based multifocus image fusion method. In: Proceedings of IEEE International Conference on Digital Image Processing (ICDIP), pp. 50–54
7. Arif, M.H., Shah, S.S.: Block level multi-focus image fusion using wavelet transform. In: Proceedings of IEEE International Conference on Signal Acquisition and Processing (ICSAP), pp. 213–216
8. Haghighat, M.B.A., Aghagolzadeh, A., Seyedarabi, H.: Multi-focus image fusion for visual sensor networks in DCT domain. Comput. Electr. Eng. **37**(2011), 789–797 (2011)
9. Li, H., Manjunath, B., Mitra, S.: Multisensor image fusion using the wavelet transform. Graph Models Image Process. **57**(3), 235–245 (1995)
10. Rockinger, O.: Image sequence fusion using a shift-invariant wavelet transform. In: Proceedings of IEEE International Conference on Image Processing, vol. 3, pp. 288–291
11. Jing, T., Li, C.: Adaptive multi-focus image fusion using a wavelet-based statistical sharpness measure. Sig. Process. **92**, 2137–2146 (2012)
12. Shreyamsha, B.K.: Multifocus and multispectral image fusion based on pixel significance using discrete cosine harmonic wavelet transform. SIViP (2012). doi:10.1007/s11760-012-0361-x
13. Tang, J.: A contrast based image fusion technique in the DCT domain. Digit. Signal Process. **14**(3), 218–226 (2004)
14. http://www.metapix.de/toolbox.htm
15. https://sites.google.com/site/eejtian

16. Qu, G.H., Zhang, D.L., Yan, P.F.: Information measure for performance of image fusion. Electron. Lett. **38**(7), 313–315 (2002)
17. Xydeas, C.S., Petrovic, V.: Objective image fusion performance measure. Electron. Lett. **36**, 308–309 (2000)
18. Mohammad, H., Ali, A., Hadi, S.: A non-reference image fusion metric based on mutual information of image features. Comput. Electr. Eng. **37**, 744–756 (2011)

Facial Emotion Recognition
Using Gravitational Search Algorithm
for Colored Images

Fatemeh Shahrabi Farahani[1(✉)], Mansour Sheikhan[2],
and Ali Farrokhi[2]

[1] Department of Mechatronic Engineering,
Islamic Azad University, South Tehran Branch, Tehran, Iran
arezo.shahrabi@yahoo.com
[2] Department of Electrical Engineering,
Islamic Azad University, South Tehran Branch, Tehran, Iran
{msheikhn,ali_farrokhi}@azad.ac.ir

Abstract. Facial expressions are the mirror of human's internal emotions. They are one of the major ways to communicate with others. Thus, they play a critical role in line with human machine communications. This paper proposes a new facial emotion recognition method based on gravitational search algorithm (GSA), from eyes and mouth features for colored images. Detection is implemented by part-based appearance manners and these attributes are used in the recognition phase. In this phase, facial attributes and their mapping to emotion space are encoded using GSA-based optimization. Applying the method on FACES facial expression database indicates 72.23 % accuracy.

Keywords: GSA · Face detection · Eye detection · Mouth detection · Emotion recognition

1 Introduction

Facial emotion recognition has become an important research field in machine vision and artificial intelligence. A facial emotion detection algorithm can be started with a face detection method [1]. These methods are classified into appearance-based and model-based [2].

A model-based approach tries to represent the face as a collection of three dimensional, geometrical primitives whereas appearance-based models only use appearance of face, which is usually captured by different two-dimensional views of the object of the interest [3]. The appearance-based methods were given better reception in comparison with model-based methods, due to their simplicity and ease of use.

The appearance-based methods are divided into two categories: part-based and holistic [4]: in part-based, unlike a holistic method, the feature vector is formed for the facial attributes, considering the fact that face emotions are mostly depicted on eyes and mouth. So, eye and mouth detection and tracking algorithms are necessary to be developed, in order to provide the features for subsequent emotion recognition [5].

© Springer International Publishing Switzerland 2014
A. Movaghar et al. (Eds.): AISP 2013, CCIS 427, pp. 32–40, 2014.
DOI: 10.1007/978-3-319-10849-0_4

Ebner et al. [6] gathered a database, entitled as FACES, of 72 facial expressions in young, middle-aged, and older women and men (including happiness, anger, disgust, fear, neutrality and sadness emotions). This free database comprises digital high-quality JPG color, front-view photographs of Caucasian faces of three different age groups, each displaying each of six expressions. All faces are standardized in terms of their production and general selection procedure and with respect to brightness, background color, and visible clothes, and show no eye-catching items such as beards or glasses. Figure 1 shows different emotions of a single person.

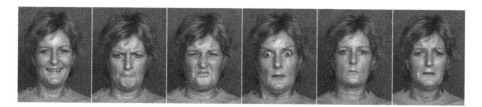

Fig. 1. Different emotions of a sample image in FACES database

In this paper, a new method is developed for human emotion detection in which gravitational search algorithm (GSA) optimization method with minimum Euclidean distance fitness function is employed for this purpose. The performance of proposed method is tested on the FACES database and is compared with the fuzzy facial expression recognition system proposed in [7, 8].

2 Gravitational Search Algorithm

GSA is a modern heuristic optimization algorithm proposed by Rashedi et al. [9]. In this algorithm, optimization is done by the laws of gravity and motion. According to these rules, each mass understands the location and position of the others through gravitational forces. Therefore, we can use this force as a tool for exchange of information. The GSA steps are represented in Fig. 2.

An optimal detector equipped with this algorithm can be used to solve optimization problem where the solution can be defined as a position in the problem space. The system space is a multidimensional coordinate system defining the problem space and search agents represent a set of objects each of which is one of the problem solutions.

The system is supposed to be a collection of m masses. The position of each agent (mass) which is a candidate solution for the problem is defined as follows:

$$X_i = \left(x_i^1; \ldots; x_i^2; \ldots x_i^D\right) \tag{1}$$

where D is the dimension of the problem and x_i^d is the position of the i-th agent in the d-th dimension. The gravitational force from agent j on agent i at time t is defined as follows:

$$F_{ij}^d(t) = \frac{G(t) \times Mg_j(t)}{R_{ij}(t) + e}(x_j^d(t) - x_i^d(t)) \tag{2}$$

where Mg_j is the active gravitational mass related to agent j, e is a small constant, $G(t)$ is the gravitational constant at time t, and $R_{ij}(t)$ is the Euclidian distance between two agents i and j that is calculated as follows:

$$R_{ij}(t) = \| X_i(t), X_j(t) \|_2 \tag{3}$$

In a problem space with the dimension d, the total force that acts on agent i is calculated by the following equation:

$$F_i^d(t) = \sum_{j=1, j \neq i}^m r_j F_{ij}^d(t) \tag{4}$$

where r_j is a random number in the interval $[0, 1]$. According to the law of motion, the acceleration of an agent is proportional to the resultant force and inverse of its mass, so the acceleration of each agent is calculated as follows:

$$a_i^d(t) = \frac{F_i^d(t)}{Mi_i(t)} \tag{5}$$

where d is the dimension of the problem, t is a specific time, and Mi_i is the inertial mass of object i. The velocity and position of agents are calculated as follows:

$$V_i^d(t+1) = r_i * V_i^d(t) + a_i^d(t) \tag{6}$$

$$x_i^d(t+1) = x_i^d(t) + V_i^d(t+1) \tag{7}$$

As can be inferred from (6) and (7), the current velocity is defined as a fraction of its previous velocity added to its acceleration. Furthermore, the current position of an agent is equal to its previous position added to its current velocity.

Agents' masses are defined using fitness evaluation; the masses of all agents are updated using the following equation:

$$Mg_i = \frac{fit_i(t) - worst(t)}{best(t) - worst(t)} \tag{8}$$

where $fit_i(t)$ is the fitness value of the agent i at time t; $best(t)$ is the strongest agent at time t, and $worst(t)$ is the weakest agent at time t. In this way, $best(t)$ and $worst(t)$ for a minimization problem are calculated as follows:

$$best(t) = \min_{j \in \{1,...,m\}} fit_j(t) \tag{9}$$

$$worst(t) = \max_{j \in \{1,...,m\}} fit_j(t) \tag{10}$$

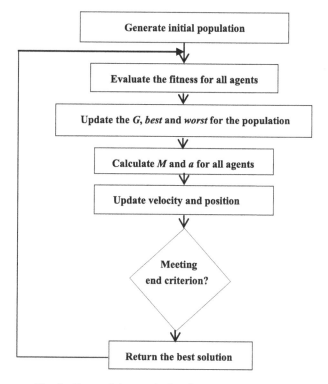

Fig. 2. Steps of the gravitational search algorithm [9]

3   Proposed Approach

A typical emotion recognition system includes four main stages [7]: face detection, feature extraction (for example, eye opening, mouth opening, eye opening/width ratio, and width of mouth), optimization, and classification. The proposed method is based on GSA capabilities for optimizing and different specifications of face in colored images [8, 10, 11].

3.1   Face Detection

Face border is recognized with red-difference Chroma components (Cr) in YCbCr color space by MATLAB image processing functions [12]. In addition, 1-D mean filter, sobel edge detection, morphological operations (Dilation and Erosion) with linear structure element and small objects removals are used [8].

3.2   Feature Extraction

Eye opening size. Eyes detection is started considering only blue-difference Chroma components (Cb) while researchers usually use a function of Cr and Cb [7–11, 13–15].

Applying MATLAB Software functions including edge detection, morphological operations (Dilate and Close) and binary connected component functions [12], the areas and bounding boxes for candidate eyes regions are obtained. The candidate regions are reduced based on eyes position in the human face, then these remaining regions are chosen as eyes and cropped from S component of HSV color space for "eye opening" calculation step. In this step, the inside of eye is filled by MATLAB edge detection, dilation with disk structure element and erosion with diamond structure element functions [12] (Fig. 3). Finally, to determine the eye opening, the pixels equal to one are counted along the center-line of eye [8].

Mouth opening size. A new parameter a × V (a in L*a*b and V in HSV color spaces) is defined on the purpose of mouth detection in this step. Mouth candidate regions are found by using morphologically open binary image, close and dilate operation with disk structure element and binary connected component MATLAB functions [12]. It is noted that the true position is gained from mouth location in the face. Also, mouth opening is considered by the cropped mouth from Cr parameter and counted zero pixels along center-line of mouth (Fig. 3) [8].

Eye opening/width ratio. For this section, the eye opening is divided by the eye width (from the width of eye region bounding box) [8].

Width of mouth. The width of mouth is obtained from width of mouth region bounding box [8].

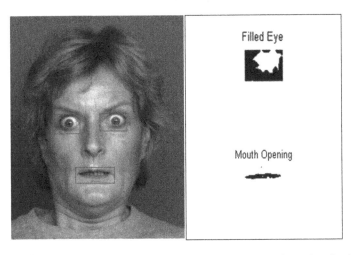

Fig. 3. An example of eye and mouth detection and extracted information for features

3.3   Optimization by GSA

In this section the average output of each emotion is used as a reference to find the best solution with Euclidean distance fitness function. By applying the proposed feature extraction method using two different threshold values in edge detection unit, output of all facial images in the same emotions are given as initial agents to the GSA algorithm (24 agents for each emotion and 26 random solutions).

This optimal solution has the minimum distance with the mean of each emotion. Table 1 shows the parameters setting for the GSA optimization and the outputs for six emotions are shown in Table 2.

Table 1. GSA parameters setting

GSA parameter	Value
Number of agents	50
Dimension of agents	4
Range of particles	[0–150]
Maximum iteration	20

Table 2. Mean and GSA best agents for each emotion

Emotion	Mean of outputs	GSA best
Sad	[1.125 11.58 2.72 84.95]	[0 14 2.07 85]
Happy	[9.79 10.45 3.07 86.2]	[8 11 2.9 84]
Anger	[0.7 9.16 4.16 71.70]	[0 7 3.71 71]
Disgust	[1.16 6.58 4.84 64.7]	[0 6 4.66 65]
Fear	[4.5 18.91 1.72 70.7]	[7 19 1.63 71]
Neutral	[0.3 14.5 2.36 75.83]	[0 14 2.24 75]

3.4   Classification

Output of last part is the best solution in every emotion and is used for emotion classification with minimum of Euclidean distance. Euclidean distance is used for classification and obtaining the level of similarity [16].

The Euclidean distance between two vectors can be obtained using Eq. (11).

$$d(x,y) = \sqrt[2]{\sum_{i}^{n}((x_i - y_i)^2)} \tag{11}$$

where n is the dimension of solution and x_i, y_i respectively are matrices of optimized and input facial image attributes. By selecting minimum of this data, their mapping to the emotion space is performed.

The functional block diagram of the proposed method is shown in Fig. 4.

4   Experimental Results

The results of present work on the FACES database are compared with the following systems tested on the same database: (a) human detection method where the recognition is performed by humans in the field of cognitive science [17], (b) Halawani's [18] work which used AdaBoost and SVM classifiers, and (c) fuzzy-based system [8].

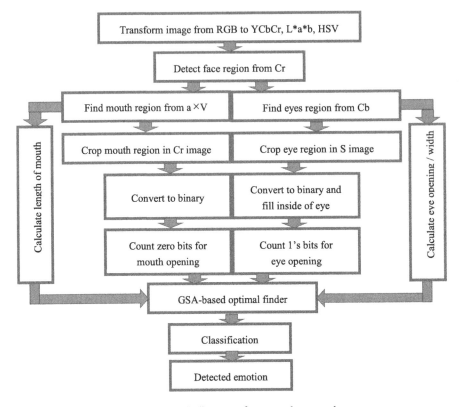

Fig. 4. Block diagram of proposed approach

As shown in Table 3 the best rates of the proposed system are achieved for Happy and Disgust emotions and the worst results occur for the Anger and Fear emotions. The proposed system acts almost similarly in recognition of Neutral and Sad emotions. By comparing the overall recognition rates of the investigated methods, it is concluded that the best recognition rate belongs to the human detection (about 86.25 %), while this rate is 77.76 % when using fuzzy-based method and is 72.23 % when using GSA.

Table 3. Recognition rate of four methods tested on the FACES database

Emotion in FACES dataset	Recognition rate			
	Human detection	SVM and AdaBoost	Fuzzy method	Proposed method
Happy	99.6 %	87.5 %	100 %	100 %
Neutral	94.8 %	–	50 %	66.7 %
Angry	77.9 %	–	91.6 %	50 %
Fear	90.4 %	91 %	100 %	50 %
Sad	78.55 %	–	75 %	66.7 %
Disgust	76.3 %	80 %	50 %	100 %

Therefore GSA shows the lowest overall recognition rate; however, its performance is outstanding for some emotions such as disgust emotion.

Because the classification phase is performed based on the distance between GSA bests and the features of each input image, and since these optimal values are obtained based on the mean of each emotion, so it seems replacing the mean by other operators (such as the geometric mean) may be investigated to achieve better performance.

5 Conclusion

In this study, a new GSA-based facial emotion recognition approach is proposed by making use of the properties of eye and mouth. This methodology discerns six emotion (happiness, sadness, neutrality, disgust, fear and anger) using GSA optimization in FACES database [6] and results in emotion accuracy rate about 72 %. According to the comparisons made, the ability of the proposed method in detecting Happy and Disgust emotions is better than other methods but for Fear and Anger emotions is worse. It is noted that the performance of proposed system is outstanding for some emotions such as disgust emotion.

References

1. DeCarlo, D., Metaxas, D.: Optical flow constraints on deformable models with applications to face tracking. Int. J. Comput. Vis. **38**(2), 99–127 (2000)
2. Azad, P., Asfour, T., Dillmann, R.: Combining appearance-based and model-based methods for real-time object recognition and 6D localization. In: 2006 IEEE/RSJ International Conference on Intelligent Robots and Systems, pp. 5339–5344 (2006)
3. Roth, P., Winter, M.: Survey of appearance-based methods for object recognition. Ph.D. Thesis, Graz University of Technology (2008)
4. Harandi, M., Nili Ahmadabadi, M., Araabi, B.N.: Optimal local basis: a reinforcement learning approach for face recognition. Int. J. Comput. Vis. **81**(2), 191–204 (2009)
5. Maglogiannis, I., Vouyioukas, D., Aggelopoulos, C.: Face detection and recognition of natural human emotion using markov random fields. Pers. Ubiquit. Comput. **13**(1), 95–101 (2009)
6. Ebner, N., Riediger, M., Lindenberger, U.: FACES - a database of facial expressions in young, middle-aged, and older women and men: development and validation. Behav. Res. Methods **42**(1), 351–362 (2010). http://faces.mpib-berlin.mpg.de/album/escidoc:57488
7. Ilbeygi, M., Shah-Hosseini, H.: A novel fuzzy facial expression recognition system based on facial feature extraction from colourfaces images. Eng. Appl. Artif. Intell. **25**(1), 130–146 (2012)
8. Shahrabi, F., Sheikhan, M., Farrokhi, A.: A fuzzy approach for facial emotion recognition. In: 13th Iranian Conference on Fuzzy Systems (2013)
9. Rashedi, E., Nezamabadi-pour, H., Saryazdi, S.: GSA: a gravitational search algorithm. Inf. Sci. **179**(13), 2232–2248 (2009)
10. Phung, S., Bouzerdoum, A., Chai, D.: Skin segmentation using color and edge information. In: Seventh International Symposium on Signal Processing and Its Applications, vol. 1, pp. 525–528 (2003)

11. Chakraborty, A., Konar, A., Chakraborty, U.K., Chatterjee, A.: Emotion recognition from facial expressions and its control using fuzzy logic. IEEE Trans. Syst. Man, Cybern. - Part A: Syst. Hum. **39**(4), 726–743 (2009)

12. Gonzalez, C., Woods, E., Eddins, L.: Digital Image Processing Using MATLAB, 2nd edn. Gatesmark Publishing, New York (2009)

13. Kalbkhani, H., Chehel Amirani, M.: An efficient algorithm for lip segmentation in colour face images based on local information. J. World's Electr. Eng. Technol. **1**(1), 12–16 (2012)

14. Nasiri, A., Sadoghi Yazdi, H., Naghibzadeh, M.: A mouth detection approach based on PSO rule mining on colour images. In: 5th Iranian Conference on Machine Vision and Image Processing, pp. 4–6 (2008)

15. Shan, C., Gong, S., McOwn, P.: Facial expression recognition based on local binary patterns: a comprehensive study. Image Vis. Comput. **27**(6), 803–816 (2009)

16. Taghizadegan, Y., Ghassemian, H., Moghaddasi, M.: 3D face recognition method using 2DPCA Euclidean distance classification. ACEEE Int. J. Control Syst. Instrum. **3**(1), 1–5 (2012)

17. Ebner, C., Johnson, M.K.: Age-group differences in interference from young and older emotional faces. Cogn. Emot. **24**(7), 1095–1116 (2010)

18. Halawani, H.: Emotion recognition system based on facial expression. M.S. Thesis, University of Sheffield (2011)

Novel Spatial Approaches for Classification of Hyperspectral Remotely Sensed Landscapes

Mostafa Borhani[✉] and Hassan Ghassemian

Faculty of Electrical and Computer Engineering,
Tarbiat Modares University, Tehran, Iran
{m.borhani,ghassemi}@modares.ac.ir

Abstract. This paper proposes some novel approaches based on spatial homogeneous regions to improve hyperspectral remotely sensed landscape's classification. Our proposed approaches are investigation of three segmentation techniques (watershed segmentation, hierarchical segmentation, partial clustering) in hyperspectral image and combination of spectral and spatial information in classification with majority vote rule. Proposed methods are compared with pixel-wise SVM and the ECHO, EMP and ML classification for University of Pavia and Indiana datasets. Empirical results showed all our proposed approaches yield higher accuracies when compared to others and the hierarchical segmentation technique resulted best most accurate. The drawback of spectral-spatial classification approaches consists in the fact that they smooth a classification map so our claim is just about remotely sensed landscape's classification.

Keywords: Support vector machine · Hierarchical segmentation · Partial clustering · Watershed segmentation · Hyperspectral landscape images · Hyperdimentional data analysis · Spatial information · Spatial homogeneous regions

1 Introduction

In hyperspectral imaging, every pixel contains a detailed spectrum of reflected light. This rich information per pixel increases the capability to distinguish materials and objects. Hyperspectral imaging leads to the potential of a more accurate classification and analysis. However, as the spectral dimension increases, image analysis becomes more complex, and methods developed for multispectral images actually fail when confronted to hyperspectral data. Therefore, to take full advantage of the rich information in spectral dimension, new algorithmic developments are required.

Hyperspectral remote sensed image classification is an important task in many application domains. First attempts to classify HS data were designed to assign each pixel to one of the classes based on its spectrum. There are methods of spectral, or pixelwise, classification that give very high classification accuracies (for example, a Support Vector Machines (SVM) classifier [1]).

Another modification to improve classification results consists in integration of spatial and spectral information. When the world is observed and analysed the world, the structures in spatial dimensions, and sizes, shapes of these structures are recognized as objects.

© Springer International Publishing Switzerland 2014
A. Movaghar et al. (Eds.): AISP 2013, CCIS 427, pp. 41–50, 2014.
DOI: 10.1007/978-3-319-10849-0_5

Therefore, the including of information about spatial structures into classifier should improve the classification. The question is how to define these structures automatically? This information is not directly accessible from camera recordings as the spectral information. The second question is how to combine spectral and spatial information?

Perhaps the most intuitive way to consider the spatial information is to assume that for a given pixel; its closest samples belong with a high probability to the same class, and thus classify a central pixel taking into account its closest samples. In the previous works, Markov Random fields [2–4] and contextual features (mean and standard deviation) [5] have been used to incorporate the information from the closest samples in classification. The main advantage of this approach is its simplicity. However, the closest fixed vicinity area does not always accurately reflect information about spatial structures, especially at the border of regions.

Pesaresi and Benediktsson have proposed to use morphological filters as an alternative way of performing joint classification. The idea behind a morphological profile consists in progressively simplifying the image [6, 7]. This means, that we include the geometrical information in classification procedure. The self-complementary area filtering removes small structures from the image based on an area criterion, and yields a map of flat connected zones [8]. The advantage of these approaches is that the proper proximity area is no more fixed, but they adapted to the structures.

However, these vicinity areas are scale dependent: here, they depend on the area criterion. The next question is what could be another way to define the structure element for each pixel?

The proposed answer of recent papers is "to exhaustive partitioning of the image into homogeneous regions". In an ideal case, each homogeneous region would correspond to one spatial object. Hence, each region in the segmentation map defines a proper proximity area for all the pixels within this region.

The first such approach, called Extraction and Classification of Homogeneous objects [9], was proposed by Kettig and Landgrebe for classification of multispectral remote sensing data, and has become a standard spectral-spatial classification technique. However, the ECHO method is based on statistical computations and involves estimation of covariance matrices. Therefore, this approach may be not well adapted for hyperspectral data. Segmentation of a hyperspectral image is a challenging task. The research groups of Linden and Huang used results from a multiscale segmentation to define a spectral-spatial feature for every pixel [10, 11]. These are efficient, but computationally demanding approaches.

The main objective of this paper was to further develop methods for classification of hyperspectral data using both spectral and spatial information. We have proposed and developed some general strategies for hyperspectral data classification. These are the contributions of this paper.

Our proposed strategies use adequate spatial vicinity area derived from segmentation results. Different segmentation techniques (watershed, Partial clustering, and hierarchical segmentation methods) are investigated and extended to the case of hyperspectral images. Then, approaches for combining the extracted spatial regions with spectral information in a classifier are proposed and developed.

Our proposed approaches are compared with spectral-spatial classification using closest fixed neighborhoods which is based on the integration of the SVM classification technique within an MRF framework [12].

Further in the rest of this paper, the details the proposed approaches for spectral-spatial classification using suitable vicinity area were derived first from unsupervised segmentation in Sect. 2. Section 3 will discuss classification using suitable vicinity area derived from unsupervised segmentation results, then, experimental results are presented in Sect. 4. Finally, conclusions and perspectives will be outlined.

2 Adequate Spatial Segmentation

Thus, our first objective is to automatically segment a hyperspectral image into homogeneous regions and to combine the obtained segmentation map with the available spectral information, aiming to improve the classification results obtained previously. Segmentation of the HS image is a challenging task, due to the high dimensionality of data. We investigated three segmentation methods.

- The first investigated technique is a watershed transformation. It is a region growing method based on the following assumptions: If we compute a gradient of the image, each minimum of the gradient corresponds to the core of a homogeneous region, and high values correspond to the edges between spatial structures.
- Region growing is performed from each local minimum, so that 1 region in the segmentation map consists of a set of pixels connected to 1 local minimum of the gradient.
- By watershed lines we mean edges between adjacent regions.

2.1 Watershed Segmentation

We investigated the use of a watershed technique to the case of HS images in this paper. A brief of the procedure leading to the best segmentation can be summarized as follow: a one-band Robust Color Morphological Gradient (RCMG) of the original image is computed. By applying watershed transformation using the algorithm of Vincent and Soille [13], the image is partitioned into a set of regions (about 11000, Fig. 1 part (d)), and one subset of watershed pixels, *i.e.*, pixels situated on the borders between regions. Finally, every watershed pixel is assigned to the spectrally most similar vicinity region.

2.2 Partial Clustering

Another type of investigated segmentation technique is partial clustering. Clustering aims at grouping pixels into C clusters, so that pixels belonging to the same cluster are spectrally similar. This paper assumes that pixels belonging to the same cluster are drawn from a multivariate Gaussian probability distribution. The parameters of the distributions are estimated by the EM algorithm [14].

In the Fig. 1 part (g) one can see a result of grouping the pixels of our HS image into 10 clusters. Spatial structures well defined by the clustering technique. However, as no spatial information is used during the clustering procedure, pixels with the same

Fig. 1. Experimental results for ROSIS image, Nine classes: asphalt, meadows, gravel, trees, metal sheets, bare soil, bitumen, bricks, shadows, (a) Spatial resolution: 1.3 m/pix Spectral resolution: 103 bands, (b) Ground-truth Map, (c) Gradient, (d) Robust Color Morphological Gradient, (e) Watershed 11802 regions, (f) Edges to adjacent regions, (g) Partial clustering (EM),10 clusters leads to 21450 regions, (h) Hierarchical segmentation, 7575 regions, (i) SVM, OA = 81.01 %, AA = 88.25 %, (j) SVM + Watershed, OA = 85.42 %, AA = 91.31 %, (k) SVM + partial clustering, OA = 94.00 %, AA = 93.13 %, (l) SVM + hierarchical segmentation, OA = 93.85 %, AA = 97.07 %

cluster label can form a connected spatial region within the spatial coordinates, or can belong to disjoint regions. Therefore, in order to obtain a segmentation map, a connected component labelling algorithm is applied to the image partitioning obtained by clustering; what means that we distinguish and label differently every adjacent group of pixels belonging to the same cluster.

2.3 Hierarchical Segmentation

The third technique investigated for segmentation is a Hierarchical Image Segmentation. This technique, developed by James Tilton [15], is a combination of region growing and spectral clustering.

In the initialization step, each pixel is considered as one region. At each iteration, the algorithm will merge the most spectrally similar adjacent and probably non-adjacent regions. We proposed to use a Spectral Angle Mapper (1) between the region mean vectors as the dissimilarity criterion between regions.

$$
SAM\left(x_i, x_j\right) = arcCos\left(\frac{\sum_{b=1}^{B} x_{ib}x_{jb}}{\left(\sum_{b=1}^{B} x_{ib}^2\right)^{\frac{1}{2}}\left(\sum_{b=1}^{B} x_{jb}^2\right)^{\frac{1}{2}}}\right) \tag{1}
$$

Where $X_i = (X_{i1}, \ldots, X_{iB})^T$ and $X_j = (X_{j1}, \ldots, X_{jB})^T$. For each iteration, our proposed approach finds the smallest dissimilarity criterion between spatially adjacent regions. Then we merge adjacent regions with the dissimilarity criterion equal to the found minimal value. Now, we merge non-adjacent regions if a dissimilarity value between them satisfies this expression. The procedure is repeated until convergence, and in the output we have a hierarchical sequence of image partitions (Fig. 1 part (h)).

We investigated more than 70 distance/similarity measures for SVM and their non-linear extensions in kernel methods titled "Extended Positive Definite Kernel Methods and Support Matrix Machines", that will we appear in IEEE Transaction of Pattern Analysis. Some of them are mentioned in Table 1.

Table 1. Some of distance/similarity measures criteria

Measure	Formula	Measure	Formula
Euclidean distance L_2	$d_{Euc} = \sqrt{\sum_{k=1}^{L} \left|x_{i,k} - x_{j,k}\right|^2}$	Canberra distance	$d_{Can} = \sum_{k=1}^{L} \frac{\left|x_{i,k} - x_{j,k}\right|}{x_{i,k} + x_{j,k}}$
City block, Manhattan metric, rectilinear distance, taxicab norm L_1	$d_{CB} = \sum_{k=1}^{L} \left|x_{i,k} - x_{j,k}\right|$	Lorentzian	$d_{Lor} = \sum_{k=1}^{L} \ln\left(1 + \left|x_{i,k} - x_{j,k}\right|\right)$
Minkowski distance L_r	$d_{Mk} = \sqrt[p]{\sum_{k=1}^{L} \left|x_{i,k} - x_{j,k}\right|^p}$	Sorensen	$d_{Sor} = \frac{\sum_{k=1}^{L} \left|x_{i,k} - x_{j,k}\right|}{\sum_{k=1}^{L} \left(x_{i,k} + x_{j,k}\right)}$

3 Spatial-Spectral Classification

Now, we must combine spectral and spatial information in classification. The proposed classification scheme based on the majority vote rule is composed of the following steps:

- Segment an image what is already done.
- Perform pixel-wise classification. We propose to use Support Vector Machines classifier for this purpose.

And then, for every region in the segmentation map, assign all the pixels to the most frequent class within this region.

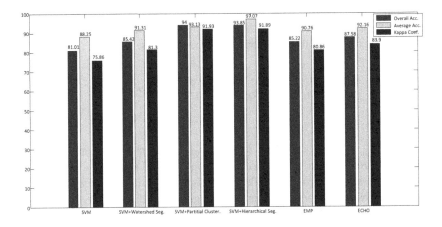

Fig. 2. Overall accuracy, average accuracy and Kappa factor for SVM, SVM + watershed segmentation, SVM + partial clustering, SVM + hierarchical segmentation, EMP and ECHO

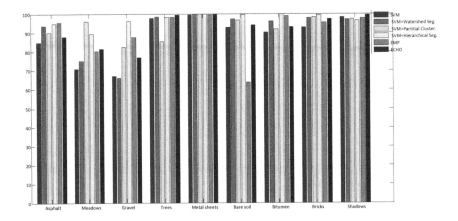

Fig. 3. Average accuracy of each class of university of Pavia for SVM, SVM + watershed segmentation, SVM + partial clustering, SVM + hierarchical segmentation, EMP and ECHO

Fig. 4. Indian *Pines* image. (a) Three-band color composite (837, 636, and 537 nm). (b) Reference data: Corn-no till, Corn-min till, Corn, Soybeans-no till, Soybeans-min till, Soybeans-clean till, Alfalfa, Grass/pasture, Grass/trees, Grass/pasture-mowed, Hay-windrowed, Oats, Wheat, Woods, Bldg-grass- tree-drives, and Stone-steel towers, (c) ML, (d) SVM, (e) ECHO, (f) SVM + watershed segmentation, (g) SVM + partial clustering, (h) SVM + hierarchical segmentation.

4 Experimental Results

The hyperspectral image of university of Pavia and ground-truth data are used for our experiments is a 103-band image, with the spatial resolution of 1.3 m/pix, recorded from the ROSIS camera in Italy, over the urban area of Pavia. The considered task is to assign every pixel to 1 of the 9 classes of interest, knowing to which class some of the image pixels belong. Results for image of Pavia are shown in Figs. 1, 2, and 3. And another image used for our experiments is a 200-band image acquired by the AVIRIS [16] sensor over the rural area in Indiana. The spatial resolution here is 20 m/pixel. It has 16 classes of interest. Results for Indiana dataset are shown in Figs. 4, 5, and 6.

An SVM classification on the original hyperspectral image were performed in Figs. 1 and 4, then the classification map of SVM with different segmentation maps obtained by proposed techniques were appeared. Figures 2 and 4 were the obtained classification maps, with the global accuracies (Overall accuracy, Average accuracy and Kappa factor) and Figs. 3 and 5 presented the average accuracy of approaches for different classes.

We can see that our approach gives higher accuracies than the previously proposed approaches. Spectral-spatial classification significantly improves accuracies for almost all the classes, except for the class shadows, where accuracies are non- considerably reduced. As can be seen, all segmentation maps lead to higher classification accuracies and classification maps with more homogeneous regions compared to pixel-wise classification. The best global accuracies are achieved when performing hierarchical image segmentation, i.e. performing segmentation both in the spatial and spectral domain.

In Figs. 1 and 4, we can take a look at classification accuracies. In order to compare the obtained results with previous works, we have included in the table accuracies of

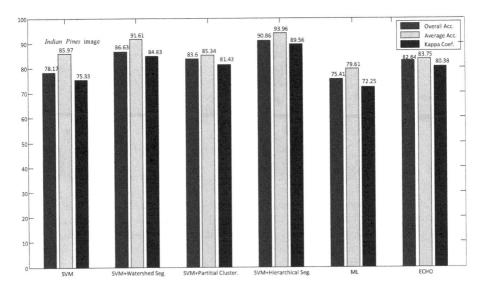

Fig. 5. Overall accuracy, average accuracy and Kappa factor for SVM, SVM + watershed segmentation, SVM + partial clustering, SVM + hierarchical segmentation, ML and ECHO

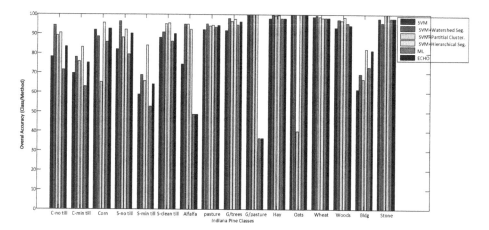

Fig. 6. Average accuracy of each class of Indiana dataset for SVM, SVM + watershed segmentation, SVM + partial clustering, SVM + hierarchical segmentation, ML and ECHO

the ECHO classification – the standard method of spectral-spatial classification in remote sensing, and of mathematical morphology-based classification using SVM and extended morphological profiles; it is one of the recently proposed and most successful methods [17].

5 Conclusions

Spectral-spatial classification improves accuracies when compared to pixelwise classification. We have proposed some new approaches of spectral-spatial classification in continue our spatial approaches [18]. It is proposed to perform segmentation in order to use every spatial region as a proper proximity area for all the pixels within this region. Several segmentation techniques are investigated for this purpose. Furthermore, the results of a pixel-wise classification and a segmentation map are combined, using the majority vote rule.

The best classification results are achieved when performing hierarchical image segmentation what means performing segmentation both in the spatial and spectral domain. Furthermore, the classification accuracies shown in this study are higher than all previous results that we have found in the literature for this data set.

References

1. Camps-Valls, G., Bruzzone, L.: Kernel-based methods for hyperspectral image classification. IEEE Trans. Geosci. Remote Sens. **43**(6), 1351–1362 (2005). doi:10.1109/TGRS.2005.846154
2. Kamandar, M., Ghassemian, H.: Linear feature extraction for hyperspectral images based on information theoretic learning. IEEE Geosci. Remote Sens. Lett. **10**(4), 702–706 (2013). doi:10.1109/LGRS.2012.2219575

3. Qiong, J., Landgrebe, D.A.: Adaptive Bayesian contextual classification based on Markov random fields. IEEE Trans. Geosci. Remote Sens. **40**(11), 2454–2463 (2002). doi:10.1109/TGRS.2002.805087

4. Farag, A.A., Mohamed, R.M., El-Baz, A.: A unified framework for MAP estimation in remote sensing image segmentation. IEEE Trans. Geosci. Remote Sens. **43**(7), 1617–1634 (2005). doi:10.1109/TGRS.2005.849059

5. Camps-Valls, G., Gomez-Chova, L., Munoz-Mari, J., Vila-Frances, J., Calpe-Maravilla, J.: Composite kernels for hyperspectral image classification. IEEE Geosci. Remote Sens. Lett. **3** (1), 93–97 (2006). doi:10.1109/LGRS.2005.857031

6. Pesaresi, M., Benediktsson, J.A.: A new approach for the morphological segmentation of high-resolution satellite imagery. IEEE Trans. Geosci. Remote Sens. **39**(2), 309–320 (2001). doi:10.1109/36.905239

7. Dell'Acqua, F., Gamba, P., Ferrari, A., Palmason, J.A., Benediktsson, J.A., Arnason, K.: Exploiting spectral and spatial information in hyperspectral urban data with high resolution. IEEE Geosci. Remote Sens. Lett. **1**(4), 322–326 (2004). doi:10.1109/LGRS.2004.837009

8. Fauvel, M., Benediktsson, J.A., Chanussot, J., Sveinsson, J.R.: Spectral and spatial classification of hyperspectral data using svms and morphological profiles. IEEE Trans. Geosci. Remote Sens. **46**(11), 3804–3814 (2008). doi:10.1109/TGRS.2008.922034

9. Kettig, R.L., Landgrebe, D.A.: Classification of multispectral image data by extraction and classification of homogeneous objects. IEEE Trans. Geosci. Electron. **14**(1), 19–26 (1976). doi:10.1109/TGE.1976.294460

10. Linden, S.V.D., Janz, A., Waske, B., Eiden, M., Hostert, P.: Classifying segmented hyperspectral data from a heterogeneous urban environment using support vector machines. J. Appl. Remote Sens. **1**(1), 013543 (2007). doi:10.1117/1.2813466

11. Huang, X., Zhang, L.: A comparative study of spatial approaches for urban mapping using hyperspectral rosis images over Pavia city, northern Italy. Int. J. Remote Sens. **30**(12), 3205–3221 (2009). doi:10.1080/01431160802559046

12. Moser, G., Serpico, S.B.: Combining support vector machines and Markov random fields in an integrated framework for contextual image classification. IEEE Trans. Geosci. Remote Sens. **51**(5), 2734–2752 (2013). doi:10.1109/TGRS.2012.2211882

13. Vincent, L., Soille, P.: Watersheds in digital spaces: an efficient algorithm based on immersion simulations. IEEE Trans. Pattern Anal. Mach. Intell. **13**(6), 583–598 (1991). doi:10.1109/34.87344

14. Tarabalka, Y., Fauvel, M., Chanussot, J., Benediktsson, J.A.: SVM and MRF-based method for accurate classification of hyperspectral images. IEEE Geosci. Remote Sens. Lett. (2010). doi:10.1109/LGRS.2010.2047711

15. Tilton, J.C.: HSEG/RHSEG, HSEGViewer and HSEGReader user's manual (version 1.40). Provided with the evaluation version of RHSEG. http://opensource.gsfc.nasa.gov/projects/HSEG/

16. Airborne Visible/Infrared Imaging Spectrometer, AVIRIS. http://aviris.jpl.nasa.gov/

17. Plaza, A., Benediktsson, J.A., Boardman, J.W., Brazile, J., Bruzzone, L., Camps-Valls, G., Chanussot, J., Fauvel, M., Gamba, P., Gualtieri, A., Marconcini, M., Tilton, J.C., Trianni, G.: Recent advances in techniques for hyperspectral image processing. Remote Sens. Environ. **113**(1), S110–S122 (2009). ISSN 0034-4257, http://dx.doi.org/10.1016/j.rse.2007.07.028

18. Borhani, M., Ghassemian, H.: Kernel grouped multivariate discriminant analysis for hyperspectral image classification. In: Symposium on Artificial Intelligence and Signal Processing, December 2013

Contourlet-Based Levelset SAR Image Segmentation

Alireza Ebrahiminia$^{(\boxtimes)}$, Mohamad Sadegh Helfroush,
Habibollah Danyali, and Shabab Bazrafkan

Department of Electrical and Electronic Engineering,
Shiraz University of technology, Shiraz, Iran
a.ebrahiminia@sutech.com,
{ms_helfroush,danyali,Shabab.bazrafkan}@sutech.ac.ir

Abstract. Segmentation in Synthetic Aperture Radar (SAR) images has become very important in recent years because of its wide range of applications. There are lots of methods introduced for this purpose in literature. In this paper we used contourlet as a new method for feature extraction. Here the levelset method is used with a statistical based kernel. The parameters of this kernel have been calculated using high order cumulants. For this purpose the estimation of energy distribution in Contourlet transform has been used. Our experimental results show that the proposed method is effective in Image segmentation containing inhomogeneity intensities such as SAR images and also outperforms wavelet based methods.

Keywords: SAR · Levelset · Segmentation · kurtosis · Contourlet

1 Introduction

SAR imaging is widely used in lots of applications in recent years. Applications such as agriculture, transportation, commercial (oil and gas resource estimation), intelligent traffic management and military (enemy position detection).

SAR can generate images from earth surface with high resolution, 10 cm in some cases. Capability for imaging in day and night and every weather conditions makes SAR imaging very useful and important. SAR waves can infiltrate tens of meters into the earth surface so it can take images from underground objects such as mines, arsenals and underground ways. The main purpose of SAR imaging is to make a powerful system for detecting, tracking and taking images with high resolution.

Segmentation is one of the primary processes for interpreting and analyzing an image. Because of this, SAR image segmentation is very important step and has lots of applications such as environmental supervision, military surveillance and geometrical mapping. The result of segmentation is to decompose the original images into homogenous regions such that each region is representing a specific texture. This process would generate suitable data for classification step. For declaring the importance of segmentation we can say that little error in segmentation would lead to a large error in classification.

The main obstacle in SAR image segmentation is to inherent speckled noise and inventible clutter [1–3] that makes segmentation such a complex problem [4].

© Springer International Publishing Switzerland 2014
A. Movaghar et al. (Eds.): AISP 2013, CCIS 427, pp. 51–59, 2014.
DOI: 10.1007/978-3-319-10849-0_6

Therefore a general method in segmentation and edge extraction in optical and infrared images is not useful in SAR images. In recent years some methods have been proposed in SAR and sonar image segmentation that based on curve evolution methods (Active Contour Methods) [5, 6]. One of the advantages of using active contours, is no need to denoising step before segmentation step. Also active contours can be modified for segmentation without using image intensity. So it can be useful for images with Inhomogeneity intensities like speckled images.

In [5] classical snake model has been used for SAR image segmentation in such a way that a predefined contour has been reshaped iteratively since it's surrounding a segment with a specific statistical criterion. In [6, 7] active contour models has been defined over level set functions, this model has the benefit of robustness on the topological variation problem. But it has serious problems on contour shape convergence. This is because of existence of lots of local minimums in energy function, that the algorithm would lead to. The other problem is the lack of a suitable criterion for stopping the process in image segmentation. The new models introduced for segmentation in [3, 8] are all depend on the homogeneous intensities in segmented regions. These models did not use the statistical property of pixels in segmented regions. Thus they cannot overcome the existence of inhomogeneous intensities in SAR images. From this we see that using statistical properties of regions would be a suitable idea for solving these problems. In [9] Akbarizadeh added a term including statistical information in the energy function. This information had been generated by estimating the energy distribution in wavelet domain. The higher order cumulants had been used for PDF parameter estimation and this distribution had been included in the energy function as a kernel. This paper is organized as follows. In Sect. 2 we introduce levelset methods for segmentation. The proposed method is described in Sect. 3. Experimental results are shown in Sect. 4 and the last section includes conclusion.

2   Level Set Methods

2.1   Definition

The level set method is a numerical technique for tracking interfaces and shapes. In this method for 2D images we have 3D surface function that intersects with the image. This intersection results in Contour shapes in 2D images. The shape of the Contour can be changed by using an energy function. The idea of segmentation by these contours comes from defining an energy function such that minimizing this function would lead to the best segmentation. There are two approaches for this definition. Reference [10] Edge based models and region base models. In this paper we focused on region based models.

2.2   Region Based Models

In 2001 Chan et al [11] introduced an energy function for region based model described such that the stopping term is independent of the image gradient. It is given by:

$$F(c_1, c_2, C) = \mu \times length(C) + \nu \times Area(inside(C))$$
$$+ \lambda_1 \int_{inside(c)} |I(x, y) - C_1|^2 dxdy + \lambda_2 \int_{outside(c)} |I(x, y) - C_2|^2 dxdy \quad (1)$$

where C is the contour, $\mu \geq 0, \nu \geq 0, \lambda_1, \lambda_2 > 0$, are fixed parameters, $I(x, y)$ is the image and C_1, C_2 are described as:

$$C_1 = \frac{\int_\Omega I(x, y) H(x, y) dxdy}{\int_\Omega H(x, y) dxdy} \quad (2)$$

$$C_2 = \frac{\int_\Omega I(x, y)(1 - H(x, y)) dxdy}{\int_\Omega (1 - H(x, y)) dxdy} \quad (3)$$

Where H, is a Heaviside function and Ω is the image region. The drawbacks of this model are its weakness in finding segments with inhomogeneous intensities.

In 2008 li et al. proposed an energy function to overcome this drawbacks. This function was given by:

$$F(f_1(x), f_2(x), C) = \mu L(\phi) + \nu \rho(\phi) + \lambda_1 \int \left[\int K_\sigma(x - y) |I(y) - f_1(x)|^2 H(\phi(y)) dy \right] dx$$
$$+ \lambda_1 \int \left[\int K_\sigma(x - y) |I(y) - f_2(x)|^2 (1 - H(\phi(y))) dy \right] dx \quad (4)$$

Where λ_1, λ_2 and H are as described before, ϕ is a zero crossing levelset of the Lipschitz function $\phi : \Omega \to R$. $L(\phi)$ And $\rho(\phi)$ are length and regularization function respectively as shown in (5) and (6).

$$\rho(\phi) = \int_\Omega \frac{1}{2} (|\nabla \phi(x)| - 1)^2 dx \quad (5)$$

$$L(\phi) = \int_\Omega \delta(\phi(x)) |\nabla \phi(x)| dx \quad (6)$$

$$f_1(x) = \frac{K_\sigma(x) * [H(\phi(x)) I(x)]}{K_\sigma(x) * H(\phi(x))} \quad (7)$$

$$f_2(x) = \frac{K_\sigma(x) * [(1 - H(\phi(x))) I(x)]}{K_\sigma(x) * [1 - H(\phi(x))]} \quad (8)$$

Where δ is the Dirac function, K is a kernel function used for localization given by:

$$K_\sigma(x) = \frac{1}{2\pi^{n/2} \sigma^n} e^{-\frac{|x^2|}{2\sigma^2}} \quad (9)$$

The weakness of this model was the absence of pixel statistic information in speckled images.

In 2012 Akbarizade [9] extracted the texture features as a kernel function by applying the wavelet transform. In this method The energy function was same as Eq. 4, but the kernel function was given by:

$$K(x) = \frac{k}{2\sqrt{x}} \exp\left(-\left(\frac{\sqrt{x}}{\alpha}\right)^{\beta}\right)$$ (10)

Where K, α, β was determined by kurtosis of energy of the wavelet coefficients. This idea overcomes the problem of inhomogeneity intensities for speckled images.

3   Proposed method

Because of spackle noise in SAR images we cannot use edge based level set method for segmentation, thus region based models are preferred. So the energy function described in Eq. 4 was used for segmentation and the kernel parameters were specified using kurtosis method. This idea comes from entering statistic properties of the image to our kernel. In other words for each image, we have a specific kernel defined for it. Using this adaptive approach leads to better result in segmentation for Speckled images as in [9]. For extracting statistic parameter we used contourlet transform.

3.1   Wavelet and Contourlet Transform

In essence, wavelets are good at catching zero dimensional singularities, but two-dimensional piecewise smooth signals resembling images have one dimensional singularities. That is, smooth regions are separated by edges, and while edges are discontinuous across, they are typically smooth curves. Intuitively, wavelets in 2-D obtained by a tensor-product of one dimensional wavelets will be good at isolating the discontinuity across the edge, but will not see the smoothness along the edge. This disappointing behavior indicates that more powerful bases are needed in higher dimensions.

A new non-separable two-dimensional signal transform, called the Contourlet Transform (CT) has recently been proposed as an alternative to an improvement on separable wavelet for representation of images. Contourlet is a directional and scalable transform describing contours and details in images. This transform is using directional scalable basis functions. This strong set of basis functions can generate anisotropic texture features. This transform scales to capture the intrinsic geometrical structure in visual information through a multiresolution, multidimensional decomposition.

In [12] zhao et al, show that the subband distribution in contourlet transforms has the form of generalized Gaussian density (GGD). The probability density function of each subband is defined as below:

$$(x; \alpha, \beta) = \frac{\beta}{2\alpha \, \Gamma(1/\beta)} e^{-\frac{|x|^{\beta}}{\alpha}}$$ (11)

Where $\Gamma(\cdot)$ is the Gamma function, α is the width of the PDF peak (Standard deviation), and β is inversely proportional to the decreasing rate of the peak (shape parameter).

The kurtosis parameter estimation was used to determine pdf parameters α and β. In such a way that subband with maximum energy was used for estimation in each scale. For parameter estimation at the first step the forth order moment of the contourlet coefficient should be calculated as below:

$$m^{(4)} = \int_0^\infty |W_c|^8 h(w_c)dw_c = \frac{k\alpha^9}{\beta}\Gamma\left(\frac{9}{\beta}\right) \tag{12}$$

Where W_c, is the according coefficients of the subband of contourlet transform. It can be shown that [9], the parameter α can be estimated by:

$$\alpha = \sqrt{\frac{m^{(4)}\Gamma\left(\frac{7}{\beta}\right)}{m^{(3)}\Gamma\left(\frac{9}{\beta}\right)}} \tag{13}$$

On the other hand the forth order cumulant of these coefficients can be described as:

$$C_x^{(4)} = E\left\{(x-\mu)^4\right\} = m^{(4)} - 4m^{(!)}m^{(3)} + 6m^{(1)^2}m^{(2)} - 3m^{(1)^4} \tag{14}$$

Kurtosis is normalized forth order cumulant and is defined by:

$$Kurtosis = \frac{C^{(4)}}{(\sigma^2)^2} \tag{15}$$

And it is shown [9] that it can be rewritten by the form:

$$F(x) = \frac{\Gamma^3\left(\frac{1}{\beta}\right)\Gamma\left(\frac{9}{\beta}\right) - 3N\Gamma^2\left(\frac{1}{\beta}\right)\Gamma^2\left(\frac{5}{\beta}\right) - 4N\Gamma^2\left(\frac{1}{\beta}\right)\Gamma\left(\frac{3}{\beta}\right)\Gamma\left(\frac{7}{\beta}\right)}{N\left(\Gamma\left(\frac{1}{\beta}\right)\Gamma\left(\frac{5}{\beta}\right) - N\Gamma^2\left(\frac{3}{\beta}\right)\right)^2}$$
$$+ \frac{12N^2\Gamma\left(\frac{1}{\beta}\right)\Gamma^2\left(\frac{3}{\beta}\right)\Gamma\left(\frac{5}{\beta}\right) - 6N^3\Gamma^4\left(\frac{3}{\beta}\right)}{N\left(\Gamma\left(\frac{1}{\beta}\right)\Gamma\left(\frac{5}{\beta}\right) - N\Gamma^2\left(\frac{3}{\beta}\right)\right)^2} \tag{16}$$

Where N, is the number of pixels in the image. So the parameter β can be determined using the inverse of kurtosis:

$$\beta = F^{-1}(kurtosis) = F^{-1}\left(\frac{C^{(4)}}{(c)^{(2)^2}}\right) \tag{17}$$

The experimental results would be illustrated at the next section.

4 Experimental Results

In order to compare the performance of proposed method and wavelet method, the experimental results are given for both real and synthetic images.

4.1 Synthetic SAR Image Segmentation

In order to evaluate the Real performance of the proposed method, the algorithm has been applied on a three-look synthetic SAR image. The synthetic SAR image generation is inspired by the procedure of radar image formation and construction. This is done by multiplying a ground truth by three independent speckle noises and averaging over them.

Here in our study we will compare the error of segmentation in the levelset model based on wavelet transform and contourlet transform. The Speckled noise power had been increased in each observation and in Fig. 1 the error is shown against the noise power for two methods. The noisy image and its ground truth are shown in Fig. 2. The parameters for two models are $\lambda_1, \lambda_2 = 1, \mu = 1, \nu = 0.02 \times 255 \times 255$ and kernel variances for two models are the same. The error was calculated as the number of non-zeros in the difference of the segmented image and the ground truth divided by the number of pixels of the image. As shown in Fig. 1, the error in the proposed method is much less than the wavelet based method and the robustness against the noise power is much larger as well.

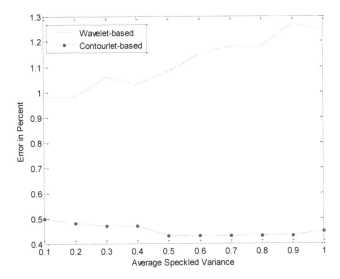

Fig. 1. Comparison between segmentation error of wavelet-based and contourlet-based algorithms

As shown in Fig. 2(c) and (d), the region selected with red circle in proposed method is more similar to ground truth image.

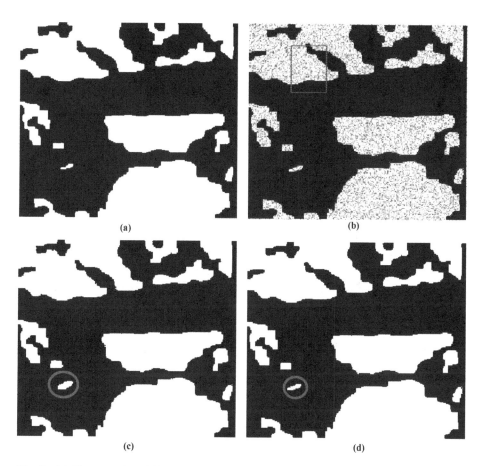

Fig. 2. (a) The ground truth image (b) The three-look synthetic SAR image and initial contour (c) Segmentation result by wavelet method (d) Segmentation result by proposed method

4.2   Real SAR Image Segmentation

In the case of real SAR Images, we cannot evaluate the performance of the proposed method objectively. Because of absence of ground truth corresponding to real SAR images. Therefore we can only evaluate these images visually.

Figure (3-a) shows an original SAR image. This image is captured from an agricultural region near the Dnieper River in Ukraine by SIR-C/X-SAR satellite in X-band with 15-m resolution.

Figure 3(b) illustrates the SAR image segmentation using proposed method and the wavelet based one is shown in Fig. 3(c) for the same image. The wavelet based method suffers from the noisy segmentation results and the given method overcame this

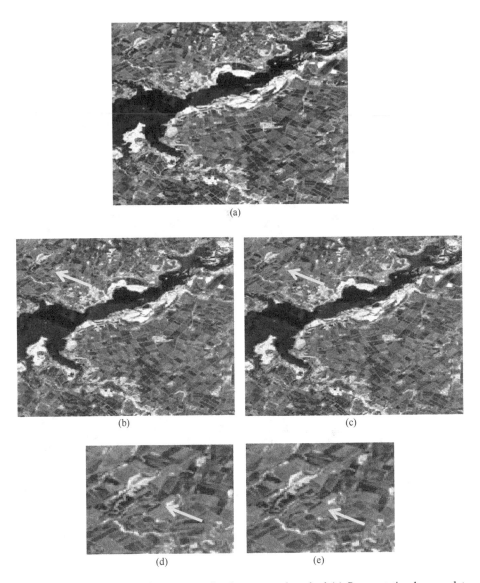

Fig. 3. (a) Original image (b) Segmentation by proposed method (c) Segmentation by wavelet method (d) Magnifying of interested region in b (e) Magnifying of interested region in c

problem. As it is obvious, the segmented regions are more accurate generated by proposed method. In Fig. 3(d) and (e) an interested region is magnified showing more detailed regions which proofs the more precision and noisy segmentation reduction given by proposed method.

5   Conclusion

In this paper we proposed a method that is effective in SAR image segmentation. It has been shown that both wavelet based and contourlet based methods are effective in image segmentations with inhomogeneous intensities. But the proposed method (contourlet based) outperforms in segmentation accuracy and is much robust against the increase in noise power. Thus we can conclude that using features that are less depend on pixel intensities leads to better models for SAR image segmentation.

Reference

1. Javidi, B.: Image Recognition and Classification, Algorithm, System, and application, p. 506. CRC Press, Boca Raton (2002)
2. Jortoft, R.F., Lopes, A., Marthon, P., Cubero-Casan, E.: An optimal multiedge detector for SAR Image segmentation. IEEE Trans. GeoSci. Remote Sens. **36**, 793–802 (1998)
3. Zhang, X., Jiao, L., Liu, F., Bo, L., Gong, M.: Sectral clustering ensemble applied to SAR image segmentation. IEEE Trans. GeoSci. Remote Sens. **46**, 2126–2136 (2008)
4. Shuai, Y., Sun, H., Xu, G.: SAR image segmentation based on levelset with stationary global minimum. IEEE Trans. Geosci. **5**, 644–648 (2008)
5. Refregier, P., Germain, O.: Edge location in SAR images: performance of the likelihood ratio filter and accuracy improvment with an activecontour approach. IEEE Trans. Image Process. **10**, 72–78 (2001)
6. Ayed, I.B., Vazquez, C., Miiche, A., Belhadj, Z.: Multiregion levelset partitioning of synthethic aperture radar images. IEEE Trans. Pattern Anal. Mach. Intell. **27**, 793–800 (2005)
7. Mitiche, A., Ayed, I.B., Vazquez, C., Belhadj, Z.: SAR image segmentation with active contours and levelsets. In: IEEE International Conference on Image Processing, vol. 4, pp. 2717–2720, October 2004
8. Li, S., Yanning, Z., Miao, M., Guangjian, T.: SAR image segmentation method uing DP mixture models. In: IEEE International Symposim on computer Science and computational Technology, vol. 2, pp. 598–601, December 2008
9. Akbarizadeh, G.: A new statistical-based kurtosis wavelet energy feature for texture recognition of SAR images. IEEE Trans. Geosci. Remote Sens. Lett. **50**(11), 4358–4368 (2012)
10. Li, C., kao, C., Gore, J., Ding, Z.: Minimization of region-scalable fitting energy for image segmentation. IEEE Trans. Image Process. **17**, 1940–1949 (2008)
11. Cha, T.F., Vese, L.A.: Active contours without edges. IEEE Trans. Image Process. **10**(2), 266–277 (2001)
12. Yifan, Z., Liangzheng, X.: Contourlet-based feature extraction on texture images. In: International Conference on Computer Science and Software Engineering, pp. 222–224 (2008)

Stereo Correspondence Using Hierarchical Belief Propagation and Cross-Based Region

Alireza Abutorabi$^{(\boxtimes)}$ and Amir Mousavinia

Department of Electrical Engineering,
K.N.Toosi University of Technology, Tehran, Iran
ar.abutorabi@ee.kntu.ac.ir, moosavie@eetd.kntu.ac.ir

Abstract. Assuming that neighboring pixels with similar colors in stereo images, share almost the same disparities, this paper presents a new global stereo matching algorithm based on Belief Propagation and cross-based aggregation method. In this approach the hierarchical Belief Propagation strategy is followed by a left-right consistency check as an initial match. Then a refinement algorithm is applied to generated disparity map, based on cross-based region method. The initial matching performed by hierarchical Belief Propagation strategy uses less memory and improves the running speed of energy minimization function. The experimental results, evaluated by the Middlebury data sets, show that the proposed method improves the accuracy of disparity map compare to other real-time stereo matching algorithms.

Keywords: Stereo matching · Hierarchical belief propagation · Cross-based region

1 Introduction

Finding an accurate disparity map from one pair of stereo images is one of the most active research areas in the field of computer vision [1, 2]. Using rectified images simplifies the matching problem by decreasing the search area into two rows in stereo images. Still, obtaining an accurate and dense disparity map is a challenge mainly due to the nature of the stereo matching problems such as disparity discontinuities, existence of texture less areas in images and especially occluded regions [3].

Many researchers have proposed their algorithms to solve parts of these problems in the past few years. The detailed review of these stereo matching algorithms can be found in [1].

Generally stereo matching algorithms can be classified into two categories: 1- the local methods and 2- the global methods. Local approach algorithms utilize details within a finite window around each pixel to determine the disparity. However, global approaches make explicit smoothness assumptions of the disparity map and determine all disparities simultaneously by minimizing a cost function for the whole image. Recently, global algorithms have attracted much attention due to their accurate experimental results. Algorithms such as Graph Cuts [4, 5] and Belief Propagation (BP) [2, 6] give a better performance compared to local methods while they are computationally expensive which makes them impractical in real-time applications. Nevertheless, some

© Springer International Publishing Switzerland 2014
A. Movaghar et al. (Eds.): AISP 2013, CCIS 427, pp. 60–68, 2014.
DOI: 10.1007/978-3-319-10849-0_7

computationally efficient global algorithms have been proposed in the past few years. Felzenszwalb et al. proposed an efficient Belief Propagation algorithm [2], which uses a hierarchical approach to reduce the computational complexity. Two step techniques which divide the matching process into two stages including initial matching and disparity refinement are also offered by many researchers [7, 8].

On the other hand the segment-based methods have attracted much attention and are used in many algorithms due to their good performance [9, 10]. Unfortunately, the Mean Shift algorithm [11], usually used for image segmentation is computationally very expensive and the real-time implementation of this algorithm is still a challenge.

In this paper, we propose a real-time stereo matching method to efficiently compute an accurate disparity map from a stereo pair of images. In the algorithm the matching procedure is divided into two main steps. In first step, initial matching is done based on a global energy minimization technique including construction of a data term and iterative optimization of a smoothness term. In second step, cross based region approach [12] using the color information (without performing any color segmentation) is used as a disparity refinement.

The rest of this paper is organized as follow. In Sects. 2 and 3 we present the hierarchical Belief Propagation and cross-based method, followed by a disparity map refinement technique. Then in Sect. 4 we give a description of our stereo matching method. The Middlebury data sets are used to evaluate the performance of our algorithm and Sect. 5 presents the results. Finally Sect. 6 concludes the paper.

2 Hierarchical Belief Propagation

The multi scale Belief Propagation technique originally proposed to perform inference on Markov random fields [2]. The computational load of the algorithm is in the order of $O(nk^2T)$ for T iterations, where n is the number of pixels in the image and k is the number of possible labels (maximum of disparity value) for each pixel.

Felzenszwalb et al. [2] proposed a new approach to compute the new messages in $O(k)$ operations with the help of discontinuity cost function, based on the bipartite graph properties. The nodes can be split into two sets, so that every edge connects one node from first set to a node from second set. Let $m_{p \to q}^t$ be the message sent from node p to node q at time t. When t is an even/odd number, the messages sent from nodes in first/second set are updated and the nodes in second/first set contain the old values. The basic idea behind message passing is that the long range pixel interaction can be captured by short paths. In [2], the multi scale hierarchical approach has been used to reduce the number of message passing iterations without changing the cost function.

The earlier implementations of hierarchical Belief Propagation [2, 13], use a window of 2×2 pixels to form the next hierarchy levels. In this paper we use a 3×3 window in the same way as proposed in [14]. The n-th level contains the blocks of $3^n \times 3^n$ pixels grouped together and the resulting blocks are connected in a grid structure. The messages sent from nodes in one set only depend on the messages sent from nodes in the other set and vice versa. Figure 1 describes the message updates protocol. Supposing a 3×3 window around pixel q the four near neighbor pixels are

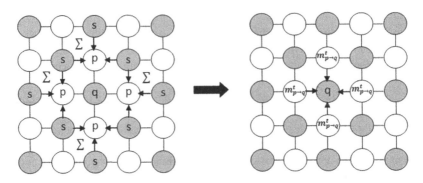

Fig. 1. General view on message passing between the nodes on alternative iterations

labeled as p and the all other far neighbors are called s. A node labeled as p receives messages send from all its adjacent nodes labeled as s (excluding node q) at time $(t - 1)$. Then all p nodes propagate their message to node q at time (t).

3   Cross Based Region

Pixels with the same color and connectivity are likely to share the same disparity value. The key idea of this approach is selecting an upright cross for each pixel as shown in Fig. 2. The cross-based algorithm searches the support region in four directions based on the color similarity and spatial connectivity. The cross-based support region is obtained by extending it first from the central pixel in directions of up and down, till the maximum arm length is received or the color difference exceeds a threshold. Then the process is repeated for each new pixel on the generated support region for left and right directions. The four arms of cross based support region around pixel p are named as $\left\{h_p^-, h_p^+, v_p^-, v_p^+\right\}$ respectively as the maximum of left, right, up and bottom arm lengths. They are used to define the horizontal and vertical segments H(p) and V(p) as Eq. (1). The support region of pixel p,U(p), is the integration of all the horizontal segments H(q) of those pixels residing on the vertical segment V(p) for pixel p as Eq. (2).

$$
\begin{cases}
H(p) = \left\{ (x,y) \mid x \in [x_p - h_p^-, x_p + h_p^+], y = y_p \right\} \\
V(p) = \left\{ (x,y) \mid x = x_p, y \in [y_p - v_p^-, y_p + v_p^+] \right\}
\end{cases}
\tag{1}
$$

$$
U(p) = \bigcup_{q \in V(p)} H(q)
\tag{2}
$$

Comparing color information of pixel p with its neighbor pixels in same row and in a finite search window in RGB format can be considered as a good real time disparity map refinement technique [14].

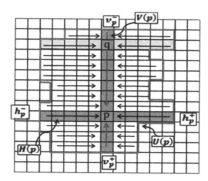

Fig. 2. The figure provides the configuration of cross-based method

4 Proposed Method

Figure 3 illustrates the block diagram of proposed stereo matching algorithms. In this method we provide a new structure that uses hierarchical Belief Propagation two times on left and right images respectively followed by a left-right consistency check as in initial match. Absolute difference (AD), squared intensity difference (SD) and cross correlation are three conventional pixel-based matching costs functions used for matching. Here absolute difference is used as cost criteria. For every pixel in the left image (reference image) it is needed to find its corresponding pixel from the right image (target image). To assign the best disparity value to a pixel we need to first compute the matching cost for all possible disparity values. Assuming the RGB format, r_p, g_p and b_p are the values of Red, Green and Blue content of pixel p. Difference $d(p, p')$ between pixel p in left image and pixel p' from right image is defined as Eq. (3):

$$d(p, p') = \sqrt{(r_p - r_{p'})^2 + (g_p - g_{p'})^2 + (b_p - b_{p'})^2} \tag{3}$$

Linear model is used to update messages in BP algorithm. For texture less areas of image the resulted disparity map is usually a false zero value. The technique proposed by Kumar in [14] has used in refinement step to solve the problem as shown in Fig. 3. The disparity map refinement is mainly based on cross based region method. A support region in four directions based on the color similarity and spatial connectivity for each pixel is defined. Then the most probable disparity values are chosen based on a voting method for refining the disparity value of each pixel. Finally algorithm updates the disparity of each pixel p with disparity of most similar pixel from reference image. Results show that this approach is very effective at objects boundaries.

5 Experimental Results and Discussion

The proposed algorithm is implemented fully in Microsoft Visual C++ and ran with a 2.00 GHz Core 2 duo computer using Windows-7 operating system. The runtime of the algorithm is related to the number of iterations and the image size. The disparity map

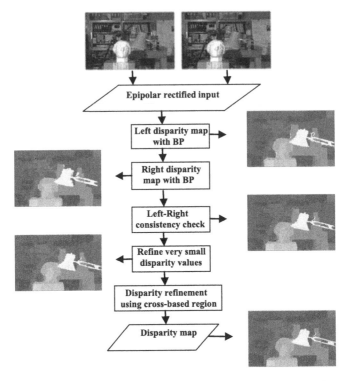

Fig. 3. Block diagram of proposed stereo matching algorithm with input data, intermediate and final results of the proposed method

calculation takes around 1.3 s for a 384 × 288 reference image. Figure 4 shows the energy of the Tsukuba dataset as a function of message update iterations in standard versus multi scale algorithm.

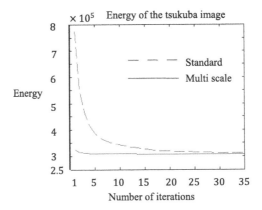

Fig. 4. The figure provides the energy as a function of message update iterations in standard and multi scale algorithm

Reference images   Ground truths   Our results   Bad pixel maps

Fig. 5. Results using the Middlebury datasets: Tsukuba, Venus, Teddy and Cones. Pixels with a disparity error greater than one pixel are displayed in the 'bad pixel' maps, where mismatches in non-occluded areas are indicated in black, in occluded areas in gray color

The results show that the proposed method converges in just a few iterations compare to the standard Belief Propagation. The comparison of the proposed method with other real-time algorithms on Middlebury evaluation table is summarized in Table 1. Table shows the percentage of the bad pixels with an absolute disparity error greater than one in whole image. We have evaluated our algorithm on the Middlebury datasets [15]. Figure 5 shows the disparity map results and bad pixels map computed using Middlebury evaluation system (for absolute disparity error >1.0). It is clear that the refinement algorithm helps to achieve a sharp disparity map by reconstructing the object boundaries.

Table 1. Middlebury stereo evaluation on the proposed method with other real-time algorithms for absolute disparity error >1, (*Not Mentioned in their paper).

Algorithm	Avg Rank	Tsukuba			Venus			Teddy			Cones			Bad pixel
		nocc	all	disc	nocc	all	disc	nocc	all	disc	nocc	all	disc	
Our method	82.4	1.51	1.84	7.80	0.79	0.90	1.84	8.88	15.7	21.0	4.59	11.6	10.8	7.27
Efficient HBP [14]	*	1.14	2.36	6.00	0.36	0.88	4.43	9.41	17.3	21.4	4.68	12.5	11.1	7.62
RealTimeBFV [16]	88.7	1.71	2.22	6.74	0.55	0.87	2.88	9.90	15.0	19.5	6.66	12.3	13.4	7.65
RealTimeBP [13]	91.2	1.49	3.40	7.87	0.77	1.90	9.00	8.72	13.2	17.2	4.61	11.6	12.4	7.69
FastAggreg [17]	94.3	1.16	2.11	6.06	4.03	4.75	6.43	9.04	15.2	20.2	5.37	12.6	11.9	8.24
RealTimeVar [18]	102.5	3.33	5.48	16.8	1.15	2.35	12.8	6.18	13.1	17.3	4.66	11.7	13.7	9.05
RealTimeGPU [19]	109.2	2.05	4.22	10.6	1.92	2.98	20.3	7.23	14.4	17.6	6.41	13.7	16.5	9.82
Tree DP [20]	118.6	1.99	2.84	9.96	1.41	2.10	7.74	15.9	23.9	27.1	10.0	18.3	18.9	11.7

6 Conclusions

In this paper we proposed a new stereo matching method with a combination of Hierarchical Belief Propagation and cross-based region strategy. In the proposed algorithm the matching process is divided into two main steps: initial matching and final disparity map refinement. We use hierarchical structure and a left-right consistency check to perform the initial matching. Disparity map refinement step uses a cross-based region that yields good results comparing to other algorithms. This algorithm computes an accurate disparity map fast, which makes it suitable to use in real-time applications. In the future, we plan to investigate some other matching cost functions to improve the initial disparity map without using left-right consistency checking in order to achieve interactive speeds.

References

1. Scharstein, D., Szeliski, R.: A taxonomy and evaluation of dense two-frame stereo correspondence algorithms. Int. J. Comput. Vis. **47**(1), 7–42 (2002)
2. Felzenszwalb, P.F., Huttenlocher, D.P.: Efficient belief propagation for early vision. In: Proceeding IEEE Conference on Computer Vision and Pattern Recognition, pp. 261–268 (2004)
3. Liang, C., Wang, L., Liu, H.: Stereo matching with cross-based region, hierarchical belief propagation and occlusion handling. In: IEEE International Conference on Mechatronics and Automation (ICMA), pp. 1999–2003 (2011)
4. Bleyer, M., Gelautz, M.: Graph-based surface reconstruction from stereo pairs using image segmentation. In: International Society for Optics and Photonics (SPIE), pp. 288–299 (2005)
5. Hong, L., Chen, G.: Segment-based stereo matching using graph cuts. In: Proceeding IEEE Conference on Computer Vision and Pattern Recognition, pp. 74–81 (2004)
6. Sun, J., Zheng, N., Shum, H.: Stereo matching using belief propagation. IEEE Trans. Pattern Anal. Mach. Intell. **25**(7), 787–800 (2003)
7. Yang, Q., Wang, L., Yang, R., Stewenius, H., Nister, D.: Stereo matching with color-weighted correlation, hierarchical belief propagation and occlusion handling. IEEE Trans. Pattern Anal. Mach. Intell. **31**(3), 492–504 (2009)
8. Taguchi, Y., Wilburn, B., Zitnick, C.L.: Stereo reconstruction with mixed pixels using adaptive over segmentation. In: IEEE International Conference on Computer Vision and Pattern Recognition, pp 1–8 (2008)
9. Klaus, A., Sormann, M., Karner, K.: Segment-based stereo matching using belief propagation and a self-adapting dissimilarity measure. In: International Conference on Pattern Recognition (ICPR), pp. 15–18 (2006)
10. Wang, Z.F., Zheng, Z.G.: A region based stereo matching algorithm using cooperative optimization. In: Proceeding IEEE Conference on Computer Vision and Pattern Recognition, pp. 1–8 (2008)
11. Comaniciu, D., Meer, P.: Mean shift: a robust approach toward feature space analysis. IEEE Trans. Pattern Anal. Mach. Intell. **24**(5), 603–619 (2002)
12. Zhang, K., Lu, J., Lafruit, G.: Cross-based local stereo matching using orthogonal integral images. IEEE Trans. Circuits Syst. Video Technol. **19**(7), 1073–1079 (2009)

13. Yang, Q., Wang, L., Yang, R., Wang, S., Liao, M., Nister, D.: Real-time global stereo matching using hierarchical belief propagation. In: British Machine Vision Conference (BMVC), pp. 989–998 (2006)
14. Gupta, R.K., Cho, S.Y.: Stereo correspondence using efficient hierarchical belief propagation. Neural Comput. Appl. **21**, 1585–1592 (2012)
15. Scharstein, D., Szeliski, R.: Middlebury Stereo Vision Page, (http://vision.middlebury.edu/stereo/)
16. Zhang, K., Lu, J., Lafruit, G., Lauwereins, R., Van Gool, L.: Real-time accurate stereo with bitwise fast voting on CUDA. In: IEEE International Conference on Computer Vision Workshop (2009)
17. Tombari, F., Mattoccia, S., Di Stefano, L., Addimanda, E.: Near real-time stereo based on effective cost aggregation. In: Proceeding IEEE Conference on Computer Vision and Pattern Recognition, pp. 1–4 (2008)
18. Kosov, S., Thormählen, T., Seidel, H.-P.: Accurate real-time disparity estimation with variational methods. In: Bebis, G., et al. (eds.) ISVC 2009, Part I. LNCS, vol. 5875, pp. 796–807. Springer, Heidelberg (2009)
19. Wang, L., Liao, M., Gong, M., Yang, R., Nister, D.: High-quality real-time stereo using adaptive cost aggregation and dynamic programming. In: Proceeding 3D Data Processing, Visualization, and Transmission, pp. 798–805 (2006)
20. Veksler, O.: Stereo correspondence by dynamic programming on a tree. In: Proceeding IEEE Conference on Computer Vision and Pattern Recognition, pp. 384–390 (2005)

Machine Vision

Incremental Discriminative Color
Object Tracking

Alireza Asvadi$^{(\boxtimes)}$, Hami Mahdavinataj, Mohammadreza Karami,
and Yasser Baleghi

Babol University of Technology, Babol, Iran
{asvadi.a,mahdavinataj}@stu.nit.ac.ir,
{mkarami,y.baleghi}@nit.ac.ir

Abstract. This paper presents an object tracking algorithm based on discriminative 3D joint RGB histograms of the object and surrounding background. Mean-shift algorithm on the object confident map is used for localization. An incremental color learning scheme with a forgetting factor is utilized to account for appearance variation of the object. Evaluated against three state of the art methods, experiments demonstrate the effectiveness of the proposed tracking algorithm where the object undergoes variation in illumination and color. Implemented in MATLAB, the proposed tracker runs at 25.7 frames per second.

Keywords: Visual tracking · Color object tracking · 3D joint RGB histogram · Incremental learning

1 Introduction

Visual object tracking is one of the most active research areas in computer vision, with numerous applications including automated surveillance, motion-based recognition, human-computer interaction and robotics. The goal of object tracking is to estimate the trajectory of an object in an image sequence given the initialized position in the first frame [1].

There is a rich literature in visual object tracking [1–4]. The object tracking algorithms mainly differ in the way they use image features and model the motion, appearance and shape of the object. Here, we focus on the most relevant online visual object tracking methods that operate directly on color images and also some state of the art methods. Generally, online object tracking algorithms can be categorized as either generative methods or discriminative methods [3].

The generative method builds a model to describe the appearance of an object and then finds the object by searching for the region most similar to the reference model in each frame. One of the most influential approaches in this category is the Mean-Shift Tracker [5] which uses a color histogram regularized by a spatially smooth isotropic kernel for object representation. Using the Bhattacharyya coefficient as a similarity metric, a mean-shift procedure is performed for object localization by finding the basin of attraction of the local maxima. One of the limitations of rectangular or ellipsoidal regions for object representation is the object model encompasses many background pixels in addition to the true target pixels. Consequently, the resulting histogram can be

© Springer International Publishing Switzerland 2014
A. Movaghar et al. (Eds.): AISP 2013, CCIS 427, pp. 71–81, 2014.
DOI: 10.1007/978-3-319-10849-0_8

corrupted by background pixels, and the tracking result degrades accordingly. To address this problem, algorithms based on fragments-based appearance model have been proposed [6]. Multiple local histograms are used to represent objects in the fragments-based method. A vote map is used to combine the votes from all the regions in the target frame. However, the computation of multiple local histograms and the vote map can be time consuming even with the use of integral histograms. In the similar vein, in [7], each target object is modeled by a small number of rectangular blocks, which their positions within the tracking window are adaptively determined. Recently, [8] proposed a histogram that takes into account contributions from pixels adaptively in a multi-region manner together with an illumination invariant feature. However, parts of the background may reside inside the object model. Therefore, the object model encompasses many background pixels in addition to the true target pixels which can degrade the object model. The advantage of generative methods is that does not require a large dataset for training, however the imperfection of the generative model is that it only focuses on the foreground without considering the background information.

Discriminative methods pose object tracking as a binary classification problem in which the task is to determine a decision boundary that distinguishes the object from the background without the need to a complex model characterizing the object. Since the discriminative model considers both the object and background information, it usually achieves better performance than the generative model. In [9] pixels color are mapped into 49 one-dimensional lines in RGB color space to build a set of 1D color histograms. Next, log-likelihood ratio of a feature value is used to select discriminative color features for tracking. In a similar manner [10, 11] adopt 13 different linear combinations of R, G, B pixel values to approximate 3D RGB color space. Approximating RGB color space using a set of 1D histograms is cheaper, however the major imperfection is it loses considerable color information that lies in 3D joint RGB histogram.

It has been shown an adaptive appearance model is the key to good performance and much attention has been paid in recent years to address this issue. The most straightforward method is to replace the current appearance model (e.g., template, color) with the visual information from the most recent tracking result [12]. However, simple update with recently obtained tracking result can lead to drift. In [13] AdaBoost algorithm is proposed to classify pixels belonging to foreground and background and update weak classifiers with new ones to adapt to the changes of the object and background during the tracking. In [14] the Boosting method is extended to an online manner. In [15] incremental subspace learning methods is proposed which present an adaptive probabilistic tracking algorithm that updates the models using an incremental update of Eigen-basis. In [16] the object is represented by a set of Haar-like features that are computed for each image patch. They used Multiple Instance Learning (MIL) to handle ambiguously labeled positive and negative data obtained online to reduce visual drift caused by classifier update.

Despite the discriminative methods generally do not model the object explicitly and only define the boundary between the target and background, here we utilize discriminative approach and incorporate an incremental learning scheme to learn and model the object color online during the tracking process. In addition, the proposed method attempts to solve unwanted effect of background pixels in the object rectangle. The contributions of this paper are summarized as follows:

- A discriminative 3D joint RGB histogram based representation of the object.
- Incremental color tracking with a forgetting factor to account for appearance variation of the object.

The remaining part of this paper is organized as follows. Section 2 describes the details of the proposed algorithm that presents an efficient incremental color object tracking. The results of the experiments and performance evaluations are presented in Sect. 3, and the conclusions and the future prospects are given in Sect. 4. The source code and videos corresponding to this work can all be found at http://www.a-asvadi.ir/idct/.

2 Proposed Method

Object tracking starts with selecting an object in the first frame approximately. A surrounding area is computed automatically such that the number of background pixels in the region surrounding the object is approximately the same as the number of pixels within the object region. Therefore, the width and height of outer rectangle are defined by $W = \sqrt{2} \times w$ and $H = \sqrt{2} \times h$. Where w and h are the width and height of the selected object region. In object tracking, first, one needs to develop a model for the object of interest. The aim of the object model is to accurately identify the object from the background in subsequent frames. Then, the object localizer estimates the target location in the subsequent frames using the object model. Next, an efficient method that incrementally updates the object model is employed to learn the appearance of the target while tracking progresses. Main steps of the proposed tracking algorithm are shown in the Fig. 1. Each step is described in the following sections.

2.1 Object Model

The object model is built and evolved based on discriminative 3D joint RGB histogram of the object and background. The quantized 3D joint RGB histograms of the region within the inner rectangle and the region between the inner and outer rectangles are computed. Positive part of the log-likelihood ratio of object region and background region surrounding the object is used to determine object model using (1),

$$L_s = max\left\{ ln\frac{max\{H_o(s), \varepsilon\}}{max\{H_b(s), \varepsilon\}}, 0\right\}$$ (1)

where $H_o(s)$ is the histogram computed within the object rectangle and $H_b(s)$ is the histogram for the region surrounding the object. The object color seeds have higher values in the computed log-likelihood ratio, background color seeds have negative values and colors that are shared by both the object and background tend towards zero. To model the object individually, negative values are rejected. Here, 8 bins for each channel are used for histogram quantization. Therefore, the index s ranges from 1 to 8^3 and 8^3 is the total number of histogram seeds. ε is a small non-zero value to avoid

---
Tracking Algorithm Outline

---
1. Object Model
The object is modeled based on the positive log-likelihood ratio of 3D joint RGB histogram.
2. Detection and Localization
The positive log-likelihood ratio is used for object detection and the mean-shift on confident map is used for object localization.
3. Model Update
Incremental color learning with a forgetting factor is applied to learn and update the object model.
4. Get the Next Frame and Go to Step 2

Fig. 1. A summary of the proposed tracking algorithm

numerical instability that prevents dividing by zero or taking the logarithm of zero. Here ε is set to 1.

2.2 Detection and Localization

The positive log-likelihood ratio provided in previous step is used for object detection and the mean-shift on confident map is used for object localization. Steps are described in the following subsections.

Detection. The positive log-likelihood ratio L_s is used as a mapping to provide a confident map, $M(x_i, y_i)$, from the object region, $I(x_i, y_i, c_j)$, i.e.,

$$L_s : I(x_i, y_i, c_j) \mapsto M(x_i, y_i) \tag{2}$$

where $[x_i, y_i]$ is the pixel location in the image coordinate. Index i ranges from 1 to N and N is the total number of pixels in the object region. c_j is the color channel of image. Index j ranges from 1 to 3 that stands for R-G-B color channels. The mapping result is a confident map image and its pixels with higher values are more likely to belong to the object.

Localization. Object localization for the next frame starts at the centroid of confident map of the object in the current frame. Since object movement is not ballistic, the mean-shift object localization on the confident map of the object provides satisfactory performance. The displacement of the object is given by the shift in the centroid of the pixel values in confident map. In each iteration, center of the object rectangle is shifted to the centroid of current confident map of the object, computed at the same iteration. The object rectangle is iteratively shifted until the object is completely placed inside the rectangle (mean-shift convergence). At each iteration, center of the object rectangle is relocated using Eqs. (3) and (4),

$$x_{new} = \frac{\sum_{i=1}^{N}(M_i \times x_i)}{\sum_{i=1}^{N} M_i} \qquad (3)$$

$$y_{new} = \frac{\sum_{i=1}^{N}(M_i \times y_i)}{\sum_{i=1}^{N} M_i} \qquad (4)$$

where x_i and y_i show the location of pixels in the frame coordinate. M_i is the confidence value, x_{new} and y_{new} show the relocated center of the object rectangle in each iteration and N is the total number of pixels in the inner rectangle. In the presented work, the maximum number of mean-shift iterations is limited to 3 and centroid movement less than 2 pixels is considered as a complete convergence.

2.3   Model Update

To account for appearance variation of the object, it is inevitable to adapt the object model to the recent observations. Here, once the object location at the current frame is provided by mean-shift, the positive log-likelihood ratio, L_p^t, is computed and used to update the previous object model, L_p^{t-1}, by (5),

$$L_p^{t+1} \leftarrow (1 - \gamma) \times L_p^{t-1} + \gamma \times L_p^t \qquad (5)$$

where $t + 1$, t and $t - 1$ are indexes for the next, current and previous frames respectively. p indicates the randomly α percent selection of the positive log-likelihood ratio seeds s. Here α is set to 5 %. γ is a forgetting factor to moderate the balance between old and new observations. Although the forgetting factor depends on the amount of changes in object appearance, here we set it to 0.1 for all the tested videos. L_p^{t+1} is the updated object model which will be used for the object detection in the next frame.

3   Experimental Results

In order to evaluate the performance of the proposed tracking algorithm, experiments were carried out using a core 2 Duo 2 GHz processor with 1 GB RAM under MAT-LAB R2011a on the Windows XP platform. The tracker has been tested on variety of challenging sequences, and six of the most representative sequences are reported in this paper (All video results are placed at our project website: http://www.a-asvadi.ir/idct/). The sequences are Basketball, David outdoor, Girl and Trellis from Tracker Benchmark v1.0[1] [17] and Sunshade and Torus from VOT2013 dataset[2] which are publicly available. Five of the sequences were taken by non-stationary cameras and one of them

---

[1] https://sites.google.com/site/trackerbenchmark/benchmarks/v10
[2] http://votchallenge.net/vot2013/evaluation_kit.html

Table 1. The detailed information of each sequence

Sequence name	No. of frames	Resolution	Challenge			
			Background clutter	Rotation & deformation	Illumination variation	occlusion
Basketball	725	576 × 432	✓	✓	✓	✓
David outdoor	252	640 × 480	✓	✓		✓
Girl	500	128 × 96		✓		✓
Sunshade	172	352 × 288	✓		✓	
Torus	264	320 × 240	✓	✓		
Trellis	569	320 × 240	✓	✓	✓	

(Torus) was taken by a stationary camera. The detailed information and challenging factors for each sequence are described in Table 1.

The proposed method (called IDCT) is evaluated against three methods which the codes are publicly available, Mean Shift tracker (MS) [5], mean-shift tracker with Corrected Background Weighted Histogram (CBWH)[3] [18] and Variance Ratio tracker (VR)[4] [9]. We compared the proposed method with the most relevant visual object tracking methods that operate directly on color images. The MS, CBWH and IDCT adopt a 3D joint RGB histogram to describe the appearance of an object and VR uses 49 candidates of one-dimensional line color features in RGB color space as a feature pool and choose the best N features at each frame.

The parameters of the proposed algorithm are set as follows: in the object detection and localization parts, we use 8 bins for histogram quantization and the maximum number of mean-shift iterations is limited to 3 as empirical values. In the model update part, α, which is the percentage of randomly selected non-empty seeds is set to 5 % and the forgetting factor, γ, is set to 0.1. For all other algorithms we use the parameters provided by the corresponding authors and run them with the adjusted parameters. All algorithm parameters were fixed for all the experiments. All algorithms assume knowledge of the object position only in the first frame. The object position is estimated in the next frames using the corresponding algorithm. The average speed of the evaluated algorithms is computed for Trellis (as a typical video with object size of 101 × 68 pixels) and together with the detailed information of each algorithm are reported in Table 2.

Our tracker (IDCT) works at 25.7 frames per second and runs faster than the other algorithms except Variance Ratio (VR) method. It should be noted VR method is implemented in C++ which is intrinsically more efficient than MATLAB.

For evaluating the performance of trackers, the average center location error is used which is a very common criterion. The error is defined by,

---

[3] http://www4.comp.polyu.edu.hk/~cslzhang/CBWH.htm

[4] http://vision.cse.psu.edu/data/vividEval/software.html

Table 2. A comparison of tracking speed (without image I/O time)

Algorithm	Feature description	Code style	Speed (fps)
MS 8 bin	Color histogram	MATLAB code	22.9
MS 16 bin			20.5
CBWH 8 bin	Color histogram	MATLAB code	22.4
CBWH 16 bin			21.1
VR	Line color feature	C++ code with OpenCV	32.5
IDCT (proposed)	Color histogram	MATLAB code	25.7

$$error = \frac{1}{n}\sum_{i=1}^{n} \sqrt{(X_i - X_i^g)^2 + (Y_i - Y_i^g)^2} \qquad (6)$$

where $[X_i, Y_i]$ shows the center location of the object determined by an algorithm. The center of the object is defined by central point of the object window. $[X_i^g, Y_i^g]$ denotes the center of the ground truth bounding box. i ranges from 1 to n and n is the total number of frames. The average center location errors of trackers are shown in Table 3 and the details of center location errors for the sequences are shown in Fig. 2. As shown in Table 3, the proposed method provides minimum error in the Basketball, David outdoor, Girl and Trellis datasets, while it is the second and third best for the Torus and Sunshade sequences respectively.

Sample screenshots of the tracking results for the video sequences are shown in Fig. 3 where each row corresponds to one video clip. The qualitative evaluation of each scenario is described in the following paragraph.

In the Basketball sequence only our method tracks the object successfully. The object trajectories provided by other methods were hijacked by the other cluttered basketball players (e.g. frame #600 and #700). In the David outdoor sequence our method and CBWH 8 and 16 have a good performance. MS 8 and 16 lose the object from fame #100 to #180 and VR drifts from frame #180 when the target object is occluded by a tree (it can be seen in frame #125 and #190). For the Girl sequence, since our object model evolves during tracking, our method successfully tracked the object while the other methods lost the object (as shown in frame #100 and #425). In the Sunshade sequence MS 8 and 16 do not perform well for the frames between #15 to #105 due to illumination variation, however other methods have reasonable results

Table 3. The average center location errors (in pixels) of the sequences. The best result is printed in bold faced letters.

Seq.\ Algorithm	MS 8	MS 16	CBWH 8	CBWH 16	VR	IDCT
Basketball	57.0	58.4	18.3	18.1	116.1	**5.4**
David outdoor	68.6	55.6	25.2	26.6	81.8	**23.1**
Girl	18.5	19.0	26.9	27.6	62.4	**12.8**
Sunshade	72.6	71.2	9.8	**9.4**	13.9	12.5
Torus	8.2	36.2	4.2	**3.4**	7.6	4.2
Trellis	54.1	38.3	23.6	18.5	60.0	**15.2**

(e.g. frame #30). In the Torus sequence MS 8 drifts to background clutter, however other methods track the object till the end of the sequence (as shown in frame #200). For the Trellis sequence the object appearance changes drastically due to the change in illumination, only the proposed method achieves good performance and is able to adapt to the illumination variation well.

4 Concluding Remarks and Future Work

In this paper, we proposed a fast effective object tracking algorithm with incremental discriminative object color modeling. The algorithm efficiently addresses tracking of an object which undergoes variation in illumination and color. The object scale was not

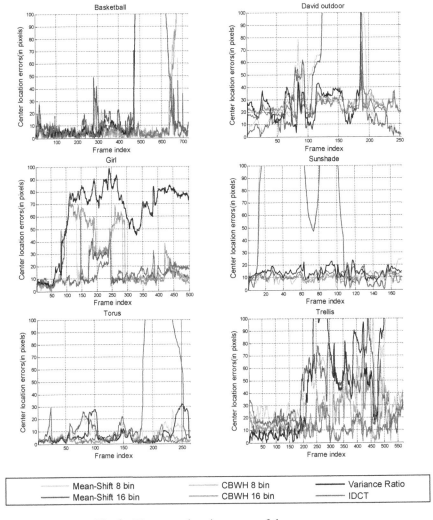

Fig. 2. The center location errors of the sequences.

| Mean-Shift 8 bin | CBWH 8 bin | Variance Ratio |
| Mean-Shift 16 bin | CBWH 16 bin | IDCT |

Fig. 3. Screenshots of tracking results presented as listed in Table 1. The object confident map provided by the proposed method (IDCT) is shown at the top-left corner of the frames.

considered here, the approach in [19] can be incorporated for scale adaption. We propose two ways for the future work. First, the motion and object model we used here are fairly simple, in future, prediction-based methods such as a Kalman filter [20] can be used. Second, inherent in the use of histograms is the complete lack of spatial information which is undesirable. Template patches can be incorporated in the object model to preserve spatial information which will be our future work.

References

1. Yilmaz, A., Javed, O., Shah, M.: Object tracking: a survey. ACM Comput. Surv. **38**, 1–45 (2006)
2. Cannons, K.: A review of visual tracking. York University, Department of Computer Science and Engineering, Technical report CSE-2008-07 (2008)
3. Yang, H., Shao, L., Zheng, F., Wang, L., Song, Z.: Recent advances and trends in visual tracking: a review. Neurocomputing **74**, 3823–3831 (2011)
4. Li, X., Hu, W., Shen, C., Zhang, Z., Dick, A., Hengel, A.V.D.: A survey of appearance models in visual object tracking. ACM Trans. Intell. Syst. Technol. **4**, 58:1–58:48 (2013)
5. Comaniciu, D., Ramesh, V., Meer, P.: Kernel-based object tracking. IEEE Trans. Pattern Anal. Mach. Intell. **25**, 564–577 (2003)
6. Adam, A., Rivlin, E., Shimshoni, I.: Robust fragments-based tracking using the integral histogram. In: Proceeding of IEEE Conference on Computer Vision and Pattern Recognition, pp. 2142–2147 (2006)
7. Shahed Nejhum, S.M., Ho, J., Yang, M.H.: Online visual tracking with histograms and articulating blocks. Comput. Vis. Image Und. **114**, 901–914 (2010)
8. He, S., Yang, Q., Lau, R.W., Wang, J., Yang, M.H.: Visual tracking via locality sensitive histograms. In: Proceeding of IEEE Conference on Computer Vision and Pattern Recognition, pp. 2427–2434 (2013)
9. Collins, R.T., Liu, Y., Leordeanu, M.: Online selection of discriminative tracking features. IEEE Trans. Pattern Anal. Mach. Intell. **27**, 1631–1643 (2005)
10. Wei, Y., Sun, J., Tang, X., Shum, H.Y.: Interactive offline tracking for color objects. In: Proceeding of International Conference on Computer Vision, pp. 1–8 (2007)
11. Wang, D., Lu, H., Xiao, Z., Chen, Y.W.: Fast and effective color-based object tracking by boosted color distribution. Pattern Anal. Appl. **16**, 647–661 (2013)
12. Asvadi, A., Karami, M., Baleghi, Y.: Object tracking using adaptive object color modeling. In: Proceeding of 4th Conference on Information and Knowledge Technology, pp. 848–852 (2012)
13. Avidan, S.: Ensemble tracking. IEEE Trans. Pattern Anal. Mach. Intell. **29**, 261–271 (2007)
14. Grabner, H., Leistner, C., Bischof, H.: Semi-supervised on-line boosting for robust tracking. In: Forsyth, D., Torr, P., Zisserman, A. (eds.) ECCV 2008, Part I. LNCS, vol. 5302, pp. 234–247. Springer, Heidelberg (2008)
15. Ross, D.A., Lim, J., Lin, R.S., Yang, M.H.: Incremental learning for robust visual tracking. Int. J. Comput. Vision **77**, 125–141 (2008)
16. Babenko, B., Yang, M.H., Belongie, S.: Robust object tracking with online multiple instance learning. IEEE Trans. Pattern Anal. Mach. Intell. **33**, 1619–1632 (2011)
17. Wu, Y., Lim, J., Yang, M. H.: Online object tracking: a benchmark. In: Proceeding of IEEE Conference on Computer Vision and Pattern Recognition (2013)

18. Ning, J., Zhang, L., Zhang, D., Wu, C.: Robust mean-shift tracking with corrected background-weighted histogram. IET Comput. Vis. **6**, 62–69 (2012)
19. Collins, R.T.: Mean-shift blob tracking through scale space. In: Proceeding of IEEE Conference on Computer Vision and Pattern Recognition, pp. II–234 (2003)
20. Jahandide, H., Mohamedpour, K., Moghaddam, H.A.: A hybrid motion and appearance prediction model for robust visual object tracking. Pattern Recogn. Lett. **33**, 2192–2197 (2012)

Aerial Target Recognition Based on High Resolution Range Profiles (HRRP)

Reza Hallaj$^{(\boxtimes)}$, Reza Mohseni, and Kamran Kazemi

Shiraz University of Technology, Shiraz, Iran
{r.hallaj,mohseni,kazemi}@sutech.ac.ir

Abstract. The fact that very small aspect changes can drastically alter the profile of an aircraft implies that a huge number of profiles would be required to characterize an aircraft from all possible aspects. This make a look-up table approach to classification impractical in the short-wavelength limit. A deterministic model and a conditionally Gaussian model for high-resolution range profiles (HRRP) are used, and the recognition performance under each model are compared by using one and more than one range profile. The experimental results show that assumption of Gaussian distribution by using 10 range profiles improve the recognition performance.

Keywords: High-resolution range profile (HRRP) · Radar automatic target recognition (RATR) · Bayesian classifier · Statistical propriety

1 Introduction

According to electromagnetic scattering theory, in the high-frequency zone where the extent of an object is much greater than the wavelength of a radar, a high-resolution range profile (HRRP) is a function of the coherent summations of the complex time returns from target scatterers in each range cell [1], which represents the projection of the complex returned echoes from the target scattering centers onto the radar line-of-sight (LOS). Since HRRP of a target contains the target structure signatures, it can be used for radar automatic target recognition (RATR).

A small change in orientation of illumination will change the HRRP time values [2, 3]. If the target recognition algorithm uses time values of signal, we will need a database of targets HRRP with little angle spacing while including all important targets [3]. So the database would be very large and hence slow recognition process [3]. For aspect changes as much as several degrees, the variations in range profile signal are mostly in amplitude but not in shape of signal. HRRPs have a same statistical properties in that range of orientation [4, 5].

If we use HRRP statistical properties instead of real time values in the range of orientation that those are constant, database will be smaller, since it only contains statistical distribution parameters of HRRPs.

The echoed HRRP can be assumed as a deterministic signal but this assumption can degenerate the recognition algorithm performance, since unpredictable effects, i.e. dust, weather conditions and difference in orientation that signal is simulated in database and

© Springer International Publishing Switzerland 2014
A. Movaghar et al. (Eds.): AISP 2013, CCIS 427, pp. 82–90, 2014.
DOI: 10.1007/978-3-319-10849-0_9

orientation of received signal [5]. Parametric statistical distribution assumption for HRRP can compensate unpredictable effects and dependence of HRRP to orientation.

We use Bayesian classifier to classify objects based on conditional probability density of HRRP given a known class. Nonparametric methods of density estimation are impractical due to the unrealistic amounts of data required for accurate density estimation. An alternative approach is to trade flexibility for robustness and to use some simple parametric forms [6]. Under the hypothesis that elements in an HRRP sample are statistically independent, some simple statistical models, i.e., Gaussian model [5], Gamma model [7], and the two distribution compounded model comprising Gamma distribution and Gaussian mixture distribution [8], were proposed for HRRP samples. In parametric methods database includes only the parameters of determined density functions.

By using more than one HRRP to make decision, performance of recognition algorithm enhances [4, 9]. This paper is intended to compare deterministic model and Gaussian model using one and 10 HRRPs in recognition rate and the elapsed time.

This paper is organized as follows, In Sect. 2, Radar range profile proprieties are explained. In Sect. 3, we explain Bayesian classifier and radar HRRP. In Sect. 4, We propose equations which are based on deterministic and Gaussian HRRP statistical distribution assumptions. In Sect. 5, recognition experiments based on simulated data are performed to compare the recognition performances of proposed statistical distribution models of HRRP and influence of using sequence of HRRPs on recognition rate. Finally, conclusions are made is Sect. 6.

2 Radar Range Profiles

Since the bandwidth of high-range resolution radar is more than several hundred megahertz, the range resolution is smaller than one meter. So the target echo is not a point, but a range profile related to scatterer distribution. A radar range profile can be thought of as the one dimensional projection of the spatial distribution of radar reflectivity of the aircraft onto the radar LOS.

If the radial range of scatterers is changed, two different effects will be caused. One is the displacement of envelope, and the other is variation of the phase difference that is typically described in terms of phase cancellation [3, 5].

Consider monochromatic illumination of a radar target of width D by a source of wavelength λ, Fig. 1. If the envelope displacement is greater than the range resolution cell, the scatterers' migration through resolution cells (MTRC) takes place, and then the scatterers' distribution of every range cell is changed. To avoid MTRC, the rotation angle must be restricted, that is, if the range resolution is Δr, the cross-direction length is D, and then the rotation angle must be confined to

$$\Delta\theta \leq \frac{\Delta r}{D} \tag{1}$$

On the range of aspects for which the radar profile can be considered the same projection of the aircraft [3]. For example, if $\Delta r = 0.5$ m and D = 10 m, we find $\Delta\theta < 3°$.

Phase cancelation is occurred if the orientation of target is changed so that scaterrer points in the same range bin move through a distance on the order of λ, the relative phases contributing to the compete return produce varying degrees of constructive and destructive interference over the rotation [3]. To avoid speckle fluctuations the aspect would stay constant to within

$$\Delta\theta \ll \frac{\lambda}{4D} \tag{2}$$

If the target is large compared with λ, then the rotation required to produce speckle is very small. If λ = 0.03 m and D = 10 m, we find Δθ < 0.04°.

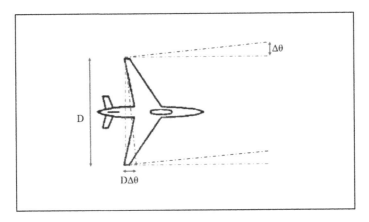

Fig. 1. Small aspect change Δθ causes relative range change of DΔθ for points separated by D.

HRRP of AN-26 aircraft is simulated by a radar backscattering simulation software [10, 11]. Radar signal is a linear FM chirp, with a center frequency of 3 GHz and a bandwidth of 360 MHz. Horizontal polarization was used during transmission and reception. Data set consists of 600 range profiles collected over an orientation bin of 0–60°. The change in orientation of illuminated aircraft with respect to the radar system between adjacent range profiles is 0.1°.

Figure 2 displays the magnitude of 20 range-profiles of AN-26 aircraft in orientation span of 30–32°. The self consistency of the range profiles in this data set is evident in that the individual traces lie nearly on top of one another.

This experiment shows that, for an aircraft over a limited range of aspects, i.e., Eq. 1, the distribution of scattering centers in range will be similar. Hence, the corresponding profiles should display common statistical proprieties, although the amplitude of the features will fluctuate from profile to profile [2, 5].

Statistical distribution of range profiles in a span of orientations is the same. If we use statistical proprieties instead of time values of target range profile the dependency of recognition algorithm to illumination aspect decreases and the targets database need only to save statistical distribution parameters instead of time values [2, 4, 5].

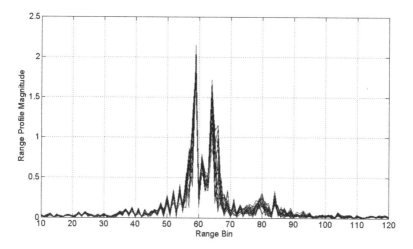

Fig. 2. Magnitude of 20 range profiles over the span of $2°$

3 Bayesian Classifier

The Bayesian classifier Eq. 3 has optimal performance if the probability density functions computed accurately [12].

$$\omega_k : arg\ max\ P(\omega_i|\boldsymbol{x})$$
$$1 \leq i \leq M \tag{3}$$

where $p(\omega_i|\boldsymbol{x})$ are posteriori probability densities of class ith (ω_i), $\boldsymbol{x}$ measured data vector, ω_k are the selected class and M is the number of classes that recognition is performed between them. The classifier chooses between classes that have the highest probability of occurrence. Equation (3) can be written in the form of Eq. 4 by using of bayesian rule Eq. 5.

$$\omega_k : arg\ max\ p(\boldsymbol{x}|\omega_i)$$
$$1 \leq i \leq M \tag{4}$$

$$P(\omega_i|\boldsymbol{x}) = \frac{p(\boldsymbol{x}|\omega_i)P(\omega_i)}{p(\boldsymbol{x})}$$
$$i = 1, 2, \ldots, M \tag{5}$$

where $p(x|\omega_i)$ are class-conditional probability densities, $P(\omega_i)$ are prior class probabilities and $p(x)$ probability density of measured data.

In obtaining Eq. 4 we assumes equal prior class probabilities and eliminates ineffective $p(x)$ element.

To specify $p(\boldsymbol{x}|\omega_i)$, We must determine the statistical distributions of $\boldsymbol{x}$ vector conditioned on every class members.

Measured data $\boldsymbol{x}$ contains the HRRP and additive complex white Gaussian noise.

$$x = s(\theta, a) + w$$
$$a \in \mathcal{A} \qquad (6)$$
$$\theta \in SO(3)$$

where $s(\theta,a)$ is HRRP vector of target a in orientation θ, W is an independent complex Gaussian random variable with mean 0 and variance N_0, $\mathcal{A}$ is a list of candidate target types and the orthogonal group $SO(3)$ is defined so orientation θ is parameterized by a 3×3 rotation matrix taking its value on it. On selecting an appropriate parametric model, we assumes that range profiles are independent from one orientation to another and that for each orientation [5].

4   Models of HRRP Data

4.1   Deterministic Model

Under deterministic model, the vector $s(\theta,a)$ is a complex vector that is known given θ and a. The log-likelihood for x is

$$T(x|\theta, a) = Re\left(\frac{2}{N_0} \sum_{l=1}^{K} x_l^* s_l(\theta, a) - \frac{E_{s(\theta.a)}}{N_0} \right) \qquad (7)$$

where Re{.} is real part of equation, (*) complex conjugate operator, k number of rang cells values, x_i and $E_{s(\theta,a)}$ energy of $s(\theta,a)$ signal. Using this model needs database of HRRPs stored on a grid in orientation space [5].

4.2   Gaussian Model

By independent Gaussian distribution assumption, then the log-likelihood for x is

$$T(x|\theta, a) = -\sum_{l=1}^{k} \ln\left(\sigma^2(l; \theta, a) + N_0 \right) + \frac{|x_l - \mu(l; \theta, a)|^2}{\sigma^2(l; \theta, a) + N_0} \qquad (8)$$

where k is dimension of x, x_i is lth entry of x, $\mu(l;\theta,a)$ and $\sigma^2(l;\theta,a)$ respectively are mean and variance of lth entry.

Recognition based on conditional Gaussian model requires a database of mean and variance vectors. To form Gaussian database for targets, the set of possible azimuth angles is divided into overlapping patches, and the libraries consist of mean range profiles and range bin variances computed from all of the range profiles in each patch. Two strategies are required in choosing size of orientation bins [5].

- The Likelihood of any range profile must be constant over the orientation bin.
- Choose size of orientation bins in which the range profiles in adjacent bins are independent.

By using Gaussian model for HRRPs, the angular sampling is more sparse than deterministic method and is not very dependent to carrier frequency [5]. The size of orientation bin that we will use is 3°, according to Eq. 1, and in view of few scatterers distributed at the edges of an aircraft-like target and with weak energy [5, 8].

5   Experimental Results

Experiments are given to verify the theory and method described above. We simulate radar range profiles data of three airplanes by a radar backscattering simulation software [10, 11], the parameters of radar signal and targets are shown in Table 1, radar signal is a linear FM chirp. As these three airplanes are all symmetrical in horizontal, we only simulate azimuth 0°–180° at interval 0.15°, and elevation angle is initialized to 0°. Range of noise variance in all experiments is from 0.6 to 4.8.

Table 1. Parameter of aircrafts and radar in experiments

Radar parameters		
	Center frequency	1.35 GHz
	Bandwidth	753 MHz
	Sampling frequency	5.02 MHz
	Number of frequency samples	150
	Number of azimuth samples	1201
Planes	Length (m)	Width (m)	Height (m)
F-15	19.43	13.05	5.73
Mig-21	15.76	7.15	4.15
Tornado	16.72	13.92	5.95

5.1   Recognition by One HRRP

In this paper we examine the difference in performance of deterministic and Gaussian models by using one range profile.

The range profile from the F-15 dataset at an azimuth angle of 70° was selected as an observation. Adding complex white Gaussian noise to the signal, the log-likelihood functions under the two models Eqs. 7 and 8 were computed for each of three aircrafts over the range of azimuth angles from 0 to 180°. The aircraft with largest log-likelihood function is chosen as the target type estimate.

Recognition rate of deterministic model and Gaussian model versus noise variance are shown in Fig. 3. The results of this experiment, show that recognition performance of the models are almost the same. It is possible by Gaussian model while using smaller libraries and considerably faster recognition process see Table 2.

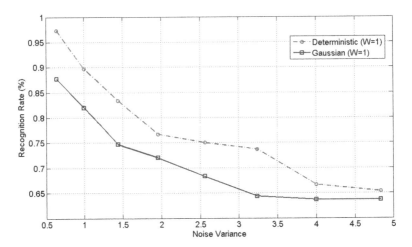

Fig. 3. Recognition performance using one HRRP

5.2   Recognition by More Than One HRRP

In the previous experiment, estimate of target type was computed individually for each illumination, in this one we are going to estimate target type by using a number of successive HRRPs. We have chosen a simple dynamical model to relate past and present target estimates; namely, that the yaw angles defining the aircraft orientation change linearly over a sliding window in time. Then, a sequence of orientations over the window are completely determined by the window end points.

After loading range profile libraries for all three aircrafts and the first W observed range profiles, estimation of target type proceeds as fallows [5].

1. The likelihood of observation number 1 is computed by Eq. 7 or Eq. 8 depend on which model is chosen, for each orientation of the F-15 range profile library. The ten orientations having the highest computed likelihood are retained. This process is repeated using observation number W, producing 100 pairs of candidate orientations at the widow endpoints.
2. For each entry of this list, linear interpolation is applied to the window endpoints to generate a sequence of orientation estimates over the widow. Each of these estimates is replaced by the nearest orientations that are orientation points in our library. These data and the sequence of observations are used to compute the joint likelihood of the sequence of orientation points corresponding to the current list entry, and the process is repeated for the entry list. A list of joint likelihood values collected for this target.
3. The entire process is repeated using the range profile library for two other targets. The target producing the highest joint likelihood is selected as the target type estimate.

For this experiment the range profiles from the F-15 dataset in azimuth orientation range from 70 to 73° were selected as observations, given that window length W is 10.

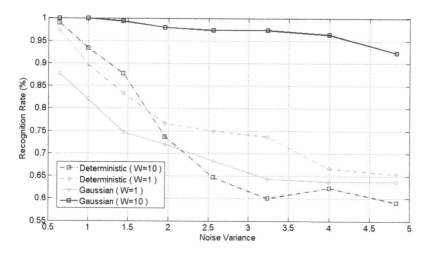

Fig. 4. Recognition performance using 10 HRRPs

Recognition rate of deterministic model and Gaussian model versus noise variance are shown in Fig. 4. The results of experiment show that recognition performance of the Gaussian model is better than the deterministic model.

Improvement in recognition performance is because of two reason. First reason is which the Gaussian model is less sensitive to orientation angle changes than the deterministic model [5] and the second one, the result of multi look classification is higher in correct recognition rate than that from single look classification [4, 9]. The results in Fig. 4 slow that using 10 HRRPs degenerates deterministic model performance in comparison with one HRRP and this is because of sensitivity of deterministic model to orientation variations. Enhanced performance in using Gaussian model by 10 HRRPs is achieved while using smaller libraries and faster recognition process see Table 2.

Table 2. Elapsed time for 300 iterations

		Elapsed time (s), 300 iterations	
		Deterministic model	Gaussian model
Window length	W = 1	805	25
	W = 10	1815	362

6   Conclusion

In this paper we use the Gaussian and the deterministic models for HRRP statistical distribution and measured the correct recognition rate by one HRRP and a group of successive HRRPs. Using one HRRP to classify the unknown target, deterministic model has better performance and lower speed of recognition process compared with

Gaussian model but when using a group of successive HRRPs, we achieve enhanced performance by Gaussian model assumption.

This improvement is obtained by lower sensitivity of Gaussian model to variation in orientation of illumination and use of more HRRPs to estimate target type.

References

1. Knott, E.F., Shaeffer, J.F., Tuley, M.T.: Radar Cross Section. Scitech, Raleigh (2004)
2. Xing, M., Bao, Z., Pei, B.: Properties of high-resolution range profiles. Opt. Eng. **41**(2), 493–504 (2002)
3. Hudson, S., Psaltis, D.: Correlation filters for aircraft identification from radar range profiles. IEEE Trans. Aerosp. Electron. Syst. **29**(3), 741–748 (1993)
4. Pei, B., Bao, Z.: Multi-aspect target recognition method based on scattering centers and HMMs classifiers. IEEE Trans. Aerosp. Electron. Syst. **41**(3), 1067–1074 (2005)
5. Jacobs, S.P., O'Sollivan, J.A.: Automatic target recognition using sequences of high resolution radar range-profiles. IEEE Trans. Aerosp. Electron. Syst. **36**(2), 364–381 (2000)
6. Du, L., Liu, H., Bao, Z.: Radar HRRP statistical recognition: parameter model and model selection. IEEE Trans. Sig. Process. **56**(5), 1931–1944 (2008)
7. Copsey, K., Webb, A.: Bayesian gamma mixture model approach to radar target recognition. IEEE Trans. Aerosp. Electron. Syst. **39**(4), 1201–1217 (2003)
8. Du, L., Liu, H., Bao, Z., Zhang, J.: A two-distribution compounded statistical model for radar HRRP target recognition. IEEE Trans. Sig. Process. **54**(6), 2226–2238 (2006)
9. Williams, R., Westerkamp, J., Gross, D., Palomino, A.: Automatic target recognition of time critical moving targets using 1D high range resolution (HRR) radar. IEEE AES Syst. Mag. **15**(4), 37–43 (2000)
10. Shirman, Y.D.: Computer Simulation of Aerial Target Radar Scattering Recognition, Detection, and Tracking. Artech House, Boston (2002)
11. Gorshkov, S.A., Leschenko, S.P., Orlenko, V.M., Sedyshev, S.Y., Shirman, Y.D.: Radar Target Backscattering Simulation Software and User's Manual. Artech House, Boston (2002)
12. Cai, Y., Cai, H.: The comparative study of different Bayesian classifier models. In: ICMLC, pp. 302–313 (2010)

Unconstrained Head Pose Estimation with Constrained Local Model and Memory Based Particle Filter by 3D Point Distribution Models

Ali Moeini[1(✉)], Mahdi Seyfipoor[1], Karim Faez[1], and Hossein Moeini[2]

[1] Amirkabir University of Technology, Tehran, Iran
{alimoeini,mahdiseyfipoor,kfaez}@aut.ac.ir
[2] Semnan University, Semnan, Iran
hosseinmoeini@aol.com

Abstract. In this paper, a novel and efficient method was proposed for unconstrained head pose estimation of the human face and robustness to changes of pose, position and facial expression. A Constrained Local Model (CLM) by a 3D Point Distribution Model (PDM) was proposed for locating 2D facial landmarks in optional poses of the human face. Also, a memory based Particle Filter (PF) was used to improve the manner of prior distribution in PF and reduce the number of particles. However, a fast search method was proposed from the trained memory of PF. In fact, instead of calculating the similarity distance between each particle and the total templates in the memory, a small number of templates were utilized. The present method was tested on two available video databases to evaluate performance of proposed method. Promising results displayed better performance than the current state-of-the-art approaches in head pose tracking with our extension of the 3D Constrained Local Model (CLM-Z).

Keywords: Head pose estimation · Face detection · Face tracking · Memory based particle filter · Constrained local model

1 Introduction

The real time head pose estimation is a fundamental problem in computer vision, computer animation, computer games for its various applications, including pose invariant face recognition [1–3], gaze estimation [4], etc. Research topics in this field include appearance template methods, detector array methods, hybrid methods, geometric methods, nonlinear regression methods, tracking methods, flexible models, and manifold embedding methods. Thus, head pose estimation in real-time, wider rotations ranges, low and variable lighting conditions, and user independence is extremely challenging. For a real-time head pose estimation system to be of general use, it should have a sufficient range of allowed motion, be invariant to identity, require no manual intervention, and should be easily deployed on conventional hardware. However, some

A. Movaghar et al. (Eds.): AISP 2013, CCIS 427, pp. 91–99, 2014.
DOI: 10.1007/978-3-319-10849-0_10

systems often assume one or more conditions that simplify the pose estimation problem such as: continuous video assumption, initialization assumption, stereo vision assumption, single Degree-Of-Freedom (DOF) assumption, synthetic data assumption and etc. Meanwhile, the majority of head pose estimation approaches assume the perspective of a rigid model, which has inherent limitations. The difficulty in creating head pose estimation systems stems from the immense variability in individual appearance coupled with differences in lighting, background, and camera geometry. Also, many existing pose estimation methods may not be suitable for achieving real times systems, both coarse, fine resolution and in 6 DOF directions.

Recently, Tadas proposed a 3D Constrained Local Model (CLM-Z) [5] for strong facial landmark tracking under different poses. This method mixes both depth and intensity data in a shared framework. He demonstrated the advantage of the CLM-Z method in both precision and convergence amounts over regular CLM formulations over investigations. The main drawback of this method is that it requires the frontal face image in initial frames of video in order to detect the facial landmarks in frontal face images. Also, the other drawback of this method is the requirement for depth information from the human face. In this work, these restrictions are resolved by employing a 3D PDM in CLM framework. Therefore, the face detection in all of the poses of the head by the present method is possible. In fact, face pose tracking based on the 3D model can be used as pose invariant face detection and tracking.

In this work, a CLM method with a 3D Point Distribution Model (PDM) was proposed for face detection and appearance models for pose estimations. Also, a Memory-based Particle Filter (M-PF) was proposed which was combined with the appearance of 3D PDM in order to carry out real-time face tracking robust to changes of pose, position and facial expression. By using MBPF, a small number of particles were distributed in appropriate poses and positions to estimate the state of the head in the next frame. In fact, rather than distribute particles in random poses and positions, the previous memory of states was used to scatter a few number of particles with proper states.

Also, experiments were provided that demonstrate the present method can achieve an accurate pose of input faces under a variety of imaging conditions, including facial expressions, gender and ethnicity. The present method was tested on Biwi Kinect Head Pose [6] and ICT database [5] in order to carry out head pose estimation.

This paper is organized as follows: Sect. 2 describes CLM with a 3D Point Distribution Model (PDM) for locating the facial landmarks in total face pose. Section 3 describes the M-PF for pose invariant head tracking. Experimental evaluations are presented in Sect. 4 and conclusions in Sect. 5.

2 Constrained Local Model with 3D Point Distribution Model for Face Pose Detection

In this section, how to construct a 3D PDM for use in the CLM was presented. A visual illustration of constructing a 3D PDM is shown in Fig. 1. Based on, a Generic Elastic Model (GEM) [7] for each expression was considered. The GEM was created by the method employed in [8, 12] and by using the 3D database Bosphorus [9]. Then, the 3D spatial location (x_{2DPDM}, y_{2DPDM}, z_{GEM}) of each 3D PDM was constructed as:

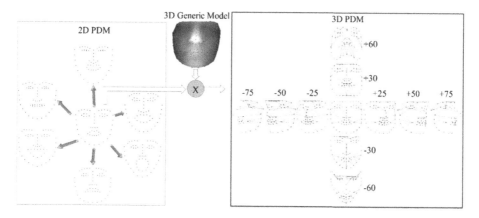

Fig. 1. Construction 3D PDM from 2D PDM and GEM.

$$(x_{2DPDM},\ y_{2DPDM},\ 0) + (0,\ 0,\ z_{GEM}) = (x_{2DPDM},\ y_{2DPDM},\ z_{GEM}) \qquad (1)$$

where x_{2DPDM} and y_{2DPDM} are 2D spatial location of each 2D PDM, and z_{GEM} is the depth of spatial location of 2D PDM in each GEM for each 2D PDM according to facial expressions. The main contributions of this section are 3D PDM construction and use in landmark localizations.

In general, the pose detection and landmark localization process can be shown in Fig. 2. Based on, pose detection performs in initial frames of input video by Haar pose detection [8]. Then, the constructed 3D PDM rotates in the detected initial pose direction and a patch is created around each facial landmark in the rotated 3D PDM. Finally, the fitting process is performed on spatial location of 3D PDM in order to fit the facial landmarks to the main location.

For the fitting process, a common two step CLM fitting strategy [10, 11] was employed, carrying out an exhaustive local search around the present estimate of spatial location of 3D PDM leading to a response map around every facial landmark, and then iteratively updating the model factors to minimize error until a convergence metric is obtained. For fitting process a Regularized Landmark Mean-Shift (RLMS) [11] was used according to the method employed in [11].

Training CLM with 3D PDM includes constructing the 3D PDM and training the patch experts. The PDM is used both to provide the prior p(p) and to make 3D PDM the shape model. The patch experts serve to calculate the response maps according to the method employed in [11]. For training, the Biwi Kinect Head Pose database [6] was used and the main training was employed according to the training method employed in [11] with a few difference. These difference are due to training of the patch experts in all face poses which in addition to training the patch experts in frontal face, the patch experts in non-frontal face were also trained.

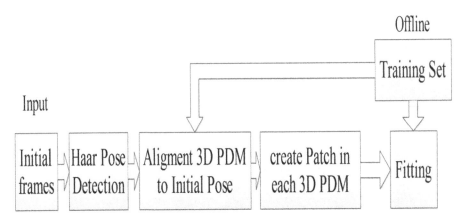

Fig. 2. An illustration of pose detection and landmark localization.

Therefore, by employing 3D PDM in the CLM landmark localization, all possible face poses are possible. This pose detection and landmark localization is rapid and the average time of this manner for pose detection and landmark localization is less than 0.1 s.

3   Facial Landmarks Tracking

3.1   Memory-Based Particle Filter (M-PF)

The M-PF provides vigorous target tracking without explicit modeling of the target's dynamics. Similar to conventional PF, M-PF uses Bayes' rule and estimates the posterior probability density function for the next state of the target by a two-stage process including prediction and update that have been presented in Eqs. (2) and (3) respectively. The first stage predicts prior distribution and the second updates particles weight by using obtained observations. Providing that the posterior probability density function of the previous state $(p(x_{t-1}|z_{1:t-1}))$ is available, the prior probability density function is obtained as:

$$p(x_t|z_{1:t-1}) = \int p(x_t|x_{t-1})p(x_{t-1}|z_{1:t-1})dx_{t-1} \tag{2}$$

where z_t and z_{t-1} are observation at times t and t − 1, respectively, and x_t and x_{t-1} are state vectors at times t and t − 1, respectively. Utilizing z_t (observation at time t), the prior probability density function obtained from Eq. (2) is updated with Bayes' rule according to Eq. (3):

$$p(x_t|z_{1:t}) = \frac{p(z_t|x_t)p(x_t|z_{1:t-1})}{\int p(z_t|x_t)p(x_t|z_{1:t-1})dx_t} \tag{3}$$

where p(zt|xt) represents the likelihood function.

The M-PF eases the Markov supposition of PF and predicts the prior distribution based on the target's long-term dynamics using the past account of the target's positions. Probability density function $p(x_t \mid x_{t-1})$ in Eq. (1) expresses the motion model of the target that demonstrates the distribution manner of particles for estimation of the next state. This model can be an explicit model of target motion such as the motion model with constant velocity, random Gaussian model or motion model based on memory. M-PF uses the memory-based motion model to predict prior distribution and scatter particles. In other words, the aim of employing PF based on memory is improving of the particles scattering using a small number of them.

The M-PF stores activist series of past state vectors $x_{1:t} = \{x_1,\ldots,x_t\}$ in the memory and assumes that the subsequent parts of the past states similar to the current state present the good estimation of the next state. Here, $x_{1:t}$ denotes a sequence of state estimates from time 1 to time t.

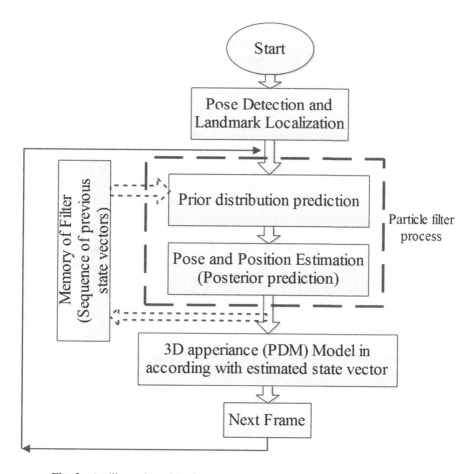

Fig. 3. An illustration of tracking method for head pose estimation approach.

3.2   Face Pose Tracking System Using M-PF

In this section, a pose invariant face tracking was proposed using M-PF that utilizes a simple memory to store past estimated state vectors. This memory only stores 7D vectors $S = \{S_1, S_2 \ldots S_{t-1}\}$, $S_i = (x, y, z, p, y, r, i)$ and no appearance models (PDMs) for which (x, y, z), (p, y, r), and i represent 3D position of the head, face pose and coefficient of light respectively. The tracking system based on M-PF uses this memory to estimate prior prediction. However, a general 3D appearance model of the face is available in order to model likelihood probability. The general 3D PDMs is illustrated in Fig. 1 in which by varying this model's parameters, the PDMs accordance with state vectors can be obtained. Therefore, no requirement is necessary to save this model in the memory.

Suppose that the 7D state vector of the target in time $t-1$ is presented by S_{t-1} which is available. To estimate the state (pose and position) of the target in time t, the memory of the filter is searched to find the vector that is the most similar to S_{t-1} and has the minimum Euclidean distance with it. Then, a small number of state vectors around this selected vector in memory are selected as possible vectors for estimation of the state vector in time t that are mentioned as particles (prior distribution prediction process). To measure of the similarity between each particle and the target model, a PDM likelihood model is required. Therefore, for each scattered particle a 3D mesh model is made and similarity between each of them and the target model is measured.

Figure 3 illustrates a block diagram of the proposed tracking system. The proposed detection algorithm expressed in the previous sections is used to detect face pose direction in the first frame. In the other frames, pose and position of the target is tracked by using the M-PF tracking method. This tracking algorithm is utilized as long as the state of the target is determined. In the first step of the algorithm, a memory-based particle filter process is used to estimate the state of the target in each frame such that it uses a sequence of previous state vectors in memory to predict prior distribution and then estimates the posterior density function by using likelihood observation (appearance model). The estimated state vector of the target is saved in memory. In the last step, an appearance model according to the estimated state vector is created. In this way, the tracking process of the target for one frame is finished.

4   Experiments

In order to quantitatively show the performance of the present pose estimation method in all possible poses of the face, the present method was tested on two available databases to estimate the face poses as sequence images. The Biwi Kinect Head Pose database [6] and ICT-3DHP database [5] are two databases that were used in the experiment. To demonstrate the accuracy of the present method, in order to detect the face in all poses, initial frames that are included in the frontal face image were removed from the databases and the test was performed on the remaining frames.

4.1   Head Pose Estimation on ICT-3DHP Database

To test the present method in this part, the ICT-3DHP database was used. The dataset contains 10 video sequences (both intensity and depth), of around 1400 frames each and is publicly available. Also in this database, for each image the pitch and yaw angles are rendered. In this database to show accuracy, the present method frontal face images are removed from the initial frames in each video. To evaluate the present method, the pose of face was initially estimated. Then, estimation error was computed by subtracting the estimated value in each frame from each person and the pitch and yaw value which are rendered for each frame. Finally, for each person a mean estimation error was calculated.

Fig. 4. Examples of CLM with 3D PDM tracking method on a sample from ICT-3DHP database. Blue meshes in each image represent 3D PDM of the target and red cubes in each frame demonstrates face pose in that frame. Each frame show: three measured angles of face pose, the number of frames per second (FPS) and number of frame.

Examples of landmark localization and tracks using CLM with 3D PDM and (present tracker) on two samples from the ICT-3DHP dataset can be seen in Fig. 4. To verify the effectiveness of face tracking method using M-PF, we used a test video sequence that included a head rotated with high degree of freedom and having rapid direction changes. Blue meshes in each image represent a 3D PDM of the target and red cubes in each frame demonstrate face pose in that frame. As illustrated in Fig. 4, this tracking algorithm can track the pose and position of the face accurately with sufficient frames per second. In Fig. 4, an effective face pose detection and landmark localization method can be seen in frame #0 which is robust to face pose and no frontal face for landmark localization is required. Results of appraising the present tracker on the ICT-3DHP database can be seen in Table 1. We see a significant progress of using the present method over other methods in trackers.

Table 1. Table showing the head pose estimation results on ICT-3DHP database. Error is measured in mean absolute distance from the ground truth.

Method	Yaw	Pitch	Roll	Mean
Regression forests [6]	7.17	9.40	7.53	8.03
CLM [10]	11.10	9.92	7.30	9.44
CLM-Z [5]	14.80	12.03	23.26	16.69
CLM-Z with GAVAM [5]	2.90	3.14	3.17	3.07
CLM with 3D PDM (our method)	**2.53**	**2.67**	**3.24**	**2.81**

Table 2. Table showing the head pose estimation results on Biwi Kinect Head Pose database. Error is measured in mean absolute distance from the ground truth.

Method	Yaw	Pitch	Roll	Mean
Regression forests [6]	9.2	8.5	8	8.6
CLM [10]	28.85	18.3	28.49	25.21
CLM-Z [5]	14.80	12.03	23.26	16.69
CLM-Z with GAVAM [5]	6.29	5.1	11.29	7.56
CLM with 3D PDM (our method)	**4.1**	**4.9**	**9.5**	**6.16**

4.2 Head Pose Estimation on the Biwi Kinect Head Pose Database

To test the present method in this part, the Biwi Kinect Head Pose database was used. The dataset contained over 15 K images of 20 people (6 females and 14 males in which 4 people were recorded twice) without facial expressions. For each frame, a depth image corresponding to the RGB image and the annotation is provided. The head pose range covers about $\pm 75°$ yaw and $\pm 60°$ pitch. A subset of 20 face images were utilized which are selected from each person including 400 images in yaw direction between -75 and $+75°$ as sequence and frame to frame images, 400 images in pitch direction between -60 and $+60°$ as sequence images. Thus, the total images utilized for each person in this experiment are 800 (400 + 400) of which frontal face images are removed from the initial frames. Also in this database, for each image the pitch and yaw angles are rendered.

Results of evaluating the present tracker on the Biwi Kinect Head Pose database can be seen in Table 2. We see a significant progress of using the present method over other methods in trackers.

5   Conclusion

In this paper a CLM method with 3D PDM was proposed which utilized a 3D PDM for face pose detection and landmark localization. In this method frontal state of face not required in initial frames of video and present method can be in all pose of face to carry out locating facial landmarks. This method was tested on available datasets and demonstrates better performance both in terms of convergence and accuracy for facial landmarks tracking from a single image non-frontal face and in frames of video.

Also, the M-PF was proposed which was combined with an appearance of 3D PDM in order to carry out real-time face tracking robust to changes of pose, position and facial expression. The drawback of the existing methods are using only frontal face for face detection and landmark localization. Hence, we extend an existing CLM tracker to be able to use the non-frontal face detection and landmark localization leading to more accuracy when tracking head pose by M-PF.

References

1. Blanz, V., Vetter, T.: Face recognition based on fitting a 3D morphable model. IEEE Trans. Pattern Anal. Mach. Intell. **25**(9), 1063–1074 (2003)
2. Prabhu, U., Heo, J., Savvides, M.: Unconstrained pose-invariant face recognition using 3D generic elastic models. IEEE Trans. Pattern Anal. Mach. Intell. **33**(10), 1952–1961 (2011)
3. Ishiyama, R., Hamanaka, M., Sakamoto, S.: An appearance model constructed on 3-D surface for robust face recognition against pose and illumination variations. IEEE Trans. Syst. Man Cybern. Part C Appl. Rev. **35**(3), 326–334 (2005)
4. Valenti, R., Sebe, N., Gevers, T.: Combining head pose and eye location information for gaze estimation. IEEE Trans. Image Proc. **21**(2), 802–815 (2012)
5. Baltrusaitis, T., Robinson, P., Morency, L.P.: 3D constrained local model for rigid and non-rigid facial tracking. In: CVPR (2013)
6. Fanelli, G., Weise, T., Gall, J., van Gool., L.: Real time head pose estimation from consumer depth cameras. In: DAGM (2011)
7. Heo, J., Savvides, M.: 3-D generic elastic models for fast and texture preserving 2-D novel pose synthesis. IEEE Trans. Inf. Forensics Secur. **7**(2), 563–576 (2012)
8. Ramirez, G.A., Fuentes, O.: Multi-pose face detection with asymmetric haar features. In: IEEE Workshop on Applications of Computer Vision (WACV 2008) (2008)
9. Savran, A., Alyüz, N., Dibekliöglu, H., Çliktutan, O., Göberk, B., Sankur, B., Akarun, L.: Bosphorus database for 3D face analysis. In: Proceedings of the 1st COST Workshop Biometrics Identity Management, pp. 47–56 (2008)
10. Cristinacce, D., Cootes. T.: Feature detection and tracking with constrained local models. In: BMVC (2006)
11. Saragih, J., Lucey, S., Cohn, J.: Deformable model fitting by regularized landmark mean-shift. Int. J. Comput. Vision **91**(2), 200–215 (2011)
12. Moeini, A., Faez, K., Moeini, H.: Facial expression invariant 3D face reconstruction from a single image using deformable generic elastic models. In: Proceeding of MVIP (2013)

Semi-dynamic Facial Expression Recognition Based on Masked Displacement Image

Hamid Sadeghi[(✉)] and Abolghasem Asadollah Raie

Electrical Engineering Department,
Amirkabir University of Technology, Tehran, Iran
{hamid.sadeghi,raie}@aut.ac.ir

Abstract. Facial expression recognition, as an interesting problem in pattern recognition and computer vision, has been performed by means of dynamic and static methods in recent years. Though dynamic information plays important role in facial expression recognition, utilizing the entire dynamic information of expression image sequences have high computational cost compared to the static cases. In order to reduce the computational cost, only neutral and emotional faces can be used instead of entire image sequence. In the previous research, this idea has been employed by means of DLBPHS method which vanish facial important small displacements by subtracting LBP features of neutral and emotional face images. In this paper, a novel semi-dynamic approach is proposed to utilize two face images by subtracting neutral image from emotional image. In this method, LBP features are extracted from masked difference image. In the masking procedure, eyes and mouth being important regions in facial expression recognition are selected for feature extraction step. Evaluation of the proposed algorithm on the standard databases shows a significant accuracy improvement compared to DLBPHS method.

Keywords: Facial expression recognition · Local Binary Patterns (LBP) · Displacement image · Difference image · Support Vector Machine (SVM)

1 Introduction

Facial expression or emotion expression in human face is an important human social interaction way. Psychological studies show that six basic emotions including anger, disgust, fear, happiness, sadness, and surprise have universal facial expressions in all cultures [1, 2]. Though different subjects express these emotions differently, we can recognize facial expression of an unfamiliar face [3]. Because of various applications, such as producing robots with human-like emotions, automatic facial expression analysis becomes an interesting problem in machine vision and pattern recognition.

Feature extraction step plays an important role in the accuracy of recognizing facial expression. The existing facial expression recognition systems can be divided according to their feature extraction method [4]. Basically, there are three types of feature extraction techniques: geometric feature-based; appearance feature-based; and hybrids of appearance and geometric feature-based. Geometric feature-based methods [5–7] utilize the geometric shape and location of facial components, such as eyebrow

© Springer International Publishing Switzerland 2014
A. Movaghar et al. (Eds.): AISP 2013, CCIS 427, pp. 100–108, 2014.
DOI: 10.1007/978-3-319-10849-0_11

and mouth, for facial representation. In the appearance feature-based methods [8–11], the texture information of facial image is employed [4, 11]. Hybrid methods [12–16] use both appearance and geometric features for facial images representation. Although geometric features have similar or more accuracy than appearance features [17, 18], geometric feature extraction generally needs perfect location of facial fiducial point.

In appearance feature-based methods, generally Gabor filter [19] was applied to the facial images [15, 20–22]. However, convolving Gabor filters in different orientations and scales have a huge calculation. In [23], another type of texture descriptors as Local Binary Patterns (LBP) have been introduced, and different version of them have been used for facial appearance feature extraction in both static and dynamic methods [9–11, 15]. A survey of facial image analysis using LBP-based feature extraction is presented in [24].

In other categorization, the existing studies can be divided into static and dynamic approaches [4]. Static methods use a single frame to recognize facial expression; while in the dynamic methods, temporal changes in the video sequence are utilized [4]. Psychological studies indicate that dynamic methods provide higher performance than static approaches [25]. Therefore, this paper tries to utilize the dynamic information of facial expression. However, utilizing the whole dynamic information of an image sequence has a huge computational cost. For this reason, this paper compares the emotional image with neutral image to extract suitable facial features. In this study, LBP are used as facial appearance features due to their accuracy in facial representation [24] and computational simplicity. All of the experiments are person-independent in such a way that the train persons are not present in the testing data. For this reason, a multiclass Support Vector Machine (SVM) classifier is used in different cross validation testing schemes. Support Vector Machine is attracted much attention in pattern recognition and facial expression recognition [9–11, 22].

The remainder of this paper is summarized as:

In the next section, the LBP texture descriptor and the proposed feature extraction method using LBP is described. Introducing the databases and evaluation of the proposed system on standard databases is presented in Sect. 3. Finally, Sect. 4 concludes this paper.

2   Facial Representation

2.1   Local Binary Patterns

Basic Local Binary Patterns (LBP) operator was introduced as a powerful texture descriptor in [23]. For each pixel, LBP operator produces 8 labels by thresholding 3×3 neighborhood of the pixel with its gray-level value (Fig. 1). Then, the histogram of corresponding decimal values as shown in is used as an image texture descriptor. The basic LBP operator produces 256 binary patterns. However, it can be shown the most appeared binary patterns in facial images are uniform [27]. Number of uniform binary patterns in the basic LBP operator is 58; accumulating the non-uniform binary patterns into a single bin yields a 59 bin histogram (LBP^{u2} operator) [27]. Figure 2 shows some examples of uniform binary patterns along with their micro-texture information.

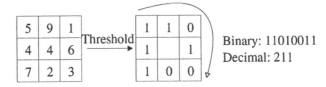

Fig. 1. An example of the basic LBP operator on an image pixel [26]

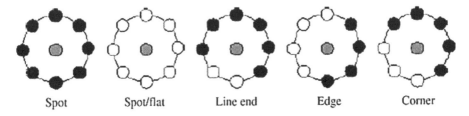

Spot   Spot/flat   Line end   Edge   Corner

Fig. 2. Five examples of texture information in LBP patterns; black and white circles represent zero and one, respectively [28].

The experimental results demonstrate that 90.6 % of appeared patterns in facial images using basic LBP operator are uniform [29]. Therefore, this paper utilizes LBP^{u2} operator for feature extraction.

2.2 Displacement Image LBP (DI-LBP)

As mentioned previously, the dynamic information of facial images sequence is utilized in this paper. Intuitively, one can say that a facial expression is a variation in the texture of facial components. Each expression has an individual variation; and the variations lie in specific regions. In this study, the facial regions containing expression-based variation are detected in the video sequence. Therefore, the difference of emotional image (EI) and one of the previous frames (here: the first frame) is calculated. Then, LBP^{u2} features are extracted from the difference/displacement image (DI). The block diagram of the proposed feature extraction method is shown in Fig. 3.

Firstly, the first and the peak frame of expression sequence are selected for our experiment. Color images are converted to grayscale. Next, all facial images are normalized to 150 × 110 pixels followed by face region localization using AAM feature points. In the next step, difference of peak frame and the first frame is calculated. To reduce the computational cost, some important regions in facial image can be used for feature extraction. Therefore, mouth and eyes regions are selected in our experiments. This method reduces computational complexity and enhances the accuracy of algorithm. Then, LBP^{u2} histogram is extracted from masked difference/displacement image (DI-LBP). Thus, the facial regions being stationary in the image sequence are appeared as flat areas in DI. Accordingly, facial stationary textures are accumulated in the flat area bin of LBP histogram.

Holistic LBP histogram cannot represent any indication about location of binary patterns. To solve this problem, the masked images are divided into 19 sub-regions with

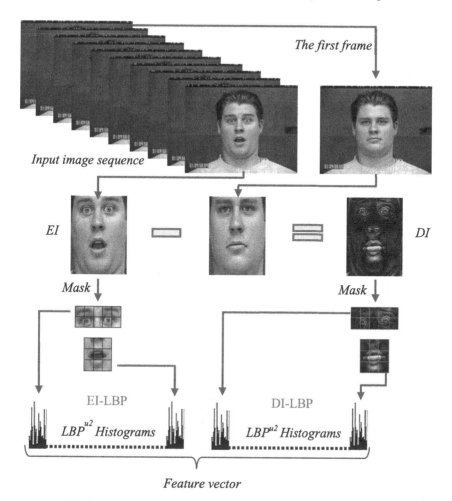

The first frame

Input image sequence

EI

DI

Mask ↓

Mask ↓

EI-LBP

DI-LBP

LBP^{u2} *Histograms*

LBP^{u2} *Histograms*

Feature vector

Fig. 3. The block diagram of proposed feature extraction method.

size of 21 × 18 pixels according to [11]. Then, the LBP^{u2} histograms of these sub-regions are concatenated to a single feature vector with the length of 1121 (59 × 19) to represent facial image. In order to keep all suitable information of facial image, the LBP histograms of masked emotional image (EI) is calculated in the same way. Finally, EI-LBP and DI-LBP are concatenated into final feature vector with length of 2242 (2 × 1121).

In [30], difference of LBP histograms calculated from emotional and neutral frames was used as DLBPHS (Difference of LBP Histogram Sequences) feature vector. One disadvantage of DLBPHS is elimination of small displacement texture information from LBP histogram by subtracting two LBP features. In contrast, the effects of small displacements are highlighted in DI. Calculating LBP histogram from DI can be appropriately used for texture description in facial image.

Another disadvantage of subtracting two LBP histograms in DLBPHS algorithm is elimination of facial stationary region information. On the contrary, in the proposed method, difference of neutral and emotional images is calculated; thus, facial stationary regions are appeared as flat area in DI. Accordingly, the texture information of these regions lies in flat area bin in the LBP histogram. As a result, feature vectors are inherently normalized. Furthermore, any information is not eliminated from feature vector; and they only lie in suitable bins in the LBP histogram.

3   Experimental Results

3.1   Dataset

In this paper, extended Cohn-Kanade database (CK+) [31], that is an extended version of original Cohn-Kanade dataset (CK) [32], are employed for evaluation of the proposed system. The database consists of 123 subjects and all prototypic emotions in addition to Contempt facial expression. Furthermore, 68 fiducial points was localized using Active Appearance Model (AAM) in CK+ [31]. Each data includes one sequence of images starting from neutral face to peak of its emotion label. In this study, three peak frames of each sequence were labeled as one of the emotions are utilized in the experiments. The AAM fiducial points are used for face region localization. Figure 4 shows some examples of CK+ facial image with maximum emotion intensity.

Fig. 4. Eight examples of CK face images and new images in CK+ are shown in the top and bottom rows, respectively. Expression labels from top left to bottom right: Disgust, Happiness, Surprise, Fear, Angry, Contempt, Sadness, and Neutral [31].

3.2   Experiments

To evaluate the performance of proposed algorithm, a multi-class Support Vector Machine (SVM) [33] classifier with linear and polynomial kernel functions is utilized on CK+ [31] database. For this reason, different testing scheme, including leave-one-subject-out (LOSO) and 10-fold cross validation are used for person-independent classification. Table 1 show the result of different region selection in facial expression recognition. The confusion matrix of six-expression recognition on CK+ database using SVM (linear) is shown in Table 2. The results of different region selection are compared with [34] in Table 3.

Table 1. 6-class average recognition rate on CK+ database in case of different region selection

SVM kernel	Measure			
Linear	10-fold	91.45	93.72	89.5	79.44
	LOSO	**93.16**	**94.68**	**91.97**	**80.24**
Polynomial	10-fold	91.67	94.16	89.72	77.71
	LOSO	92.29	94.68	91.86	79.26

Table 2. Confusion matrix of six-class expression recognition on CK+ database using SVM (linear) classifier and leave-one-subject-out measure

Expression	Angry (%)	Disgust (%)	Fear (%)	Happiness (%)	Sadness (%)	Surprise (%)
Angry	**92.59**	5.19	0	0	2.22	0
Disgust	1.72	**97.70**	0	0.57	0	0
Fear	4.17	2.78	**88.89**	0	0	4.17
Happiness	0	2.42	1.45	**96.14**	0	0
Sadness	8.33	0	0	0	**88.10**	3.57
Surprise	0	1.20	1.20	1.2	0	**96.39**
Average	**94.68 %**					

Table 3. Comparison of algorithm accuracy to [34] on CK+ dataset using different face regions

	Whole face	Best region selection	Mouth	Eyes
Ours	**93.16**	**94.68**	**91.97**	**80.24**
[34] (%)	88	91.4	81.0	64.8

CK+ database includes contempt expression, which makes it more challenging than CK dataset. In this section, 7-class facial expression recognition including contempt and six basic emotions is performed using SVM (polynomial) classifier. Table 4 compares the accuracy of the proposed algorithm with the existing work on CK+ dataset. As shown in Table 4, the proposed method has the highest accuracy on CK+.

3.3   Evaluation on JAFFE Database

To provide a fair comparison of the proposed algorithm with DLBPHS [30], we conduct experiments in the same ways as [30]. In [30], JAFFE database [35] was used in the experiments. JAFFE database consists of 10 Japanese female subjects. Each subject has 3 or 4 images for each basic facial expression and the neutral face (totally 213 images with size of 256×256 pixels).

Table 4. Comparison of the algorithm performance with the existing work on CK+ database

	Classes	Cross validation	Accuracy (%)
Ours	6	leave-one-subject-out	94.68
Ours	6	10-fold	94.16
Ours	7	leave-one-subject-out	94.41
Ours	7	10-fold	94.05
[31]	7	leave-one-subject-out	88.33
[36]	7	10-fold	90.1
[37]	7	leave-one-subject-out	82.6
[38]	7	10-fold	89.3
[34]	7	leave-one-subject-out	91.4

Table 5. Comparisons between DLBPHS method [30] and our method

	Database	6-calss recognition (%)
Ours	**CK+**	**94.16**
Ours	**JAFFE**	**91.23**
DLBPHS	CK+	82.36
DLBPHS [30]	JAFFE	80.33

In [30], 2 images of each subject from each expression were selected in training step, and the rest images from each expression were used as test images. In this section, the experiments are conducted in the same way as [30]. Moreover, we implement the DLBPHS method [30], which was discussed in Sect. 2.2, with the same results as [30] on JAFFE database. Then, this method is experimented on CK+ database in a 10-fold cross validation person-independent testing scheme. Table 5 compares the result of our method with DLBPHS on both CK+ and JAFFE databases.

4   Conclusion

In this paper, we present a facial expression recognition method which utilizes semi-dynamic information of emotional and neutral frames. Therefore, the first frame of each image sequence (neutral face) is subtracted from the emotional face instead of subtracting their LBP features. Next, LBP is used for efficient facial feature extraction. According to the experimental results on the standard datasets, it can be concluded that feature extraction from difference image provides better accuracy than subtracting LBP features. Moreover, utilizing important region instead of whole face (masking process) improves the accuracy of proposed facial expression recognition systems.

The major of dynamic facial expression methods utilize whole facial expression image sequence. The proposed algorithm can be utilized in these dynamic systems to reduce the computational cost. Furthermore, difference/displacement image (DI) can be obtained from emotional frame and one of the previous frames with low emotion intensity instead of neutral face in future work.

References

1. Fasel, B., Luettin, J.: Automatic facial expression analysis: a survey. Pattern Recogn. **36**, 259–275 (2003)
2. Ekman, P., Friesen, W.V.: Constants across cultures in the face and emotion. J. Pers. Soc. Psychol. **17**(2), 124–129 (1971)
3. Ekman, P.: Facial expressions of emotion: an old controversy and new findings. Philos. Trans. Royal Soc. Lond. **B335**, 63–69 (1992)
4. Tian, Y., Kanade, T., Cohn, J.: Chapter 11. Facial expression analysis. In: Handbook of Face Recognition. Springer, Heidelberg (2005)
5. Pai, N.S., Chang, S.P.: An embedded system for real-time facial expression recognition based on the extension theory. Comput. Math. Appl. **61**(8), 2101–2106 (2011)
6. Kobayashi, H., Hara, F.: Recognition of six basic facial expression and their strength by neural network. In: Proceedings of International Workshop Robot and Human Communication, pp. 381–386 (1992)
7. Kobayashi, H., Hara, F.: Recognition of mixed facial expression by neural network. In: IEEE International Workshop Robot and Human Communication, pp. 387–391 (1992)
8. Ma, L., Khorasani, K.: Facial expression recognition using constructive feedforward neural networks. IEEE Trans. Syst. Man Cybern. Part B Cybern. **34**(3), 1588–1595 (2004)
9. Zhao, G., Pietikäinen, M.: Dynamic texture recognition using local binary patterns with an application to facial expressions. IEEE Trans. Pattern Anal. Mach. Intell. **29**(6), 915–928 (2007)
10. Sadeghi, H., Raie, A.A., Mohammadi, M.R.: Facial expression recognition using geometric normalization and appearance representation. In: 8th Iranian Conference on Machine Vision and Image Processing (MVIP 2013), Zanjan, Iran, pp. 856–860 (2013)
11. Shan, C., Gong, Sh, McOwan, P.W.: Facial expression recognition based on local binary patterns: a comprehensive study. Image Vis. Comput. **27**(6), 803–816 (2009)
12. Lanitis, A., Taylor, C., Cootes, T.: Automatic interpretation and coding of face images using flexible models. IEEE Trans. Pattern Anal. Mach. Intell. **19**(7), 743–756 (1997)
13. Cootes, T., Edwards, G., Taylor, C.: Active appearance models. IEEE Trans. Pattern Anal. Mach. Intell. **23**(6), 681–685 (2001)
14. Edwards, G.J., Cootes, Tim F., Taylor, C.J.: Face recognition using active appearance models. In: Burkhardt, H., Neumann, B. (eds.) ECCV 1998. LNCS, vol. 1407, pp. 581–595. Springer, Heidelberg (1998)
15. Xiao, R., Zhao, Q., Zhang, D., Shi, P.: Facial expression recognition on multiple manifolds. Pattern Recogn. **44**(1), 107–116 (2011)
16. Zhang, L., Chen, S., Wang, T., Liu, Z.: Automatic facial expression recognition based on hybrid features. In: International Conference on Future Electrical Power and Energy Systems, Energy Procedia, vol. 17, pp. 1817–1823 (2012)
17. Valstar, M., Patras, I., Pantic, M.: Facial action unit detection using probabilistic actively learned support vector machines on tracked facial point data. In: Proceedings of CVPR, vol. 3, pp. 76–84 (2005)
18. Valstar, M., Pantic, M.: Fully automatic facial action unit detection and temporal analysis. In: Proceedings of CVPR, p. 149 (2006)
19. Daugmen, J.: Complete discrete 2d Gabor transforms by neutral networks for image analysis and compression. IEEE Trans. Acoust. Speech Signal Process. **36**(7), 1169–1179 (1988)
20. Bashyal, S., Venayagamoorthy, G.K.: Recognition of facial expression using Gabor wavelets and learning vector quantization. Eng. Appl. Artif. Intell. **21**(7), 1056–1064 (2008)

21. Gu, W., Xiang, C., Venkatesh, Y.V., Huang, D., Lin, H.: Facial expression recognition using radial encoding of local Gabor features and classifier synthesis. Pattern Recogn. **45**, 80–91 (2012)
22. Zhang, L., Tjondronegoro, D.: Facial expression recognition using facial movement features. IEEE Trans. Affect. Comput. **2**(4), 219–229 (2011)
23. Ojala, T., Pietikäinen, M., Harwood, D.: A comparative study of texture measures with classification based on featured distribution. Pattern Recogn. **29**, 51–59 (1996)
24. Huang, D., Shan, C., Ardabilian, M., Wang, Y., Chen, L.: Local binary patterns and its application to facial image analysis: a survey. IEEE Trans. Syst. Man Cybern. Part C Appl. Rev. **41**(6), 765–781 (2011)
25. Bassili, J.N.: Emotion recognition: the role of facial movement and the relative importance of upper and lower area of the face. J. Pers. Soc. Psychol. **37**(11), 2049–2058 (1979)
26. Ahonen, T., Hadid, A., Pietikäinen, M.: Face recognition with local binary patterns. In: Pajdla, T., Matas, J. (eds.) ECCV 2004. LNCS, vol. 3021, pp. 469–481. Springer, Heidelberg (2004)
27. Ojala, T., Pietikäinen, M., Maenpaa, T.: Multiresolution gray-scale and rotation invariant texture classification with local binary patterns. IEEE Trans. Pattern Anal. Mach. Intell. **24** (7), 971–987 (2002)
28. Hadid, A., Pietikäinen, M., Ahonen, T.: A discriminative feature space for detecting and recognizing faces. In: Proceedings of CVPR, pp. 797–804 (2004)
29. Ahonen, T., Hadid, A., Pietikäinen, M.: Face description with local binary patterns: Application to face recognition. IEEE Trans. Pattern Anal. Mach. Intell. **28**(12), 2037–2041 (2006)
30. Liu, W.F., Wang, Y.J.: Expression feature extraction based on difference of local binary pattern histogram sequences. In: Proceedings of IEEE International Conference on signal processing, pp. 2082–2084 (2008)
31. Lucey, P., Cohn, J.F., Kanade, T., Saragih, J., Ambadar, Z., Matthews, I.: The extended cohn-kanade dataset (ck+): a complete expression dataset for action unit and emotion-specified expression. In: Proceedings of the Third International Workshop on CVPR for Human Communicative Behavior Analysis, San Francisco, USA, pp. 94–101 (2010)
32. Kanade, T., Cohn, J.F., Tian, Y.: Comprehensive database for facial expression analysis. In: Proceedings of the Fourth IEEE International Conference on Automatic Face and Gesture Recognition (FG'00), Grenoble, France, pp 46–53 (2000)
33. Chang, C.C., Lin, C.J.: (2012) LIBSVM: a library for support vector machines. ACM Trans. Intell. Syst. Technol. http://www.csie.ntu.edu.tw/∼cjlin/papers/libsvm.pdf
34. Ptucha, R., Savakis, A.: manifold based sparse representation for facial understanding in natural images. Image Vis. Comput. **31**(5), 365–378 (2013)
35. Lyons, M.J., Budynek, J., Akamatsu, S.: Automatic classification of single facial images. IEEE Trans. Pattern Anal. Mach. Intell. **21**(12), 1357–1362 (1999)
36. Islam, M.S., Auwatanamongkol, S.: A novel feature extraction technique for facial expression recognition. Int. J. Comput. Sci. Issues **10**(3), 9–14 (2013)
37. Yang, S., Bhanu, B.: Understanding discrete facial expressions in video using an emotion avatar image. IEEE Trans. Syst. Man Cybern. Part B Cybern. **42**(4), 980–992 (2012)
38. Rivera, A.R., Castillo, J.R., Chae, O.: Local directional number pattern for face analysis: face and expression recognition. IEEE Trans. Image Process. **22**(5), 1740–1752 (2013)

Medical Image Processing

Needle Detection in 3D Ultrasound Images Using Anisotropic Diffusion and Robust Fitting

Leila Malekian$^{(\boxtimes)}$, Heidar Ali Talebi, and Farzad Towhidkhah

Amirkabir University of Technology, Tehran, Iran
leila.malekian@aut.ac.ir

Abstract. Needle insertion is a minimally invasive medical procedure with a vast domain of applications. 3D localization of the needle is important in needle visual tracking by a physician and robotic automatic needle guidance. This paper investigates detection of the needle position in 3D ultrasound images. Ultrasound is a fast and non-invasive medical imaging modality that is suitable for intra-operative imaging. But unfortunately, ultrasound images suffer from speckle noise and other artifacts that degrade the image quality. We combined the RANSAC robust fitting algorithm with a structure adopted denoising method called anisotropic diffusion. The results show more accuracy compared to the previous method and significant improvement in the processing time.

Keywords: 3D ultrasound image · Needle segmentation · Nonlinear anisotropic diffusion · Robust fitting

1 Introduction

Needle insertion is an important operation in many medical applications such as biopsy, brachytrapy and neural signal recording. Precise localization and navigation of the needle reduce the damage to tissue and decrease the number of unsuccessful insertions. Image guided procedures can achieve this goal by tracking the surgical instrument in intra-operative images. Among various medical imaging modalities, ultrasound is popular because of acquisition speed, non-ionizing radiation, compatibility with metallic objects and low cost.

Despite current advances in imaging and processing technologies, automatic needle detection in 3D ultrasound data is still challenging. Speckle noise that is inherent property of the ultrasound images degrades the image quality. Needle diameter in the image is low and comparable to ultrasound image resolution. There are other bright structures with similar intensity as a needle in the background. Resolution and intensity of pixels decrease in higher distances from the transducer. The 3D image volume is a large data that should be processed in high speed.

The problem of needle localization in 3D ultrasound images has been studied in many previous researches. Novotny et al. [1] used the principle component analysis (PCA) method. The thresholded pixels are divided into clusters and the cluster with longest line and highest intensities is selected using PCA as a needle. Minimization of parallel projection is introduced by Ding et al. [2]. This method is based on the fact that if the projection is parallel to needle axis, the needle area in the projected image will be

© Springer International Publishing Switzerland 2014
A. Movaghar et al. (Eds.): AISP 2013, CCIS 427, pp. 111–120, 2014.
DOI: 10.1007/978-3-319-10849-0_12

minimized. Ding et al. [3] also proposed the method of needle segmentation in two orthogonal projections. This technique reduces the processing time and makes the algorithm independent of initial projection direction. This method is used by Aboofazeli et al. [4] for curved needle segmentation. Cao et al. [5] proposed a catheter segmentation algorithm based on Aboofazeli 's approach that detects the catheter absence in the image.

The Hough transform is a well-known method for line and curve detection. Zhou et al. [6] used the randomized version of 3D Hough transform because of its memory and time efficiency. Qiu et al. [7] introduced the Quick Randomized Hough transform that employs a coarse to fine search strategy. They [8] also used Roberts line representation for needle axis, because of low computational memory. Neshat et al. [9] considered the needle axis model as a third order Bezier curve and employed the generalized Hough transform. They implement the algorithm on a Graphical Processing Unit (GPU).

The Parallel Integral Projection (PIP) transform is a form of Radon transform. Barva et al. [10] showed that needle axis can be found by maximization of PIP transform. The hierarchical mesh-grid technique is used to speed up this method. Uhercik et al. [11] introduced the faster multi-resolution PIP approach. Wei et al. [12] acquired two images before and after insertion. The needle is segmented in the difference image using least square method. Yan et al. [13] employed the level set segmentation approach. This method is not automatic and need user input data. Novotny et al. [14] used the generalized Radon transform. The image is divided into smaller regions that are processed on a GPU. Adebar et al. [15] vibrated the needle with high frequency and segmented it in the resulting 3D power Doppler image. They fitted a third order polynomial to the thresholded Doppler response.

Most of the introduced needle detection techniques-such as Hough and Radon transform and PIP-are projection based. These methods suffer from high computational time and robustness problem in case of cluttered background. The faster and more robust model fitting RANSAC approach is introduced by Uhercik et al. [16]. They also employed a linear classifier [17] to identify tool pixels using intensity and tubularity features. This modification leads to a more robust algorithm but decreases the speed. Zhao et al. [18] considered detection and tracking of needle in the sequence of 3D images. In their method, a Kalman filter estimated the needle tip position using speckle tracking speed estimation and RANSAC tip localization. Chatelain et al. [19] also studied the needle tracking problem. They found the ROI that contained the needle using predictive Kalman filtering. The predicted model is used in the RANSAC procedure to reject improbable configurations.

In this paper, we take advantage of nonlinear anisotropic diffusion (AND) to achieve faster and more accurate result, in RANSAC based needle localization. The anisotropic diffusion is first introduced by Perona et al. [20] as an edge preserving denoising method. The success and time performance of model fitting algorithms are very much affected by the number of outliers. Realizing the fact that outliers are mainly due to speckle noise and existence of other bright structures in the background, we reduced the effect of these parameters using anisotropic diffusion (AND). The major advantage of AND is that it can reduce the noise without removing specific structures (such as lines) and even enhance them. This is an important feature because of needle low diameter and possible loss of needle pixels in the denoising process. The results show the effectiveness of this scheme in reducing the needle localization error and processing time.

2   Method

The needle appears in the ultrasound images as a thin tubular high intensity structure that is surrounded by a noisy and inhomogeneous background. The position of the needle is found in three consecutive steps: anisotropic diffusion, thresholding and RANSAC robust fitting. The two first steps assure less noisy and erroneous input data for RANSAC procedure.

2.1   Nonlinear Anisotropic Diffusion

To preserve the specific structure of interest, the local image structure in each pixel should be known. The structure tensor of the image I is defined as

$$J(\nabla I) = \nabla I \cdot \nabla I^T = \begin{bmatrix} I_x^2 & I_xI_y & I_xI_z \\ I_xI_y & I_y^2 & I_yI_z \\ I_xI_z & I_yI_z & I_z^2 \end{bmatrix} \tag{1}$$

The subscript means derivative with respect to spatial coordinates.

After Gaussian smoothing the input image, the structure tensor in each pixel is found. The eigenvalues and eigenvectors of J contain information about the local image structure in the specific pixel. Three mutually perpendicular eigenvectors v_1, v_2, v_3 describe the local orientation and the eigenvalues μ_1, μ_2, μ_3 measure average contrast along eigendirections. The eigenvector v_1 is perpendicular to the local structure. In needle detection problem, we should preserve lines. High level of smoothing perpendicular to the eigenvector v_1 will realize this goal.

In physics, the difference in density cause mass transport without creating and destroying mass. This process is called diffusion and is similar to image smoothing when there is a difference in gray levels. The diffusion equation for the image u is expressed as

$$\partial_t u = div(D \cdot \nabla u) \tag{2}$$

The subscript t denotes derivative with respect to diffusion time t. "div" is the divergence operator

$$div\,\vec{p} = \partial_x p_1 + \partial_y p_2 + \partial_z p_3 \tag{3}$$

where $\vec{p} = [p_1, p_2, p_3]$ is an arbitrary vector. D is the diffusion tensor and the term $j = -D\nabla u$ is called flux. If D is constant over the image, the resulting linear diffusion will excessively smooth the image. In nonlinear diffusion, D is a function of image structure. Nonlinearity allows controlling the amount of diffusion and reducing it on lines. In anisotropic diffusion, we can make the diffusion direction-dependent by defining the diffusion tensor. The diffusion tensor D changes the orientation and intensity of the flux to preserve the structures of interest in the image. D can be found using its eigenvalues and eigenvectors

$$D = \begin{bmatrix} v_1 & v_2 & v_3 \end{bmatrix} \cdot \begin{bmatrix} \lambda_1 & 0 & 0 \\ 0 & \lambda_2 & 0 \\ 0 & 0 & \lambda_3 \end{bmatrix} \cdot \begin{bmatrix} v_1^T \\ v_2^T \\ v_3^T \end{bmatrix} \tag{4}$$

The values of the eigenvalues $\lambda_1, \lambda_2, \lambda_3$ are obtained by extending Weickert 's 2D equation [21] to 3D case [22] for line enhancement

$$\begin{cases} \lambda_1 = c_1 \\ \lambda_2 = c_2 \\ \lambda_3 = c_1 + (1 - c_1) \cdot \exp\left(\dfrac{-c_2}{(\mu_1 - \mu_2)^2}\right) \end{cases} \tag{5}$$

where $\mu_1 \geq \mu_2 \geq \mu_3$ are eigenvalues of the structure tensor J and $c_1 \in (0, 1)$ and $c_2 \geq 0$ are smoothing constants.

The diffusion equation is continuous in both space and time. To solve it numerically, it should be discretized.

$$\begin{aligned} \partial_t u = div(D \cdot \nabla u) &= \partial_x \left(a \, \partial_x u + d \, \partial_y u + e \, \partial_z u\right) \\ &+ \partial_y \left(d \, \partial_x u + b \, \partial_y u + f \, \partial_z u\right) + \partial_z \left(e \, \partial_x u + f \, \partial_y u + c \, \partial_z u\right) \end{aligned} \tag{6}$$

where D is

$$D = \begin{bmatrix} a & d & e \\ d & b & f \\ e & f & c \end{bmatrix} \tag{7}$$

We used standard discretization method [22] with the central difference approximation for spatial derivatives

$$\partial_y(d \, \partial_x u) = \frac{1}{2}\left(d_{x,y+1,z} \frac{u_{x+1,y+1,z} - u_{x-1,y+1,z}}{2}\right) - \frac{1}{2}\left(d_{x,y-1,z} \frac{u_{x+1,y-1,z} - u_{x-1,y-1,z}}{2}\right) \tag{8}$$

The subscript in the right side of (8) denotes spatial coordinate indices. The iterative forward difference method approximates the term $\partial_t u$ in (6)

$$\partial_t u \approx \frac{u_{x,y,z}^{K+1} - u_{x,y,z}^K}{h} \tag{9}$$

where K is the time step and h is the step size. $u_{x,y,z}^K$ is the approximation of u in location (x,y,z) and time Kh.

The (2) can be written as convolution of a $3 \times 3 \times 3$ time and space varying mask with the image

$$\frac{u_{x,y,z}^{K+1} - u_{x,y,z}^{K}}{h} = A_{x,y,z}^{K} * u_{x,y,z}^{K} \tag{10}$$

$$u_{x,y,z}^{K+1} = \left(1 + h.A_{x,y,z}^{K}\right) * u_{x,y,z}^{K} \tag{11}$$

The entries of mask A that is calculated in [23] is showed in Fig. 1.

$\dfrac{-d_{x-1,y,z} - d_{x,y+1,z}}{4h_1 h_2}$	$\dfrac{b_{x,y+1,z} + b_{x,y,z}}{2h_2^{\ 2}}$	$\dfrac{d_{x+1,y,z} + d_{x,y+1,z}}{4h_1 h_2}$
$\dfrac{a_{x-1,y,z} + a_{x,y,z}}{2h_1^{\ 2}}$	$-\dfrac{a_{x-1,y,z} + 2a_{x,y,z} + a_{x+1,y,z}}{2h_1^{\ 2}}$ $-\dfrac{b_{x,y-1,z} + 2b_{x,y,z} + b_{x,y+1,z}}{2h_2^{\ 2}}$ $-\dfrac{c_{x,y,z-1} + 2c_{x,y,z} + b_{x,y,z+1}}{2h_3^{\ 2}}$	$\dfrac{a_{x+1,y,z} + a_{x,y,z}}{2h_1^{\ 2}}$
$\dfrac{d_{x-1,y,z} + d_{x,y-1,z}}{4h_1 h_2}$	$\dfrac{b_{x,y-1,z} + b_{x,y,z}}{2h_2^{\ 2}}$	$\dfrac{-d_{x+1,y,z} - d_{x,y-1,z}}{4h_1 h_2}$

(a)

	$\dfrac{f_{x,y,z+1} + f_{x,y+1,z}}{4h_2 h_3}$	
$\dfrac{-e_{x,y,z+1} - e_{x-1,y,z}}{4h_1 h_3}$	$\dfrac{c_{x,y,z+1} + c_{x,y,z}}{2h_3^{\ 2}}$	$\dfrac{e_{x,y,z+1} + e_{x+1,y,z}}{4h_1 h_3}$
	$\dfrac{-f_{x,y,z+1} - f_{x,y-1,z}}{4h_2 h_3}$	

(b)

	$\dfrac{-f_{x,y,z-1} - f_{x,y+1,z}}{4h_2 h_3}$	
$\dfrac{e_{x,y,z-1} + e_{x-1,y,z}}{4h_1 h_3}$	$\dfrac{c_{x,y,z-1} + c_{x,y,z}}{2h_3^{\ 2}}$	$\dfrac{-e_{x,y,z-1} - e_{x+1,y,z}}{4h_1 h_3}$
	$\dfrac{f_{x,y,z-1} + f_{x,y-1,z}}{4h_2 h_3}$	

(c)

Fig. 1. The convolution mask, (a) for z = 0, (b) z =+1 and (c) z = −1

3   RANSAC

RANSAC (Random Sample Consensus) [24] is a robust fitting method that can find the model parameters when the data contains a high percentage of outliers. The algorithm iteratively selects N_s random samples of data and fits a model to them. Next, the number of data points that are consistent with the hypothesized model is specified. If this number is big enough, the model will be accepted; otherwise iteration continues. The Maximum number of iterations is updated at the end of each iteration as follows

$$L = \frac{\log(p)}{\log\left(1 - p_g^{N_s}\right)} \tag{12}$$

$$p_g = \frac{N_{inl}}{N_{data}} \tag{13}$$

where N_{inl} is the number of inliers (model consistent points) and N_{data} is the number of all data points. Consistent data have a shorter distance than τ from the model. The threshold τ is defined as needle observed radius in the image. p is the probability of L consecutive failures and is set by user. N_s is the minimum number of data that is required to fit the specific type of model.

4   Result

To evaluate the proposed method, we used a 3D ultrasound dataset that consists of various needle positions and orientations. The dataset contains 28 ultrasound images that are produced by previous researchers [16] using the software Field II. The background scatterers are created using real ultrasound breast images. The dimension of the

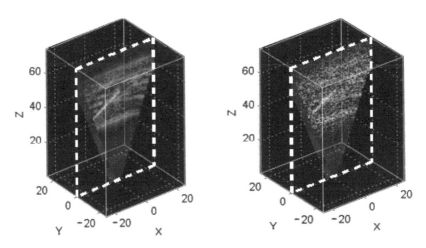

Fig. 2. A plane of the 3D ultrasound image that contains the needle, in low and high noise levels.

initial RF data is 53 planes of 71 RF beams. Each RF beam consists of 164 data samples. The resulting 3D ultrasound image resolution is $53 \times 71 \times 160$ pixels.

Results are measured in various levels of the speckle noise. An example of the high and low noise level images is shown in Fig. 2. At each noise level, we repeated the algorithm 30 times for each of the dataset images and reported the average value.

Figure 3 shows the average axis localization error. Axis error is the maximum Cartesian distance between actual and found needle axes. A failure occurs when the error value is greater than 3 mm. Figure 4 shows the average failure rate. The figures demonstrate that the proposed AND-RANSAC method yields smaller error and greater accuracy than RANSAC, while failure rates are nearly equal.

Figure 5 shows the average elapsed time of the needle detection algorithm. The processing time of the AND-RANSAC approach is not very much affected by amount of speckle noise in the image and is significantly lower than RANSAC.

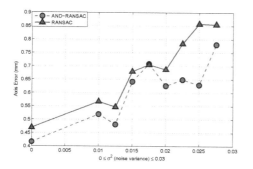

Fig. 3. Needle axis localization error, in different variances of the speckle noise

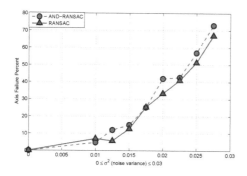

Fig. 4. Needle axis localization failure percent, in different variances of the speckle noise

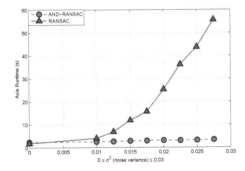

Fig. 5. The elapsed time of the needle localization procedure, in different variances of the speckle noise

5 Conclusion

Regarding the main challenges of needle detection in 3D ultrasound images, such as high dimensionality and noisy nature of data, we have investigated improving the speed and accuracy of the model fitting RANSAC needle localization method. The amount of speedup that can be achieved by anisotropic diffusion has a trade-off relation with size of the 3D data. In the large volumes further acceleration can be made using GPU or parallel implementation. Automatic detection of ROI using image itself or prior information will increase the speed and accuracy. Techniques such as guided sampling or partial evaluation can improve the RANSAC computational time.

Acknowledgments. The authors would like to thank M. Uhercik and J. Kybic for providing the access to the 3D ultrasound data.

References

1. Novotny, P.M., Cannon, J.W., Howe, R.D.: Tool localization in 3D ultrasound images. In: Ellis, R.E., Peters, T.M. (eds.) MICCAI 2003. LNCS, vol. 2879, pp. 969–970. Springer, Heidelberg (2003). doi:10.1007/978-3-540-39903-2_127
2. Ding, M., Cardinal, H.N., Guan, W., Fenster, A.: Automatic needle segmentation in 3D ultrasound images. In: SPIE Medical Imaging: Visualization, Image-Guided Procedures, and Display, vol. 4681, pp. 65–76 (2002). doi:10.1117/12.466907
3. Ding, M., Cardinal, H.N., Fenster, A.: Automatic needle segmentation in three-dimensional ultrasound images using two orthogonal two-dimensional image projections. J. Med. Phys. **30**(2), 222–234 (2003). doi:10.1118/1.1538231
4. Aboofazeli, M., Abolmaesumi, P., Mousavi, P., Fichtinger, G.: A new scheme for curved needle segmentation in three-dimensional ultrasound images. In: IEEE International Symposium on Biomedical Imaging: From Nano to Macro, pp. 1067–1070. IEEE Press (2009). doi:10.1109/ISBI.2009.5193240
5. Cao, K., Mills, D., Patwardhan, K.A.: Automated catheter detection in volumetric ultrasound. In: 10th IEEE International Symposium on Biomedical Imaging, pp. 37–40. IEEE Press (2013). doi:10.1109/ISBI.2013.6556406

6. Zhou, H., Qiu, W., Ding, M., Zhang, S.: Automatic needle segmentation in 3D ultrasound images using 3D improved Hough transform. In: SPIE Medical Imaging: Visualization, Image-guided Procedures, and Modeling, vol. 6918, pp. 691821-1–691821-9 (2008). doi:10. 1117/12.770077

7. Qiu, W., Ding, M., Yuchi, M.: Needle segmentation using 3D quick randomized Hough transform. In: First International Conference on Intelligent Networks and Intelligent Systems ICINIS'08, pp. 449–452. IEEE Press (2008). doi:10.1109/ICINIS.2008.41

8. Qiu, W., Yuchi, M., Ding, M., Tessier, D., Fenster, A.: Needle segmentation using 3D Hough transform in 3D TRUS guided prostate transperineal therapy. Med. Phys. **40**(4), 042902 (2013). doi:10.1118/1.4795337

9. Neshat, H.R.S., Patel, R.V.: Real-time parametric curved needle segmentation in 3D ultrasound images. In: 2nd IEEE RAS & EMBS International Conference on Biomedical Robotics and Biomechatronics, pp. 670–675. IEEE Press (2008). doi:10.1109/BIOROB. 2008.4762877

10. Barva, M., Uhercik, M., Mari, J.M., Kybic, J., Duhamel, J.R., Liebgott, H., Hlaváč, V., Cachard, C.: Parallel integral projection transform for straight electrode localization in 3D ultrasound images. IEEE Trans. Ultrason. Ferroelectr. Freq. Control **55**(7), 1559–1569 (2008). doi:10.1109/TUFFC.2008.833

11. Uhercik, M., Kybic, J., Liebgott, H., Cachard, C.: Multi-resolution parallel integral projection for fast localization of a straight electrode in 3D ultrasound images. In: 5th IEEE International Symposium on Biomedical Imaging: From Nano to Macro, pp. 33–36. IEEE Press (2008). doi:10.1109/ISBI.2008.4540925

12. Wei, Z., Gardi, L., Downey, D.B., Fenster, A.: Oblique needle segmentation for 3d trus-guided robot-aided transperineal prostate brachytherapy. In: IEEE International Symposium on Biomedical Imaging: From Nano to Macro, pp. 960–963. IEEE Press (2004). doi:10. 1109/ISBI.2004.1398699

13. Yan, P., Cheeseborough, J.C., Chao, C.K.: Automatic shape-based level set segmentation for needle tracking in 3D TRUS-guided prostate brachytherapy. Ultrasound Med. Biol. **38**(9), 1626–1636 (2012). doi:10.1016/j.ultrasmedbio.2012.02.011

14. Novotny, P.M., Stoll, J.A., Vasilyev, N.V., Del Nido, P.J., Dupont, P.E., Zickler, T.E., Howe, R.D.: GPU based real-time instrument tracking with three-dimensional ultrasound. Med. Image Anal. **11**(5), 458–464 (2007). doi:10.1016/j.media.2007.06.009

15. Adebar, T.K., Okamura, A.M.: 3D segmentation of curved needles using doppler ultrasound and vibration. In: Barratt, D., Cotin, S., Fichtinger, G., Jannin, P., Navab, N. (eds.) IPCAI 2013. LNCS, vol. 7915, pp. 61–70. Springer, Heidelberg (2013). doi:10.1007/978-3-642-38568-1_7

16. Uhercik, M., Kybic, J., Liebgott, H., Cachard, C.: Model fitting using ransac for surgical tool localization in 3D ultrasound images. IEEE Trans. Biomed. Eng. **57**(8), 1907–1916 (2010). doi:10.1109/TBME.2010.2046416

17. Uhercik, M., Kybic, J., Cachard, C., Liebgott, H.: Line filtering for detection of microtools in 3D ultrasound data. In: IEEE International Ultrasonics Symposium (IUS), pp. 594–597. IEEE Press (2009). doi:10.1109/ULTSYM.2009.5441538

18. Zhao, Y., Liebgott, H., Cachard, C.: Tracking micro tool in a dynamic 3D ultrasound situation using kalman filter and ransac algorithm. In: 9th IEEE International Symposium on Biomedical Imaging (ISBI), pp. 1076–1079. IEEE Press (2012). doi:10.1109/ISBI.2012. 6235745

19. Chatelain, P., Krupa, A., Marchal, M.: Real-time needle detection and tracking using a visually servoed 3D ultrasound probe. In: IEEE International Conference on Robotics and Automation (ICRA), pp. 1668–1673 (2013). doi:10.1109/ICRA.2013.6630795

20. Perona, P., Malik, J.: Scale-space and edge detection using anisotropic diffusion. IEEE Trans. Pattern Anal. Mach. Intell. **12**(7), 629–639 (1990). doi:10.1109/34.56205

21. Weickert, J., Scharr, H.: A scheme for coherence-enhancing diffusion filtering with optimized rotation invariance. J. Vis. Commun. Image Represent. **13**(1), 103–118 (2002). doi:10.1006/jvci.2001.0495

22. Frangakis, A.S., Hegerl, R.: Noise reduction in electron tomographic reconstructions using nonlinear anisotropic diffusion. J. Struct. Biol. **135**(3), 239–250 (2001). doi:10.1006/jsbi.2001.4406

23. Fritz, L: Diffusion-based applications for interactive medical image segmentation. In: Proceedings of CESCG (Central European Seminar on Computer Graphics) (2006)

24. Fischler, M.A., Bolles, R.C.: Random sample consensus: a paradigm for model fitting with applications to image analysis and automated cartography. Commun. ACM **24**(6), 381–395 (1981). doi:10.1145/358669.358692

A Robust and Invariant Keypoint Extraction Algorithm in Brain MR Images

Hossein Sarikhani[✉], Ebrahim Abdollahian, Mohsen Shirpour,
Alireza Javaheri, and Mohammad Taghi Manzuri

Department of Computer Engineering,
Sharif University of Technology, Tehran, Iran
{sarikhani, ebiabdollahian, mshirpour,
javaheri}@ce.sharif.edu,
manzuri@sharif.edu

Abstract. In this paper a method for extracting keypoints from human brain MR images is proposed. These keypoints are obtained based on curved structures in the brain MR images. In this method, a keypoint is center of a circle which includes circular boundaries in the image and is selected based on gradients of the image. These keypoints and their descriptors are scale and rotation invariant. The proposed method is compared with other well-known methods with repeatability measure and ROC curves. Experimental results show that proposed method performs better than other well-known methods, specially, when deformations are remarkable.

Keywords: Keypoint extraction · Center of curve · Rotation invariance · Scale invariance · Hill pattern · Valley pattern · Repeatability

1 Introduction

Extracting keypoints from an image is one of the most important fields in image processing that is used as a principal step in many applications, such as pattern recognition, image registration, image classification, object tracking and many other applications in computer vision. Most features that are extracted from an image as keypoint are based on human visual system. An appropriate keypoint extraction algorithm should have the following characteristics:

- Invariance: extracted keypoints and their descriptors should be invariant to supposed transform functions. One of the transform families that has mostly been investigated by previous works is affine transform, specially rotation and scaling. Each invariant keypoint has the following characteristic. First, the corresponding point in the second image should be selected as a keypoint. Also, these two points should have same descriptors. This is very important, because more corresponding extracted points will make next manipulations more simple and accurate.
- Rarity: with extracting so many keypoints, number of not-matched keypoints increases. Therefore, finding corresponding points become more difficult and time consuming.

© Springer International Publishing Switzerland 2014
A. Movaghar et al. (Eds.): AISP 2013, CCIS 427, pp. 121–130, 2014.
DOI: 10.1007/978-3-319-10849-0_13

- Dispersion: extracted keypoints should be spread all over the image. This is very useful in applications like image registration, because distribution of keypoints in the image can accurate reconstruction of the local deformations.

Many different methods have been proposed in feature extraction step, such as corner detection [1–3], closed-boundary area detection [4], edge and line intersection detection [3]. Corner detection algorithm is one of the most important keypoint extraction algorithms. Harris corner detector is one of these methods that has a very high accuracy [5]. The main problem with this method is its time complexity. In recent years many corner detection methods have tried to solve this problem, but none of them could achieve its accuracy [6, 7].

Another well-known keypoint extraction method that have been used successfully in many machine vision applications, is SIFT algorithm. This method is based on the image gradients and is scale and rotation invariant. It is also robust to other more complex transforms and luminance variations [8, 9].

One another feature that is used as keypoint is salient area. This method uses the idea that the more complex is a part of a signal; it can be more invariant to complex transforms. This feature has a high consistency with human visual system. In this method, center of circular areas that have the maximum entropy, are considered as the keypoint.

Alhichri used virtual circles as the keypoints [10]. The virtual circle is a circle with the maximum radius that does not include any edge pixel. This feature is rotation and scale invariant. Another advantage of virtual circles is their extraction speed; due to use of distance transform [11]. The local maximums of distance transform are the center of the virtual circles.

In this paper, we have proposed a keypoint extraction method that is useful in medical applications, especially for brain MR images. The paper is organized as follows. In Sect. 2 the proposed method for extracting keypoints is represented. In Sect. 3 the experimental results are analyzed and performance of the proposed method is compared with other well-known methods. Finally we conclude in the last section.

2 Proposed Method

Curved like areas that are abundant in MR images have unique characteristics which are matched with anatomical structures of human brain. Figure 1 shows two examples of brain MR images. These anatomical structures remain unchanged through the time and only may be stretched, scaled and rotated. Thus, these curved like areas are invariant to severe changes too. In this method, a keypoint is center of a circle which includes circular boundaries in the image. These keypoints which have high structural information are called center of curves (COC). In contrast to COC, keypoints like corner are completely unstable and variant to common deformations in MR images of brain. Curved like anatomical structures of brain are spread all over it and COC keypoints are selected based on these structures. Thus, another advantage of these points is their dispersion throughout the image. This is very important for applications such as image registration, because for precise reconstruction of local deformations, keypoints should be available in all over the image.

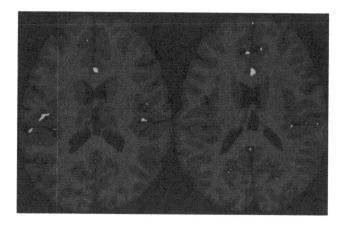

Fig. 1. Two examples of brain MR images

2.1 Keypoint Extraction

In first step, a measure should be defined to determine how much a pixel is center of a curve. This method uses direction and magnitude of gradients on the perimeter of circles which their centers are candidate for a keypoint and have different radiuses.

Suppose that the candidate pixel is in the (x, y) coordinate. If N samples are selected from a circle with radius R and center of (x, y) uniformly, the coordinates of these samples are calculated as follows:

$$u = x - R \times \sin(\frac{2\pi n}{N}) \qquad n = 0, 1, \ldots, N - 1, \tag{1}$$

$$v = y + R \times \cos(\frac{2\pi n}{N}) \qquad n = 0, 1, \ldots, N - 1, \tag{2}$$

where (u, v) is coordinate of sample point on the circle. These coordinates are calculated for radiuses between R_0 to R_1. Direction and magnitude of gradients is calculated with interpolation. N is supposed to be 8 and R_0 and R_1 are tuned with respect to average size of the curve structures in image. In all experiments of this paper, these two parameters are 1 and 15.

Next step is finding a measure to determine the probability that these samples are placed on edge of a circle with center of $P_0 = (x, y)$. This measure for a point in coordinate $P_1 = (u, v)$ is calculated with respect to angle between direction of gradient in P_1 and vector $\overrightarrow{P_0 P_1}$. This angle is shown with α. The more this angle is closer to 0 or 180; this point can be placed on edge of a curve with center of P_0 with more probability. In a specific case which P_0 exactly is in the center of a circle, α is 0 ore 180 for all point on the edge. If the area in the circle is darker than the area out of the circle, for points on the edge of the circle, α is 0 and if area in the circle is lighter than the area out of the circle, for points on the edge of the circle, α is 180. In the first case, center of the circle is called a COC of valley type and in the second case; it is called a COC of hill type.

For each sample two measures are defined. First measure estimates the probability that sample $P_1 = (u, v)$ is placed on the edge of a valley curve with center of $P_0 = (x, y)$ and the second measure estimates the probability that this sample is placed on the edge of a hill curve with center of $P_0 = (x, y)$. These two probabilistic measures are calculated with the assumption that different samples are independent from each other. These measures are shown with $Hill(P_1)$ and $Valley(P_1)$ and are calculated as follows:

$$Valley(P_1) = \begin{cases} 1 - \frac{\alpha}{90} & (\alpha < 90) \ and \ (G(P_1) \geq G_{TH}) \\ 0 & o.w. \end{cases} \tag{3}$$

$$Hill(P_1) = \begin{cases} \frac{\alpha}{90} - 1 & (\alpha \geq 90) \ and \ (G(P_1) \geq G_{TH}) \\ 0 & o.w. \end{cases} \tag{4}$$

where $G(P_1)$ is magnitude of gradient vector in P_1 and G_{TH} is a threshold for magnitude of gradient vector in P_1. If the magnitude of gradient vector of a point is smaller than a threshold, without calculating the α angle, it can be concluded that P_1 is not an edge point and the probabilities of $Hill$ and $Valley$ are 0. Figure 2 illustrates an example of calculating the $Hill$ and $Valley$ measures for samples around a pixel which with a high probability is a COC. In this figure, point A is a strong valley COC. Two patterns of $Hill$ and $Valley$ probabilities of point A are shown in right and center of Fig. 2. These patterns that are called Hill Pattern (HP) and Valley Pattern (VP) are used to determine that how much point A is a COC.

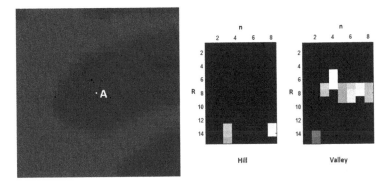

Fig. 2. An example of HP and VP calculation. The left image is part of a MRI image that the center pixel is shown with A in it. The center and the right show the patterns of Hill and Valley probabilities for point A.

Intuitively, it can be apprehended that a point which its Hill or Valley pattern has consequent values near 1 in a row, can be a good COC. In these two patterns, first and last columns are supposed to be connected. This idea still has a problem. Only for candidate points that are included in a completely circular area, it results in a high COC value and if the areas are nearly circular, the value of COC will be very low or even zero. This problem is more common for areas with high radiuses. To solve this problem two new patterns are defined from previous ones. These two new patterns are called Final Hill Pattern (FHP) and Final Valley Pattern (FVP) and are defined as follows:

$$
\begin{cases}
FHP(i,j) = \max\{HP(-k,j), HP(-k+1,j), \ldots, HP(k-1,j), HP(k,j)\} \\
\quad j = 1, 2, \ldots, N \quad i = R_0, R_0 + 1, \ldots, R_1
\end{cases} \tag{5}
$$

$$
\begin{cases}
FVP(i,j) = \max\{VP(-k,j), VP(-k+1,j), \ldots, VP(k-1,j), VP(k,j)\} \\
\quad j = 1, 2, \ldots, N \quad i = R_0, R_0 + 1, \ldots, R_1
\end{cases} \tag{6}
$$

where HP and VP are Hill and Valley patterns and k is defined as follow:

$$
k = \lfloor \log(i) \rfloor - 1. \tag{7}
$$

Finally a minimum Filter of size $1 \times (N/2)$ is applied to FHP and FVP to obtain matrices A_{Hill} and A_{Valley}. Then the measure for amount of being COC for a point is calculated as follow:

$$
M = \max\{\max\{A_{Hill}\}, \max\{A_{Valley}\}\}, \tag{8}
$$

where $\max\{A_{Hill}\}$ is maximum element in matrix A_{Hill}. After calculating value of M for all pixels of image, local maximums of these values which are greater than a threshold are selected as keypoints. For each selected keypoint, type, direction and radius (scale) are also extracted. Type of a point, determines if it is center of a Hill or Valley. Radius and direction of a point are calculated as follows:

$$
(Scale, Direction) = \begin{cases}
\arg\max_{(i,j)} A_{Hill}(i,j) & if \quad area \ is \ a \ Hill \\
\arg\max_{(i,j)} A_{Valley}(i,j) & if \quad area \ is \ a \ Valley
\end{cases} \tag{9}
$$

According to Fig. 2, scaling the image, results in a vertical shift in both HP and VP. Consequently, values of FHP, FVP, A_{Hill} and A_{Valley} are shifted in the same manner. According to Eq. 9, obtained *Scale* of the keypoint is proportional to amount of the scale, applied to the image. Rotation of the image results in a horizontal circular shift in both HP and VP. Using a similar conclusion, it can be shown that obtained *Direction* of the keypoint is proportional to the degree of image rotation. Therefore, COC keypoints are scale and rotation invariant. Selected keypoints are obtained based on gradient information of the image and are independent of luminance value of the pixels. So they have an acceptable robustness to luminance variations. Figure 3 shows an output example of the COC keypoint extraction algorithm on original and deformed MR images of brain.

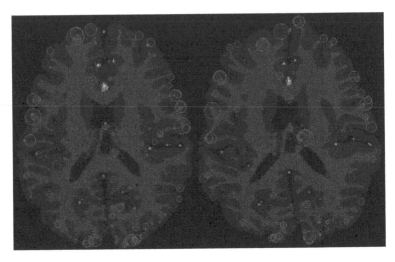

Fig. 3. An example output of COC keypoint extraction algorithm on original and deformed images. Pink circles are hills and blue circles are valleys (Color figure online).

3 Extracting Descriptor for Keypoints

In the previous step, for each keypoint, the direction and radius of the curve was extracted. These two features are useful for obtaining a descriptor that is scale and rotation invariant. Descriptor for keypoint located in *(x, y)* coordinate is obtained by sampling from luminance values in the following points of the original image:

$$\begin{cases} u = x - r \times \sin(\frac{\alpha+2\pi n}{N}) & n = 0, 1, \ldots, N-1 \\ v = y + r \times \cos(\frac{\alpha+2\pi n}{N}) & r = \frac{4R}{10}, \frac{8R}{10}, \frac{12R}{10}, \frac{16R}{10}, \frac{20R}{10}, \end{cases} \tag{10}$$

where α is direction of the keypoint, R is scale of the keypoint and N is 24. The length of the feature vector is 120. To robust the feature vector against intensity bias, all elements of feature vector are subtracted from luminance of the center point, like Local Binary Pattern method (LBP) [12].

4 Experimental Results

Experiments of this article are done using 180th horizontal slice of "BrainWeb" dataset. To analyze the performance of algorithm precisely, for each of the 20 images in the dataset, four images with different degrees of deformation are produced using thin plate spline transform [13]. Images are divided to 40 × 40 blocks and then for each block, movement in *x* and *y* directions is calculated. These movements are random and calculated as follows:

$$\Delta x = 20 \times (-1)^k (\alpha_1 + (\alpha_2 - \alpha_1) \times U) \tag{11}$$

$$\Delta y = 20 \times (-1)^k (\alpha_1 + (\alpha_2 - \alpha_1) \times U) \tag{12}$$

where α_1 and α_2 are parameters of movement amount, k is a discrete uniform random variable, which has value of 0 or 1. U is a continuous uniform random variable in $[0, 1]$. $[\alpha_1, \alpha_2]^T$ Vector is considered for levels of deformation of low, medium, high and very high as $[0, 0.2]^T$, $[0.1, 0.4]^T$, $[0.2, 0.6]^T$ and $[0.3, 0.7]^T$. Figure 4 shows three set of these simulated images.

Fig. 4. Three set of simulated images. From left to right, the first column is original images from the data set. Other columns are produced images with deformations of low, medium, high and very high respectively.

If point (x, y) is selected in the first image as the keypoint, the method which selects $f(x, y)$ as the corresponding point to (x, y) with more probability, is more suitable (f is transform function). Two corresponding point should have the following conditions. First, both (x, y) and $f(x, y)$ should be selected as a keypoint. Second, $f(x, y)$ should be selected as the exactly most similar point to the point (x, y). The probability of selecting $f(x, y)$ as the corresponding point to (x, y) is calculated as follows:

$$P([x, y] \mapsto [f(x, y)]) = P([f(x, y)] \in P_2) \times P([x, y] \mapsto [f(x, y)] | [f(x, y)] \in P_2), \tag{13}$$

where P_2 is set of selected points from second image. This equation is multiplication of two probabilistic terms. First term models the local accuracy of the keypoints and second term measures the quality of the descriptor of the keypoint. In this paper repeatability measure is used to evaluate the first term and ROC curve is used to evaluate the second term. Equation 13 shows that a method which has an acceptable repeatability and ROC curve simultaneously is more suitable. Figures 5 and 6 show the results of comparison of COC keypoint extraction method with other well-known methods with two measures of repeatability and ROC curve respectively.

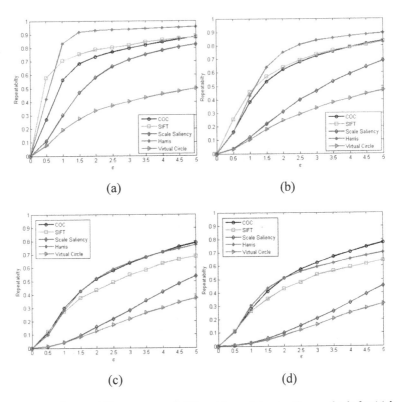

Fig. 5. Results of repeatability measure of different keypoint extraction methods for (a) low, (b) medium, (c) high and (d) very high level of deformation respectively.

Figure 5 shows that COC keypoint extraction method is very successful in establishing the correspondence between the points in two images. COC method is more robust than other methods against more severe deformations. The value of repeatability measure for other methods sinks sharply as the level of deformation becomes higher. The reason for such level of robustness is high structural information in the COC features that are not in other methods.

According to Fig. 6, although the scale saliency method has an appropriate ROC curve, but it has not a good performance, because the value of repeatability is low for this method. The Harris and virtual circles methods do not include the descriptor extracting phase. Therefore, it is not possible to draw ROC curve for them. As illustrated in two last figures COC method have a better performance compared to SIFT and Scale Saliency methods.

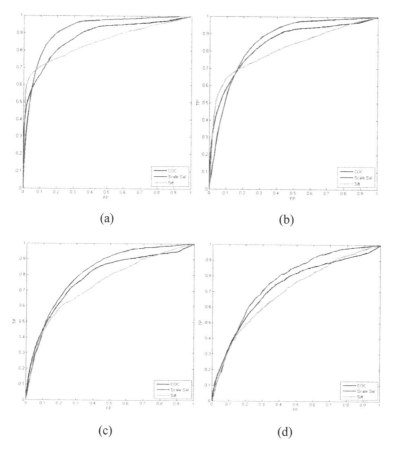

Fig. 6. ROC curve of different keypoint extraction methods for (a) low, (b) medium, (c) high and (d) very high level of deformation respectively.

5 Conclusion

In this paper a method for extracting keypoints from brain MR images is proposed. Keypoints in this method are extracted based on curved like areas in the image. These keypoints and their corresponding descriptors are invariant to scaling, rotation and luminance variations. As illustrated in Figs. 5 and 6, in experimental result section, this method has a better performance from other well-known methods.

References

1. Lin, H., Du, P., Zhao, W., Zhang, L., Sun, H.: Image registration based on corner detection and affine transformation. In: 3rd International Congress Image and Signal Processing (CISP), pp. 2184–218 (2010)

2. Pei, Y., Wu, H., Yu, J., Cai, G.: Effective image registration based on improved harris corner detection. In: International Conference on Information Networking and Automation (ICINA), pp. V1-93–V96-1 (2010)
3. Harris, C., Stephens, M.: A combined corner and edge detector. In: Alvey Vision Conference, pp. 147–151 (1988)
4. Davatzikos, C., Prince, J.L., Bryan, R.N.: Image registration based on boundary mapping. IEEE Trans. Med. Imaging **15**, 112–115 (1996)
5. Vasileisky, A., Zhukov, B., Berger, M.: Automated image coregistration based on linear feature recognition. In: Proceedings of the Second Conference Fusion of Earth Data, Sophia Antipolis, France, pp. 59–66 (1998)
6. Rosten, E., Drummond, T.W.: Machine learning for high-speed corner detection. In: Leonardis, A., Bischof, H., Pinz, A. (eds.) ECCV 2006, Part I. LNCS, vol. 3951, pp. 430–443. Springer, Heidelberg (2006)
7. Rosten, E., Porter, R., Drummond, T.: Faster and better: a machine learning approach to corner detection. IEEE Trans. Pattern Anal. Mach. Intell. **32**, 105–119 (2010)
8. Lowe, D.G.: Distinctive image features from scale-invariant keypoints. Int. J. Comput. Vision **60**, 91–110 (2004)
9. Lowe, D.G.: Object recognition from local scale-invariant features. In: The Proceedings of the Seventh IEEE International Conference on Computer Vision, pp. 1150–1157 (1999)
10. Alhichri, H.S., Kamel, M.: Virtual circles: a new set of features for fast image registration. Pattern Recogn. Lett. **24**, 1181–1190 (2003)
11. Borgefors, G.: Distance transformations in digital images. Comput. Vision Graph. Image Proc. **34**, 344–371 (1986)
12. Guo, Z., Zhang, L., Zhang, D.: A completed modeling of local binary pattern operator for texture classification. IEEE Trans. Image Proc. **19**, 1657–1663 (2010)
13. Bookstein, F.L.: Principal warps: thin-plate splines and the decomposition of deformations. IEEE Trans. Pattern Anal. Mach. Intell **6**, 567–585 (1989)

Automated Retinal Blood Vessel Segmentation Using Fuzzy Mathematical Morphology and Morphological Reconstruction

Razieh Akhavan[1($\boxtimes$)] and Karim Faez[2]

[1] Department of Electrical, Computer and Biomedical Engineering
Qazvin Branch, Islamic Azad University, Qazvin, Iran
R.akhavan.a@gmail.com
[2] Electrical Engineering Department,
Amirkabir University of Technology, Tehran, Iran
Kfaez@aut.ac.ir

Abstract. Assessment of blood vessels in retinal images is an important factor for the many medical disorders. The retinal vessel evaluation can be done by first extracting the retinal images from the background. The changes in the retinal vessels due to the pathologies can be easily identified by segmenting the retinal vessels. In this paper we describe an automatic method for retinal blood vessels segmentation. Segmentation of retinal vessels is done to identify the early diagnosis of the disease like glaucoma, diabetic retinopathy, macular degeneration, hypertensive retinopathy and arteriosclerosis. In this the blood vessel is segmented using fuzzy morphological operation with the disc shaped structuring element and morphological reconstruction. This method is applied on the publicly available DRIVE database and the experimental results obtained by using green-channel images have been presented. This algorithm has been shown to be a very effective method to detect retinal blood vessels. Our proposed algorithm is simple, easy to be implemented, and the best suited for fast processing applications.

Keywords: Blood vessel segmentation · Fuzzy morphological operations · Morphological reconstruction · Retinal images

1 Introduction

The diagnosis of the fundus image is widely used in many medical diagnosis. Image segmentation [1] in the fundus image is the important factor for identifying the retinal pathology. The analysis of the human retina helps the ophthalmologists to identify the retinal disease. The disease such as the diabetes, hypertension and arteriosclerosis affect the retina and causes the changes in the retinal blood vessels [2]. The changes in the blood vessel and the retinal pathology can be identified by first segmenting the retinal vessels and by proper analysis of the retinal blood vessels.

Automatic segmentation of retinal vessels is important for early diagnosis of eye diseases like diabetic retinopathy [3]. There are various segmentation methods for segmenting the retinal vessels in the fundus image which segments the retinal vessels using two dimensional matched filters and by piecewise threshold probing [4, 5].

© Springer International Publishing Switzerland 2014
A. Movaghar et al. (Eds.): AISP 2013, CCIS 427, pp. 131–140, 2014.
DOI: 10.1007/978-3-319-10849-0_14

There are other segmentation processes which include segmentation of retinal vessels using the Mumford-Shah model and Gabor wavelet filter [6]. Extraction of retinal blood vessels is done using Weiner filter and the Morphological operations like open and close operation [7]. This paper focuses on segmentation of the retinal vessels to identify the changes in the retinal vessel which occurs due to retinal pathologies like diabetic retinopathy [8]. Vessel segmentation is done using Max-Tree to represent the image and the branches filtering approach to segment the image [9]. Mathematical morphology is mostly used for analysis the shape of the image. The two main processes which involves are dilation and erosion. The algorithms of open and close are based on these processes. These algorithms are combined to detect the edges and identifying the specific shapes in the image and also for the background removal [10]. Retinal vessel segmentation is done to classify the pixel as the vessel and non-vessel using morphological thresholding. The retinal blood vessel is extracted by first smoothening the image and enhanced by applying the fuzzy c-means clustering algorithm [11].

In this paper we used the morphological operation and double threshold on the image to get the properly segmented output image.

2   Methods

2.1   Systematic Overview

This paper proposes a novel method for retinal blood vessels segmentation. The fundus image used in this research is obtained from Digital Retinal Images for vessel extraction (DRIVE database). The segmentation of the retinal blood vessel should be automatic and accurate for the diagnosis of the retinal disease. The main parts of the algorithm are as follows: Color image (RGB) to green conversion, contrast enhancement, image segmentation, and morphological reconstruction and background exclusion.

2.2   RGB to Green Channel Conversion

In this part, the color fundus image is converted to green channel image to make the segmentation process more easy and to decrease the computational time. The green channel image provides the maximum contrast between the image and the background, because the retinal blood vessel information in the green channel image is more clear [12, 13].

2.3   Contrast Enhancement

Low contrast images could occur often due to several reasons, such as poor or non-uniform lighting condition, nonlinearity or small dynamic range of the imaging sensor, i.e., illumination is distributed non-uniformly within the image. Therefore, it is necessary to enhance the contrast of these images to provide a better transform representation for subsequent image analysis steps. CLAHE technique is an acceptable and satisfactory method to improve contrast. This technique enhances the contrast adaptively across the image by limiting the maximum slope in the transformation function. Moreover, background of retinal images often have a gradual intensity variation from the periphery of the retina towards the central macular area; other retinal regions, like the optic disc, also have distinctive intensity values. Vessels are retinal structures that stand out from the background, but a more detailed analysis of local vessel intensities can reveal significant changes (typically dependent from neighboring conditions), which can negatively affect the process of complete vessel segmentation. In order to decrease this influence, the contrast-enhanced image is normalized by subtracting an estimate of the background, which is the result of a filtering operation with a large median kernel (Fig. 1).

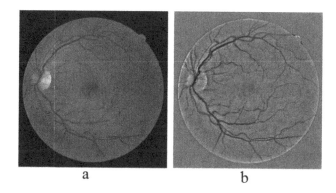

a   b

Fig. 1. (a) Original green channel (b) Background normalized image.

2.4 Fuzzy Mathematical Morphology

Morphological operations are a set of image processing operations that analyzes the shapes within the image. It applies a structuring element to the image and output the image of the same size. The output value of each pixel is determined by the neighboring pixels with its corresponding pixel of input image. The size and shape of the structuring element affects the number of pixels being added or removed from the object in the image.

The Mathematical Morphology (MM) has been applied successfully to a large number of image processing problems. However, MM does not allow a complete representation of the uncertainties in images with high texture or a high degree of uncertainty in structural components. From the binary MM different extensions have been made for grayscale images. One of them is the fuzzy extension of mathematical morphology (FMM). The advantages of the fuzzy sets to represent uncertainty in the images has led them to become a useful tool for segmentation. The FMM has been applied successfully in medical image segmentation. Here, we introduce the following operators, which are used in this paper.

In what follows μ and ν represent two fuzzy sets, where the first is a grayscale image and the second corresponds to the structuring element. Importantly, in most cases the gray level intensity at each pixel of the gray level images are defined to be an integer value belonging to the natural range [0,255]. Therefore, to be able to apply the FMM operators, we need to use a function that converts the scale of these images to the range [0,1]. This process of scaling is called "fuzzification", while the reverse process is called "defuzzification". For the development of this work fuzzification function g: $\{0,1,2...,255\} \rightarrow [0,1]$ used is:

$$g(x) = x/255 \tag{1}$$

The reverse process by which the intensities of the gray levels of an image, belonging to the interval [0,1], are brought to the set $\{0,1,2,...,255\}$ is defined from the function $h:[0,1] \rightarrow \{0,1,2,...,255\}$ given by:

$$h(x) = [255x] \tag{2}$$

where $[0]:R \rightarrow Z$ represents the integer part function, i.e., [a] is the nearest integer to a with $a \in |R$.

Importantly, this process does not convert the image into a fuzzy representation of an object, but can models a grayscale image as a fuzzy set in order to apply the theory of fuzzy sets.

The basic operations of FMM are fuzzy dilation (Max filter) and fuzzy erosion (Min filter).

Fuzzy dilation and fuzzy erosion of the image μ by the structuring element (v) are given respectively:

$$\mu \oplus v = sup_{y \in U}[t(\mu(y), v(y - x))] \tag{3}$$

$$\mu \odot v = inf_{y \in U}[s(\mu(y), c(v(y - x)))] \tag{4}$$

where t[a,b] and s[a,b] are t-norm and s-norm, respectively.

Close operation is defined as dilation followed by erosion. Dilation is an operation that thickens or expands objects in a binary image. Erosion is an operation that extenuates objects in a binary image. The specific manner and extent of this thickening and narrowing is controlled by a shape referred to a structuring element [14]. Fuzzy morphological close of the image μ by the structuring element (v) is given by:

$$\mu \cdot v = (\mu \oplus v) \odot v \tag{5}$$

2.5   Image Segmentation

In this paper the retinal blood vessel segmentation is done using fuzzy morphological close operation. It applies the disk shaped structuring element to the image and output the image of the same size. The structuring element used is of two different sizes. One with a big size for the higher structuring element and one with a small size for the lower structuring element. Then, the image with higher structuring element is subtracted from image with lower structuring element. Herein we applied CLAHE technique as a post processing technique to provide an optimal image of the vessels. The output image obtained is the retinal blood vessel extracted from the background.

2.6   Morphological Reconstruction and Background Exclusion

In the last part, we apply the threshold on the extracted retinal vessels. After applying the threshold the background is eliminated and the properly segmented binary image of the retinal vessel is obtained. For this task, we selected a binary morphological reconstruction method, called the double threshold operator. This operator uses two different values for thresholding the image. One of them is bigger than the other. The image obtained with the big threshold value (marker image) is used as a seed for the reconstruction using the image obtained with the small threshold value (mask image) [15]. This morphological operator is used to reconstruct vessel segments from the enhanced vessel representation. Figure 2 shows the maker and mask and the output of the morphological reconstruction operator.

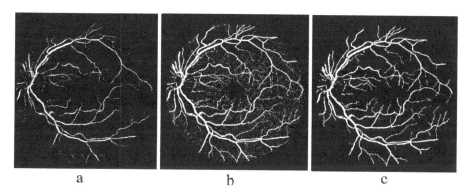

a   b   c

Fig. 2. Result of morphological reconstruction operator for enhanced image (a) Marker image (b) Mask image (c) Output of morphological reconstruction operator.

3   Result

Figure 3 shows the sample results of the segmentation process obtained from the fundus image taken from DRIVE database. To validate the obtained segmented image, we used the gold standard image obtained from manual blood vessels segmentation by an expert. In Fig. 3, first of all the original image is shown, then the segmented image using the operators of the FMM and finally the gold standard image obtained from manual blood vessels segmentation is presented. The results demonstrated herein indicate that automated identification of retinal blood vessels based on fuzzy Morphological operations can be very successful. Hence, eye care specialists can potentially monitor larger populations using this method. Furthermore, observations based on such a tool would be systematically reproducible.

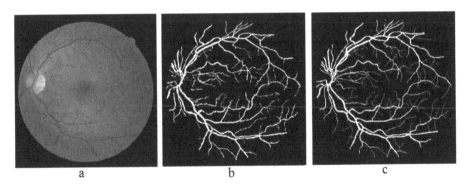

a   b   c

Fig. 3. (a) The original image (b) segmented image using the operators of the FMM (c) gold standard image obtained from manual blood vessels segmentation.

The evaluation results are given as the pixel-wise sensitivity, specificity and accuracy of all the segmentation in comparison with ground truth provided by experts, where sensitivity is a normalized measure of true positives, specificity measures the proportion of true negatives, and accuracy represents the proportion of the total number of correctly classified pixels relative to the total number of pixels.

$$\text{Sensitivity} = \frac{TP}{TP + FN}$$
$$\text{Specificity} = \frac{TN}{TN + FP}$$
$$\text{Accuracy} = \frac{(TP + TN)}{TP + TN + FP + FN}$$

True positive (TP) is a number of blood vessels correctly detected, false positive (FP) is a number of non-blood vessels which are detected wrongly as blood vessels, false negative (FN) is a number of blood vessels that are not detected and true negative (TN) is a number of non-blood vessels which are correctly identified as non-blood vessels.

Table 1. Average percentage of vessel segmentation methods

Method	Accuracy	Sensitivity	Specificity
Proposed method	95.37	72.26	97.81
Fraz [16]	94.30	71.52	97.68
Espona et al. [17]	93.16	66.34	96.82
Al-Diri [18]	92.58	67.16	–
Mendonca [19]	94.52	73.44	97.64
Espona et al. [20]	93.52	74.36	96.15
Vlachos [21]	92.85	74.68	95.51
Nilanjan Dey [22]	95.03	54.66	99.62
Baisheng Dai [23]	94.60	70.91	98.06

Table 1 compares evaluation results of proposed method with the listed approaches. In comparison with the methods of [16–18], our proposed method have the highest accuracy, sensitivity and specificity. In addition, it has the highest accuracy and specificity compared to [19–21]. Finally, our method has the best accuracy and sensitivity than the approaches of [22, 23].

Figure 4 represents other sample results of the segmentation process obtained from the fundus images taken from DRIVE database.

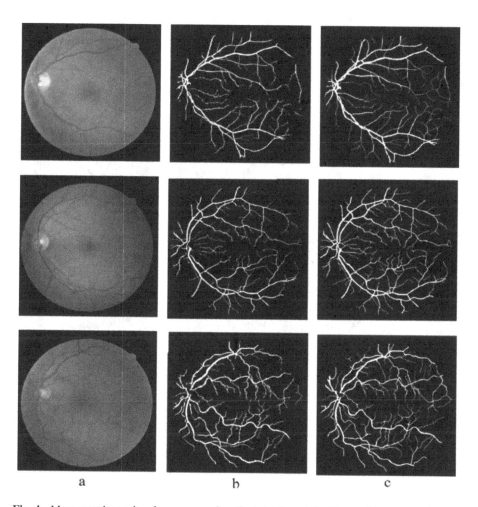

a   b   c

Fig. 4. More sample results of our proposed method: (a) the original image (b) segmented image using the operators of the FMM (c) gold standard image obtained from manual blood vessels segmentation.

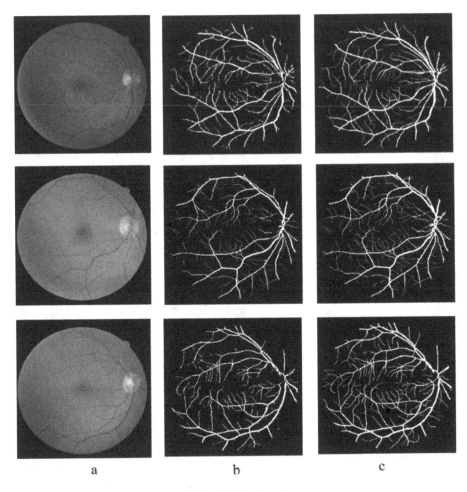

a   b   c

Fig. 4. *(Continued)*

4 Conclusion

The retinal blood vessel segmentation technique describe in this paper is based on fuzzy morphological operation and apply on a large number of images. Our proposed technique is a simple and computationally efficient algorithm for retinal blood vessel segmentation and it is successful and robust in representing the directional model of the retinal vessels surrounding the optic disk. Our proposed vessel extraction technique does not require any user intervention, and has consistent performance in both normal and abnormal images.

To validate the proposed method we used images provided from the public database DRIVE, which includes the ideal segmentation, a tool necessary to carry out the validation of any method of segmentation. As a result of the processing of the 40 images, were obtained that our proposed method has the great specificity 97.81, accuracy 95.37 and sensitivity 72.26.

References

1. Jain, K.: Fundamentals of Digital Image Processing, vol. 3. Prentice-Hall, Englewood Cliffs (1989)
2. Pedersen, L., Grunkin, M., Ersbøll, B., Madsen, K., Larsen, M., Christoffersen, N., et al.: Quantitative measurement of changes in retinal vessel diameter in ocular fundus images. Pattern Recogn. Lett. **21**, 1215–1223 (2000)
3. Sinthanayothin, C., Boyce, J., Williamson, T., Cook, H., Mensah, E., Lal, S., et al.: Automated detection of diabetic retinopathy on digital fundus images. Diabet. Med. **19**, 105–112 (2002)
4. Chaudhuri, S., Chatterjee, S., Katz, N., Nelson, M., Goldbaum, M.: Detection of blood vessels in retinal images using two-dimensional matched filters. IEEE Trans. Med. Imag. **8**, 263–269 (1989)
5. Hoover, A., Kouznetsova, V., Goldbaum, M.: Locating blood vessels in retinal images by piecewise threshold probing of a matched filter response. IEEE Trans. Med. Imag. **19**, 203–210 (2000)
6. Du, X., Bui, T.D.: Retinal image segmentation based on Mumford-Shah model and Gabor wavelet filter. In: 2010 20th International Conference on, Pattern Recognition (ICPR), pp. 3384–3387 (2010)
7. Kumari, V.V., Suriyanarayanan, N.: Blood vessel extraction using wiener filter and morphological operation. Int. J. Comput. Sci. Emerg. Technol **1**, 7–10 (2010)
8. Foracchia, M., Grisan, E., Ruggeri, A.: Extraction and quantitative description of vessel features in hypertensive retinopathy fundus images. In: Book Abstracts 2nd International Workshop on Computer Assisted Fundus Image Analysis, p. 6 (2001)
9. Yang, Y., Huang, S., Rao, N.: An automatic hybrid method for retinal blood vessel extraction. Int. J. Appl. Math. Comput. Sci. **18**, 399–407 (2008)
10. Patton, N., Aslam, T.M., MacGillivray, T., Deary, I.J., Dhillon, B., Eikelboom, R.H., et al.: Retinal image analysis: concepts, applications and potential. Prog. Retinal Eye Res. **25**, 99–127 (2006)
11. Noronha, K., Nayak, J., Bhat, S.: Enhancement of retinal fundus Image to highlight the features for detection of abnormal eyes. In: 2006 IEEE Region 10 Conference TENCON 2006, pp. 1–4 (2006)
12. Bouchet, A., Brun, M., Ballarin, V.: Morfología Matemática Difusa aplicada a la segmentación de angiografías retinales. Revista Argentina de Bioingeniería **16**, 7–10 (2001)
13. Bouchet, A., Pastore, J.I., Ballarín, V.L.: Segmentation of medical images using fuzzy mathematical morphology. J. Comput. Sci. Technol. **7**, 256–262 (2007)
14. Gasparri, J., Bouchet, A., Abras, G., Ballarin, V., Pastore, J.: Medical image segmentation using the HSI color space and Fuzzy Mathematical Morphology. J. Phys. Conf. Ser. **332**(1), 012033 (2011)
15. Michielsen, K., De Raedt, H., Kawakatsu, T.: Morphological image analysis. In: Landau, D. P., Lewis, S.P., Schüttler, H.-B. (eds.) Computer Simulation Studies in Condensed-Matter Physics XIII, pp. 87–91. Springer, New York (2001)

16. Fraz, M.M., Remagnino, P., Hoppe, A., Uyyanonvara, B., Owen, C.G., Rudnicka, A.R., Barman, S.A.: Retinal vessel extraction using first-order derivative of gaussian and morphological processing. In: Bebis, G. (ed.) ISVC 2011, Part I. LNCS, vol. 6938, pp. 410–420. Springer, Heidelberg (2011)
17. Espona, L., Carreira, M.J., Ortega, M., Penedo, M.G.: A Snake for retinal vessel segmentation. In: Martí, J., Benedí, J.M., Mendonça, A.M., Serrat, J. (eds.) IbPRIA 2007. LNCS, vol. 4478, pp. 178–185. Springer, Heidelberg (2007)
18. Al-Diri, B., Hunter, A., Steel, D.: An active contour model for segmenting and measuring retinal vessels. IEEE Trans. Med. Imag. **28**, 1488–1497 (2009)
19. Mendonca, A.M., Campilho, A.: Segmentation of retinal blood vessels by combining the detection of centerlines and morphological reconstruction. IEEE Trans. Med. Imag. **25**, 1200–1213 (2006)
20. Espona, L., Carreira, M.J., Penedo, M., Ortega, M.: Retinal vessel tree segmentation using a deformable contour model. In: 19th International Conference on Pattern Recognition, 2008, ICPR 2008, pp. 1–4 (2008)
21. Vlachos, M., Dermatas, E.: Multi-scale retinal vessel segmentation using line tracking. Comput. Med. Imag. Graph. **34**, 213–227 (2010)
22. Dey, N., Roy, A.B., Pal, M., Das, A.: FCM based blood vessel segmentation method for retinal images. arXiv preprint: arXiv:1209.1181 (2012)
23. Dai, B., Bu, W., Wu, X., Teng, Y.: Retinal vessel segmentation via iterative geodesic time transform. In: 2012 21st International Conference on Pattern Recognition (ICPR), pp. 561–564 (2012)

Diagnosing of Fatty and Heterogeneous Liver Diseases from Ultrasound Images Using Fully Automated Segmentation and Hierarchical Classification

Mehri Owjimehr$^{(\boxtimes)}$, Habibollah Danyali,
and Mohammad Sadegh Helfroush

Shiraz University of Technology, Shiraz, Iran
{m.owjimehr, danyali, ms_helfroush}@sutech.ac.ir

Abstract. In this paper, a fully automatic approach to select the regions of interest (ROIs) of the liver images and an automatic hierarchical procedure to characterize normal, fatty and heterogeneous livers, using textural analysis of liver ultrasound images are described. The proposed algorithm contains two stages. The first stage, automatically assigns some ROIs in a liver ultrasound. In the second stage, discrimination between heterogeneous, fatty and normal livers is performed in a hierarchical method. This stage, first, classifies focal and diffused livers and then discriminates fatty and normal ones. The wavelet packet transform is used to analyze liver texture and obtaining a number of statistical features. A support vector machine classifier is employed to classify three classes. The fully automatic scheme to select the ROIs with low computational cost and the hierarchical classification scheme outperformed the non-hierarchical one-against-all schemes, achieving an overall accuracy of 97.9 %.

Keywords: Liver diseases · Automatic segmentation · Hierarchical classification · WPT

1 Introduction

Liver is a vital organ of body and is necessary for survival and moreover, there is no way to compensate for the absence of liver function, therefore, liver diseases have attracted much attention [1].

Liver diseases can be classified into two main categories. The first category is heterogeneous diseases that abnormalities are concentrated within a small area in one or both of the liver lobes while the rest of the liver tissue remains normal such as solid lesion and fluid lesions. The second category is Diffused or homogenous diseases that the disease is distributed over the whole liver tissues such as fatty liver [1–3].

Fatty liver disease is caused by the accumulation of fat tissue in the liver. The most common causes of fatty liver are obesity, alcoholism, high blood triglycerides, diabetes and hepatitis [2, 5–7].

The best way to diagnose fatty liver disease is liver biopsy. In biopsy, a small sample of tissue is taken from the liver using a needle [10]. This method is highly invasive and costly. However, medical imaging techniques such as Ultrasound (US),

© Springer International Publishing Switzerland 2014
A. Movaghar et al. (Eds.): AISP 2013, CCIS 427, pp. 141–151, 2014.
DOI: 10.1007/978-3-319-10849-0_15

Computed Tomography (CT) and Magnetic Resonance Imaging (MRI), are used for examination and since US is non-radiological, noninvasive, inexpensive, easy to operate and portable it is the most preferred diagnostic method for fatty liver. Extract information from the fatty liver ultrasound images are based on the changes of scanned image intensity. Fatty liver causes an increase of echogenicity or brightness in the liver tissue [2].

In order to find a gold standard method to diagnose and detect fatty liver disease, some authors recently proposed methods and tools based on computer-aided diagnosis (CAD) to help the physicians and experts to detect and classify fatty liver from normal liver or heterogeneous one using ultrasound images [1–4, 6–9].

Liver segmentation and classification are the main steps of CAD system. There are several methods to segment a proper region of liver. Most of them are manual and a few others are semi-automatic and automatic. Manual approaches require medical experts to determine the Region Of Interest (ROI) before leaving to the computer for processing. Whereas, automated segmentation methods segment with minimal user input or without the need of any medical expert assistance. In [18], the ROI for each image in the patient database is selected manually in the training phase. The threshold value to generate extremely stable edge pattern for the template image is then learned and stored back to the database. In the test phase, the ROI is detected from a query image based on a representative template using generalized Hough transform (GHT) to map the edge pattern of a database template to the edge pattern of image. Authors of [6] proposed a method to extract ROI semi-automatically. In their method, a medical expert has manually extracted ROIs from the training ultrasound images and the final ROIs are selected based on Continuous Wavelet Transform (CWT) and one-class support vector machine (SVM) classifier. The aim of the CAD systems is to minimize the user intervention, therefore automatic approaches are preferred. However, the ROI selection in [6, 18] is semi-automatic which results in high computational cost. Another semi-automatic method to select ROI is proposed in [19], this method is used for the liver surface detection, based on an image processing procedure that decomposes the US images of the liver parenchyma into two fields: the speckle image containing textural information and the de-speckled image containing intensity and anatomical information of the liver. Features extracted from the liver contour detected in the de-speckled field. The detected contour distinguishes the liver anatomy from its neighbors and the selected region is used as ROI, however, an efficient ROI should not include hepatic vessels, bile stores and other anomalies, therefore the segmentation stage of this scheme may not be efficient due to lack of anomalies removal.

Several approaches have been proposed for feature extraction and classification in liver tissue based on ultrasound images. The most common features used for diagnosis of fatty liver are the first order and the second order statistical features based on texture analysis of the ultrasound images [11, 12]. Texture analysis approaches can be divided in two groups: one based on the relation of neighbor pixels in spatial domain such as the Gray Level Concurrence Matrix (GLCM) [4, 14, 15], the Gray Level Difference Statistical (GLDS) [15], the Gray Level Run Length Matrix (GLRLM) [4] and fractal parameters [16]; and one based on the analysis of transform coefficients such as Fourier Power Spectrum (FPS) [16], Discrete Wavelet Transform (DWT) [13, 17] and Wavelet Packet Transform (WPT) [6, 17, 21].

As mentioned above, a fully automatic and efficient CAD system includes automatic selection of ROI, efficient feature extraction method and effective classification approach. In our proposed method, the ROIs are selected completely automatic without the need of radiologist assistance. In this method some ROIs have been selected by partitioning the ultrasound image, inspired by the clinical practice, and classification is performed by the use of these ROIs. This procedure presents a considerable low computational cost. Then the WPT is employed to extract some statistical features. Finally, in the classification part, we proposed a novel classification strategy based on a hierarchical method. The first stage of this method classifies heterogeneous liver from others and in the second stage, discrimination of fatty and normal is performed.

The rest of this paper is organized as follows. Section 2 explains the main methodology. Section 3 introduced the dataset used in this work. Segmentation part and the procedure of selecting the ROIs are described in Sect. 4. Sections 5 and 6 study texture analyzer and feature extraction, respectively. Section 7 provides detailed information of classifiers. In Sect. 8 the results are presented and Sect. 9 concludes the paper.

2   Methodology

Block diagram of the proposed method is illustrated in Fig. 1. In this method after acquiring ultrasound images of liver, some optimum ROIs are selected in segmentation section. Then, WPT is applied to extract statistical features. Finally the hierarchical classification approach is employed.

3   Image Acquisition

The ultrasound images of 88 subjects contain 30 fatty, 39 normal and 19 heterogeneous liver images. The images are of size 560 × 450 and saved in bitmap format. All images were obtained using a Toshiba SSA 550 digital ultrasound imaging system at a 5 MHz frequency. This dataset is which has been used in [6] to enable us to have comparison results. Paper [6] is one of the most efficient and newest studies in classification of liver diseases and is the only study to discriminate fatty, normal and heterogeneous livers. Authors of [6] proposed an effective semi-automatic method to select a proper ROI in each ultrasound image.

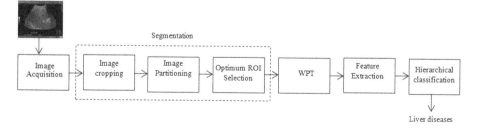

Fig. 1. The block diagram of the proposed method.

4 Segmentation

The purpose of this section is to automatically select the proper regions of interest to perform accurate classification and diagnosis.

In the proposed method, as illustrated in Fig. 1, given ultrasound image of liver is first cropped to extract a wide region near the central lobe and the black region around the main part is removed. This is performed in order to reduce the computational cost of the process. Figure 2 shows a sample of the cropped image. Partitioning this wide region is performed in three levels. The wide region is partitioned to 9 equal size neighboring blocks without overlap in the first level. In order to utilize more information of image, overlapped blocks are also required. Therefore, in the second level, some other blocks formed at the intersection of each two blocks in each row. Thus, 6 blocks are generated which each one has 50 % overlap with each of two adjacent blocks. This process results in obtaining 15 overlapped blocks. The partitioning is continued at the intersection of each two blocks from 15 blocks in each column in the third level. Finally, 25 equal overlapped blocks are specified. Figure 3 shows this procedure. In order to find the proper ROIs, we select 64 × 64 regions in the center of each block, therefore, 25 ROIs of size 64 × 64 is obtained for each ultrasound image. However, using all the ROIs in classification is not efficient and increases the computational cost. Therefore, a v -linear support vector classifier ($v - LSVC$) [27] is employed as a preprocessing stage, and after classification process, 8 ROIs which have better results are selected. Finally, these selected ROIs are used in classification phase. The features which are used in this classification are explained in Sect. 6.

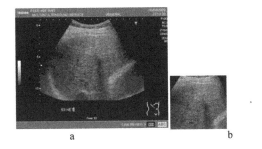

Fig. 2. An example of the cropped liver ultrasound image.

5 Wavelet Packet Transform (WPT)

Multi-resolution analysis feature extraction can be performed in the spatial domain which exists over small neighborhoods for example by using GLCM, GLDS and GLRLM, etc. Feature extraction in transform domain is performed over various scales by using multi-resolution schemes such as DWT and WPT. Using texture descriptors in transform domain is much more reasonable in the sense that human visual system

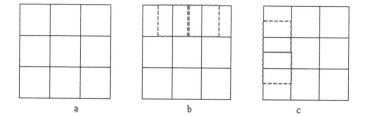

Fig. 3. (a) The first level of partitioning (9 non-overlapped equal size blocks), (b) The second level of partitioning (the process of forming two overlapped blocks at the intersection of two previous blocks in each row), (c) The third level of partitioning (the process of forming two overlapped blocks at the intersection of two previous blocks in each column)

processes images in a multi-scale way and scale is a dominant aspect for analysis of texture [20, 21].

In case of DWT, as only the low frequency subband is recursively decomposed, it may not be efficient for texture characterization as most significant texture information usually appears in the middle and high frequency bands [23]. The wavelet packet transform, in comparison, decomposes the detailed information of the image in the high frequency bands [22, 23]. The WPT tree up to second level of decomposition results in 16 subbands. Therefore, 4 and 16 subbands are obtained at the first and the second level of decomposition, respectively, that result totally in 20 subbands. The desired features are extracted from these 20 subbands as well as original ROIs.

6   Feature Extraction

The extracted features from WPT coefficients are Median, standard deviation and interquartile range. Median of the image shows the numerical value of intensity separating the higher half of pixel intensities in a window of the image, from the lower half. The median value of intensity in ultrasound fatty liver images is higher than the intensity of normal ones due to their increased echogenicity caused by fat accumulation [6]. This characteristic also exists in WPT subbands of ultrasound fatty liver images. Standard deviation shows the variation from the mean. The interquartile range measures the dispersion and is the difference between the upper and lower quartiles. The standard deviation and the interquartile range of the image represent the regularity or smoothness of the ultrasound texture. These two features may be good indicators to distinguish ultrasound images of focal and diffused diseases of liver.

As a spatial domain feature, the ratio of the maximum to the minimum value in the original image is computed the same as [6]. Therefore, by calculating the three explained features from each of 20 subbands and one feature from the original ROI image, the total number of 61 features is obtained.

7 Classification

In this section, it is aimed to discriminate normal, fatty and heterogeneous livers. To reach this aim, a hierarchical classification scheme is proposed. A block diagram of this scheme is illustrated in Fig. 4. The proposed hierarchical classification scheme is organized in two steps. The first step distinguishes heterogeneous liver from others and classification of fatty and normal livers is performed in the second step.

As already mentioned, in normal case, both lobes of liver are homogeneously clear and in fatty case, as it is a diffused disease, at least one lobe is accumulated homogeneously by fat, however, heterogeneous case is focal and a small region of liver is only affected. Therefore, the fatty and normal cases can be placed in the diffused category and the heterogeneous case placed in the focal category. In order to have a hierarchical scheme, in the first classification step, focal case is discriminated from diffused case, if a liver is classified as diffused in the first step, discrimination of fatty and normal is attempted in the second step.

For the classification in each step, the SVM classifier is implemented. The purpose of SVM is to find a decision plane that has a maximum distance (margin) from the nearest training pattern [24, 25]. In order to perform this aim, SVM maps the feature vector to a higher-dimensional space. In this space the SVM finds a hyperplane to separate the two classes with a decision boundary set by support vectors [24, 25]. An appropriate kernel function can reduced the high computational cost of mapping process. In this paper, a binary SVM classifier is adopted using the polynomial kernel.

8 Implementation Results

The first part of implementation is selecting ROIs which is performed as a fully automatic segmentation. The simplicity and reduction of computational cost of this method in comparison with the semi-automatic method of selecting ROI in [6], without degrading the classification performance, is noticeable. After selecting proper ROIs, classification is performed. At the first step of classification, the diffused and focal classes are denoted as class 1 and 2, respectively and at the second step, repeatedly, the fatty class is marked as class 1 and the normal one as class 2.

This experiment contains three tests over automatically selected ROIs and a comparison with the results of [6]. The first test is performed on only the 9 non-overlapped blocks. These blocks have the size of 76 × 84 pixels. 9 ROIs are formed by selecting 64 × 64 pixel regions at the center of each block. Each of these 9 ROIs are examined by SVM classifier, therefore, the total number of 9 class labels are obtained for each liver image. The performance of the SVM classifier is evaluated by means of leave one out cross validation (LOOCV) method, same as the method used in [6] to have a fair comparison with its results. Furthermore, this method is useful in cases with small amount of available data, as normally observed in medical problems. In LOOCV method, one case is left out as the testing set and the rest of the data is used as the training set. This process is repeated so that each case is given a chance as the testing case [26].

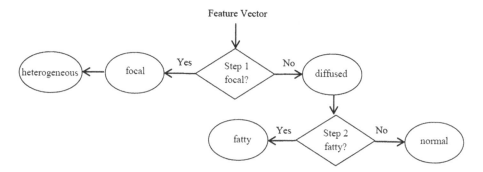

Fig. 4. The proposed hierarchical classification scheme

The performance of the algorithm was investigated by the following measures:

(1) Sensitivity (Se):

$$Se = \frac{TP}{TP + FN}$$

(2) Positive Predictive Value (PPV):

$$PPV = \frac{TP}{TP + FP}$$

(3) Accuracy (Acc):

$$Acc = \frac{TN + TP}{TN + TP + FN + FP}$$

TP (True Positives): TP is the number of instances of each class which have been correctly labeled to belong to that class [6, 28]. TN (True Negative): TN is the number of instances of other classes that have been labeled to belong to their class [6, 28]. FN (False Negatives): FN is the number of instances of each class which have been labeled to belong to any other class [6, 28]. FP (False Positives): FP is the number of instances of other classes that have been labeled to belong to a specified class [6, 28].

Tables 1, 2 and 3 illustrate the sensitivity and positive predictive value of each class in each step and the accuracy of each step using leave one out cross validation method of first, second and third tests, respectively. As these three Tables show, the sensitivity and the positive predictive value of each class and the accuracy of each step are

Table 1. Results of Leave One Out cross validation and hierarchical classification scheme at the first test (considering 9 non-overlapped blocks).

		Sensitivity (Se)	Positive predictive value (PPV)	Accuracy (Acc)	Overall accuracy
Step 1	Focal (heterogeneous)	71.5 %	62.7 %	85.3 %	88.4 %
	Diffused	87.9 %	94.2 %		
Step 2	Fatty	97.1 %	86.7 %	91.4 %	
	Normal	90.3 %	94.9 %		

Table 2. Results of Leave One Out cross validation and hierarchical classification scheme at the second test (considering 15 overlapped blocks).

		Sensitivity (Se)	Positive predictive value (PPV)	Accuracy (Acc)	Overall accuracy
Step 1	Focal (heterogeneous)	86.7 %	70.5 %	90.9 %	93.3 %
	Diffused	91.8 %	97.1 %		
Step 2	Fatty	100 %	90 %	95.7 %	
	Normal	92.9 %	100 %		

Table 3. Results of Leave One Out cross validation and hierarchical classification scheme at the third test (considering 25 overlapped blocks) in comparison with method of [6].

			Sensitivity (Se)	Positive predictive value (PPV)	Accuracy (Acc)	Overall accuracy
The proposed algorithm	Step 1	Focal (heterogeneous)	100 %	92.7 %	98.7 %	97.9 %
		Diffused	96.1 %	100 %		
	Step 2	Fatty	100 %	93.3 %	97.1 %	
		Normal	95.1 %	100 %		
Algorithm of [6]		Heterogeneous	94.7 %	100 %	–	95.4 %
		Fatty	93.3 %	93.3 %		
		Normal	96.4 %	95 %		

increased by increasing the number of blocks. This fact shows the importance of selecting appropriate ROIs in diagnosing the diseases. The ROIs are placed at the center of blocks and cover 65 % of each one. Therefore, decreasing the number of blocks results in losing the regions around the edges. These regions may contain useful texture information which can be applied in the classification process by considering the overlapped blocks.

According to the results in Table 3, by considering 25 ROIs, the proposed method gives the sensitivity of 100 % for detecting both heterogeneous and fatty liver at the first and the second steps which shows the complete detection and quite correct diagnosis of these diseases. The high values of PPV given in this Table, also depicts the high precision of this method. Furthermore, we have achieved the overall accuracy of 97.9 % which is higher compare to the approach of [6] with overall accuracy of 95.4 % in the same condition. In addition, the method of selecting ROIs in the proposed scheme is completely automatic with lower computational cost than the method of [6]. In [6] the segmentation process is semi-automatic with high computational complexity and moreover, their classification method is not such a hierarchical scheme.

9 Conclusion

In this paper, an automatic segmentation and classification method to discriminate normal, fatty and heterogeneous liver images is proposed. The proposed algorithm is performed in two stages. The first stage, automatically selects some ROIs in a liver ultrasound. The WPT is applied to the selected ROIs as a multi-scale texture analyzer to extract some statistical features. In the second stage, a hierarchical binary classification method using SVM classifier is employed. The proposed hierarchical classification algorithm discriminates the heterogeneous case from the diffused case at the first step and classifies the fatty and the normal cases at the second step. The overall accuracy of 97.7 % indicates the efficiency of the hierarchical classification scheme. The implementation results illustrate the suitability of the proposed system to be used in a clinical environment to help radiologists in liver disease classification and improve diagnostic accuracy which can avoid biopsies in some cases. The completely automatic scheme to select the ROIs with the noticeable low computational cost is the other advantage of this system.

References

1. Suganya, R., Rajaram, S., Classification of liver diseases from ultrasound images using a hybrid kohonen SOM and LPND speckle reduction method. In: 2012 IEEE International Conference on Signal Processing, Computing and Control (ISPCC), pp. 1–6 (2012)
2. Icer, S., Coskun, A., Ikizceli, T.: Quantitative grading using grey relational analysis on ultrasonographic images of a fatty liver. J. Med. Syst. **36**, 2521–2528 (2012)
3. Kadah, Y.M., Farag, A.A., Zurada, J.M., Badawi, A.M., Youssef, A.M.: Classification algorithms for quantitative tissue characterization of diffuse liver disease from ultrasound images. IEEE Trans. Med. Imag. **15**(4), 466–478 (1996)
4. Andrade, A., Silva, J.S., Santos, J., Belo-Soares, P.: Classifier approaches for liver steatosis using ultrasound images. Procedia Technol. **5**, 763–770 (2012)
5. Radu, C., Grigorescu, M., Lupsor, M., Vicas, C., Nedevschi, S., Badea, R., Grigorescu, M. D., Sparchez, Z., Crisan, D., Feier, D.: The diagnostic performance of attenuation coefficient computed on the ultrasound image compared to a biochemical marker - SteatoTest - for steatosis quantification in non-alcoholic fatty liver disease. In: 2010 IEEE International Conference on Automation Quality and Testing Robotics (AQTR), vol. 2, pp. 1–5 (2010)

6. Afsar Minhas, A., Sabih, D., Hussain, M.: Automated classification of liver disorders using ultrasound images. J. Med. Syst. **36**, 3163–3172 (2012)
7. Mihailescu, D.M., Gui, V., Toma, C. I., Popescu, A., Sporea, I.: Automatic evaluation of steatosis by ultrasound image analysis. In: 2012 10th International Symposium on Electronics and Telecommunications (ISETC), pp. 311–314 (2012)
8. Yang, Y., He, Q., Hu, C., Liao, J., Meng, M.: Method of edge energy template for detection of ultrasonic based fatty liver. In: 2010 3rd International Congress on Image and Signal Processing (CISP), vol. 2, pp. 994–998 (2010)
9. Moldovanu, S., Moraru, L., Bibicu, D.: Computerized decision support in liver steatosis investigation. Int. J. Biol. Biomed. Eng. **6**, 69–76 (2012)
10. Ceylan, R., Ceylan, M., Ozbay, Y., Kara, S.: Fuzzy clustering complex-valued neural network to diagnose cirrhosis disease. Expert Syst. Appl. **38**, 9744–9751 (2011)
11. Wun, Y.T., Chung, R.: Ultrasound characterization by stable statistical patterns. Comput. Methods Prog. Biomed. **55**(2), 117–126 (1998)
12. Badawi, A.M., Derbala, A.S., Youssef, A.B.M.: Fuzzy logic algorithm for quantitative tissue characterization of diffuse liver diseases from ultrasound images. Int. J. Med. Inf. **55**(2), 135–147 (1999)
13. Yeh, W.C., Jeng, Y.M., Li, C.H., Lee, P.H., Li, P.C.: Liver fatty change classification using 25 MHz high frequency ultrasound. In: 2004 IEEE Ultrasonics Symposium, vol. 3, pp. 2169–2172 (2004)
14. Mukherjee, S., Chakravorty, A., Ghosh, K., Roy, M., Adhikari, A., Mazumdar, S.: Corroborating the subjective classification of ultrasound images of normal and fatty human livers by the radiologist through texture analysis and SOM. In: International Conference on Advanced Computing and Communications, 2007, ADCOM 2007, pp. 97–202. IEEE (2007)
15. Yali, H., Han, X., Tian, X., Zhao, Z., Zhao, J., Hao, D.: Texture analysis of ultrasonic liver images based on spatial domain methods. In: 2010 3rd International Congress on Image and Signal Processing (CISP), vol. 2, pp. 562–565 (2010)
16. Singh, M., Singh, S., Gupta, S.: A new measure of echogenicity of ultrasound images for liver classification. In: 2011 24th Canadian Conference on Electrical and Computer Engineering (CCECE), pp. 317–320 (2011)
17. Ribeiro, R., Marinho, R.T., Sanches, J.M.: Global and local detection of liver steatosis from ultrasound. In: Conference Proceedings: Annual International Conference of the IEEE Engineering in Medicine and Biology Society. pp. 5547–5550 (2012)
18. Wu, Y.H., Lo, Y.C., Cheng, S.C., Lin, C.L.: Adaptive ultrasound image matching for automatic liver disease diagnosis using generalized hough transform. In: 2010 Sixth International Conference on Intelligent Information Hiding and Multimedia Signal Processing (IIH-MSP). IEEE (2010)
19. Ribeiro, R., Marinho, R., Velosa, J., Ramalho, F., Sanches, J.M.: Diffuse liver disease classification from ultrasound surface characterization, clinical and laboratorial data. In: Vitrià, J., Sanches, J.M., Hernández, M. (eds.) IbPRIA 2011. LNCS, vol. 6669, pp. 167–175. Springer, Heidelberg (2011)
20. Daugman, J.: An information-theoretic view of analog representations in the striate cortex. In: Schwartz, E.L. (ed.) Computational Neuroscience. MIT Press, Cambridge (1990)
21. Virmani, V., Kumar, V., Kalra, N., Khandelwal, N.: SVM-based characterization of liver ultrasound images using wavelet packet texture descriptors. J. Digit. Imag. pp. 1–14 (2013)
22. Gao, R.X., Yan, R.: Wavelet packet transform. In: Wavelets, pp. 69–81. Springer, US (2011)
23. Chang, T., Kuo, C.C.J.: Texture analysis and classification with tree structured wavelet transform. IEEE Trans. Image Process. **2**(4), 429–441 (1993)

24. Sudha, S., Suresh, G.R., Sukanesh, R.: Speckle noise reduction in ultrasound images using context-based adaptive wavelet thresholding. IETE J. Res. **55**(3), 135–143 (2009)
25. Duda, R.O., Hart, P.E., Stork, D.G.: Pattern Classification, 2nd edn. Wiley-Interscience, New York (2000)
26. Cawley, G., Talbot, N.: Efficient leave-one-out cross-validation of kernel fisher discriminant classifiers. Pattern Recogn. **36**, 2585–2592 (2003)
27. Chen, P.H., Lin, C.J., Scholkopf, B.: A tutorial on v-support vector machines. Appl. Stoch. Models Bus. Ind. **21**(2), 111–136 (2004)
28. Zhu, W., Zeng, N., Wang, N.: Sensitivity, specificity, accuracy, associated confidence interval and ROC analysis with practical SAS® implementations, In: NESUG proceedings: health care and life sciences, Baltimore, Maryland, pp. 1–9 (2010)

Signal Processing

A New Sparse Representation Algorithm for Semi-supervised Signal Classification

Azam Andalib$^{(\boxtimes)}$ and Seyed Morteza Babamir

Department of Computer Engineering, University of Kashan, Kashan, Iran
azam.andalib@grad.kashanu.ac.ir, babamir@kashanu.ac.ir

Abstract. The performance of many Sparse Representation (SR) based signal classification tasks is highly dependent on the availability of the datasets with a large amount of labeled data points. However, in many cases, accessing to sufficient labeled data may be expensive or time consuming, whereas acquiring a large amount of unlabeled data is relatively easy. In this paper, we propose a new SR based classification method which utilizes the information of the unlabeled data as well as the labeled data. Experimental results show that the proposed method outperforms the state of the art SR based classification methods.

Keywords: Local linear embedding · Dictionary learning · Semi-supervised learning · Sparse representation

1 Introduction

In the last decade, sparse representation has attracted much attention to itself from signal processing community [1]. This attention is because many natural signals (i.e. images) are inherently sparse that can be reconstructed by their sparse codes such that the reconstructed signals are fairly close to the original signals. More precisely, original signals can be represented efficiently by linear combination of some features (atoms). A set of atoms is called a dictionary.

Generally speaking, there are two ways for determining dictionary atoms: (i) using of-the shelf features such as Fourier Basis, (ii) learning dictionary atoms from data itself. Recently, Wright et al. [1] have shown that learning dictionary directly from data can lead to more accurate reconstruction of the original data. Learning the elements of a dictionary from the training signals can be described as determining dictionary atomes such that the reconstructed signals based on the atoms are very similar to the original signals. The following optimization problem demonstrates the dictionary learning procedure [1].

$$[D, A] = \underset{D,A}{argmin} \sum_{i=1}^{n} \left(\|x_i - D\alpha_i\|_2^2 + \beta\|\alpha_i\|_1 \right), \tag{1}$$

In the above equation, $X = [x_1, x_2, ..., x_n]$ is the $m \times n$ matrix of the original signals, $D = [d_1, d_2, ..., d_K]$ is the $m \times K$ Dictionary matrix, $A = [\alpha_1, \alpha_2, ..., \alpha_n]$

© Springer International Publishing Switzerland 2014
A. Movaghar et al. (Eds.): AISP 2013, CCIS 427, pp. 155–163, 2014.
DOI: 10.1007/978-3-319-10849-0_16

is the $K \times n$ matrix of the sparse codes, β is a free parameter which determines the importance of the reconstruction term ($\|x_i - D\alpha_i\|_2^2$) respect to the sparsity term ($\|\alpha_i\|_1$), and $\|.\|_1$ is the l_1 norm, which is defined as [4]

$$\|y\|_1 = \sum_i^m |y_i| \tag{2}$$

where, y denotes a m dimensional signal and y_i is the i-th element of that signal. Unfortunately, the optimization problem of Eq. 1 is not convex respect to A and D simultaneously, however, by considering one of the variables as constant, the optimization problem become convex respect to the other variable. There have been proposed lots of method for solving the optimization problem of the Eq. 1 among which K-SVD [2] and MOD [3] have attracted much attention due to their efficiency.

2   Related Work

In the last decade, there have been proposed many DL algorithms for signal classification applications which use label information of the data points to learn a discriminative dictionary [4–10].

Wright et al. [11] considered the training data points as atoms of the dictionary for face recognition task. This method determines the class of an unknown face image based on evaluating which class leads to the minimal reconstruction error. The main disadvantage of this method is that it cannot utilize the discriminative information of the training data that is vital in discriminative DL tasks.

Yang et al. [12] incorporated a discriminative term based on Fisher Discriminat Analysis (FDA) algorithm into the DL learning framework, in which a sub-dictionary for each class is learned. Ramirez et al. [6] added a structured inherence penalty term to the objective function of the class specific sub-dictionary learning problem to make the sub-dictionaries incoherent. Mairal et al. [4] proposed a method in which, a classifier and a dictionary are jointly learned by utilizing a logistic loss function instead of canonical least square loss function. Jiang et al. [13] modified the K-SVD algorithm by adding a label consistent term to this algorithm to increase the discrimination power of the sparse codes. The main shortcoming of the above DL methods is that the number of the labeled signals has a strong impact on the performance of these methods. Unfortunately, in many applications, accessibility to a large amount of labeled samples is not possible due to the fact that labeling data is expensive and time consuming. On the other hand, a large set of unlabeled data points are easily accessible which have motivated many researchers to develop semi-supervised learning methods which utilize the unlabeled data as well as the labeled data, to build better models for classification tasks.

A canonical example for semi-supervised classification (SSL) methods is Semi-Supervised Support Vector Machine (S3VM) [14], which incorporates not only the labeled data, but also the information of the unlabeled samples into the max-margin framework. Another well-known method for semi-supervised learning is

Co-training [15], which assumes that features (data points) have multiple views. Based on this assumption, this algorithm utilizes the confident samples in one view to update the other view. The problem with this method is that in many applications (i.e., image classification), for each signal (i.e., image) there is only one feature vector which makes Co-Training unusable.

Very recently, Shrivastava et al. [16] have introduced a dictionary learning pattern classification method taking advantages of the information of unlabeled signals as well as the labeled signals. Although this method is more accurate than the previous discriminative DL methods, it has two main shortcomings. Firstly, because this method learns one dictionary for each class, it cannot scale to problems with large number of classes. Secondly, it does not consider the topological structure of all data points.

To circumvent these drawbacks, in this paper, we propose a new discriminative DL method for data classification, by which we learn a classifier and a dictionary simultaneously with the capability of sharing features among different classes. Moreover, we utilize the idea of Locally linear Embedding (LLE) method [17] to hold the geometrical structure of data, by which we can prevent overfitting.

The rest of this paper is organized as follows. Section 3 presents the proposed SR based semi-supervised classification method. In Sect. 4 the experimental results are depicted and at last, we conclude our work in the conclusion section.

3 Proposed Method

In this section, we present our method which exploit the information of both the labeled and the unlabeled data. More precisely, the proposed method tries to improve the discrimination in the dictionary and to prevent overfitting over the (small-size) labeled data points by adding a classifier error term and a geometrical preserving term into the proposed objective function respectively.

3.1 Problem Formulation

Let $X_l = \{(x_i, y_i), i = 1, ..., n_l\}$ be the set of labeled data, and $X_u = \{x_j, j = n_l+1, ..., n\}$ be the set of unlabeled data, where n_l and n are the number of labeled and total samples, respectively. Here, $x_j \in R^m$ denotes the j-th sample, $y_i \in \{+1, -1\}$ is the corresponding class label of the i-th data point (for the problems with more than two classes, we use the *one versus all* classification procedure), and $n_u = n - n_l$ is the number of the unlabeled data points. Let $D = [d_1, ..., d_K] \in R^{m \times K}$ be the dictionary with K atoms and $A = [A_l, A_u]_{K \times n}$ be the matrix of the sparse codes, where $A_l = [\alpha_1, ..., \alpha_l]_{K \times n_l}$ and $A_u = [\alpha_{n_l+1}, ..., \alpha_n]_{K \times n_u}$ show the matrices of the sparse codes of the labeled and unlabeled data respectively. Our goal is to learn jointly a single dictionary D adapted to the classification task and a function f which should be positive for any signal in class $+1$ and negative otherwise. In this paper, we consider a linear classifier which uses the sparse code α for the classification task:

$$f(x, \alpha, \theta) = w^T \alpha + b, \tag{3}$$

where $\theta = \{w \in R^K, b \in R\}$ is the parameter of the linear classifier.

Motivated by the idea of [4], we use the logistic loss function to incorporate the error of the classifier to the proposed objective function. By solving the following optimization problem, we can learn the sparse codes A, the dictionary D and the classifier θ simultaneously.

$$[\hat{A}, \hat{D}, \hat{\theta}] = \underset{A,D,\theta}{argmin} \sum_{i=1}^{n_l} C(y_i f(x_i, \alpha_i, \theta))$$

$$+ \sum_{j=1}^{n} \lambda_0 \|x_j - D\alpha_j\|_2^2 + \lambda_1 \|\alpha_j\|_1 + \lambda_2 \|\theta\|_2^2 \qquad (4)$$

where C is the logistic loss function which is defined as

$$C(x) = \log(1 + e^{-x}), \qquad (5)$$

and $\lambda_0, \lambda_1, \lambda_2$ are the regularization parameters.

The problem with the optimization of the Eq. 4 is that whenever the number of the training data is small, the overfitting risk on training data will increase. Furthermore, the topological structure of all the data may not be preserved in sparse feature space. To address the above problems, we utilize the LLE algorithm and modify the above objective function based on that idea. In the following, we first briefly describe the LLE algorithm, then we describe the proposed objective function based on that idea.

3.2   Local Linear Embedding (LLE)

Local Linear Embedding [17] is one of the algorithms that tries to preserve the topological structure of data by retaining locally linear relationships between close data points in the transformed space (the transformed space in this paper is the sparse feature space).

This method assumes that the data is linear in each neighborhood, which means that any data point p can be approximated by a weighted average of its neighbors.

Given the set of data points, this method constructs a k-nearest neighbor graph which models the relations between close data points. The algorithm finds weights that minimize the cost of representing the point by its neighbors under the l_2-norm. The optimal weight matrix $S^* = [s_{ij}^*]$ providing minimal error for the linear reconstruction of data points from their neighbors is obtained according to:

$$S^* = \underset{S=[s_{ij}]}{argmin} \sum_{i=1}^{n} \|x_i - \sum_{x_j \in N_k(x_i)} s_{ij} x_j\|^2$$

$$\text{subject to. } \forall i, \sum_{x_j \in N_k(x_i)} s_{ij} = 1 \qquad (6)$$

where $N_k(x_i)$ shows the set of k nearest neighbors of x_i. This problem can be solved as a constrained least-squares problem [17].

After finding the optimal weight matrix S^*, we define the penalty term $J(A)$ as:

$$J(A) \equiv \sum_{i=1}^{n} \|\alpha_i - \sum_{x_j \in N_k(x_i)} s^*_{ij}\alpha_j\|^2 = tr(AEA^T) \tag{7}$$

where,

$$E = (I - S^*)^T(I - S^*). \tag{8}$$

In the Eq. 7, tr shows the trace operator, and I is the Identity matrix. In (7), $J(A)$ denotes the locally linear reconstruction error of the sparse codes according to the weight matrix S^*. Indeed, it reflects the assumption of preserving the geometrical structure of data in the sparse feature space.

By incorporating $J(A)$ into Eq. 4, the proposed objective function for computing the sparse codes A, the dictionary D, and the classifier θ can be formulated as

$$[\hat{A}, \hat{D}, \hat{\theta}] = \underset{A,D,\theta}{argmin} \sum_{i=1}^{n_l} C(y_i f(x_i, \alpha_i, \theta)) + \lambda_2\|\theta\|_2^2$$

$$+ \sum_{j=1}^{n} \lambda_0\|x_j - D\alpha_j\|_2^2 + \lambda_1\|\alpha_j\|_1 + \lambda_3 tr(AEA^T),$$

$$s.t \ \forall k = 1, ..., K, \|d_k\|_2 \leq 1, \tag{9}$$

where d_k denotes the k-th atom of the dictionary, and λ_3 is a regularization term which controls the balance between preserving the topological structure of the all labeled and unlabeled data, and the discriminativeness of the dictionary, the sparse codes, and the classifier. Since the values of the atomes of D can be arbitrary large, the values of the sparse codes can be relatively low. Therefore, it is common to normalize the atoms of the dictionary such that each column has $\|d_k\|_2 \leq 1$.

3.3   Optimization Procedure

In this section, we describe the optimization procedure for the proposed objective function (Eq. 9). Solving (9) is a challenging task due to the fact that the objective function is not convex respect to A, D and θ simultaneously. To address this problem, we can easily observe that the objective function is convex with respect to each of the parameters when the others are fixed. Hence, we resort to a coordinate descent method, in which unknown parameters are updated through an iterative process which updates each parameter by fixing the other parameters in each step.

Since the proposed objective function is convex respect to the sparse codes (D and θ are fixed in this step) under an l_1 penalty, we use the fixed-point continuation method (FPC) [18] to update the sparse codes. By fixing the sparse codes, our objective function is equivalent to the objective function of the SDL-G (Supervised Dictionary Learning, Generative) method [4], hence we use the optimization procedure of [4] to update the dictionary and the classifier.

3.4   Class Label Prediction

After learning A, D and θ, based on the idea of [4], we estimate the label of a new signal x with an unknown label y as

$$\hat{y} = \underset{y \in \{+1, -1\}}{argmin} \left(\underset{\alpha}{min}\, C(yf(x, \alpha, \theta)) + \lambda_0 \|x - D\alpha\|_2^2 + \lambda_1 \|\alpha\|_1 \right) \qquad (10)$$

It should be noted that the above classification procedure is usable only for binary classification. For multi-class classification problem, we use *one vs all* classification method based on the above binary classification method.

4   Experimental Results

In order to show the effectiveness of the proposed method, we present experimental results on applications such as Handwritten Digit Recognition, Object Recognition, and Letter Recognition. Details of the databases are summarized in Table 1 (in that table, L-examples and U-examples denote the labeled examples and the unlabeled examples respectively). MNIST [19] and USPS [20] are standard handwritten digit databases where MNIST dataset consists of 70,000 images, 60,000 for training, 10,000 for testing, and USPS is composed of 7291 training images and 2007 test images. ISOLET dataset [21] comprises of examples of letters from the alphabet spoken in isolation by 30 individual speakers and COIL2 [22] is two class object recognition dataset. All of the experimental results are averaged over several runs of randomly generated splits of the data. For digit datasets, 40 samples per class are randomly chosen from the training data as the labeled samples and 500 samples per class is used as the unlabeled data. For each class of ISOLET dataset, we randomly select 10 samples as labeled data, 150 samples as unlabeled data, and for COIL2 dataset, 100 samples per class are randomly chosen from the training data as the labeled samples and 500 samples per class is used as the unlabeled data.

We also compare our method with some state of the art supervised dictionary learning methods such as SDL-D [4], SDL-G [4], FDDL [12], and two well-known classification methods SVM and S3VM [14]. We also compare our method with S2D2 [16] which is a recently introduced semi-supervised dictionary learning algorithm.

In order to determine an appropriate number of dictionary atoms (K), and nearest neighbors of data samples (k) for computing the LLE matrix (E), Five-fold cross validation is performed to find the best pair (K, k). The tested values for K are $\{64, 128, 256, 512\}$ and for k, $\{3, 5, 7, 9, 11\}$. Since determining the values of the regularization parameters $\lambda_0, \lambda_1, \lambda_2$ and λ_3 using the cross validation technique is time consuming, we set them manually for all experiments as

$$\lambda_0 = 0.01, \; \lambda_1 = 0.15, \; \lambda_2 = 0.01, \; \lambda_3 = 0.1, \qquad (11)$$

Table 1. Properties of data sets and experimental parameters.

	MNIST	USPS	ISOLET	COIL2
L-examples (train)	400	400	100	200
U-examples (train)	5000	5000	1500	1000
Examples (test)	10000	2007	1000	300
Classes	10	10	10	2
Input dimensions	784	256	617	1025
Features after PCA	256	256	100	50
Runs	10	10	10	10

Table 2. Classification accuracy using different methods.

	MNIST	USPS	ISOLET	COIL2
SVM	82.6	83.7	86.1	77.6
S3VM	86.1	85.3	88.4	80.4
FFDL	83.9	84.2	83.5	77.9
SDL-G	84.2	84.4	83.8	78.2
SDL-D	82.8	83.7	83.1	77.7
S2D2	89.0	88.3	90.1	85.6
PM	**90.1**	**89.2**	**91.5**	**86.3**

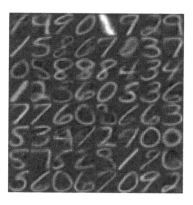

Fig. 1. The Dictionary with 64 atoms for USPS database.

The average recognition accuracies over 10 runs are shown in Table 2, from which, we can see that the proposed method outperforms all other methods. The improvement in performance compared to supervised dictionary learning (sdl) methods is because of two reasons. Firstly, the number of labeled data is small, hence the sdl methods may overfit to the labeled data. Secondly, these methods cannot utilize unlabeled data for learning dictionary. Moreover, S3VM and S2D2 does not consider the topological structure of all data, hence both of them are less accurate than our method. The learned Dictionary for USPS dataset using $K = 64$ is demonstrated in Fig. 1.

5   Conclusion

In this paper, we proposed a novel sparse representation method which uses the information of unlabeled data as well as labeled data for signal classification tasks. We incorporated the information of the unlabeled data into the proposed classification method using the LLE algorithm, by which the geometrical structure of all labeled and unlabeled data is preserved and it leads to immunity of the proposed method against overfitting to small-sized labeled training data. Experimental results using different datasets demonstrate the superiority of the proposed method over the state-of-the-art SR based classification methods.

References

1. Wright, J., Ma, Y., Mairal, J., Sapiro, G., Huang, C., Yan, S.: Sparse representation for computer vision and pattern recognition. In: Proceedings of the IEEE (2010)
2. Aharon, M., Elad, M., Bruckstein, A.: K-SVD: an algorithm for designing overcomplete dictionaries for sparse representation. IEEE Trans. Signal Process. **54**(11), 4311–4322 (2006)
3. Kreutz-Delgado, K., Murray, J., Rao, B., Engan, K., Sejnowski, T.: Dictionary learning algorithms for sparse representation. Neural Comput. **15**, 349–396 (2003)
4. Mairal, J., Bach, F., Ponce, J., Sapiro, G., Zisserman, A.: Supervised dictionary learning. In: Proceedings of Neural Information Processing Systems (NIPS) (2009)
5. Zhang, Q., Li, B.X.: Discriminative K-SVD for dictionary learning in face recognition. In: IEEE Conference on Computer Vision and Pattern Recognition (CVPR) (2010)
6. Ramirez, I., Sprechmann, P., Sapiro, G.: Classification and clustering via dictionary learning with structured incoherence and shared features. In: IEEE Conference on Computer Vision and Pattern Recognition (CVPR) (2010)
7. Yang, J.C., Yu, K., Huang, T.: Supervised translation-invariant sparse coding. In: IEEE Conference on Computer Vision and Pattern Recognition (CVPR) (2010)
8. Yang, M., Zhang, L., Yang, J., Zhang, D.: Metaface learning for sparse representation based face recognition. In: IEEE International Conference on Image Processing (ICIP) (2010)
9. Mairal, J., Bach, B., Ponce, J., Sapiro, G., Zissserman, A.: Learning discriminative dictionaries for local image analysis. In: IEEE Conference on Computer Vision and Pattern Recognition (CVPR) (2008)
10. Pham, D., Venkatesh, S.: Joint learning and dictionary construction for pattern recognition. In: IEEE Conference on Computer Vision and Pattern Recognition (CVPR) (2008)
11. Wright, J., Yang, A.Y., Ganesh, A., Sastry, S.S., Ma, Y.: Robust face recognition via sparse representation. In: IEEE Transaction on Pattern Analysis and Machine Intelligence (TPAMI), pp. 210–227 (2009)

12. Yang, M., Zhang, L., Feng, X., Zhang, D.: Fisher discrimination dictionary learning for sparse representation. In: International Conference on Computer Vision (ICCV) (2011)
13. Jiang, Z., Lin, Z., Davis, L.: Learning a discriminative dictionary for sparse coding via label consistent K-SVD. In: IEEE Conference on Computer Vision and Pattern Recognition (CVPR) (2011)
14. Keerthi, S.S., Sindhwani, V.: Large scale semisupervised linear SVMS. In: ACM SIGIR (2006)
15. Blum, B., Mitchell, T.: Combining labeled and unlabeled data with co-training. In: ACM COLT (1998)
16. Shrivastava, A., Patel, V.M., Chellappa R., Jaishanker, K.P.: Learning discriminative dictionaries with partially labeled data. In: IEEE International Conference on Image Processing (ICIP) (2012)
17. Roweis, S.T., Saul, L.K.: Nonlinear dimensionality reduction by locally linearembedding. J. Science **290**, 2323–2326 (2000)
18. Hale, E.T., Yin, W., Zhang, Y.: A fixed-point continuation method for l1-regularized minimization with applications to compressed sensing. CAAM Technical report (2007)
19. LeCun, Y., Bottou, L., Bengio, Y., Haffner, P.: Gradient-based learning applied to document recognition. In: Proceedings of the IEEE, vol. 86, (1998)
20. Hull, J.J.: A database for handwritten text recognition research. IEEE Trans. Pattern Anal. Mach. Intell **16**, 550–554 (1994)
21. Blake, C.L., Merz, C.J.: Uci repository of machine learning databases. Department of Information and Computer Science, University of California (1998)
22. Nene, S., Nayar, S., and Murase, H.: Columbia object image library (coil- 20). Department of Compututer Science, Columbia University, New York (1996)

Decoding the Long Term Memory Using Weighted Thresholding Union Subspaces Based Classification on Magnetoencephalogram

Sahar Tavakoli$^{(\boxtimes)}$ and Emad Fatemizadeh

Biomedical Signal and Image Processing Lab (BiSIPL),
Department of Electrical Engineering, Sharif University of Technology,
Tehran, Iran
stavakoli@ee.sharif.ir, fatemizadeh@sharif.edu

Abstract. In this paper Long Term Memory (LTM) process during leftward and rightward orientation recalling have been analyzed using Magnetoencephalogram (MEG) signals. This paper presents a novel criterion for decision making using union subspace based classifier. The proposed method involves the Eigenvalues from Singular Value Decomposition (SVD) of each subspace not only to select basis for each subspace but also to weight the decision making criterion to discriminate two classes. The proposed method has provided orientation detection from recalling signal with 6.75 percent increase in classification accuracy compared to better results on this data.

Keywords: Long term memory (LTM) · Magnetoencephalogram (MEG) signal · Singular value decomposition (SVD) · Union subspace based classifier · Dictionary learning · Leftward and rightward orientation detection

1 Introduction

Several works have been done on fMRI data in decoding human's memory using pattern recognition [1–4], but fMRI limitation in time resolution persuaded researchers to utilize MEG to investigate that subject.

MEG is a noninvasive method with proper time resolution and also acceptable spatial resolution. These properties make MEG appropriate to use pattern recognition methods [5]. This capability has been applied in differentiation and recognition between two directions of observed grating using frequency information of Gamma band [6]. Researchers also have been studied short term memory involving high frequency phase [7]. Other papers also have been published showing that time information can be useful in MEG classification [8, 9]. From the classification point of view, many methods such as SVM, LDA or elastic net classifier have been used in MEG classification [10–12]. The novel method presented in this paper is based on new decision making in subspace based classifier on the BioMag 2012 competition data [13] that resulted in better accuracy in orientation detection than best reported ones. The database will be explained in Sect. 2, afterwards, mathematical theory and results will be described in order.

© Springer International Publishing Switzerland 2014
A. Movaghar et al. (Eds.): AISP 2013, CCIS 427, pp. 164–171, 2014.
DOI: 10.1007/978-3-319-10849-0_17

1.1   Introduction to Problem

Data that is used in this paper is from BioMag2012 competition. Following experiment is designed to record this data. 48 pictures of usual objects are selected. Each picture is matched to a grating (rightward or leftward). This paired picture and grating is fixed during the whole experiment sequences. In Fig. 1 two of these pairs have been depicted, a glass is matched to grating with right orientation and a duck is matched to left orient one.

Fig. 1. Two cue pictures of 48 pictures. Each picture is matched to a grating (rightward or leftward).

During the experiment, as it will be explained in the following, those 48 pairs are trained to the subject. The whole experiment was performed in three days. First day was the stage of decoding in memory that was included several direct training blocks and feedback blocks. In each block, all 48 pairs have been shown to the subject in random order with the different that in training block clue picture have been presented for 1 s and after 2 s delay its corresponding grating have been appeared. But in feedback block, process is according to Fig. 2.

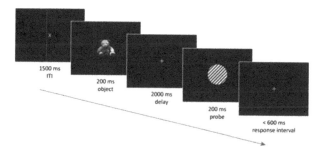

Fig. 2. The feedback block process. Source: [12]

In feedback block there is an opportunity for incorrect ones to be shown (50 % of them will be incorrect) and subject is asked to declare it true or false. He is supposed to answer by pushing a bottom immediately after seeing the grating. After his answer, the correct grating will appear to feedback him. This is what happened during first day to teach subject the pairs. During the day after, the feedback training block have been applied on subject. Learning process has been continued until that subject performance reached to 90 %.

Third day was final stage that MEG signal have been recorded at that time. In that day, all 48 clues were asked subject to recognize its grating orientation 18 times. From all recorded signals, 681 correct answers are saved that are including 344 trains from right orientation class and 337 left ones. Time interval of this recorded signal is from 200 ms before clue appearance to 220 ms after its disappearance.

2   Material and Method

Overall process is depicted in Fig. 3. After generating features for each experiment, PCA has been used to select best basis for subspaces, then union subspace based classification has been applied. Details of process will be explained following.

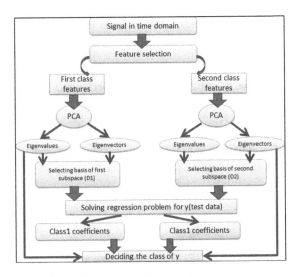

Fig. 3. The overall diagram of methodology

2.1   Subspace Based Classification

Let each vector that contains features of each train experiment be a column of D_1 (assigned for first class) and D_2 (for second class). Then two classes can be supposed in following order:

$$\begin{cases} H_0 : y \in \text{span}(D_1) \\ H_1 : y \in span(D_2) \end{cases}$$

Columns of D_1 will be basis for first subspace and it will be the same for D_2 and second subspace. With this assumption, two types of classifications can be designed:

Separated Subspaces Classifier. In this classification, each subspace will be considered separately and regression problem will be solved for each of them in the number of classes. If y is a test vector (features of test experiment that its class is unknown) then projection of y from first subspace view will be:

$$y_1 = D_1 (D_1^T D_1)^{-1} D_1^T y$$

And from second subspace view it will be:

$$y_2 = D_2 (D_2^T D_2)^{-1} D_2^T y$$

These reconstruction equations are coming from answer of regression problem [14].

$$\min_x \|y - Ax\|_2^2$$

The answer is obtained from following optimization process:

$$x = (A^T A)^{-1} A^T y$$

Having mentioned constructed terms and comparing following two differences, the class that y is belonging to can be determined.

$$\|y - y_1\| \le \|y - y_2\| \rightarrow \text{Class1 is selected}$$
$$\|y - y_1\| \ge \|y - y_2\| \rightarrow \text{Class2 is selected}$$

This classification is also named as Nearest Subspace classifier [15].

Union Subspaces Classifier. Instead of solving a separate regression for each class, and finding minimum for a metric criterion, one regression with high dimensions can be done. In this regression, the basis of all classes will be used. Rather than D_1 and D_2, on matrix that is named D will be formed according below formula.

$$D = [D_1 \quad D_2]$$

The only regression problem for y as test data will be:

$$\min_x \|y - Dx\|_2^2$$

The answer will be:

$$x = (D^T D)^{-1} D^T y$$

In this case, the solution (x) will be a vector that its component can be used to decide the class of test data. If we name first part of x (the part that is related to first class basis) x_1 and second part x_2, then following logical relations will guide us to declare the selected class.

$$\|x_1\|_1 \leq \|x_2\|_1 \rightarrow \text{Class1 is selected}$$
$$\|x_1\|_1 \geq \|x_2\|_1 \rightarrow \text{Class2 is selected}$$

This method will result better, because of using both classes information.

Developing mentioned method, and setting some constraint behind regression problem will guide us to ridge, lasso, and elastic net regression classifiers.

Ridge problem:

$$\min_x \|y - Dx\|_2 + \lambda \|x\|_1$$

Lasso problem:

$$\min_x \|y - Dx\|_2 + \lambda \|x\|_2$$

Elastic net problem:

$$\min_x \|y - Dx\|_2 + \lambda_1 \|x\|_1 + \lambda_2 \|x\|_2$$

Lasso is the most famous linear regression that has been improved several applications.

2.2   Proposed Method

As choosing all the experiments as basis for subspaces causes over learning, (Principle Components Analysis) PCA is used to subspace identification and choosing best basis. PCA has been used before in feature and dimension reduction [17], but here, PCA is applied in reducing the basis number of subspaces and avoiding over learning. PCA is based on SVD decomposition that gives us Eigenvalues. A sample of this Eigenvalues amounts are depicted in Fig. 4. According to this diagram, for each class the number of useful Eigenvectors as subspace basis can be selected.

The number of Eigenvalues that provide acceptable percentage of total energy determines the number of required Eigenvectors from SVD as subspace basis.

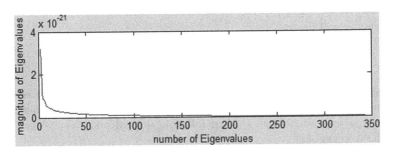

Fig. 4. Magnitude versus number of Eigenvalues for one class

Not only this Eigenvalues are used in mentioned decision but also they affect the class determination that will be explained in the following:

After formation of D_1 and D_2 with selected Eigenvectors, D matrix will be formed by putting D_1 and D_2 together, and regression problem will be solved that gives x solution.

Former decision criteria on x have been comparing norm of two parts of it, but a novel method in decision making is involving mentioned Eigenvalues to multiply to x elements and to weight them. Therefore, elements corresponding to larger Eigenvalues will have more influence in comparing. If λ_1 contains Eigenvalues from SVD decomposition related to class1, and λ_2 contains Eigenvalues from SVD decomposition related to class2, following logical relations will decide the unknown class. n_1 and n_1 are the number of required Eigenvectors from SVD as subspace basis for class1 and class2.

$$\sum_{i=1}^{n1} x_1(i)\lambda_1(i) \leq \sum_{i=1}^{n2} x_2(i)\lambda_2(i) \rightarrow \quad \text{Class1 is selected.}$$

$$\sum_{i=1}^{n1} x_1(i)\lambda_1(i) \geq \sum_{i=1}^{n2} x_2(i)\lambda_2(i) \rightarrow \quad \text{Class2 is selected.}$$

3 Results

As mentioned before, wide types of features have been used in classifying MEG signal. Two new features introduced in this paper that have shown better results than previous ones are differential spectrum and correlation between two adjacent channels in Fourier space. Our results comparing to previous report from winner of BioMag competition have been shown in Table 1.

Table 1. Accuracy percent in classifying leftward versus rightward

Our Method						BioMag 2012
Feature type	Time	DCT coefficients	FFT coefficients	differential spectrum	Correlation in Fourier space	67 %
Accuracy	65 %	63.75 %	70 %	72.5 %	73.75 %	

Involving each part of brain separately in classification process, one can decide the influence of different channels and brain parts in recalling left or right direction perception (Fig. 5).

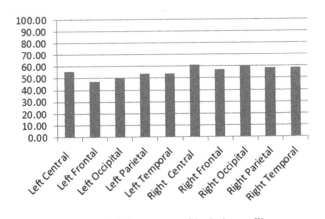

Fig. 5. Influence of different parts of brain in recalling process

4 Conclusion

In summary, the classification accuracy can be improved involving Eigenvalues of PCA, not only in selecting basis of subspaces but also in weighted decision making. Furthermore, feature selection can help this method to reach better accuracy. It is proved that differential spectrum and correlation between two adjacent channels will give better result in recalling left or right direction perception. Results show that the right hemisphere of brain has most effect on mentioned process.

References

1. Harrison, S.A., Tong, F.: Decoding reveals the contents of visual working memory in early visual areas. Nature **458**(7238), 632–635 (2009). doi:10.1038/nature07832. Nature Publishing Group
2. Johnson, J.D., McDuff, S.G.R., Rugg, M.D., Norman, K.A.: Recollection, familiarity, and cortical reinstatement: a multivoxel pattern analysis. Neuron **63**(5), 697–708 (2009). doi:10.1016/j.neuron.2009.08.011. Elsevier Ltd
3. Lewis-Peacock, J.A., Postle, B.R.: Temporary activation of long-term memory supports working memory. J. Neurosci. **28**(35), 8765–8771 (2008). doi:10.1523/JNEUROSCI.1953-08.2008
4. Xue, G., Dong, Q., Chen, C., Lu, Z., Mumford, J.A., Poldrack, R.A.: Greater neural pattern similarity across repetitions is associated with better memory. Science **330**(97), 97–101 (2010). doi:10.1126/science.1193125
5. Besserve, M., Jerbi, K., Laurent, F., Baillet, S., Martinerie, J., Garnero, L.: Classification methods for ongoing EEG and MEG signals. Biol. Res. **40**(4), 415–437 (2007). doi:/S0716-97602007000500005
6. Duncan, K.K., Hadjipapas, A., Li, S., Kourtzi, Z., Bagshaw, A., Barnes, G.R.: Identifying spatially overlapping local cortical networks with MEG. Hum. Brain Mapp. **1016**, 1003–1016 (2009). doi:10.1002/hbm.20912

7. Fuentemilla, L., Penny, W.D., Cashdollar, N., Bunzeck, N., Düzel, E.: Theta-coupled periodic replay in working memory. Curr. Biol. **20**(7), 606–612 (2010). doi:10.1016/j.cub. 2010.01.057
8. Chan, A.M., Halgren, E., Marinkovic, K., Cash, S.S.: Decoding word and category-specific spatiotemporal representations from MEG and EEG. NeuroImage (2010). doi:10.1016/j. neuroimage.2010.10.073. Elsevier Inc
9. Simanova, I., van Gerven, M., Oostenveld, R., Hagoort, P.: Identifying object categories from event- related EEG: toward decoding of conceptual representations. PloS ONE **5**(12), e14465 (2010). doi:10.1371/journal.pone.0014465
10. Kumar, Y., Dewal, M.L., Anand, R.S.: Relative wavelet energy and wavelet entropy based epileptic brain signals classification. Biomed. Eng. lett. **2**(3), 147–157 (2012)
11. Waldert, S., et al.: Hand movement direction decoded from MEG and EEG. J. Neurosci. **28** (4), 1000–1008 (2008). doi:10.1523/JNEUROSCI.5171-07.2008
12. Backus, A., Jensen, O., Meeuwissen, E., Gerven, M.V., Dumoulin, S.: Investigating the temporal dynamics of long-term memory representation retrieval using multivariate pattern analyses on magnetoencephalography data. M.Sc. major internship. Utrecht university (2012)
13. WWW.biomag2012.org
14. Wright, J., Yang, A.Y., Ganesh, A., Sastry, S., Ma, Y.: Robust face recognition via sparse representation. IEEE Trans. Pattern Anal. Mach. Intell. **31**, 210–227 (2009)
15. Cohen, M.C., Paliwal, K.K.: Classifying microarray cancer datasets using nearest subspace classification. In: PRIB 2008 Supplementary Conference, pp. 170–180 (2008)
16. Naseem, I., Togneri, R., Bennamoun, M.: Linear regression for face recognition. IEEE Trans. Pattern Anal. Mach. Intell. **32**(11), 2106–2112 (2010)
17. Xu, Y., Zhang, D., Yang, J.-Y.: A feature extraction method for use with bimodal biometrics. Pattern Recogn. **43**, 1106–1115 (2010)

An Adaptive Automatic EEG Signal Segmentation Method Based on Generalized Likelihood Ratio

Hamed Azami[1]([⊠]), Seyed Mahmoud Anisheh[2],
and Hamid Hassanpour[3]

[1] Department of Electrical Engineering,
Iran University of Science and Technology, Tehran, Iran
hamed_azami@ieee.org
[2] Department of Computer and Electrical Engineering,
Khaje Nasir Toosi University of Technology, Tehran, Iran
s_m_anisheh@yahoo.com
[3] Faculty of Information Technology and Computer Engineering,
Shahrood University, Shahrood, Iran
h.hassanpour@ieee.org

Abstract. In many signal processing applications, it is often needed to segment signals into small epochs with similar characteristics such as amplitude and/or frequency that are particularly meaningful to clinicians and for assessment by neurophysiologists. This paper presents a novel adaptive segmentation method based on the time-varying autoregressive (TVAR) model, integral, and basic generalized likelihood ratio (GLR). Since autoregressive (AR) model for the GLR method is valid for only stationary signals, TVAR is employed as a valuable and powerful tool for non-stationary signals. Moreover, to improve the performance of the basic GLR and increase its speed, we propose to use moving steps more than one sample for successive windows in the basic GLR method. Performance of the proposed method is compared with existing GLR and wavelet GLR (WGLR) methods using both the synthetic signal and real EEG data. The simulation results indicate the high accuracy of the proposed method.

Keywords: Adaptive signal segmentation · Generalized likelihood ratio · Time-varying autoregressive model · Integral

1 Introduction

The recording of electrical activity along the scalp, namely electroencephalogram (EEG), represents not only the brain function but also the status of the whole body [1]. Understanding of neuronal functions and neurophysiological properties of the brain together with the mechanisms underlying the generation of signals and their recordings is critical for those who deal with these signals for detection, diagnosis, and treatment of brain disorders and the related diseases [1].

A great automatic EEG analysis during long-term monitoring consists of four basic steps: (1) segmentation; (2) feature extraction; (3) classification; and (4) presentation [2].

© Springer International Publishing Switzerland 2014
A. Movaghar et al. (Eds.): AISP 2013, CCIS 427, pp. 172–180, 2014.
DOI: 10.1007/978-3-319-10849-0_18

Dividing a signal into parts that in each part, its statistical characteristics such as amplitude and frequency do not change, namely segmentation, plays a significant role in these steps. Today, segmenting a signal has variety and great applications in many engineering and clinical fields [3–7].

In the literature, two basic approaches exist for signal segmentation, namely constant segmentation and adaptive segmentation [8]. In the constant segmentation, the signal is divided into small epochs with a fixed length. In general, this type of segmentation is the simplest and fastest one. The attained epochs, yet, may not be necessarily stationary. In order to overcome the restriction in using constant segmentation, it is necessary to employ a segmentation method that automatically detects the true segment boundaries. In adaptive segmentation approach, for automatic detection of the true boundaries, segmentation is done based on change in statistical characteristics (such as amplitude and/or frequency variations) of the original signal [8]. There are a number of adaptive segmentation methods suggested by researchers such as those in [9–17].

Azami et al. have proposed a method to segment a signal in general and real EEG signal in particular using standard deviation, integral operation, discrete wavelet transform (DWT), and variable threshold [17]. In this paper, they have illustrated that the standard deviation can indicate changes in the amplitude and/or frequency. To remove the effect of shifting and smooth the signal, the integral operation has been used as a pre-processing step [17]. However, although the segments the performance of the method is still dependent on the noise components. Moreover, in this method, the length of the window must be selected empirically.

In order to detect the anomalies in the traffic signal of computer networks, a new method called generalized likelihood ratio (GLR) is proposed [15]. To enhance the GLR method, it has been suggested to use wavelet as a post-processing stage. This new method was named wavelet GLR (WGLR) method [15].

There are two shortages in the basic GLR and WGLR methods: (1) In these methods, autoregressive (AR) model was used and this model can only consider stationary signals. This is very important shortage in biomedical signals that are often non-stationary; (2) Moving 1 sample in successive windows for GLR method causes the method to become slow and unreliable for signal segmentation. Moreover, in the vicinity of each segments' boundaries, there are some boundaries detected incorrectly by the use of GLR/WGLR method.

In order to overcome these problems, in this paper, we propose to use time-varying AR (TVAR) model that can be employed for non-stationary signals as well as stationary ones. Integral as a pre-processing step is applied to increase the performance of the method. In addition, we propose that the successive windows are moved more than 1 sample that this technique not only enhances the CPU time, but also it increases the performance of the basic GLR method considerably.

This article is organized as follows: Sect. 2 clarifies the proposed method in three steps. The performance assessment of the suggested approach and results compared with existing methods are provided in Sect. 3. Finally, the conclusions are given in Sect. 4.

2 Proposed Adaptive Segmentation

This proposed method consists of three steps as briefly described below:

1. First, in order to smooth or filter the signal we use integral as a pre-processing step. In addition, using the integral causes that the frequency is shown in the amplitude. If we assume $f(x) = a\cos(wx)$, the integral of $f(x)$ becomes $f(x) = \frac{a}{w}\sin(wx)$. In other words, it causes the frequency is shown in amplitude (term $\frac{1}{w}$). This policy helps that the proposed method becomes better than the previous version (basic GLR).

2. In this method two sliding windows move alongside the entire signal. The signal in each window of this method is modeled by the TVAR model instead of the conventional AR which is only applicable for stationary signals. In the standard AR structure, a discretely sampled signal is modeled by representing the voltage level at time t as a linear combination of voltage levels at times t-1, t-2, ..., t-p for $p > 0$ an addition a random (driving noise) component. The relationship is supposed to be fixed over time in that the regression parameters defining the linear combination are constant for the whole period of recording. While in the TVAR model these parameters differ over time, adapting to changes evidenced in the signals, and therefore, potentially provide the kinds of time-evolving structure evident in many non-stationary signals. Such models can specially answer to and adequately capture the forms of change in the frequency structure of oscillations in EEG data [18]. Therefore because EEG is considered as a non-stationary signal, this model improves the performance of the basic GLR. If the sliding windows fall within a segment, since the both windows have the same statistical properties, the modeling error between the two windows is low. However, if both sliding windows are not placed in the same segments, the modeling error rises. As stated previously, since in the vicinity of each segments' boundaries, there are some boundaries detected incorrectly by the use of GLR/WGLR method and increase the speed and reliability of the basic GLR/WGLR, in this paper we propose to use moving steps more than 1 sample for the successive windows.

3. Determining a threshold is one of the important problems in segmentation of the signal. In many researches, the mean value or the mean value added to standard deviation or something like those are proposed as a threshold. If the defined threshold is large, several boundaries of segments may not be indicated. Whereas the threshold value is low, several boundaries of segments may be selected inaccurately. In this paper the mean value of $G(\bar{G})$ is defined as the threshold. When the local maximum is bigger than the threshold, the current time is selected as a boundary of the segment.

3 Data Simulation and Results

The following methods were implemented using MATLAB R2009a from MathWorks. The performance and efficiency of all the proposed and existing methods were evaluated using 50 synthetic multi-component and real EEG signals.

3.1   Synthetic Signal

In order to assess the performance of the suggested method, these algorithms are applied on a set of synthetic multi-component signals which each epoch is selected as a stationary signal. One piece of these signals includes the following seven epochs:

Epoch 1: $0.5\cos(\pi t) + 1.5\cos(4\pi t) + 4\cos(5\pi t)$,
Epoch 2: $0.7\cos(\pi t) + 2.1\cos(4\pi t) + 5.6\cos(5\pi t)$,
Epoch 3: $1.5\cos(2\pi t) + 4\cos(8\pi t)$,
Epoch 4: $1.5\cos(\pi t) + 4\cos(4\pi t)$,
Epoch 5: $0.5\cos(\pi t) + 1.7\cos(2\pi t) + 3.7\cos(5\pi t)$,
Epoch 6: $2.3\cos(3\pi t) + 7.8\cos(8\pi t)$,
Epoch 7: $0.8\cos(\pi t) + \cos(3\pi t) + 3\cos(5\pi t)$.

Figures 1.a and b show 50 s of the mentioned signal and the result of applying the basic GLR, respectively. Figure 1.b shows that this algorithm cannot detect some segments boundaries of the signal. These undetected boundaries are named miss boundaries (MBs). Also, obtained output shows that this method has many false boundaries (FBs).

The signal in Fig. 1.a is also segmented using the WGLR as shown in Fig. 2. Although Fig. 2 shows that the WGLR method can detect segments boundaries better than the GLR, the WGLR is still not reliable and there are some FBs and MBs.

As mentioned before, in order to increase the speed and boundaries detection accuracy of the GLR method, we propose to use a step more than 1 sample for moving successive windows. In Fig. 3 we use this idea. By comparing Figs. 1, 2 and 3, we can realize that the proposed method is much better than the WGLR and basic GLR methods. However, the method still cannot detect one boundary correctly.

To improve the performance of the GLR method, integral is applied as a pre-processing step. The output of the method is shown in Fig. 4. As can be seen in Fig. 4.c, the boundaries for all seven segments can be perfectly detected.

To increase the reliability of the performance of the proposed methods, in this paper 50 synthetic multi-component signals are used. Also, in order to make the signals more similar to real signals, Gaussian noise with SNRs = 5, 10, and 15 dBs are added to each 50 original signals and then, the performance of the proposed methods are assessed. Three parameters are used to assess the performance of the proposed methods: True Positive (TP) Miss or False negative (FN) and False Alarm or False Positive (FP) ratios. These parameters are $TP = \left(N_t/N\right)$, $FN = \left(N_m/N\right)$ and $FP = \left(N_f/N\right)$, where N_t, N_m and N_f represent the number of true, missed, and falsely detected and N shows actual number of segment boundaries.

In Table 1, the results of segmentation for 50 synthetic data using the proposed methods are shown next to the results of conventional methods, namely, GLR and WGLR method. The parameters used for the proposed methods and existing methods are completely equal and are selected by trials and errors. As can be seen in the table TPs and FNs are approximately equivalent. However, FP for proposed method by using integral is much better than GLR and WGLR that are known as conventional methods. Moreover, an important reason to cause the performance of the proposed method

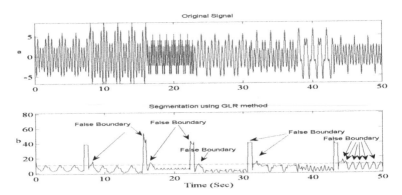

Fig. 1. Signal segmentation for synthetic signal, (a) original signal, and (b) output of the basic GLR.

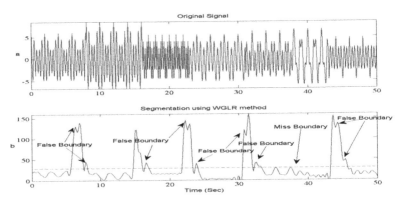

Fig. 2. Signal segmentation for synthetic signal, (a) original signal, and (b) output of the WGLR.

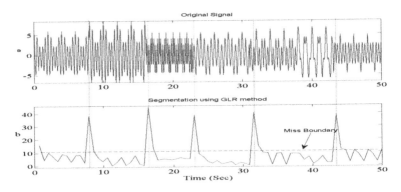

Fig. 3. Signal segmentation for synthetic signal, (a) original signal, and (b) output of the proposed method without using integral.

Table 1. Effect of applying the proposed methods and conventional methods on set of synthetic data.

Proposed method with integral as a pre-processing step				
SNR	5 dB	10 dB	15 dB	Without Noise
TP	94.1%	95.6%	100%	100%
FN	5.9%	4.4%	0%	0%
FP	43.2%	25%	17.6%	12.4%
Proposed method				
SNR	5 dB	10 dB	15 dB	Without Noise
TP	92.6%	95.6%	98.5%	98.5%
FN	7.4%	4.4%	1.5%	1.5%
FP	48%	33.8%	26.4%	22.6%
WGLR method				
SNR	5 dB	10 dB	15 dB	Without Noise
TP	97%	97%	98.5%	98.5%
FN	3%	3%	1.5%	1.5%
FP	260%	180%	120%	110%
Basic GLR				
SNR	5 dB	10 dB	15 dB	Without Noise
TP	97%	97%	98.5%	98.5%
FN	3%	3%	1.5%	1.5%
FP	350%	220%	180%	140%

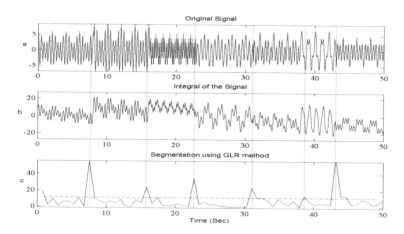

Fig. 4. Signal segmentation for synthetic signal, (a) original signal, (b) filtered signal by integral, and (c) output of the proposed method.

increase significantly is that we use the TVAR model instead of the AR model employed in the conventional GLR.

3.2   Real EEG Signal

EEG is the neurophysiologic measurement of the electrical activity of the brain using electrodes placed on the scalp. As described before, signal segmentation is an important pre-processing step for EEG signals processing. In this part, we have used a real newborn EEG signal that is shown in Fig. 4.a. The length of this signal and the sampling frequency are 500 ms and 256 Hz, respectively. The results of applying the basic GLR and the proposed method are shown in Fig. 5.b and 6.c, respectively. In Fig. 5.c can be seen that all five segments have segmented accurately. Also, basic GLR detects many segments inaccurately. We can see the influence of this method by comparing of these figures.

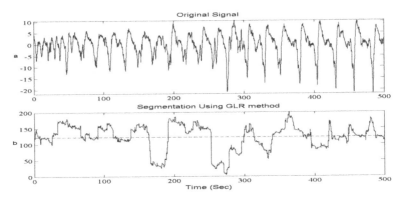

Fig. 5. Signal segmentation for real EEG data, (a) original signal, and (b) output of the basic GLR.

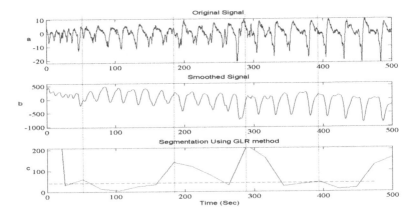

Fig. 6. Signal segmentation for real EEG data, (a) original signal, (b) filtered signal by integral, and (c) output of the proposed method.

4   Conclusions

An improved method for EEG signal segmentation has been proposed in this paper. After smoothing the signal by using integral operation, EEG signals have been modeled using TVAR. TVAR is applicable to analyze non-stationary signals, while the AR is only applicable for stationary signals. Unlike other smoothing methods such as wavelet transforms and Kalman filter, integral does not need to any parameters adjustment. In addition, it can detect the effect of frequency of the signal on the amplitude. In order to reduce the computational load of the proposed method, we have proposed to use moving steps more than one sample for successive windows. The proposed algorithm has been applied on the both synthetic data and real EEG signal. The results have indicated the superiority of the proposed method in signal segmentation.

Acknowledgment. The authors wish to thank Prof. Saeid Sanei in University of Surrey, UK and Prof. William D. Penny in University College London, UK, for their so valuable and kind guidance.

References

1. Sanei, S., Chambers, J.: EEG Signal Processing. Wiley, New York (2007)
2. Agarwal, R., Gotmana, J., Flanagana, D., Rosenblatt, B.: Automatic EEG analysis during long-term monitoring in the ICU. Electroencephalogr. Clin. Neurophysiol. **107**(1), 44–58 (1998)
3. Jellema, R.H., Krishnan, S., Hendriks, M.M.W.B., Muilwijk, B., Vogels, J.T.W.E.: Deconvolution using signal segmentation. Chemometr. Intell. Lab. Syst. **104**(1), 132–139 (2010)
4. Albaa, A., Marroquínb, J.L., Arce-Santanaa, E., Harmonyc, T.: Classification and interactive segmentation of EEG synchrony patterns. Pattern Recogn. **43**(2), 530–544 (2010)
5. Micó, P., Mora, M., Cuesta-Frau, D., Aboy, M.: Automatic segmentation of long-term ECG signals corrupted with broadband noise based on sample entropy. Comput. Methods Progr. Biomed. **98**(2), 118–129 (2010)
6. Homaeinezhad, M.R., Ghaffari, A., Toosi, H.N., Rahmani, R., Tahmasebi, M., Daevaeiha, M.M.: Ambulatory Holter ECG individual events delineation via segmentation of a wavelet-based information-optimized 1-D feature. Scientia Iranica **18**(1), 86–104 (2011)
7. Leea, J., Steeleb, C.M., Chau, T.: Swallow segmentation with artificial neural networks and multi-sensor fusion. Med. Eng. Phys. **31**(9), 1049–1055 (2009)
8. Anisheh, M., Hassanpour, H.: Designing an adaptive approach for segmenting non-stationary signals. Int. J. Electron. **98**(8), 1091–1102 (2011)
9. Azami, H., Sanei, S.: Automatic signal segmentation based on singular spectrum analysis and imperialist competitive algorithm. In: 2nd International Conference on Computer and Knowledge Engineering, pp. 50–55. IEEE Xplore (2012)
10. Azami, H., Sanei, S., Mohammadi, K., Hassanpour, H.: A hybrid evolutionary approach to segmentation of non-stationary signals. Digit. Signal Proc. **23**(4), 1–12 (2013)
11. Azami, H., Mohammadi, K., Bozorgtabar, B.: An improved signal segmentation using moving average and Savitzky-Golay filter. J. Signal Inf. Process. **3**(1), 39–44 (2012)

12. Hassanpour, H., Anisheh, S.M.: An improved adaptive signal segmentation method using fractal dimension. In: International Symposium on Signal Processing and Its Applications, pp. 720–723 (2010)

13. Kosar, K., Lhotská, L., Krajca, V.: Classification of long-term EEG recordings. In: Barreiro, J.M., Martín-Sánchez, F., Maojo, V., Sanz, F. (eds.) ISBMDA 2004. LNCS, vol. 3337, pp. 322–332. Springer, Heidelberg (2004)

14. Kirlangic, M.E., Perez, D., Kudryavtseva, S., Griessbach, G., Henning, G., Ivanova, G.: Fractal dimension as a feature for adaptive electroencephalogram segmentation in epilepsy. IEEE Int. EMBS Conf. **2**, 1573–1576 (2001)

15. Wang, D., Vogt, R., Mason, M. Sridharan, S.: Automatic audio segmentation using the generalized likelihood ratio. In: 2nd IEEE International Conference on Signal Processing and Communication Systems, pp. 1–5 (2008)

16. Azami, H., Khosravi, A., Malekzadeh, M., Sanei, S.: A new adaptive signal segmentation approach based on Hiaguchi's fractal dimension. In: Huang, D.-S., Gupta, P., Zhang, X., Premaratne, P. (eds.) ICIC 2012. CCIS, vol. 304, pp. 152–159. Springer, Heidelberg (2012)

17. Azami, H., Sanei, S., Mohammadi, K.: A novel signal segmentation method based on standard deviation and variable Threshold. J. Comput. Appl. **34**(2), 27–34 (2011)

18. Krystal, A.D., Prado, R., West, M.: New methods of time series analysis of non-stationary EEG data: eigenstructure decompositions of time varying autoregressions. Clin. Neurophysiol. **110**(12), 2197–2206 (1999)

Speech Processing

Speech Synthesis Based on Gaussian Conditional Random Fields

Soheil Khorram[✉], Fahimeh Bahmaninezhad, and Hossein Sameti

Department of Computer Engineering,
Sharif University of Technology, Tehran, Iran
{khorram,bahmaninezhad}@ce.sharif.edu,
sameti@sharif.edu

Abstract. Hidden Markov Model (HMM)-based synthesis (HTS) has recently been confirmed to be the most effective method in generating natural speech. However, it lacks adequate context generalization when the training data is limited. As a solution, current study provides a new context-dependent speech modeling framework based on the Gaussian Conditional Random Field (GCRF) theory. By applying this model, an innovative speech synthesis system has been developed which can be viewed as an extension of Context-Dependent Hidden Semi Markov Model (CD-HSMM). A novel Viterbi decoder along with a stochastic gradient ascent algorithm was applied to train model parameters. Also, a fast and efficient parameter generation algorithm was derived for the synthesis part. Experimental results using objective and subjective criteria have shown that the proposed system outperforms HSMM substantially in limited speech databases. Moreover, Mel-cepstral distance of the spectral parameters has been reduced considerably for any size of training database.

Keywords: Gaussian conditional random field · Statistical parametric speech synthesis · HSMM extension

1 Introduction

Statistical Parametric Speech Synthesis (SPSS) has reportedly been a dominant research area due to its peculiarities since the last decade [1, 2]. Modeling in the domain of SPSS is of prime importance and it is naïve to assume unnecessary simplifying assumptions in modeling as it may reduce the quality of synthetic speech. This work extends Hidden Semi Markov Model (HSMM) synthesis [3] by eliminating some of its simplifying assumptions. In the next subsection we will briefly discuss related works.

1.1 Related Work

Many research activities have already been performed to improve the quality of basic HTS. The progresses such as Hidden Semi Markov Model (HSMM) [3], Trajectory HMM [4] and Multi-Space Distribution HMM [5] have made HTS the most powerful statistical approach. However, these systems do not lead to an acceptable quality with

© Springer International Publishing Switzerland 2014
A. Movaghar et al. (Eds.): AISP 2013, CCIS 427, pp. 183–193, 2014.
DOI: 10.1007/978-3-319-10849-0_19

limited databases (less than 30 min). This deficiency is a direct result of applying decision-tree-based context clustering which cannot exploit contextual information efficiently, because each training sample is associated in modeling only one context cluster. This study is an attempt to improve SPSS quality even for limited training data.

The rest of the paper is organized as follows. In Sect. 2, GCRF is introduced. Sections 3 and 4 propose a context-dependent model for speech using GCRF and its application in speech synthesis. Experimental results are presented in Sect. 5 and final remarks are given in Sect. 6.

2   Gaussian Conditional Random Field

To define GCRF, first a brief description of Markov Random Field (MRF) and Conditional Random Field (CRF) is given.

Definition 1. Let $G = (V, E)$ be an undirected graph, $X = (X_v)_{v \in V}$ be a set of random variables indexed by nodes of G, X is modeled by MRF iff $\forall A, B \subseteq V, P(X_A|X_B) = P(X_A|X_S)$, where S is a border subset of A such that every path from a node in A to a node in B passes through S [6].

Definition 2. (X, C) is a CRF iff for any given set of random variables C, X forms an MRF [6].

In the speech synthesis framework, given an utterance contextual information C, sufficient statistics of speech (acoustic features) can be considered as an MRF.

Hammersley-Clifford's Theorem. Suppose (x, c) is an arbitrary realization of a CRF (X, C) defined based on a graph G with positive probability, then $P(x|c)$ can be factorized by the following Gibbs distribution [7].

$$P(x|c) = \frac{1}{Z(c)} \prod_{\mathcal{A}} \Psi_a(x, c), \tag{1}$$

where $\mathcal{A}$ denotes a set of all maximal cliques of G. $Z(c)$ is called partition function which ensures that the distribution sums to one. In other words,

$$Z(c) = \iint_x \prod_{\mathcal{A}} \Psi_a(x, c). \tag{2}$$

The theorem also states that for any choice of positive local functions $\{\Psi_a(x)\}$ (potential functions) a valid CRF is generated. One of the simplest choices of a potential function is Gaussian function. CRF with Gaussian potential function is named GCRF which is introduced in the next section.

3 Context-Dependent Speech Modeling Using GCRF

For modeling speech, the proposed system primarily splits each segment into a fixed number of states. Then, acoustic and binary contextual features (sufficient statistics) are extracted for each state. The goal is to model and generate acoustic features provided that contextual features are present. The following notations are taken into account henceforth.

L,I: Total number of acoustic and linguistic features.

$\mathcal{J}$: Total number of states for the current utterance.

V: All acoustic parameters. (Extracted from frame samples)

x_{lj} : l-th acoustic feature of state j. (Extracted from V)

x_l : l-th acoustic feature vector, $x_l \overset{\text{def}}{=} [x_{l1}, \ldots, x_{l\mathcal{J}}]^T$.

X: All acoustic features, $X \overset{\text{def}}{=} [x_1, \ldots, x_L]$.

c_{ji} : i-th binary linguistic feature of state j.

c_j : Linguistic feature vector of state j, $c_j \overset{\text{def}}{=} [c_{j1}, \ldots, c_{jI}]^T$.

C: All linguistic features, $C \overset{\text{def}}{=} [c_1, \ldots, c_{\mathcal{J}}]$.

3.1 GCRF Graphical Structure

Factor graph [8] of the proposed GCRF (with order one) is depicted in Fig. 1. As it is obvious in the figure, GCRF is a set of L linear chain CRF [8] (with order one) which are independent when C is given. Each rectangular node Ψ_{lj} represents a potential function describing the effect of a maximal clique $(x_{lj}, x_{l(j-1)}, c_j)$ in the random field distribution. This figure can be extended to higher order linear chain CRFs. As a result, if GCRF extends with order o, Ψ_{lj}. becomes a function of $(x_{lj}, \ldots, x_{l(j-o)}, c_j)$.

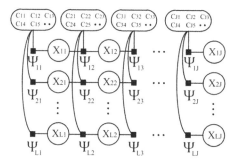

Fig. 1. Factor graph of the first order GCRF.

3.2 GCRF Distribution

Having described the graphical model, this subsection investigates the probability distribution provided by GCRF. Markov property of MRFs implies the following equality.

$$P(X|C;\theta) = \prod_{l=1}^{L} P(x_l|C;\theta), \tag{3}$$

where θ is the set of all model parameters. This paper assumes that the partition function, Ψ_{lj}, is formulated by Eq. 4 which is a Gaussian function with parameters H_{lji} and u_{lji}.

$$\Psi_{lj} \overset{\text{def}}{=} \exp\left\{ -\frac{1}{2} \sum_{i=1}^{I} \left[\left(x_l^T H_{lji} x_l + u_{lji}^T x_l \right) c_{ji} \right] \right\}. \tag{4}$$

In this equation, H_{lji} has to be a symmetric and positive definite matrix. If H_{lji} is not restricted to a positive definite matrix, the distribution may be realized by a number greater than one. Thus, considering positive definite condition seems to be necessary. Moreover, in GCRF with order o, H_{lij} and u_{lij} contain only $(o+1) \times (o+1)$ and $(o+1)$ nonzero elements respectively. The overall form of model parameters is shown as follows.

$$H^{lij} = \begin{bmatrix} 0 & 0 & \cdots & 0 & 0 & \cdots \\ 0 & h^{lij}_{(j-o)(j-o)} & \cdots & h^{lij}_{(j-o)j} & 0 & \cdots \\ \vdots & \vdots & \ddots & \vdots & \vdots & \ddots \\ 0 & h^{lij}_{j(j-o)} & \cdots & h^{lij}_{jj} & 0 & \cdots \\ 0 & 0 & \cdots & 0 & 0 & \cdots \\ \vdots & \vdots & \ddots & \vdots & \vdots & \ddots \end{bmatrix}, u^{lij} = \begin{bmatrix} 0 \\ u^{lij}_{j-o} \\ \vdots \\ u^{lij}_{j} \\ 0 \\ \vdots \end{bmatrix}. \tag{5}$$

By considering defined potential function and according to the fundamental theorem of Hammersley and Cliffort the final expression for $P(x_l|C;\theta_l)$ is given by

$$P(x_l|C;\theta_l) = \frac{1}{Z_l(C;\theta_l)} \exp\left\{ -\frac{1}{2} \left(x_l^T H_l x_l + u_l^T x_l \right) \right\}, \tag{6}$$

where $H_l = \sum_{j=1}^{J} \sum_{i=1}^{I} c_{ji} H_{lji}$ and $u_l = \sum_{j=1}^{J} \sum_{i=1}^{I} c_{ji} u_{lji}$.

Z_l is the partition function and is computed by Eq. 2. Fortunately, for Gaussian distribution of Eq. 4 there is a closed formula for the partition function as:

$$Z_l(C;\theta_l) = (2\pi)^{\frac{J}{2}} \left(\det\left(H_l^{-1} \right) \right)^{\frac{1}{2}} \exp\left(\frac{1}{8} u_l^T H_l^{-1} u_l \right). \tag{7}$$

A marvelous point is that conventional CD-HSMM can be considered as a type of GCRF with order zero and mutually exclusive contextual features.

4   Speech Synthesis Based on GCRF

Figure 2 shows an overview of the proposed GCRF-based speech synthesis system. All blocks in the figure are identical to classical SPSS [1], except the three further blocks added with a different color. In the training part, acoustic sufficient statistics or features (X) are extracted according to both speech parameters (V) and state boundaries (T). State boundaries are latent and the added Viterbi block is employed to train them in an unsupervised manner. It should be noted that only sufficient statistics are modeled in the training phase; therefore synthesis phase has to generate them first. After generating features, speech parameters and speech signal are successively synthesized.

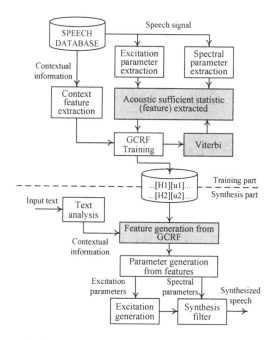

Fig. 2. An overview of the proposed architecture.

4.1   Estimation of Model Parameters

In this section, we discuss how to train model parameters θ. We are given a set of T iid training data $\{X^t, C^t\}_{t=1}^T$, the goal is to find the best set of parameters, $\widehat{\theta}$, which maximizes the conditional log likelihood:

$$\widehat{\theta} = \text{argmax}_\theta \, L(\theta), \tag{8}$$

$$L(\theta) \stackrel{\text{def}}{=} \frac{1}{T} \sum_{t=1}^T \log P(X^t | C^t; \theta). \tag{9}$$

The problem is that, acoustic feature Matrix X^t, wholly depends on the state boundaries which are latent. Hence, it is impossible to compute $L(\theta)$. A correct solution for this problem that converges to the Maximum Likelihood (ML)-estimate is given by the Expectation Maximization (EM) algorithm; however, EM is computationally expensive. Another commonly used method which is computationally efficient and works well in practice is to compute first X^t and then $L(\theta)$ on the Viterbi path. Appling this approach and substituting $P(X^t|C^t;\theta)$ with Eq. 6 gives

$$L(\theta) = -\frac{1}{2T} \sum\nolimits_{t=1}^{T} \sum\nolimits_{l=1}^{L} \{L_l^t(\theta_l)\}, \tag{10}$$

$$L_l^t(\theta_l) \stackrel{\text{def}}{=} x_l^{tT} H_l^t x_l^t + u_l^{tT} x_l^t + \mathcal{J} \log 2\pi - \log \det H_l^t + \frac{1}{4} u_l^{tT} H_l^{t-1} u_l^t. \tag{11}$$

In general, this function cannot be maximized in closed form, therefore numerical optimization is used. The partial derivatives of $L(\theta)$ are calculated as follows.

$$\frac{\partial L(\theta)}{\partial u_{lij}} = -\frac{1}{2T} \sum\nolimits_{t=1}^{T} \frac{\partial L_l^t(\theta_l)}{\partial u_{lij}}, \tag{12}$$

$$\frac{\partial L_l^t(\theta)}{\partial u_{lij}} = \left[\left(x_l^t + \frac{1}{2} H_l^{t-1} u_l^t\right) c_{ji}^t\right] \star \mathbb{b}(\mathcal{J}, j, o), \tag{13}$$

$$\frac{\partial L(\theta)}{\partial H_{lij}} = -\frac{1}{2T} \sum\nolimits_{t=1}^{T} \frac{\partial L_l^t(\theta_l)}{\partial H_{lij}}, \tag{14}$$

$$\frac{\partial L_l^t(\theta_l)}{\partial H_{lij}} = \left[\left(x_l^t x_l^{tT} - H_l^{t-1} - \frac{1}{4} H_l^{t-1} u_l^t u_l^{tT} H_l^{t-1}\right) c_{ji}^t\right] \star \mathbb{B}(\mathcal{J}, j, o). \tag{15}$$

where o denotes the order of model, $\star$ denotes element-by-element product operator and $\mathbb{B}$ ($\mathbb{b}$) is a $\mathcal{J}$-by-$\mathcal{J}$ ($\mathcal{J}$) Boolean matrix (vector) defined by an indicator function I as:

$$\mathbb{b}(\mathcal{J}, j, o) \stackrel{\text{def}}{=} [\mathbb{b}_m(\mathcal{J}, j, o)]_{\mathcal{J} \times 1}, \tag{16}$$

$$\mathbb{b}_m(\mathcal{J}, j, o) \stackrel{\text{def}}{=} I(j - o \leq m \leq j),$$

$$\mathbb{B}(\mathcal{J}, j, o) \stackrel{\text{def}}{=} [\mathbb{B}_{mn}(\mathcal{J}, j, o)]_{\mathcal{J} \times 1}, \tag{17}$$

$$\mathbb{B}_{mn}(\mathcal{J}, j, o) \stackrel{\text{def}}{=} I((j - o \leq m \leq j)\&(j - o \leq n \leq j)).$$

A common solution of this optimization problem is to take entire training samples into account and update model parameters using an optimization algorithm such as *BFGS*. Unfortunately, this in turn leads to large computational complexity. This paper proposes the application of *stochastic gradient ascent* [9] method which is faster than above-mentioned algorithm by orders of magnitude. This method has proven to be effective [9]. Following equations express its updating rule:

$$u^t_{lij} = u^{t-1}_{lij} - \alpha^t \frac{\partial L^k_l(\theta_l)}{\partial u_{lij}}\bigg|_{u^t_{lij}, H^t_{lij}}, \tag{18}$$

$$H^t_{lij} = H^{t-1}_{lij} - \alpha^t \frac{\partial L^t_l(\theta_l)}{\partial H_{lij}}\bigg|_{u^t_{lij}, H^t_{lij}}. \tag{19}$$

A variable step size algorithm described by [10] is utilized in our experiments.

4.2 Viterbi Algorithm for GCRF

Given a sequence of acoustic parameters (V), sentence contextual features (C) and a trained GCRF parameters (θ), this section presents an algorithm to find the most likely state boundaries ($\hat{T}$). Thus the aim is to estimate $\hat{T}$ such that

$$\hat{T} \stackrel{def}{=} \text{argmax}_T P(T|V, C; \theta) = \text{argmax}_T P(X(T, V)|V, C; \theta). \tag{20}$$

From Eq. 6 we have

$$\hat{T} = \text{argmin}_T \sum_{j=1}^{\mathcal{J}} \phi_j(T, V, C, \theta), \tag{21}$$

where $\phi_j(T, V, C, \theta) \stackrel{def}{=} \sum_{l=1}^{L} \sum_{i=1}^{I} \left(x^T_{lj} H_{lij} x_{lj} + b^T_{lij} x_{lj} \right) c_{ji}$.

Let t_j be the j-th state boundary (j-th element of T), then for a GCRF with order o, ϕ_j becomes a function of $t_{j-o-1}, ..., t_j$ instead of entire elements of T. This fact gives us an ability to exploit dynamic programming for performing a complete search on T. Inspired by the other Viterbi algorithms, we need to define an auxiliary variable δ_j.

$$\delta_j(t_{j-o}, ..., t_j) \stackrel{def}{=} \min_{t_1, ..., t_{j-o-1}} \sum_{j=1}^{j} \phi_j(t_{j-o-1}, ..., t_j). \tag{22}$$

δ_j can be calculated from δ_{j-1} by following recursion.

$$\delta_{j+1}(t_{j-o+1}, ..., t_{j+1}) = \min_{t_{j-o}}[\delta_j(t_{j-o}, ..., t_j) + \phi_{j+1}(t_{j-o}, ..., t_{j+1})]. \tag{23}$$

Using this recursion, it is straightforward to obtain Viterbi algorithm.

4.3 Parameter Generation Algorithm

This section, for a given GCRF, derives an algorithm to estimate the best synthesized speech parameters ($\hat{V}$) by maximizing the likelihood criteria, i.e.

$$\hat{V} \overset{\text{def}}{=} \text{argmax}_V P(V|\theta) = \text{argmax}_V \sum_{\mathcal{T}} P(X(V, \mathcal{T})|\theta). \tag{24}$$

The synthesis part needs to respond quickly, however, solving this problem directly is challenging. Hence, the algorithm derived from Eq. 24 is not practical.

A two-step algorithm is proposed here which approximates $\hat{V}$ fast.

Step 1. For a given θ, compute the ML-estimate of X:

$$\hat{X} \overset{\text{def}}{=} \text{argmax}_X P(X|\theta). \tag{25}$$

Step 2. For a given X, compute the ML-estimate of V:

$$\hat{V} \overset{\text{def}}{=} \text{argmax}_V P(V|X). \tag{26}$$

The first step is simply obtained by considering the distribution discussed in Sect. 3. Since different acoustic features are statistically independent (given in Eq. 3), the algorithm can generate features independently, i.e.

$$\hat{x}_l = \text{argmax}_{x_l} P(x_l|C; \theta_l). \tag{27}$$

Optimizing the Gaussian distribution $P(x_1|C; \theta_1)$, expressed by Eq. 6, results in the set of linear equations below:

$$H^l \hat{x}_l = -\frac{1}{2} b^l. \tag{28}$$

H^l is symmetric and positive definite, so Eq. 28 can be efficiently solved using the Cholesky decomposition.

Second step depends heavily on the selected acoustic features. For the set of acoustic features extracted in our system, Tokoda et al. [11] algorithm was used in this step.

5 Experiments

5.1 Experimental Conditions

To evaluate the proposed system, a Persian speech database [12] consisting of 1000 utterances with an average length of 8 s was employed. Experiments were conducted on a fixed test set of 200 utterances and 5 different training sets with remaining 50, 100, 200, 400 and 800 utterances. It should be noted that the average length of each utterance is about 8 s. Speech parameters including mel-cepstral coefficients, bandpass aperiodicity and fundamental frequency were extracted by STRAIGHT [13]. Sample mean and variance of each static and dynamic parameter, in addition to the voicing probability and duration are computed as the acoustic state features. For contextual state features a set of 150 well designed binary questions are employed. Following subsections evaluate the proposed method in contrast to the HSMM-based technique.

5.2   Objective Evaluation

As Fig. 3 shows, three objective measures were calculated to evaluate the proposed and HSMM-based systems, namely the average mel-cepstral distortion (expressed in dB) [14], the Root-Mean-Square (RMS) error of fundamental frequency logarithm (expressed in cent) and the RMS error of phoneme durations (expressed in terms of number of frames). Computing the first and second measures needs an assumption about state boundaries that was estimated here using the Viterbi algorithm. Since F0 value is not observed in unvoiced regions, only voiced frames of speech were taken into account for the second measure.

From Fig. 3, it is noticeable that GCRF always outperforms HSMM in generating mel-cepstral and duration parameters, but HSMM is superior in synthesizing fundamental frequency when the number of training data is larger than 200 utterances. This drawback is a result of weak estimation of F0 parameters during the training process. Table 1 compares the accuracy of voiced/unvoiced detection in proposed system with its counterpart in HSMM-based synthesis.

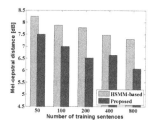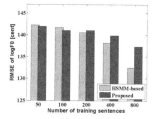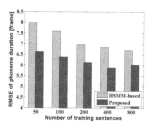

Fig. 3. Objective evaluation of HSMM-based and proposed speech synthesis systems. (Left) Mel-cepstral distance [dB]; (Middle) RMSE of log F0 [cent]; (Right) RMSE of phoneme duration [frame].

5.3   Subjective Evaluation

We conducted preference score measure to compare the proposed and HSMM-based systems subjectively. 20 subjects were presented with 10 randomly chosen pairs of synthesized speech from the two models and then asked for their preference.

Figure 4 shows the average preference score. The result confirms that the synthetic speech generated by proposed system has been favorable when training data are limited.

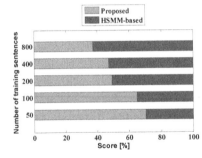

Fig. 4. Subjective evaluation of HSMM and proposed systems using preference score.

Table 1. Accuracy of Voiced/Unvoiced Detector.

# train data	Proposed accuracy	HSMM accuracy
50	0.9184	0.8851
100	0.9241	0.8828
200	0.9157	0.8903
400	0.9104	0.8783
800	0.9037	0.8809

6 Conclusion

This paper improves HSMM-based synthesis in the following ways:

1. The independence assumption of states distribution in HTS is removed.
2. In contrast to HMM, the proposed model does not limit its potential functions to be a probability distribution.
3. CD-HMM uses decision-tree-based context clustering that does not provide efficient generalization in limited training data, because each speech parameter vector is associated in modeling of only one context cluster. In contrast, our method contributes each training vector in many clusters to offer an efficient generalization.

Despite the advantages, which made our system to outperform in small training data, a drawback such as difficult training procedure is noticed in large databases.

References

1. Black, A.W., Zen, H., Tokuda, K.: Statistical Parametric Speech Synthesis. In: ICASSP'2007, Honolulu, Hawai'i, USA, pp. IV-1229–IV-1232 (2007)
2. Zen, H., Tokuda, K., Black, A.W.: Statistical parametric speech synthesis. Speech Commun. Elsevier **51**(11), 1039–1064 (2009)
3. Zen, H., Tokuda, K., Masuko, T., Kobayashi, T., Kitamura, T.: Hidden semi-markov model based speech synthesis. In: Interspeech'2004, Jeju Island, Korea, pp. 1393–1396, October 4–8 2004
4. Zen, H., Tokuda, K., Kitamura, T.: An introduction of trajectory model into hmm-based speech synthesis. In: SSW5, pp. 191–196. Carnegie Mellon University, June 2004
5. Tokuda, K., Masuko, T., Miyazaki, N., Kobayashi, T.: Multi-space probability distribution HMM. IEICE Trans. Inf. Syst. **E85-D**(3), 455–464 (2002)
6. Lafferty, J., McCallum, A., Pereira, F.: Conditional random fields: probabilistic models for segmenting and labeling sequence data. In: Proceedings of the Eighteenth International Conference on Machine Learning, pp. 282–289 (2001)
7. Grimmett, G.R.: A theorem about random fields. Bull. Lond. Math. Soc. **5**, 81–84 (1973)

8. Sutton, C., McCallum, A.: An introduction to conditional random fields for relational learning. In: Getoor, L., Taskar, B. (eds.) Introduction to statistical Relational Learning. MIT Press, Cambridge (2006)

9. Gardner, W.A.: Learning characteristics of stochastic-gradient-descent algorithms: a general study, analysis and critique. Sig. Process. **6**(2), 113–133 (1984)

10. Vrahatis, M.N., Androulakis, G.S., Lambrinos, J.N., Magoulas, G.D.: A class of gradient unconstrained minimization algorithms with adaptive stepsize. J. Comput. Appl. Math. **114** (2), 367–386 (2000)

11. Tokuda, K., Yoshimura, T., Masuko, T., Kobayashi, T., Kitamura, T.: Speech parameter generation algorithms for HMM-based speech synthesis. In: ICASSP'2000, vol. 3, Istanbul, pp. 1315–1318, June 2000

12. Bijankhan, M., Sheikhzadegan, J., Roohani, M.R., Samareh, Y., Lucas, C., Tebiani, M.: The speech database of farsi spoken language. In: Proceedings of 5th Australian International Conference on Speech Science and Technology (SST'94), pp. 826–831 (1994)

13. Kawahara, H., Masuda-Katsuse, I., de Cheveigné, A.: Restructuring speech representations using a pitch-adaptive time-frequency smoothing and an instantaneous-frequency-based F0 extraction: possible role of a repetitive structure in sounds. Speech Commun. **27**(3–4), 187–207 (1999)

14. Kubichek, R.F.: Mel-cepstral distance measure for objective speech quality assessment. In: Proceedings of the IEEE Pacific Rim Conference on Communications, Computers, and Signal Processing, pp. 125–128 (1993)

Discriminative Spoken Language Understanding Using Statistical Machine Translation Alignment Models

Mohammad Aliannejadi[1]([⊠]), Shahram Khadivi[1], Saeed Shiry Ghidary[1], and Mohammad Hadi Bokaei[2]

[1] Department of Computer Engineering and Information Technology,
Amirkabir University of Technology, Tehran, Iran
{m.aliannejadi,khadivi,shiry}@aut.ac.ir
[2] Department of Computer Engineering, Sharif University of Technology,
Tehran, Iran
bokaei@ce.sharif.edu

Abstract. In this paper, we study the discriminative modeling of Spoken Language Understanding (SLU) using Conditional Random Fields (CRF) and Statistical Machine Translation (SMT) alignment models. Previous discriminative approaches to SLU have been dependent on *n-gram* features. Other previous works have used SMT alignment models to predict the output labels. We have used SMT alignment models to align the abstract labels and trained CRF to predict the labels. We show that the *state transition* features improve the performance. Furthermore, we have compared the proposed method with two baseline approaches; Hidden Vector States (HVS) and baseline-CRF. The results show that for the F-measure the proposed method outperforms HVS by 1.74 % and baseline-CRF by 1.7 % on ATIS corpus.

Keywords: Spoken language understanding · Statistical machine translation · Conditional random fields · Hidden vector state · Discriminative modeling · Sequential labeling · Natural language processing

1 Introduction

Spoken Language Understanding (SLU) is the problem of extracting the intention and aim of the user's utterance. More specifically, a SLU system tries to find a mapping from user's utterance in natural language, which follows no rules or restrictions, to the limited set of concepts that is structured and meaningful for the computer. The only restriction for the user's input is the domain of the utterance, i.e. a SLU system trained in Air Travel domain, can be used only in this domain.

Below is an example of Air Travel Information System (ATIS) [1] corpus. The input utterance is:

I want to return to Dallas on Thursday

and its corresponding output is:

© Springer International Publishing Switzerland 2014
A. Movaghar et al. (Eds.): AISP 2013, CCIS 427, pp. 194–202, 2014.
DOI: 10.1007/978-3-319-10849-0_20

```
    GOAL : RETURN
TOLOC.CITY = Dallas
RETURN.DATE = Thursday .
```

The output indicates that the goal of the utterance is to get the list of *RETURN* flights. The arrival city of the flights is "Dallas" (which is labeled as *TOLOC.CITY*) and the desired date of the flights is "Thursday" (which is labeled as *RETURN.DATE*). A simple algorithm is able to generate a SQL command from the system's output. Therefore the list of return flights to Dallas on Thursday will be available for the user automatically.

The first statistical method for SLU was based on Hidden Markov Model (HMM) using a finite state semantic tagger which was a part of AT&T's CHRONUS system [2]. In [2] semantic representation was flat-concept but later Hidden Vector State (HVS) extended the representation to a hierarchical structure and modeled the problem using a Push-down automaton [3].

The problem can been converted to a sequential labeling problem. Discriminative methods deal directly with the aligned data (fully annotated) using sequential classification and Conditional Random Fields (CRF) [4,5]. Discriminative sequence labeling was a success because of its power in utilizing problem specific features, comparing to HMM. Linear-chain CRF combines the advantage of discriminative modeling and sequence modeling [6].

In [7–9] the problem of SLU was dealt by SMT approaches. S.D. Pietra et al. In [7] have used fertility models to predict labels in ATIS corpus and R. Macherey et al. In [8] and later in [9] have applied numerous alignment models for this task where the source language is the user's utterance and the target langauge is a formal language of the labels. All these works have used SMT alignment models to *predict* the labels. These models are not able to capture many dependnecies and difficulties of this problem, thus they will not be appropriate for predicting the labels. On the other hand, these models are able to *align* the training data to their abstract (unaligned) labels at high accuracy.

In this paper we automatically annotate the training data using SMT alignment models in order to have a better flat-concept version of the hierarchical semantic representation and trained CRF using the new annotated corpus. We show that this method outperforms other flat-concept fully annotation methods proposed before trained using CRF and also outperforms other methods dealing with abstract annotation directly.

The remainder of paper is organized as follows. Section 2 briefly describes CRF for sequential labeling. Section 3 briefly presents basic SMT alignment models. Section 4 presents the combination of SMT alignment for annotation and linear-chain CRF for sequential labeling task. The experimental evaluation using ATIS is presented in Sect. 5 and finally Sect. 6 concludes the paper.

2   Conditional Random Fields

Discriminative modeling of the problem leads to linear-chain CRFs for the task of mapping the input sequence ($\mathbf{x}$) to the sequence of labels ($\mathbf{y}$) [6]. $\mathbf{x}$ ranges over all natural language sentences but $\mathbf{y}$ ranges over the finite label set $\mathcal{Y}$. In our problem the label set consists of labels such as `FLIGHT`, `TOLOC`, `FROMLOC`, etc. $\mathbf{x}$ and $\mathbf{y}$ are jointly distributed, but using CRF as a discriminative framework, the marginal $p(\mathbf{x})$ is not explicitly modeled, instead $\mathbf{x}$ and $\mathbf{y}$ are conditionally modeled as $p(\mathbf{y}|\mathbf{x})$ [6]. A linear-chain CRF is defined by a dependency graph G and a set of features f_k which the weights λ_k are associated with them. The main difference of CRF as a dicriminative method to generative methods such as HMM is that CRF models the conditional probability $p(\mathbf{y}|\mathbf{x})$ directly utilizing problem-specific features, whereas HMM decomposes the probability function using Bayes theorem.

The conditional probability of a sequence of labels given a sequence of observations is given by:

$$p(\mathbf{y}|\mathbf{x}) = \frac{1}{Z(x)}\exp(\{\sum_{k=1}^{K} \lambda_k f_k(y_t, y_{t-1}, \mathbf{x}_t)\} \tag{1}$$

with

$$Z(\mathbf{x}) = \sum_{y} \exp\{\sum_{k=1}^{K} \lambda_k f_k(y_t, y_{t-1}, \mathbf{x}_t)\}. \tag{2}$$

Feature functions are used to encode semantic features, concept relations, etc. in the model [4]. Mostly, these features are used in binary form, i.e. if the feature triggers, it returns 1 and otherwise 0. The parameters of the model are the weights of the features, λ_k, and the learning phase is the process of finding the optimum set of weights.

3   IBM Alignment Models

Given a source sentence $\mathbf{f} = f_1, \ldots, f_j, \ldots, f_J$, the best target sentence $\mathbf{e} = e_1, \ldots, e_i, \ldots, e_I$ is the one which maximizes $p(\mathbf{e}|\mathbf{f})$ [9–11]:

$$\hat{\mathbf{e}} = \arg\max_{\mathbf{e}} \{p(\mathbf{e}|\mathbf{f})\}$$

$$= \arg\max_{\mathbf{e}} \{p(\mathbf{f}|\mathbf{e}).p(\mathbf{e})\}. \tag{3}$$

Introducing $\mathbf{a} = a_1 \ldots a_j \ldots a_J$ as the *hidden* alignment set, where each $a_j \in \{1, \ldots, I\}$, Eq. 3 will be updated as [10,12]:

$$p(\mathbf{f}|\mathbf{e}) = \sum_{\mathbf{a}} p(\mathbf{f}, \mathbf{a}|\mathbf{e})$$

$$= p(J|\mathbf{e}) \cdot \sum_{\mathbf{a}} \prod_{j=1}^{J} p(f_j, a_j | f_1, \ldots, f_{j-1}, a_1, \ldots, a_{j-1}, \mathbf{e}) \tag{4}$$

$$= p(J|\mathbf{e}) \cdot \sum_{\mathbf{a}} \prod_{j=1}^{J} p(a_j | a_1 \ldots a_{j-1}, f_1, \ldots, f_{j-1}, \mathbf{e})$$

$$\cdot p(f_j | f_1 \ldots f_{j-1}, a_1, \ldots, a_{j-1}, \mathbf{e}). \tag{5}$$

The first term of Eq. 5 is the *length* model, the second is the *alignment/ distortion* model and the last is the *lexicon/translation* model [9]. Different alignment models were proposed in [10, 12], which are the base of the alignment phase of this work. The base of all these alignment models are the same as the HMM principle used in speech recognition [13] which we briefly introduce here.

3.1   HMM and IBM-1,2

Assuming a first-order dependence for a_j in Eq. 5 and other suitable modeling assumptions [10] the HMM alignment model will be:

$$p(\mathbf{f}|\mathbf{e}) = p(J|I) \cdot \sum_{\mathbf{a}} \prod_{j=1}^{J} p(a_j|a_{j-1}, I) \cdot p(f_j|e_{a_j}). \tag{6}$$

IBM-1 and IBM-2 alignment models are obtained analogously by assuming zero-order dependencies.

3.2   IBM-3,4,5

In models of IBM-3 and 4, a new concept was introduced, *fertility*. Using the concept of *inverted alignment* to perform a mapping from target position i to a set of source positions j, the fertility of a target word is the number of source words it can generate. Considering mappings $\mathcal{B}$ of the form:

$$\mathbf{b} : i \rightarrow b_i \subset \{1, \ldots, j, \ldots, J\},$$

with the constraint to cover each source position j exactly once, Eq. 4 is rewritten using $\mathbf{a} = \mathbf{b}$:

$$p(\mathbf{f}, \mathbf{b}|\mathbf{e}) = p(J|I) \cdot \prod_{i=1}^{I} \left[p(b_i|b_1, \ldots, b_{i-1}) \cdot \prod_{j \in b_i} p(f_i|e_i) \right].$$

IBM-3 and 4 has the problem which a source position could be chosen twice. Keeping track of the empty source positions IBM-5 overcomes this problem [10].

4   Training the Model Using IBM Alignments

In this section we show how to use IBM alignment results to train a linear-chain CRF for the sequence labeling task and describe the main advantage of it over previous works.

4.1   Alignment

The problem with discriminative models is that the data should be fully annotated, and because of that, in previous works some efforts were done to obtain

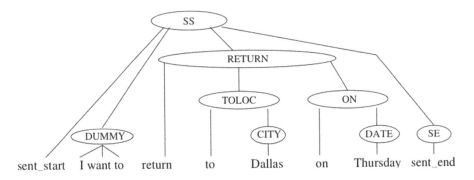

Fig. 1. The final parsed treed using HVS model [3]

fully annotated corpus from the unaligned annotation [4,5]. Figure 1 shows the annotation which was used in [3]. Note that in [3] the data is *unaligned*, so for the example shown in Fig. 1 the annotation for the sentence "sent_start I want to return to Dallas on Thursday sent_end" is:

`SS(RETURN(TOLOC(CITY) ON(DATE)) SE)`

In this example, the hierarchical semantic relationships [3] are presented in an abstract manner. In [4] a simple algorithm is proposed. Using this simple algorithm, a fully annotated data can be obtained in the following form:

$$\underbrace{I}_{null}\ \underbrace{want}_{null}\ \underbrace{to}_{null}\ \underbrace{return}_{null}\ \underbrace{to}_{null}\ \underbrace{Dallas}_{toloc.city}\ \underbrace{on}_{null}\ \underbrace{Thursday}_{return.date}$$

The only words that are tagged non-*null* are *Dallas* and *Thursday* and their tags are in two parts, the first part is the parent node in Fig. 1 and the second is the child. The main disadvantage of this annotation is that many words are labeled as *null*. In Fig. 1 it is obvious that many words such as "return" could be labeled to non-*null* (*RETURN*) labels. We will call this alignment method *Raymond's alignment*[1] in the remainder of the paper.

Another full annotation which was proposed in [5] is:

$$\underbrace{I}_{SR.ACity.pre}\quad \underbrace{want}_{SR.ACity.pre}\quad \underbrace{to}_{SR.ACity.pre}\quad \underbrace{return}_{SR.ACity.pre}$$

$$\underbrace{to}_{SR.ACity.pre}\quad \underbrace{Dallas}_{SR.ACity.start}\quad \underbrace{on}_{SR.RDate.pre}\quad \underbrace{Thursday}_{SR.RDate.start}$$

This annotation presents the labels in three parts. The first part indicates the goal of the utterance. In this example the goal of the utterance is "ShowReturn", therefore the first part of all the labels is *SR*. The second part indicates the slot and the third part indicates the state of the current word regarding to its slot. "Dallas" is the ArrivalCity (which is labeled *toloc.city* in Raymond's alignment),

---

[1] The first author of [4] is Christian Raymond, so we name this alignment in such way.

therefore the second part of its label is *A City*. It is the first word of the *A City* slot, so its status is *start*[2] This alignment labels "Dallas" and "Thursday" exaclty like Raymond's alignment, but main difference is that instead of labeling other words as *null*, it labels them regarding to the nearest labeled word, e.g. the nearest labeled word to "return" is "Dallas" - which is labeled as *SR.A City.start* - so "return" is labeled as *SR.A City.pre* which means the next labeled word has *ST.A City.start* labels [5].

In this work, we propose another full annotation method, using the abstract annotation of [3] to train linear-chain CRF. This annotation is:

$$\underbrace{\text{I}}_{DUMMY} \ \underbrace{\text{want}}_{DUMMY} \ \underbrace{\text{to}}_{DUMMY} \ \underbrace{\text{return}}_{RETURN} \ \underbrace{\text{to}}_{TOLOC} \ \underbrace{\text{Dallas}}_{CITY} \ \underbrace{\text{on}}_{ON} \ \underbrace{\text{Thursday}}_{DATE}$$

Many useful information is saved by using this annotation, e.g. the word "return" is labeled as *RETURN* instead of *null* and this label is more informative. We have trained IBM alignment models on the parallel corpus taking the natural sentences as the source language and the labels as the target language.

4.2 Sequential Labeling

In order to bring the advantages of discriminative modeling and sequence modeling together, the problem should be modeled by linear-chain CRF [6].

Using this annotation, the probabilistic model of labels $p(\mathbf{y})$ which is modeled in linear-chain CRF plays its real role. $p(\mathbf{y})$ is modeled by the feature function $f(x_t, y_t, y_{t-1})$ i.e. the label transition from y_{t-1} to y_t [6]. In [4] label transitions are going from *null* state to other states, or going to *null* state from other states and or staying at *null* state. In [5] some words which could have better labels, such as *return* have labels depending on the nearest slot in the future or past.

Investigating the nature of SLU and the hierarchical semantic labels of [3], it is obvious that $p(\mathbf{y})$ is important, i.e. knowing that a word at time $t - 1$ has been labeled as TOLOC, the word at time t is highly probable to be labeled as CITY and so on. It is also possible to reduce the number of features because somehow we are keeping track of the history, so the number of words used as features in previous works [4,5] could be reduced to zero and the features are only the current word and future words. In other works such as [4] because many informative labels have been thrown out, actually existence of $p(\mathbf{y})$ will make no improvement and in order to overcome this information loss, they had to expand the features to see the words at even time $t - 4$ but we will show that using this annotation $p(\mathbf{y})$ improves the model and the reduced number of features are enough for this task.

---

[2] City names may contain more than one words and so the other labels, in this case the other words' status will be *cont*, e.g. for the city name "Los Angeles", "Los" is labeled as *SR.A City.start* and "Angeles" is labeled as *SR.A City.cont*.

5   Experiments

In this section we evaluate our work on ATIS [1] which consists of 4978 training utterances selected from Class A in ATIS-2 and ATIS-3 corpora. The test set contains both ATIS-3 NOV93 and DEC94 test sets. In order to evaluate our work, results for HVS [3] and results from [4] are included.

5.1   Experimental Setup

We have used GIZA++ [14] for aligning the parallel corpus and used CRF++ [15] to train CRF. The resulting alignment is then corrected using the output alignment of [4]. This assures that no alignment errors will be injected to the CRF model. The features are indicators for lexical classes of words in a window around the decision state. We first trained the model using $[-4, 2]$ window using first order Markov chain dependency graph (linear-chain CRF) in order to have comparable results. We also trained the CRF using the zero order Markov chain to show the impact of the label model on the performance.

5.2   Results

We have post processed the sequence of labels to obtain the slots and their values. The slot-value pair is compared to the reference test set and the result is reported in precision (P) and recall (R) and F-measure (F) of slot classification.

Table 1 compares our method with the results of HVS baseline model and the baseline-CRF. The feature window for both CRF models is $[-4, 2]$. Our method outperforms both models. It shows the impact of our alignment method on the performance of CRF by utilizing state transitions or in other words $p(\mathbf{y})$. It shows that a more precise and informative labeling method could improve the performance. It's because an output decision at time t is not only dependent on the lexical features but also on the previous decisions, i.e. if the model decides FLIGHT at time $t - 1$, it will be very probable for TOLOC to be chosen at time t.

Table 1. Results of HVS, CRF and CRF + SMT on ATIS corpus

Model	Recall	Precision	F-measure
HVS	89.82 %	88.75 %	89.28 %
CRF	89.25 %	89.41 %	89.32 %
CRF + SMT	91.21 %	90.83 %	91.02 %

In order to show the impact of $p(\mathbf{y})$ on the performance, we have trained zero order CRF using Raymond's alignment and our method. The results can be found in Table 2. Both CRF models use same feature window $[-4, 2]$. It is obvious when we used one order Markov chain in the CRF model, the results on

Table 2. Results of using first-order and zero-order dependecy in CRF and CRF + SMT on ATIS corpus

Model	Recall		Precision		F-measure	
	0 order	1 order	0 order	1 order	0 order	1 order
CRF	90.00 %	89.25 %	89.84 %	89.41 %	89.92 %	89.32 %
CRF + SMT	89.46 %	91.21 %	88.67 %	90.83 %	89.07 %	91.02 %

our annotation have significant improvement. On the other hand, surprisingly the performance of CRF which is trained using Raymond's alignment is degraded when involving state transitions. That's because it has thrown many informative data away, therefore the decisions depend only on the lexical features.

6 Conclusion

In this paper we proposed a new method to convert the abstract annotation automatically and without any human effort to full annotation, avoiding the loss of informative labels, reshaping the annotation from the hierarchical to a flat-concept annotation. We showed that using statistical machine translation alignments, improve the model's performance comparing to similar works. The results show that using this annotation improves the F-measure by 1.74 % comparing to HVS and using the same features comparing to CRF improves it by 1.7 %.

References

1. Dahl, D.A., Bates, M., Brown, M., Fisher, W., Hunicke-Smith, K., Pallett, D., Pao, C., Rudnicky, A., Shriberg, E.: Expanding the scope of the atis task: the atis-3 corpus. In: Proceedings of the workshop on Human Language Technology, Association for Computational Linguistics, pp. 43–48 (1994)
2. Pieraccini, R., Tzoukermann, E., Gorelov, Z., Gauvain, J.L., Levin, E., Lee, C.H., Wilpon, J.G.: A speech understanding system based on statistical representation of semantics. In: IEEE International Conference on Acoustics, Speech, and Signal Processing 1992, ICASSP-92, vol. 1, pp. 193–196. IEEE (1992)
3. He, Y., Young, S.: Semantic processing using the hidden vector state model. Comput. Speech Lang. **19**(1), 85–106 (2005)
4. Raymond, C., Riccardi, G.: Generative and discriminative algorithms for spoken language understanding. In: International Conference on Speech Communication and Technologies, Antwerp, Belgium, August 2007, pp. 1605–1608 (2007)
5. Wang, Y.Y., Acero, A.: Discriminative models for spoken language understanding. In: International Conference on Speech Communication and Technologies, Citeseer (2006)
6. Lafferty, J., McCallum, A., Pereira, F.C.: Conditional random fields: Probabilistic models for segmenting and labeling sequence data. In: Proceedings of 18th International Conference on Machine Learning, Morgan Kaufmann, pp. 282–289 (2001)

7. Pietra, S.D., Epstein, M., Roukos, S., Ward, T.: Fertility models for statistical natural language understanding. In: Proceedings of the 35th Annual Meeting of the Association for Computational Linguistics and Eighth Conference of the European Chapter of the Association for Computational Linguistics, Association for Computational Linguistics, pp. 168–173 (1997)
8. Macherey, K., Och, F.J., Ney, H.: Natural language understanding using statistical machine translation. In: INTERSPEECH, Citeseer, pp. 2205–2208 (2001)
9. Macherey, K., Bender, O., Ney, H.: Applications of statistical machine translation approaches to spoken language understanding. IEEE Trans. Audio Speech Lang. Process. **17**(4), 803–818 (2009)
10. Brown, P.F., Pietra, V.J.D., Pietra, S.A.D., Mercer, R.L.: The mathematics of statistical machine translation: parameter estimation. Comput. Linguist. **19**(2), 263–311 (1993)
11. Khadivi, S., Ney, H.: Automatic filtering of bilingual corpora for statistical machine translation. In: Montoyo, A., Muñoz, R., Métais, E. (eds.) NLDB 2005. LNCS, vol. 3513, pp. 263–274. Springer, Heidelberg (2005)
12. Vogel, S., Ney, H., Tillmann, C.: Hmm-based word alignment in statistical translation. In: Proceedings of the 16th conference on Computational Linguistics- Volume 2, Association for Computational Linguistics, pp. 836–841 (1996)
13. Khadivi, S., Zolnay, A., Ney, H.: Automatic text dictation in computer-assisted translation. In: International Conference on Speech Communication and Technologies, pp. 2265–2268 (2005)
14. Och, F.J., Ney, H.: Giza++: Training of statistical translation models (2000)
15. Kudo, T.: Crf++: Yet another crf toolkit. Software available at http://crfpp. sourceforge.net (2005)

Noise Aware Sub-band Locality Preserving Projection for Robust Speech Recognition

Zahra Karevan[1](✉), Ahmad Akbari[1], and Babak Nasersharif[2]

[1] Iran University of Science and Technology, Tehran, Iran
zahra.karevan@gmail.com
[2] K.N. Toosi University of Technology, Tehran, Iran

Abstract. Recovering the nonlinear low dimensional embedding for the speech signals in the clean environment using the manifold learning techniques has become of substantial interest recently. However, the issue of manifold learning for feature transformation in domains involving noise corrupted speech can be quite different. We tackle this issue by presenting a new approach for reducing noise effect on different Mel Frequency Cepstral Coefficients (MFCCs) and so Mel sub-bands. We introduce our method in the framework of Locality Preserving Projection (LPP) as a manifold learning technique where we construct the manifold on each Mel sub-band by considering noise effects on it. We propose to learn one manifold for each MFCC and so Mel sub-band using noisy speech, and we name this method as sub-band LPP. The experimental results on AURORA-2 database show that the noise aware sub-band LPP improves the noisy speech recognition rate in comparison to conventional LPP for SNR values greater than 0 dB.

1 Introduction

The first step in all speech recognition systems is feature extraction from raw speech signal. These features should represent different characteristics of speech signals like temporal evolution of the speech spectral envelope. This, however, leads to a high dimensional feature space which is a curse for any pattern recognition problem, both from a performance and a computational point of view. Thus, finding a lower dimensional embedding space is of great interest.

To this end, linear Embedding techniques such as principle component analysis (PCA) [1] and Linear Discriminant Analysis (LDA) [2] have been successfully used in speech community for a long time. In recent years, however, many nonlinear algorithms like manifold learning techniques have found their way in this community [3]. The reason is that, the speech production mechanisms define a nonlinear mapping from a low dimensional configuration space to a high dimensional observation space. The existence of such a nonlinear embedding space for specific classes of speech sound has been proven many years ago [4], but it has been formalized in [3]. Since then, many researches have been conducted to find a proper embedding space for speech features based on manifold learning

© Springer International Publishing Switzerland 2014
A. Movaghar et al. (Eds.): AISP 2013, CCIS 427, pp. 203–211, 2014.
DOI: 10.1007/978-3-319-10849-0_21

techniques. Some examples of them are Laplacian Eigenmaps [5], ISOMAPS [6], Diffusion Maps [7], and Locally Linear Embedding [8].

However, these techniques have their own drawbacks. The extension to out-of-sample data is limited and they suffer from computational complexity. To remedy these problems, successful linear and nonlinear variants have been proposed such as : Locality Preserving Projection (LPP) [9,10], and Intrinsic Spectral Analysis (ISA) [3,11]. Although there have been plenty of works done in the realm of manifold learning, very small number of them investigate how the speech manifold can be affected in noisy environments. It is clear that noises can obscure the manifold structure; so, a critical issue of manifold learning is whether the method is robust to noise or not. Recently, the effect of choosing proper heat kernel parameters for different levels of signal to noise ratio has been investigated for a variant of LPP [12].

So far, however, dealing with speech manifold regarding the speech features and noises' characteristics has not been investigated. In this paper, we focus on the speech manifold learning in the noisy environments with respect to noise effects on different speech frequency sub-bands. In other words, various classes of speech sounds show different behaviors in frequency domain; for example: in vowels, most of the energy is concentrated in low frequencies while for a fricative like's', there are high energy components in higher frequencies. Besides, different types of noises (except the white noise) affect frequency sub-bands in different ways. These facts motivated us to deal with different frequency bands separately for the noisy speech.

In this paper, we choose LPP as an example manifold learning technique primarily because of a good performance obtained using LPP in previous works [10]. However, it is worth mentioning that there is no good reason that our proposed idea cannot be used in other manifold learning frameworks.

The rest of this paper is structured as follows. An introduction and theoretical background of LPP is presented in Sect. 2. Then, we suggest our new approach named sub-band LPP in Sect. 3. Section 4 contains the conducted experiments. Finally, this paper is concluded in Sect. 5.

2   Locality Preserving Projection

Locality Preserving Projection (LPP) is a linear extension of Laplacian Eigenmaps for features transformation. This method is interesting because it preserves the locality of data and minimizes a different objective criterion from the classical linear techniques. As LPP is a linear technique, it is faster and more suitable for practical application rather than nonlinear methods. Furthermore, in nonlinear methods, the evaluation of mapping has to be recomputed for new test data points, while in the LPP we simply apply the mapping on any out-of-sample data.

Considering a collection of n samples $X = [x_1, x_2, ..., x_n] \subset \mathcal{R}^H$ that forms a mesh of data points that lie on the manifold, it is typical in manifold learning methods to construct an undirected adjacency weighted (or binary) graph

$G = (X, \mathbf{W})$ with one vertex per data point. The similarity matrix $\mathbf{W}$ is defined such that whose element, w_{ij}, represents the similarity between x_i and x_j if x_i is one of the K nearest neighbors of x_j (or vice versa) and 0 otherwise. To exploit structural information from data, gaussian similarity function is usually used as a weight between pairs of data points:

$$w_{ij} = exp(-\|x_i - x_j\|^2/2\sigma^2). \tag{1}$$

Then, the graph Laplacian is defined, $\mathbf{L} = \mathbf{D} - \mathbf{W}$, where $\mathbf{D}$ is the diagonal vertex degree matrix with elements $D_{ii} = \sum_{j=1}^{n} w_{ij}$. Assume that y_i is the mapping of x_i by the linear transformation P, i.e. $y_i = P^T x_i$. The objective function of LPP is given by:

$$\begin{aligned} min\sum_{i\neq j} \|y_i - y_j\|^2 w_{ij} \\ = min \ 2P^T X\mathbf{L}X^T P \end{aligned} \tag{2}$$

such that $P^T X\mathbf{D}X^T P = 1$. This constraint removes the arbitrary scaling factor in the embedding. To solve the aforementioned minimization problem, we use the lagrangian formulation of it:

$$\mathcal{L} = P^T X\mathbf{L}X^T P - \lambda P^T X\mathbf{D}X^T P \tag{3}$$

It is easy to show that the following generalized eigenvalue problem gives the solution to the above-mentioned minimization problem:

$$L'P = \lambda D'P \tag{4}$$

where $D' = X\mathbf{D}X^T$ and $L' = X\mathbf{L}X^T$, and both are symmetric and positive semi-definite. D' and L' are $\mathcal{H} \times \mathcal{H}$ matrices and $\mathcal{H}$ is the dimensionality of the ambient space.

3   Sub-band Locality Preserving Projection

The performance of any speech manifold learning technique can be degraded in the presence of the noise. However, all frequency bands are not affected in the same way. This depends mostly on the type of the noise. For example, pink noise changes the low frequency components more than the high ones. However, generally, we don't have much information about this behavior of various types of noises. This motivates us to look into different frequency bands separately in the training phase. This approach interestingly makes much sense for the speech signals since speech features are mostly extracted from the frequency domain.

Assuming an arbitrary data point $x_i = [x_i^1, x_i^2, ..., x_i^{\mathcal{H}}]$ representing a frame of speech in frequency domain in $\mathcal{H}$-dimensional speech feature space, let's say MFCC, we can consider a set of data points X^l including only the lth MFCC feature of original dataset X. For example, for the typical 13-dimensional MFCCs, i.e. $\mathcal{H} = 13$, including log energy ($C0$) and first 12 Mel Cepstral coefficients ($C1 - C12$), we have 13 new datasets. Now, we can rewrite the formulation of LPP for each of the new datasets $\{X^l\}_{l=1}^{13}$. It leads to a set of eigen value problems similar to Eq. 4:

$$L'^l P^l = \lambda D'^l P^l, \quad l = 1, ..., 13 \tag{5}$$

Thus, a set of linear transformation matrices $\{P^l\}_{l=1}^{13}$ is achieved each corresponding to a specific Mel frequency Cepstral coefficient. Since the training process is done for each Mel frequency Cepstral coefficient individually, we believe that more information regarding the noise would be learnt. It is important to note that even though we construct our new datasets based on one Mel frequency band, it is always possible to construct them using a number of them.

Having the transformation matrices, we transformed the new datasets in the new embedding space:

$$Y^l = (P^l)^T X^l \tag{6}$$

By concatenating the mapped datasets, $\{Y^l\}_{l=1}^{13}$, we reach the full embedding space of the original dataset, i.e. $Y = [Y^1, Y^2, ..., Y^{13}]$.

3.1 Computational Issues of Sub-band LPP

For sub-band Locality Preserving Projection introduced here, the same computation as LPP should be done for different frequency bands. The computational issues can be explained from two points of view: 1- Graph Construction: this part includes finding nearest neighbors using Euclidean distance; to calculate the Euclidean distance, dealing with low dimensional data is a benefit ; however, finding the nearest neighbors should be done for number of datasets, $\{X^l\}_{l=1}^{13}$, and it makes our approach computationally expensive for large datasets; because the search to find nearest neighbors should be done among n data points for each Mel sub-band individually. 2- Eigen value problem: solving the problem in Eq. 6 should also be performed for different sub-bands. The eigen decomposition complexity is highly reduced since the dimension of Laplacian matrix is the same as the number of frequency bands we choose in each sub-band.

4   Experimental Results

Our experiments in this work are conducted on the European Telecommunications Standards Institute's Aurora-2 speech in noise corpus (multi-condition data). The training set consists of 8440 utterances collected from 55 male and 55 female speakers. It represents 4 different noise scenarios at 5 different SNRs. The 4 noises are suburban train, babble, car and exhibition hall. The SNRs are 20 dB, 15 dB, 10 dB, 5 dB and the clean condition. Three different test sets are defined. 4004 utterances from 52 male and 52 female speakers are split into 4 subsets with 1001 utterances in each. Recordings of all speakers are present in each subset. One noise signals is added to each subset of 1001 utterances at SNRs of 20 dB, 15 dB, 10 dB, 5 dB, 0 dB and -5 dB. Test set C, contains 2 of the 4 subsets with 1001 utterances in each. This time speech and noise are filtered with a MIRS characteristic before adding them at SNRs of 20 dB, 15 dB, 10 dB, 5 dB, 0 dB and -5dB [13].

To examine the validity and the efficiency of our proposed approach, a series of experiments for connected speech recognition are performed. The baseline features are configured as 39-dimensional Mel frequency cepstral coefficients (MFCC), consisting of 12 static coefficients, normalized log energy, and their first and second order derivations. Then, cepstral gain normalization (CGN) [14] is applied to these features. The Automatic Speech Recognition (ASR) system is configured using whole word CDHMM models with 16 states and 3 Gaussian mixtures per state. The HMMs are trained by the multi-condition training data including clean and noisy data [13]. The first experiment represents the performance of ASR system for MFCC features with no transformation (Table 1). Then we apply conventional LPP explained in Sect. 2. To examine our proposed sub-band LPP, we train 13 LPP transformation matrix for each MFCC + CGN coeffcient together with its first and second derivatives. Thus, each P^l is a 3×3 dimensional matrix. The word accuracy for different test sets are shown in Tables 2 and 3.

Table 1. Word Accuracy for MFCC + CGN features on Aurora2 dataset.

Testset-Noises	Clean	20 dB	15 dB	10 dB	5 dB	0 dB	-5 dB	Average (0–20 bB)
TestSetA-Subway	95.98	95.43	94.26	91.37	82.96	62.91	31.44	87.15
TestSetA-Babble	95.74	96.74	95.19	91.87	83.89	60.40	26.45	87.30
TestSetA-Car	95.56	96.0	94.78	92.42	86.7	71.43	43.33	89.48
TestSetA-Exhibition	96.45	95.74	94.26	89.57	79.30	60.91	31.26	86.03
TestSetB-Restaurant	95.98	95.49	94.20	91.4	82.28	61.77	27.17	86.85
TestSetB-Street	95.74	96.01	94.98	91.75	83.37	64.54	32.22	87.73
TestSetB-Airport	95.56	95.47	94.63	92.72	86.88	69.55	39.52	89.13
TestSetB-Station	96.45	96.3	95.06	92.04	84.08	66.28	37.21	88.36
TestSetC-Subway M	95.86	94.9	93.74	90.08	80.75	57.97	25.91	85.55
TestSetC-Street M	96.07	96.19	94.17	90.05	80.56	58.74	27.99	85.96

We can see that in the case of using sub-band LPP, the word accuracy improves compared to LPP for those levels of signal to noise ratio that exist in the training phase. Thus, we can conclude that using individual transformation matrix for different sub-band frequencies leads to a better ASR performance in the noisy environment. The word acurrencies in Table 3 are shown in bold for those cases where our approach outperforms typical LPP. For each experiment, proper parameters for K and σ are indicated in the top of the Table. These parameters can be derived from some huristic techniques like cross validation. But, it is worth noting that for the wide ranges of these parameters we observed almost

Table 2. Word Accuracy for conventional LPP on Aurora2 dataset. $K = 10, \sigma = 50$

Testset-Noises	Clean	20 dB	15 dB	10 dB	5 dB	0 dB	-5 dB	Average (0–20 bB)
TestSetA-Subway	95.7	95.7	93.86	91.43	84.19	65.15	34.76	87.67
TestSetA-Babble	96.04	96.07	94.98	91.90	84.85	63.69	31.44	87.92
TestSetA-Car	95.56	95.68	94.81	92.69	87.29	71.46	42.53	89.58
TestSetA-Exhibition	95.96	95.43	94.05	89.97	81.33	62.54	33.85	86.54
TestSetB-Restaurant	95.70	95.46	94.35	91.71	83.85	65.31	31.04	87.73
TestSetB-Street	96.04	95.68	94.71	91.20	84.07	64.75	33.40	87.74
TestSetB-Airport	95.56	95.7	94.39	92.87	87.83	71.76	40.77	89.68
TestSetB-Station	95.96	96.02	94.26	92.22	84.73	68.53	39.90	88.62
TestSetC-Subway M	95.76	95.09	93.80	90.30	82.13	62.54	29.17	86.60
TestSetC-Street M	95.86	95.86	94.11	89.84	81.77	62.00	29.69	86.57

Table 3. Word Accuracy for Sub-band LPP on Aurora2 dataset. $K = 20, \sigma = 50$

Testset-Noises	Clean	20 dB	15 dB	10 dB	5 dB	0 dB	-5 dB	Average (0–20 bB)
TestSetA-Subway	**96.19**	**96.07**	**94.17**	**91.80**	**84.22**	**65.52**	33.28	**87.99**
TestSetA-Babble	**96.1**	**96.67**	**95.34**	**92.11**	**84.95**	60.79	27.81	87.66
TestSetA-Car	**95.94**	**96.30**	**95.29**	**92.87**	**87.32**	**71.76**	**43.42**	**89.91**
TestSetA-Exhibition	**96.45**	**95.87**	**94.54**	**90.44**	**81.40**	**63.47**	33.42	**87.02**
TestSetB-Restaurant	**96.19**	**95.64**	**94.50**	**91.89**	**83.90**	63.56	29.97	87.61
TestSetB-Street	**96.1**	**96.16**	**95.28**	**92.05**	**84.15**	**65.63**	33.37	**88.22**
TestSetB-Airport	**95.94**	95.50	**94.75**	92.87	87.24	70.41	40.02	89.45
TestSetB-Station	**96.45**	**96.51**	**95.09**	**92.50**	**84.85**	67.23	37.58	**88.77**
TestSetC-Subway M	**96.10**	**95.21**	**93.95**	**90.64**	**82.44**	61.10	27.48	86.57
TestSetC-Street M	**96.34**	**96.19**	**94.80**	**90.69**	**81.81**	59.98	28.90	**86.63**

the same results. To have a better visualization of performance we present the accuracies for those SNRs seen in training phase in Figs. 1, 2 and 3.

This improvement is more visible for the higher ratio of signal to noise. This can be explained by noting to the fact that we trained the sub-band LPPs for only 20 dB, 15 dB, 10 dB, 5 dB and the clean condition. However, for all SNRs the average of word accuracy over all types of noises and all test sets are shown in Table 3. We can see for the SNR values equal to 0, -5 dB, LPP outperforms Sub-band LPP which shows the relation between sub-bands are not preserved in low SNRs; besides, there was no information for these levels of SNRs in the training phase (Table 4).

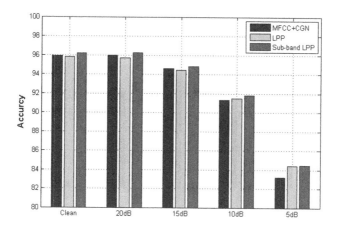

Fig. 1. Average of Word Accuracy over different types of noises in test set A for various SNRs.

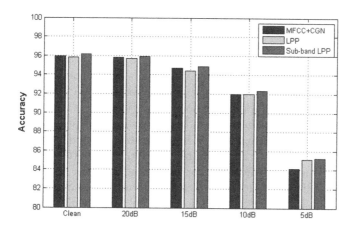

Fig. 2. Average of Word Accuracy over different types of noises in test set B for various SNRs.

Table 4. Average of Word Accuracy for different features over all test sets

Feature	Clean	20 dB	15 dB	10 dB	5 dB	0 dB	-5 dB
MFCC+CGN	95.94	95.83	94.53	91.33	83.08	63.45	32.25
LPP	95.82	95.67	94.34	91.42	84.20	**65.77**	**34.65**
Sub-band LPP	**96.18**	**96.02**	**94.77**	**91.78**	**84.22**	64.94	33.52

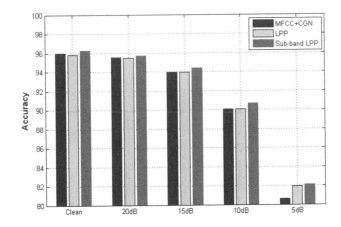

Fig. 3. Average of Word Accuracy over different types of noises in test set C for various SNRs.

5   Conclusion

We proposed to improve Locality Preserving Projection (LPP) as a linear manifold learning techniques to apply it to robust speech recognition problem. To this end, first we proposed to apply LPP to each Mel frequency cepstral coefficient(MFCC) and its first and second order derivatives to take into account the effect of noise on each Mel sub-band. We name this method as sub-band LPP. This is due to our logic that the relation between frequency sub-bands can be represented by a manifold under the noisy condition, where normal LPP finds a manifold for representing the relation between whole feature vectors extracted from the frame. As the second step of improvement, we proposed that manifold should be determined based on noisy training data for a better representation of noise effects on mel sub-bands and corresponding MFCCs. Our results showed that sub-band LPP has a better performance than LPP in SNR values in range of 5–20 dB while its performance is lower than LPP in SNR values equal to 0,-5 dB. This show that relation between frequency sub-bands can not be learned and predicted in low SNRs while the realtion between whole frequency bands is better saved.

As future works, although we proposed our method for a linear manifold based transformation, but it can be also used for nonlinear versions of manifold learning techniques; however, it is worth mentioning that this approach is computationally expensive for nonlinear ones.

References

1. Jolliffe, I.T.: Principle Component Analysis. Springer Series in Statistics. Springer, New York (1986)
2. Fukunaga, K.: Introduction to Statistical Pattern Recognition. Elsevier, Amsterdam (1990). (Online)

3. Jansen, A., Niyogi, P.: Intrinsic Fourier analysis on the manifold of speech sounds. In: Proceedings of International Conference on Acoustics, Speech, and Signal Processing, pp. 241–244 (2006)
4. Fant, G.: Acoustic Theory of Speech Production. Mouton, Paris (1970)
5. Belkin, M., Niyogi, P.: Laplacian Eigenmaps for dimensionality reduction and data represenation. Neural Comput. **16**, 1373–1396 (2003)
6. Tenenbaum, J.B., De Silva, V., Langford, J.C.: A global geometric framework for nonlinear dimensionality reduction Science. Am. Assoc. Adv. Sci. **290**, 2319–2323 (2000)
7. Nadler, B., Lafon, S., Coifman, R.R., Kevrekidis, I.G.: Diffusion maps, spectral clustering and reaction coordinates of dynamical systems. Appl. Comput. Harmonic Anal. **21**, 113–127 (2006)
8. Roweis, S.T., Saul, L.K.: Nonlinear dimensionality reduction by locally linear embedding. Science **290**, 2323–2326 (2000)
9. He, H., Niyogi, P.: Locality preserving projection. In: Proceedings of Advances in Neural Information Processing Systems (2003)
10. Ghoyenlikor, S., Nasersharif, B., Harsini, J.: Robust speech recognition using discriminant locality preserving projections. In: Proceedings of the Sixth Iran Data Mining Conference (IDMC) (2012)
11. Jansen, A., Niyogi, P.: Intrinsic spectral analysis. IEEE Trans. Signal Process. **61**, 1698–1710 (2013)
12. Tomar, V.S., Rose, R.C.: Noise aware manifold learning for robust speech recognition. In: IEEE International Conference on Acoustics Speech and Signal Processing (2013)
13. Pearce, D., Hirsch, H.G.: The aurora experimental framework for the performance evaluation of speech recognition systems under noisy conditions. In: INTERSPEECH, pp. 29–32 (2000)
14. Yoshizawa, Sh., Hayasaka, N., Wada, N., Miyanaga, Y.: Cepstral gain normalization for noise robust speech recognition. In: IEEE International Conference on Acoustics, Speech, and Signal Processing (2004)

A New Signal Segmentation Approach Based on Singular Value Decomposition and Intelligent Savitzky-Golay Filter

Hamed Azami[1(✉)], Morteza Saraf[2], and Karim Mohammadi[3]

[1] Department of Electrical Engineering,
Iran University of Science and Technology, Tehran, Iran
hamed_azami@ieee.org
[2] Institute for Research in Fundamental Sciences (IPM), Tehran, Iran
msaraf@ipm.ir
[3] Faculty of Electrical Engineering,
Iran University of Science and Technology, Tehran, Iran
mohammadi@iust.ac.ir

Abstract. Signal segmentation, dividing non-stationary signals into semi-stationary parts that each has rather equal statistical characteristics is necessary in many signal analysis approaches. In this article, a novel signal segmentation approach based on the modified singular value decomposition (SVD) and intelligent Savitzky-Golay filter is proposed. First, Savitzky-Golay filter is used to minimize the least-squares error in fitting a polynomial to frames of noisy data. There are two parameters in this filter adjusted by many trials. In this paper we propose to use new particle swarm optimization (NPSO) for appropriate selecting of these parameters. Then, we employ two approaches based on the modified SVD to attain the boundaries of each segment. The proposed methods are applied in the both comprehensive synthetic signal and real EEG data. The results of using the proposed methods compared with three well-known algorithms, demonstrate the superiority of the proposed method.

Keywords: Adaptive signal segmentation · Singular value decomposition · Savitzky-Goaly filter · New particle swarm optimization

1 Introduction

It is frequently required to label the electroencephalogram (EEG) signals by segments of similar characteristics that are particularly meaningful to clinicians and for the assessment by neurophysiologists. Within each segment, the signals are considered pseudo-stationary, often with similar temporal and spectral information. For instance, an EEG recorded from an epileptic patient may be separated into three segments of preictal, ictal, and postictal segments and each one can have a different duration [1].

The segmentation may be fixed or adaptive. Dividing the signals into fixed (rather small) size segments is easy and fast to implement. However, it cannot precisely follow the epoch boundaries [2]. On the other hand, in adaptive segmentation the boundaries

© Springer International Publishing Switzerland 2014
A. Movaghar et al. (Eds.): AISP 2013, CCIS 427, pp. 212–224, 2014.
DOI: 10.1007/978-3-319-10849-0_22

are accurately and automatically followed [2]. Some adaptive segmentation methods have been published within the last few years [3–7].

Azami et al. proposed a method for segmentation of the EEG signals based on singular spectrum analysis (SSA) and imperialist competitive algorithm [6]. First, SSA was employed to reduce the effect of noise. Then, fractal dimension (FD) of the signal was estimated and used as a feature for automatic segmentation. To select two acceptable parameters related to the FD, imperialist competitive algorithm was applied [6].

In generalized likelihood ratio (GLR) method, to obtain the boundaries of signal segments, it was suggested to use two windows that slide along the signal. The signal within each window of this method is modeled by an autoregressive (AR) process. Within stationary segments the AR parameters well describe the data. Therefore, any change in the data provoked by sliding a window over the data changes the AR coefficients or increases the prediction error when the same parameters are used [7].

In this paper, first we use a Savitzky-Golay filter to reduce the noise effect. In places where the noise average is known we propose to use the new particle swarm optimization (NPSO) for selecting two main parameters of this filter. Then, an approach based on successive windows and singular value decomposition is suggested.

The next section explains the NPSO and SVD. The proposed method is clarified in Sect. 3. The performance evaluation of the proposed method and the comparison results are provided in Sect. 4. Finally, the conclusions are derived in Sect. 5.

2 Background Knowledge

2.1 New Particle Swarm Optimization

PSO is an evolutionary computing algorithm inspired by nature and is based on repetition [8]. PSO begins with a random matrix as an initial population. Each member of the population is called a particle. There are two parameters for each particle, namely, position and velocity of the particle, which are defined by a space vector and a velocity vector, respectively. These particles form a pattern in an n-dimensional space and move to the desired value. The best position of each particle in the past and the best position among all particles are stored separately. According to the experience from the previous moves, the particles decide how to make the next move. In each iteration, the position and velocity of each particle can be modified according to the following equations:

$$v_i(t+1) = wv_i(t) + C_1 r_1 \left(p_{best_i}(t) - x_i(t) \right) + C_2 r_2 \left(g_{best_i}(t) - x_i(t) \right) \tag{1}$$

$$x_i(t+1) = x_i(t) + v_i(t+1) \tag{2}$$

where n represents the dimension ($1 \leq n \leq N$), C_1 and C_2 are positive constants, generally considered 2.0. r_1 and r_2 are random numbers uniformly between 0 and 1; w is inertia weight that can be constant [8].

Equation (1) expresses that the velocity vector of each particle is updated ($v_i(t+1)$) and the new and previous values of the vector position ($x_i(t)$) create the new position vector ($x_i(t+1)$). In fact, the updated velocity vector affects both local and global values. The best response of the local positions is the best solution of the particle until current execution time (p_{best}) and the best global solution is the best solution of the entire particles until current execution time (g_{best}).

Since in many cases the PSO stays in local minimums of fitness function, we use NPSO. In each iteration, as was said in PSO, global best particle and local best particle are computed. NPSO strategy uses the global best particle and local "worst" particle, the particle with the worst fitness value of the particle until current execution time [8]. It can be defined as:

$$v_i(t+1) = wv_i(t) + C_1r_1\left(p_{worst_i}(t) - x_i(t)\right) + C_2r_2\left(g_{best_i}(t) - x_i(t)\right) \qquad (3)$$

2.2 Singular Value Decomposition

Assume $\mathbf{A} \in \mathbb{R}^{m \times n}$, $m \geq n$. Any $\mathbf{A}$ can be factored as:

$$\mathbf{A} = \mathbf{U}\mathbf{D}\mathbf{V}^{\mathrm{T}} \qquad (4)$$

where $\mathbf{A} = \mathrm{diag}(\sigma_1, \sigma_2, \ldots, \sigma_n)$ with $\sigma_1 \geq \sigma_2 \geq \ldots \geq \sigma_n$, $\mathbf{U}$ is an $m \times m$ orthogonal matrix whose columns are the eigenvectors of $\mathbf{A}\mathbf{A}^{\mathrm{T}}$, and $\mathbf{V}$ is an $n \times n$ orthogonal matrix whose columns are the eigenvectors of $\mathbf{A}^{\mathrm{T}}\mathbf{A}$. The $\sigma_i(1 \leq i \leq n)$ are the singular values and the columns $\boldsymbol{u}_i$ of $\mathbf{U}$ and $\boldsymbol{v}_i$ of $\mathbf{V}$ are named the left and right singular vectors of $\mathbf{A}$, respectively [9]. The singular values ($\sigma_i(1 \leq i \leq n)$) describe the significance of individual singular vectors in the composition of the matrix. The singular vectors corresponding to the larger singular values have more contribution to the structure of patterns embedded in the matrix than the other singular vectors [9].

3 Proposed Adaptive Segmentation

First, in order to filter the signal we use a powerful, fast, and flexible filter widely used in biomedical signal processing, namely Savitzky-Golay, as a pre-processing step [10, 11]. The coefficients of a Savitzky-Golay filter, when applied to a signal, perform a polynomial P of the degree K, is fitted to $N = N_r + N_l + 1$ points of the signal, where N is the window size and N_r and N_l are signal points in the right and left of a current signal point, respectively. One of the best advantages of this filter is that it tends to keep the distribution features such as maxima and minima which are often flattened by other smoothing techniques such as the moving average filters [10, 11]. This property makes the Savitzky-Golay filter a favorable tool to detect the spikes. However, this filter, like almost all the filters, has an important short-coming, i.e. there are some parameters to be adjusted using a large number of trials. Sometimes we know the range or average of the signal-to-noise ratio (SNR). In this case, we propose a new method based on the NPSO. Assume a Gaussian noise with SNR = 5 dB is added to $x_1 = \sin(5\pi t)$. There are many ways for choosing the two parameters of Savitzky-Golay filter, i.e. N and K. The filtering process for a particular signal is sensitive to selection of these parameters. When N and K are selected too large, some important information of the original signal is removed by this filter. For too small N and K, however, this filter cannot attenuate destructive noises sufficiently. Moreover, in many applications due to lack of information about the best polynomial order to fit a signal, selecting K is very difficult. To overcome this problem, in this study, we propose to use the NPSO with the following fitness function:

$$H = \left| SNR - \overline{SNR} \right| = \left| 10 \cdot \log_{10} \left(\sum_{i=1}^{n} (x_f(i))^2 \Big/ \sum_{i=1}^{n} (x(i) - x_f(i))^2 \right) - \overline{SNR} \right| \quad (5)$$

where n, x, x_f, and $\overline{SNR}$ are length of the signal, noisy signal, filtered signal, and SNR average of a signal, respectively. $x - x_f$ is the noise. In other words, the NPSO tries to reduce H by changing K and N for the Savitzgy-Golay filter. It should be mentioned that we use the proposed improved filter where the SNR average or at least the range of noise power is known.

Assume a Gaussian noise with SNR = 5 dB is added to $x_1 = \sin(5\pi t)$. The results for three different sets of K and N are shown in Fig. 1. As can be seen in Fig. 1a, $K = 3$ and $N = 19$ are not large enough for filtering the signal with an SNR = 5 dB. In Fig. 1b, $K = 5$ and $N = 31$, and in Fig. 1c $K = 3$ and $N = 61$ are chosen. It is evident that in both figures the amplitudes decrease considerably for an original signal with amplitude 1. Figure 1b shows abnormalities in about 280 and 770 samples and Fig. 1c demonstrates irregularities in the first and the last time samples. Here, NPSO is used to select suitable sets of filter parameters primarily for SNR = 5 dB. The result of employing the proposed filter is shown in Fig. 2c. In the proposed approach, the parameters of the NPSO method, as for other evolutionary algorithms, are chosen by trial and error and are as follows: population size = 30; $C_1 = C_2 = 2$; dimension = 2; iteration = 50; w = 1; $2 \leq K \leq 10; 3 \leq N \leq 201$. Note that in this filter, K must be less than N and N must be odd.

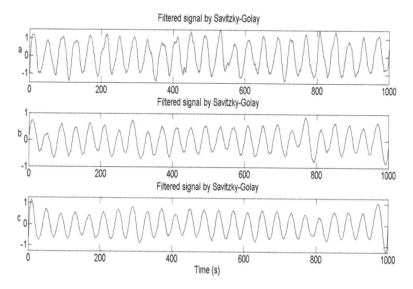

Fig. 1. Results of applying three different sets of K and N for the Savitzky-Golay filter; (a) $K = 3$ and $N = 19$, (b) $K = 5$ and $N = 31$, and (c) $K = 3$ and $N = 61$.

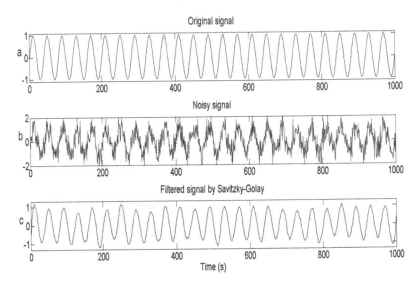

Fig. 2. Improved Savitzky-Golay filter by NPSO (a) original signal, (b) noisy signal (SNR = 5 dB), and (c) optimal filtered signal.

Let $x_1 = \sin(5\pi t)$, $x_2 = \sin(10\pi t)$, and $x_3 = 3\sin(5\pi t)$. For a signal $1 \times n$, $\mathbf{U}$ is a 1×1 matrix and $\mathbf{D}$ is a $1 \times n$ matrix as $\mathbf{D}(i) = 0, 2 \le i \le n$. $\mathbf{D}$ of x_1 and $\mathbf{D}$ of x_2 are equal as well as $\mathbf{U}$ and $\mathbf{V}$ of x_1 and $\mathbf{U}$ and $\mathbf{V}$ of x_2 can be correspondingly different. Therefore, $\mathbf{U}$ and $\mathbf{V}$ can demonstrate the changes in frequency. Moreover, $\mathbf{V}$ of x_1 and $\mathbf{V}$ of x_3 are approximately equal. In addition, $\mathbf{U}$ and $\mathbf{D}$ of x_1 and $\mathbf{U}$ and $\mathbf{D}$ of x_2 can be correspondingly different. Therefore, $\mathbf{U}$ and $\mathbf{D}$ can display the changes in amplitude. From Eq. (4) and for this application, we have:

$$
\begin{aligned}
\mathbf{D} * \mathbf{V}^T &= \begin{bmatrix} D_1 & 0 & 0 & \cdots & 0 \end{bmatrix} \begin{bmatrix} V_{11} & V_{12} & \cdots & V_{1n} \\ V_{21} & V_{22} & \cdots & V_{2n} \\ \vdots & \vdots & \ddots & \vdots \\ V_{n1} & V_{n2} & \cdots & V_{nn} \end{bmatrix}^T \\
&= \begin{bmatrix} D_1 & 0 & 0 & \cdots & 0 \end{bmatrix} \begin{bmatrix} V_{11} & V_{21} & \cdots & V_{n1} \\ V_{12} & V_{22} & \cdots & V_{n2} \\ \vdots & \vdots & \ddots & \vdots \\ V_{1n} & V_{2n} & \cdots & V_{nn} \end{bmatrix} \\
&= \begin{bmatrix} D_1.V_{11} & D_1.V_{21} & D_1.V_{31} & \cdots & D_1.V_{n1} \end{bmatrix}
\end{aligned}
\tag{6}
$$

.

Thus, for this application only $V_{11}, V_{21} = V_{12}, \ldots, V_{n1} = V_{1n}$ have information about the time domain of x and it can be assumed the other terms are equal to 0.

In [15] was shown that $\mathbf{V}$ contains the time domain information of a signal. Considering frequency generally depends on the change in the amplitude of a signal in the time domain, we propose to use $\sum_{i=1}^{n-1} |\mathbf{V}(i+1,1) - \mathbf{V}(i,1)|$ for detecting the changes in frequency of a signal. From these points and that the purpose of signal segmentation is that we detect the changes in amplitude and frequency of a signal, in this paper two combination methods are proposed for feature extraction as follows:

$$SVDS = h_1.\mathbf{U}(1) + h_2.\mathbf{D}(1) + h_3. \sum_{i=1}^{n-1} |\mathbf{V}(1,i+1) - \mathbf{V}(1,i)| \tag{7}$$

$$SVDP = \mathbf{U}^{g_1}.\mathbf{D}(1)^{g_2}. \left(\sum_{i=1}^{n-1} |\mathbf{V}(1,i+1) - \mathbf{V}(1,i)| \right)^{g_3} \tag{8}$$

The reason of using h_1, h_2, and h_3 in $SVDS$ is that in many applications only the change of the frequency of the signal is important, based on the aforementioned states, h_1 and h_2, which depend on the amplitude of a signal, can be equaled to 0 and while only the change of the signal amplitude is significant, h_3, which depends on the frequency of a signal, can be equaled to 0. g_1, g_2, and g_3 are the same situation, i.e. if in an application $g_i = 0(1 \leq i \leq 3)$, it means the corresponding term is not important for that application and vice versa. As mentioned before, when we consider a signal $1 \times n$, $\mathbf{U}$ is a 1×1 matrix or $\mathbf{U} = m$. Therefore, we can consider $\mathbf{U} = 1$, and multiply m in $\mathbf{D}$ that is a signal $1 \times n$ that only $\mathbf{D}(1) \neq 0$. Thus, we reduce three parameters to two parameters, i.e. $\mathbf{D}$ and $\mathbf{V}$. Equations (7) and (8) can be modified as follows:

$$SVDP = (\mathbf{D}(1))^{\alpha_1}. \left(\sum_{i=1}^{n-1} |\mathbf{V}(1,i+1) - \mathbf{V}(1,i)| \right)^{\alpha_2} \tag{9}$$

$$SVDS = \beta_1.\mathbf{D}(1) + \beta_2. \sum_{i=1}^{n-1} |\mathbf{V}(1,i+1) - \mathbf{V}(1,i)| \tag{10}$$

All in all, when amplitude and frequency of a signal change, $\mathbf{D}$ and $\sum_{i=1}^{n-1} |\mathbf{V}(1,i+1) - \mathbf{V}(1,i)|$ respectively change and when $\sum_{i=1}^{n-1} |\mathbf{V}(1,i+1) - \mathbf{V}(1,i)|$ or $\mathbf{D}$ changes, $SVDP/SVDS$ will change. Thus, $SVDP/SVDS$ includes information in both the amplitude and frequency of the signal and is a good feature for the signal segmentation. After, filtering signal, two successive windows are slide along the signal as is shown in Fig. 3. In order to detect the segments' boundaries, GP and GS variations are computed as follows:

$$GP_t = |SVDP_{t+1} - SVDP_t|, \quad t = 1, 2, \ldots, L - 1 \tag{11}$$

$$GS_t = |SVDS_{t+1} - SVDS_t|, \quad t = 1, 2, \ldots, L - 1 \tag{12}$$

where t and L are the number of current window and the total number of analyzed windows, respectively. If the windows are placed in a segment, their statistical properties don't change, in other words, the achieved *SVDP/SVDS* remains approximately constant and equal. However, as can be seen in Fig. 3 when the sliding windows fall in the different segments, *SVDP/SVDS* of each sliding window is not equal, thus their GP_t or GS_t respectively changes and the boundary will be detected.

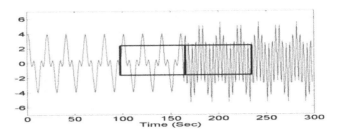

Fig. 3. A window positioned around the change point.

The mean value of $G(\overline{G})$ is selected as the threshold level, meaning that when the local maximum is bigger than this threshold, the current time sample is chosen as a boundary of the segment.

4   Data Simulation and Results

In order to evaluate the performance of the suggested method, we use two kinds of signals, namely, the synthetic data and real EEG signals. The synthetic signal includes the following seven epochs:

Epoch 1: 0.5cos(πt) + 1.5cos(4πt)
+ 4cos(5πt),
Epoch 3: 1.5cos(2πt) + 4cos(8πt),
Epoch 5: 0.5cos(πt) + 1.7cos(2πt)
+ 3.7cos(5πt),
Epoch 7: 0.8cos(πt) + cos(3πt) + 3cos(5πt).

Epoch 2: 0.7cos(πt) + 2.1cos(4πt)
+ 5.6cos(5πt)
Epoch 4: 1.5cos(πt) + 4cos(4πt),
Epoch 6: 2.3cos(3πt) + 7.8cos(8πt),

It is worthy to note that the mentioned signal is a general and comprehensive signal because Epochs 1 and 2 are different only in terms of amplitude, Epochs 3 and 4 are different only in terms of frequency, and the other adjacent epochs have the different amplitude and frequency characteristics at the same time. Thus, we have all possible states in only one signal. In Fig. 4a and b, the synthetic data described above and the filtered signal by Savitzky-Golay are shown, respectively. The result of using *SVDP/SVDS* is shown in Figs. 4c/5c. As can be seen in these figures, all segments are attained correctly. In order to demonstrate the performance of the proposed method, it is compared with three well-known existing ones including FD-based [2], wavelet GLR (WGLR) [7], and modified Varri [12] methods respectively in Figs. 6, 7, and 8. As can be seen, the FD-based method has a boundary selected inaccurately, the WGLR has many wrongly detected boundaries, and the modified Varri method not only cannot detect a segment boundary (missed boundary) but also detect two boundaries incorrectly.

As noted before, signal segmentation is a pre-processing step for EEG signals. Figure 9a shows a real newborn EEG signal which the length of this signal and the sampling frequency are 7500 samples and 256 Hz, respectively [13]. The results of applying the proposed method with using *SVDP* and *SVDS* functions are shown in

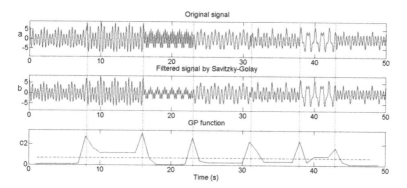

Fig. 4. Result of the proposed technique for the synthetic signal; (a) original signal, (b) filtered signal by improved Savitzky-Goaly filter, and (c) *GP* function result.

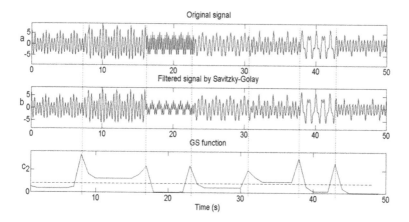

Fig. 5. Result of the proposed technique for the synthetic signal; (a) original signal, (b) filtered signal by improved Savitzky-Goaly filter, and (c) *GS* function result.

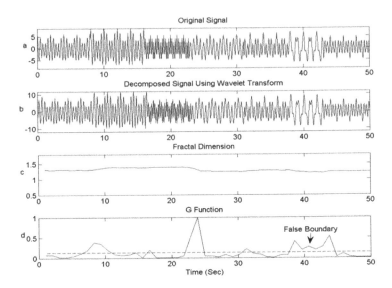

Fig. 6. Signal segmentation based on the fractal dimension for the synthetic signal; (a) original signal, (b) filtered signal by wavelet transform, and (c) fractal dimension of the filtered signal, and (d) G function [2].

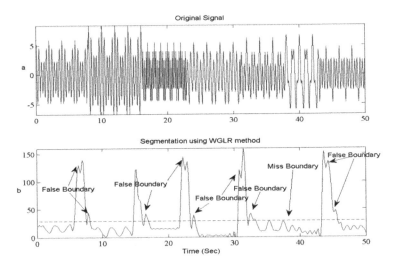

Fig. 7 Signal segmentation by using the WGLR method for the synthetic signal; (a) original signal, (b) output of the WGLR method [7].

Figs. 9c and 10c, respectively. In addition, we test our proposed method by using another EEG signal in Figs. 11 and 12. As can be seen in these four figures, all the segments' boundaries are accurately detected. The importance of using Savitzky-Golay filter is depicted in these two figures, especially in Figs. 11 and 12.

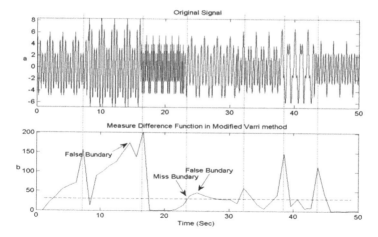

Fig. 8. Signal segmentation based on the modified Varri method for the synthetic signal; (a) original signal, and (b) output of the modified Varri method [12].

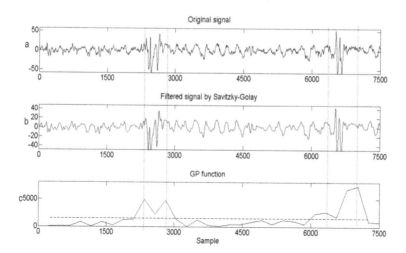

Fig. 9. Result of the proposed technique for the real EEG signal; (a) original signal, (b) filtered signal by improved Savitzky-Goaly filter, and (c) *GP* function result. As can be seen the boundaries for all five segments can be accurately detected.

It should be added that since we wanted to detect changes in both of the frequency and amplitude of the signals, in this article for *SVDS* and *SVDP*, we assign $\alpha_1 = \alpha_2 = \beta_1 = \beta_2 = 1$.

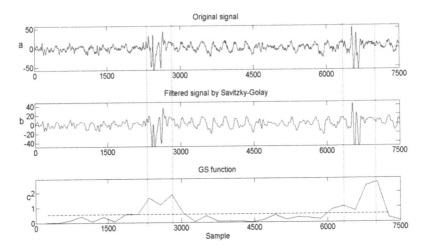

Fig. 10. Result of the proposed technique for the real EEG signal; (a) original signal, (b) filtered signal by improved Savitzky-Goaly filter, and (c) *GS* function result. As can be seen the boundaries for all five segments can be accurately detected.

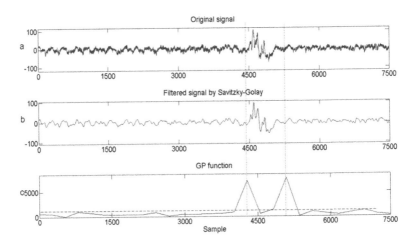

Fig. 11. Result of the proposed technique for the real EEG signal; (a) original signal, (b) filtered signal by improved Savitzky-Goaly filter, and (c) *GP* function. As can be seen the boundaries for all three segments can be accurately detected.

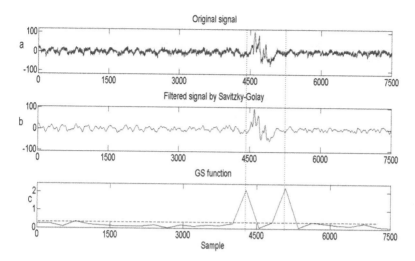

Fig. 12. Result of the proposed technique for the real EEG signal; (a) original signal, (b) filtered signal by improved Savitzky-Goaly filter, and (c) *GS* function result. As can be seen the boundaries for all three segments can be accurately detected.

5 Conclusions

The aim of this work is to investigate and demonstrate the ability of the modified SVD and intelligent Savitzky-Golay filter in segmenting the non-stationary signals such as EEG. Since noise can significantly influence the performance of the segmentation method, the Savitzky-Golay filter is employed. In this article, to select appropriate parameters of this filter, NPSO as a powerful evolutionary algorithm is proposed. It is worthy to mention that providing an intelligent method to reduce the effect of the noise resources based on the Savitzky Golay filter and NPSO is proposed in this article as the first time and can be used in every signal processing applications. Then, two approaches based on the combination of singular values and right-singular vectors of a signal are proposed for segmenting the signals. The results indicate superiority of the proposed method comparing with three well-known methods.

Acknowledgment. The authors wish to thank Prof. Saeid Sanei for his so valuable and kind guidance.

References

1. Sanei, S., Chambers, J.: EEG Signal Processing. Wiley, New York (2007)
2. Anisheh, M., Hassanpour, H.: Designing an adaptive approach for segmenting non-stationary signals. Int. J. Electron. **98**(8), 1091–1102 (2011)
3. Jellema, R.H., Krishnan, S., Hendriks, M.M.W.B., Muilwijk, B., Vogels, J.T.W.E.: Deconvolution using signal segmentation. Chemom. Intell. Lab. Syst. **104**(1), 132–139 (2010)

4. Azami, H., Sanei, S., Mohammadi, K., Hassanpour, H.: A hybrid evolutionary approach to segmentation of non-stationary signals. Digit. Sig. Process. **23**(4), 1–12 (2013)
5. Albaa, A., Marroquínb, J.L., Arce-Santanaa, E., Harmonyc, T.: Classification and interactive segmentation of EEG synchrony patterns. Pattern Recogn. **43**(2), 530–544 (2010)
6. Azami, H., Sanei, S.: Automatic signal segmentation based on singular spectrum analysis and imperialist competitive algorithm. In: 2nd International eConference on Computer and Knowledge Engineering, pp. 50–55 (2012)
7. Wang, D., Vogt, R., Mason, M., Sridharan, S.: Automatic audio segmentation using the generalized likelihood ratio. In: 2nd IEEE International Conference on Signal Processing and Communication Systems, pp. 1–5 (2008)
8. Azami, H., Malekzadeh, M., Sanei, S., Khosravi, A.: Optimization of orthogonal polyphase coding waveform for MIMO radar based on evolutionary algorithms. J. Math. Comput. Sci. **6**(2), 146–153 (2012)
9. Hassanpour, H., Mesbah, M., Boashash, B.: Time-frequency feature extraction of newborn EEG seizure using SVD-based techniques. EURASIP J. Appl. Sig. Process. **16**, 2544–2554 (2004)
10. Savitzky, A., Golay, M.J.: Smoothing and differentiation of data by simplified least square procedure. Anal. Chem. **36**(8), 1627–1639 (1964)
11. Lue, J., Ying, K., Bai, J.: Savitzky-Golay smoothing and differentiation filter for even number data. Sig. Process. **85**(7), 1429–1434 (2005)
12. Kosar, K., Lhotská, L., Krajca, V.: Classification of long-term EEG recordings. In: Barreiro, J.M., Martín-Sánchez, F., Maojo, V., Sanz, F. (eds.) ISBMDA 2004. LNCS, vol. 3337, pp. 322–332. Springer, Heidelberg (2004)
13. Signal Processing Research Centre at Queensland University of Technology

Natural Language Processing

Improving Reordering Models with Phrase Number Feature for Statistical Machine Translation

Neda Noormohammadi[(✉)], Zahra Rahimi[(✉)],
and Shahram Khadivi[(✉)]

Human Language Technology Lab,
Amirkabir University of Technology, Tehran, Iran
noor@ce.sharif.edu, {zah-ra,khadivi}@aut.ac.ir

Abstract. Reordering models in statistical machine translation are crucial for many language pairs. Specifically those with very different sentence structure like Persian and English. In this paper, we enhance the well-known lexical model by taking into account the position of the phrase in the target language. We observe over 1.7 percent relative improvement in BLEU score when comparing the baseline lexical reordering model with the proposed model in an English-Persian task.

Keywords: Statistical machine translation · Reordering model · Lexicalized reordering model · Phrase number feature · Distance based reordering model · Reordering graph

1 Introduction

Variance in syntactic structure of languages is one of the main reasons that machine translation is a hard task. Since, different languages put words in different orders; one of the fundamental challenges of statistical machine translation (SMT) is to translate phrases in the right order.

In recent years several methods have been introduced to solve this challenge. The basic reordering model used in many SMT systems is distance based distortion model (Koehn et al. 2003). Although several complex reordering models have been introduced in the literature, still this simple reordering model is extensively used. At the other hand, lexical reordering model (Tillmann et al. 2004; Koehn et al. 2005; Zens et al. 2006; Xiong et al. 2006; Galley and Manning, 2008) shows its superiority in many SMT tasks.

In this paper due to the disadvantages of distance-based model (Matusov et al. 2010) we propose a new model that is based on distance. Specifically, this model estimates the position of a phrase in the target sentence which is called phrase number feature. To learn this model from the training corpus, we use reordering graph (Su et al. 2010). This reordering model is applied on English-Persian data set and show experimentally that proposed method in combination with reordering model perform better than distance-based distortion model and lexicalized reordering model.

© Springer International Publishing Switzerland 2014
A. Movaghar et al. (Eds.): AISP 2013, CCIS 427, pp. 227–233, 2014.
DOI: 10.1007/978-3-319-10849-0_23

This paper is structured as follows. In the second section, we review related work on reordering in statistical machine translation. In Sect. 3, we first describe the distance-based model and the lexicalized reordering model and then briefly illustrate the reordering graph concept. In Sect. 4, we focus on our new reordering model. We report the translation results on English-Persian translation task in Sect. 5. The last section is assigned to the conclusion of the paper.

2 Related Works

As already mentioned, one of the principal challenges in SMT is how to reorder the translated phrases in the generated target sentence. SMT decoders attempt to put words in the right order by trying many possible phrase orders and evaluating them during the translation process. Trying all possible word reorderings are an NP-complete problem (Knight 1999) therefore many decoders attempt to limit phrase permutations by placing reordering constraints. Monotone translation despite its simplicity is not appropriate for some language pairs.

Another method is distance-based distortion model which often limits movement over a small number of words (Koehn et al. 2003). This model is not appropriate for the language pairs with very different sentence structure. In these language pairs, the long range reordering occurs frequently for some type of phrases so the integration of lexical information into reordering model is recommended.

Some researchers (Tillmann et al. 2004; Koehn et al. 2005; Zens et al. 2006; Xiong et al. 2006; Galley and Manning 2008) propose some lexicalized reordering model that learns different behavior for each specific phrase pair during phrase extraction process. This model should predict for a given phrase whether the next phrase should be oriented to its left or right. These models decide just based on examining the orientation type of adjacent phrase in alignment matrix. But Su et al. (2010) have argued that it is important to consider the number of adjacent phrases in model for better estimations of reordering models. To achieve this goal, they have introduced a structure named reordering graph which is constructed using alignment matrices. Reordering graph presents all possible segmentations for each sentence pair. Another distortion (Al-Onaizan et al. 2006) model assigns a probability distribution over possible relative jumps conditioned on source words. In this model for example adjectives would have a different distribution than verbs or nouns.

3 Reordering Models

Among the models mentioned in previous section, the most relevant ones to our work are investigated in this section. First, distance-based reordering model is presented. Then the lexicalized reordering model is illustrated and at the end, a description on reordering graph concept is stated.

3.1   Distance Based Model

This model that proposed by Koehn, et al. (2003) is a relative distortion model. The model is defined based on the difference between the position of the current phrase and the position of the previous phrase in the source sentence.

Although this model is simple and fast, it has some disadvantages (Matusov et al. 2010). It is obvious that this model is limited to jump over a maximum number of words. So it is not a good reordering model for translation tasks in which the source side language has SOV structure and the target side language has SVO structure or vice versa.

A good example is a translation task including English-Persian language pair. English has a verb-begin structure, whereas Persian is a verb-last language. For these language pairs, the long range reordering for a phrase including a verb is highly penalized by the distance based model.

3.2   Lexicalized Reordering Model

Lexicalized reordering model plays a central role in phrase-based statistical machine translation systems. This model is learned based on the orientation type of a phrase with respect to its adjacent phrases in the alignment matrix. It just checks the previous and next cells of each phrase pair in alignment matrix for determining the orientation type.

There are various approaches for lexicalized reordering model. In the traditional one (Koehn et al. 2005), it collects bilingual phrases from training corpus and determines their orientations according to previous phrase.

The probability distribution for lexicalized reordering model is estimated based on the maximum likelihood principle where $count(O, \bar{f}_{a_i}, \bar{e}_i)$ is calculated from training data. O is orientation of current phrase with respect to previous phrase. $\bar{f}_{a_i}$ is the current source phrase that align with i_{th} target phrase $(\bar{e}_i)$.

$$p(O|\bar{f}_{a_i}, \bar{e}_i) = \frac{count(O, \bar{f}_{a_i}, \bar{e}_i)}{\sum_{o'} count(O', \bar{f}_{a_i}, \bar{e}_i)} \qquad (1)$$

O is monotone (m) or swap (s) or discontinuous (d). These orientations are defined as follows:

$$O = \begin{cases} m & if \ a_i - a_{i-1} = 1 \\ s & if \ a_i - a_{i-1} = -1 \\ d & if \ |a_i - a_{i-1}| \neq 1 \end{cases} \qquad (2)$$

3.3   Reordering Graph

As mentioned before, the traditional lexicalized reordering model just considers the presence of an adjacent phrase. This model does not consider the number of available phrases around a given phrase. To overcome this problem and achieve maximum efficiency, Su et al. (2010) have introduced the reordering graph concept. In their work, for each pair of sentence, reordering graph presents all available paths and derivations to generate the target sentence. In the following, we will briefly describe the necessary steps for constructing the reordering graph for a given bilingual sentence:

Steps for constructing the reordering graph for a given bilingual sentence:

- Extract bilingual phrases as graph nodes
- Determine adjacent phrases for each phrase pair
- Connect each phrase to its adjacent phrases as graph edges

If there is not any phrase around a specific phrase, it is connected to the nearest available phrase in the reordering graph. Also a start node is added to the graph and is linked to all phrase pairs which start the target sentence, and an end node is connected to all phrase pairs which end the target sentence. An example of reordering graph is illustrated in Fig. 1.

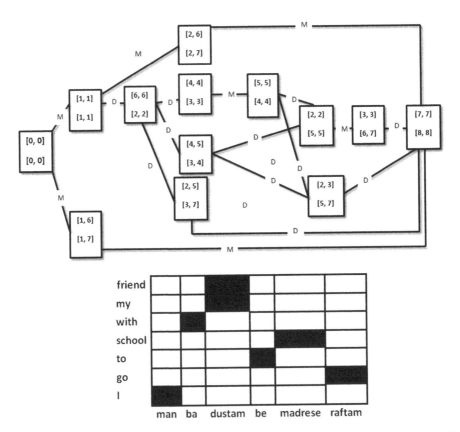

Fig. 1. Each rectangle is a bilingual phrase and each edge is the orientation of each phrase with respect to previous phrase, phrase number for each phrase is the length of path from start node of the graph to that node for example for phrase [2, 2; 5, 5] phrase numbers are 4, 5.

In such a graph, each edge has a label. The label shows the orientation type between two adjacent phrases and the weight indicates what percentage of the total paths goes through this edge. The edge weight is given by:

$$count(o, p', p) = \frac{(\alpha(p)\beta(p'))}{\beta(b_s)} \tag{3}$$

In Eq. 3, α is the number of paths from the start node to node p, $\beta(p')$ is the number of paths from the end node to node p', and o is the label of edge. Then, the fractional count of node p is given by:

$$count(o, p) = \sum_{\forall_{p'}} count(o, p, p') \tag{4}$$

The probability distribution is estimated with applying Eq. 4 in Eq. 1.

4 Proposed Approach

As mentioned above long range reordering is a fundamental challenge in statistical machine translation, for this reordering the position of the phrase in the sentence can be considered as a good feature. This feature is helpful for detecting the type of the phrase. For example Persian have a SOV structure, if a phrase is placed at the end of a sentence; we can guess it is a phrase which probably includes a verb.

In this paper, we propose a new feature for reordering problem, named "phrase number". Phrase number is the translation order of phrases when translating from source language to target language, phrase number is determined for each phrase.

This new model that is called the phrase number reordering model tries to guess the position of a phrase in the target sentence and penalizes phrases based on the phrase number feature. The proposed reordering model is defined in Eq. 5 where δ is the length of jump and $phr\#$ is the phrase number.

$$p(\delta|phr\#) = \frac{count(\delta, phr\#)}{\sum_{\forall_\delta} count(\delta, phr\#)} \tag{5}$$

$count(\delta, phr\#)$ is computed by reordering graph. Equation 6 shows the $count(\delta, phr\#)$ where $\alpha_N(phr\#)$ is number of paths from first node to node N the phrase number of which is phr# and $\beta_N(phr\#)$ is number of paths from last node to node N the phrase number of which is phr#. $\beta(0)$ is sum of all paths in the graph.

$$count(\delta, phr\#) = \frac{\sum_{\substack{\forall N \\ \exists \delta_N = delta}} \alpha_N(phr\#)\beta_N(phr\#)}{\beta(0)} \tag{6}$$

The phrase numbers for each phrase are extracted from the reordering graph. Based on the number of paths to each node in the graph, its phrase numbers are different. Therefore, we must extract all phrase numbers for each phrase.

In the training step, the model using reordering graph is learned which jumps are normal for each phrase number. Since the model does not use any lexical information and just utilizes the number of phrase, so we consider it as a content independent model.

We smooth Eq. 5 as follows where $p_s(\delta)$[1] is a probability distribution which is used for smoothing and α[2] is a linear-mixture parameter.

$$p_{smooth}(\delta|phr\#) = (1 - \alpha)p(\delta|phr\#) + \alpha p_s(\delta) \qquad (7)$$

This model adds as a feature to Moses decoder. When the sentence is translated in decoding step, its segments are selected based on an order. Phrase number is number of selection of phrase in this sequence. In other word, the phrase that is selected before has a smaller phrase number.

5 Experimental Results

The training corpus is used in our experiment is Persian-English Verbmobil Corpus. The direction of translation is English to Persian. Test set of this corpus is four reference set. A statistical summary of this corpus is given in Table 1.

Table 1. Statistical summary of English-Persian Verbmobil Corpus

	English	Persian
Train: sentences	23145	23145
Running words	249335	216577
Singleton	2501	2415
Tune sentences	276	276
Test sentences	250	250

We choose Moses (Koehn et al. 2007) as experimental decoder. GIZA ++ (Och and Ney 2003) and the "grow-diag-final-and" heuristic are used for generating word alignments. A 3-gram language model is generated by SRILM toolkit (Stolcke, 2002). MERT (Och 2003) is used for tuning various feature weights.

The translation quality is evaluated by BLEU score (Papineni et al. 2002). We compared the following setups: (Table 2)

Table 2. The BLEU score for methods

Reordering model	BLEU
Distance based distortion model	24.6
Lexicalized reordering model	26
Lexicalized + phrase number	**27.9**

---

[1] The smoothing method is a geometrically decreasing distribution.
[2] For the experiments reported in this paper, we use $\alpha = 0.1$, which is set empirically.

6   Conclusions

In this study, we focus on improving reordering using phrase number feature and propose new reordering model. Experimental results on test set demonstrate the effectiveness of our method. we use reordering graph concept to extract phrase numbers.

Experimental results on Persian-English corpus shows the effectiveness of our method on languages with long distance reordering. Our method in combination with lexical reordering model performs better than lexical reordering model and distance-based reordering model alone.

We plan to use weighted reordering graph for extracting phrase numbers. Also, we decide to integrate lexical information with phrase number model and investigate the impact of it.

References

Al-Onaizan, Y., Papineni, K.: Distortion models for statistical machine translation. In: Proceedings of ACL, pp. 529−536 (2006)

Galley, M., Manning, C.D.: A simple and effective hierarchical phrase reordering model. In: Proceedings of EMNLP 2008, pp. 848-856 (2008)

Koehn, P., Och, F.J., Marcu, D.: Statistical phrase-based translation. In: Proceedings of HLT-NAACL 2003, pp. 127−133 (2003)

Koehn, P., Axelrod, A., Mayne, A.B., Callison-Burch, C., Osborne, M., Talbot, D.: Edinburgh system description for the 2005 IWSLT speech translation evaluation. In: Proceedings of IWSLT (2005)

Koehn, P., Hoang, H., Birch, A., Callison-Burch, C., Federico, M., Bertoldi, N., Cowan, B., Shen, W., Moran, C., Zens, R., Dyer, C., Bojar, O., Constantin, A., Herbst, E.: Moses: open source toolkit for statistical machine translation. In: Proceedings of ACL 2007, Demonstration Session, pp. 177−180 (2007)

Matusov, E., Kopru, S.: Improving reordering in statistical machine translation from farsi. In: AMTA the Ninth Conference of the Association for Machine Translation (2010)

Knight, K.: Squibs and discussions: de-coding complexity in word-replacement translation models. Comput. Linguist. 25(4), 607–616 (1999)

Och, F.J., Ney, H.: *Giza ++:* Training of statistical translation models (2000)

Och, F.J.: Minimum error rate training in statistical machine translation. In: Proceedings of ACL 2003, pp. 160−167 (2003)

Papineni, K., Roukos, S., Ward, T., Zhu, W.-J.: BLEU: a method for automatic evaluation of machine translation. In: Proceedings of ACL, pp. 311−318 (2002)

Stolcke, A.: SRILM - An extensible language modeling toolkit. In: Proceedinge of ICSLP, vol. 2, pp. 901−904 (2002)

Su, J., Liu, Y., Lü, Y., Mi, H., Liu, Q.: Learning lexicalized reordering models from reordering graphs. In: Proceedings of ACL 2010, Short Papers, pp. 12−16 (2010)

Tillmann, C.: A unigram orientation model for statistical machine translation. In: Proceedings of HLT-NAACL 2004, Short Papers, pp. 101−104 (2004)

Zens, R., Ney, H.: Discriminative reordering models for statistical machine translation. In: Proceedings of Workshop on Statistical Machine Translation 2006, pp. 521−528 (2006)

An Automatic Prosodic Event Detector Using MSD HMMs for Persian Language

Fatemeh Sadat Saleh$^{(\boxtimes)}$, Boshra Shams, Hossein Sameti,
and Soheil Khorram

Sharif University of Technology, Tehran, Iran
{saleh, bshams, khorram}@ce.sharif.edu,
sameti@sharif.edu

Abstract. Automatic detection of prosodic events in speech such as detecting the boundaries of Accentual Phrases (APs) and Intonational Phrases (IPs) has been an attractive subject in recent years for speech technologists and linguists. Prosodic events are important for spoken language applications such as speech recognition and translation. Also in order to generate natural speech in text to speech synthesizers, the corpus should be tagged with prosodic events. In this paper, we introduce and implement a prosody recognition system that could automatically label prosodic events and their boundaries at the syllable level in Persian language using a Multi-Space Probability Distribution Hidden Markov Model. In order to implement this system we use acoustic features. Experiments show that the detector achieves about 73.5 % accuracy on accentual phrase labeling and 80.08 % accuracy on intonation phrase detection. These accuracies are comparable with automatic labeling results in American English language which has used acoustic features and achieved 73.97 % accuracy in syllable level.

Keywords: Prosody · Accentual · Intonational · Hidden Markov Model · Multi-Space Probability Distribution HMM

1 Introduction

Prosody is comprised of information including variations of the pitch contour, rhythm, and lexical stress patterns of spoken utterance. These prosodic events are suprasegmental effects that operate at a level higher than the local phonetic context. Speakers use these prosodic effects to provide cues to the listener and help for better interpretation of their speech and better spoken language understanding [1].

In this paper, we introduce and build an automatic detector for labeling prosodic events trained with a small number of manually labeled samples, and after that could automatically label large corpora in real time.

Previous models were widely focused on prosody labeling at the phone level. It is important to note that, prosodic characteristics are often not related to the information of the phonetic level and are only associated with phrase semantics [2]. Therefore, it is more preferable to consider prosodic features at syllable level.

Wightman and Ostendorf [3] proposed Automatic detection of prosodic events for the first time at syllable level. Their modeling was based on posterior probabilities

© Springer International Publishing Switzerland 2014
A. Movaghar et al. (Eds.): AISP 2013, CCIS 427, pp. 234–240, 2014.
DOI: 10.1007/978-3-319-10849-0_24

computed from acoustic features using decision tree. In [4] the prosodic features were combined and applied to time series modeling framework and in works such as [5], GMM and ANN have been used to classify phrase boundaries using features extracted from syllable level. In [6] a prosody recognition system that detects prosodic boundaries at word and syllable level in American English language using CHMM was introduced. It is believed that the acoustic features of prosodic events consist of multiple streams of information that are correlated but are not always synchronous [6]. Thus, we can take advantage of HMM models with multiple feature streams to deal with asynchrony between acoustic features.

Moreover, one of the problems with fundamental frequency ($F0$) modeling as one of the most important prosodic features is that $F0$ values are not defined in the unvoiced region. MSD-HMM [7] is a practical solution to deal with this problem. In this paper we design an automatic prosodic labeling that can detect Intonational Phrases and Accentual Phrases boundaries in syllable level for Persian language, based on MSD-HMM modeling.

The remainder of this paper is organized as follows. The prosodic event definitions are proposed in Sect. 2. Section 3 presents the proposed methodology. Section 4 presents some experimental results, and finally some conclusions are given in Sect. 5.

2 Prosodic Events Definitions

There are two prosodic constituents in the prosodic structure of the Persian language. The smallest prosodic unit in Persian is the Accentual Phrase (APs) [8]. According to linguistic experts, 6 types of APs are defined for Persian language. Although there may be minor differences in the definitions of these types, in this research we define APs as shown in Table 1. The next level of prosodic events in Persian language is Intonational Phrase (APs) that consists of one or more APs.

Table 1. Persian prosodic AP's definitions [8]

H*	For initially stressed words and phrases and also one-syllable words
L+H*	For words and phrases with final stress
l,h	The part of an Accentual Phrase between the pitch accent and the AP end is handled by a boundary tone, which can be high or low, named here as h and l
L+	For words and phrases losing their stress in sentence
p	For showing silence in sentences

The right boundary of an IPs is determined with a low or high boundary tone that is specified with L% or H% [8].

3 Methodology

In this part, we explain our methodology in two sections. First, we introduce the feature used and then the structure of the model.

3.1 Features

In this paper three features are used for modeling. Each feature is introduced in below. In order to compute feature vectors, the frame length is considered to be 5 ms.

Fundamental Frequency (F0). Fundamental Frequency is one of the most important characteristics of the speech signal. In voiced frames, speech signal is periodic with period T in time domain. The numeric value of $F0$ in each frame is $F_0 = \frac{1}{T}$. $F0$ with its first and second derivative are applied as features in three different streams in HMM model. These features efficiently affect detector performance. The speech analysis software used throughout this work to extract pitch track is Praat (Boersma and Weenink 2007) [9].

$F0$ values are not defined in the unvoiced region and the observation sequence of an $F0$ pattern is composed of one-dimensional continuous value and discrete value which represent "unvoiced". However, we cannot apply both the conventional discrete and continuous HMMs to such observations like $F0$. In this paper we model the fundamental frequency ($F0$) with a kind of HMM in which the state output probabilities are defined by Multi-Space Probability Distributions. This kind of HMM model is called MSD-HMM [7].

MSD-HMM can model the sequence of observation vectors with different dimensionalities. So we can model observed $F0$ values in a one-dimensional space and the "unvoiced" segments in a zero-dimensional space.

Intensity. Intensity is a measure of the energy flux, averaged over the period of the signal. To obtain the intensity values we have employed these steps: first hamming windows of the length 400 samples are applied to the signal and the result is squared. Then an averaging is performed on the results. Consecutive frames are processed with a shift of 80 samples.

Duration. In each syllable, the repetition of vowel phonemes determine the duration of that syllable. Therefore, we can generate a vector of duration values for each utterance.

3.2 MSD-HMM

In order to model $F0$ patterns, we assume two spaces, named Ω_1 and Ω_2 representing one-dimensional space for $F0$ in voiced regions and single zero-dimensional space for the unvoiced regions, respectively. In general, we consider Ω_g as one of G sub-spaces with its own dimensionality and probability w_g of observation space Ω of an event E, so we have,

$$\Omega = \bigcup_{g=1}^{G} \Omega_g, \quad \sum P(\Omega_g) = 1 \tag{1}$$

If the dimensionality of each space n_g, is greater than zero, then it has a probability distribution function $N_g(x)$ and if it equals zero, this sub-space contains only one sample point. Here, event E is representing an observation O that consists of a set of space indices X and a random variable $x \in R^n$, that is $O = (X, x)$.

Note that dimensionality of each sub-spaces is depicted by n in X and observation probability of o is defined as below,

$$b(o) = \sum_{g \in s(o)} w_g N_g(V(o)) \tag{2}$$

where $s(o) = X$, $V(o) = x$ and $N_g(V(o))$ is a pdf in the sub-space in which random variable x is distributed. In Eq. (2), w_g is the mixture weight for g-th Gaussian, so it is considered as the prior probability of g-th sub-space.

As described before, in order to obtain an automatic prosody recognizer, $F0$ contour curve plays an important role in recognition process, so since the observation sequences of $F0$ patterns are regarded as one-dimension continuous values in voiced regions and as a discrete symbol in unvoiced regions, we employ multi-space distribution probability HMM (MSD-HMM) for modeling discontinuity of fundamental frequency.

To start modeling, first we consider an HMM model λ of the appointed type with N number of states in which the initial states, transition and the state output probability distribution is specified as, $\pi = \{\pi_j\}_{j=1}^{N}$, $A = \{a_{ij}\}_{i,j=1}^{N}$ and $B = \{b_i(.)\}_{i=1}^{N}$ respectively, where,

$$b_i(o) = \sum_{g \in s(o)} w_{ig} N_{ig}(V(o)), \; i = 1, 2, \ldots, N \tag{3}$$

Each state i has G pdfs $N_{i1}(.), N_{i2}(.), \ldots, N_{iG}(.)$ with their corresponding weights $w_{i1}(.), w_{i2}(.), \ldots, w_{iG}(.)$, so that we can calculate the observation probability of sequence O as follows;

$$P(o|\lambda) = \sum_{allq} \prod_{t=1}^{T} a_{q_{t-1}q_t} b_{q_t}(o_t) = \sum_{allq,X} \prod_{t=1}^{T} a_{q_{t-1}q_t} w_{q_t X_t} N_{q_t X_t}(V(o_t)) \tag{4}$$

where $q = \{q_1, q_2, \ldots, q_T\}$ denotes state sequence, $X = \{X_1, X_2, \ldots, X_T\} \in \{s(o_1), s(o_2), \ldots, s(o_T)\}$ is a sequence of possible space indices for the observation sequence O and $a_{q_0j} = \pi_j$. The modified forward and backward algorithms are utilized for computing observation probabilities. The modified Viterbi algorithm is utilized for the decoding. These algorithms are similar to traditional HMM algorithms [7].

3.3   Structure of Model

The main structure of the proposed automatic prosody detector system is similar to an automatic speech recognizer. In fact the prosodic event sequences with maximum likelihood probability are defined as below,

$$P^* = \operatorname*{argmax}_{P} p(A|P) \cdot p(P) \tag{5}$$

where $A = \{a_1, a_2, \ldots, a_n\}$ is set of acoustic features and P is a candidate sequence of prosodic events. Also $p(P)$ is the probability of a given prosodic event sequences.

Finally a prosodic event sequences $P^* = \{p_1^*, p_2^*, \ldots, p_n^*\}$ with the maximum probability will be found through the Viterbi algorithm. In this paper, we have used a left to right MSD-HMM with 5 states and 5 streams. Three streams are $f0, \Delta f0, \Delta^2 f0$ each consisting of two Gaussian distributions. One is defined with zero variance and mean that is for modeling MSD-HMM and the other is a usual Gaussian distribution. Another stream for intensity is a 3-dimensional Gaussian distribution and includes $I, \Delta I, \Delta^2 I$. Finally the fifth stream is a one dimensional Gaussian distribution and contains the duration values. Figure 1 shows the structure of MSD-HMM which used in this paper. As the figure clearly shows, this model is a 5-state left to right HMM with 5 streams.

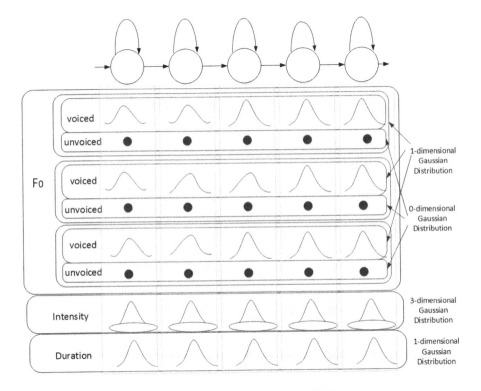

Fig. 1. The structure of used MSD-HMM

4 Experiments

4.1 Experiments Conditions

In order to evaluate the performance of this automatic prosodic detector, a speech database in Persian language was used. This database has been designed after Arctic database in English and contains the speech utterances of two speakers. These utterances are designed in order to satisfy the following conditions [10]:

- Each sentence is short enough to be recorded easily.
- The utterances are phonetically balanced and contain Persian diphones and syllables.

The sentences have been selected from Peykare corpus [11]. The selected sentences contain 5 to 20 words. Final sentences are selected in a way to cover most frequent Persian words and also most frequent syllables. There are some questions and exclamatory sentences, too.

4.2 Experiments Results

Among 1300 available utterances, 1000 utterances were used for training the models and 300 utterances were used for evaluation. There is no overlap between training data and evaluation data. It should be noted that this database is tagged manually with prosodic labels by a linguist. Table 2 shows the results of this automatic prosody detector. The accuracy is the ratio of truly labeled prosodic events by the proposed system to all prosodic events of the utterances.

Figure 2 shows an utterance tagged by prosodic labels. As it is obvious from the figure, pitch contour is an important factor to recognize the prosodic labels. Also the results in Table 2 show that $F0$ is the most important factor in this detector system, but intensity and duration have certain effects on detecting these labels.

In [6] a prosody recognition system that detects stress and prosodic boundaries at the word and syllable level in American English using a coupled Hidden Markov

Table 2. The accuracy results of automatic prosodic event detector

Features	AP	IP
F0	56.5 %	68.8 %
F0, intensity	63.33 %	77.35 %
F0, intensity, duration	73.5 %	80.08 %

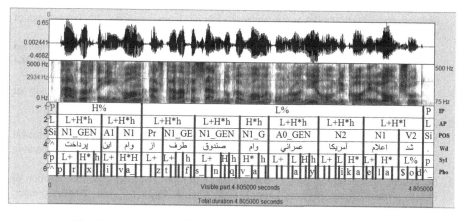

Fig. 2. An utterance which has been tagged with prosodic events.

Model (CHMM) has been introduced. Experiments show that the recognizer achieves 72.03 % accuracy at word level 73.97 % accuracy at the syllable level using acoustic features. The results of our algorithm for Persian language is comparable with these results in American English language.

5   Conclusion

In this paper, we introduced and implemented an automatic prosodic event detector for Persian language. This system is able to detect the Accentual Phrases and Intonational Phrases for Persian utterances. We used fundamental frequency ($F0$), intensity and duration as features. In this article MSD-HMM is used and finally the most probable prosodic sequence is obtained using maximum likelihood criterion. The proposed method reaches 73.5 % accuracy for Accentual Phrase detection and 80.08 % for Intonational Phrase detection.

References

1. Sridhar, V., Bangalore, S., Narayanan, S.: Exploiting acoustic and syntactic features for automatic prosody labeling in a maximum entropy framework. IEEE Trans. Audio Speech Lang Process. **16**(4), 797–811 (2008)
2. Milone, D.H., Rubio, A.J.: Prosodic and accentual information for automatic speech recognition. IEEE Trans. Speech Audio Process. **11**(4), 321–333 (2003)
3. Wightman, C., Ostendorf, M.: Automatic labeling of prosodic patterns. IEEE Trans. Speech Audio Process. **2**(4), 469–481 (1994)
4. Chen, K., Hasegawa-Johnson, M., Borys, S.: Prosody dependent speech recognition with explicit duration modeling at intonational phrase boundaries. In: Proceedings of Eurospeech (2003)
5. Chen, K., Hasegawa-Johnson, M., Cohen, A.: An automatic prosody labeling system using ANN based syntactic-prosodic model and GMM-based acoustic-prosodic model. In: International Conference on Acoustics, Speech and Signal Processing, vol. 1, pp. 509–512 (2004)
6. Ananthakrishnan, S., Narayanan, S.S.: An Automatic prosody recognizer using a coupled multi-stream acoustic model and a syntactic-prosodic language model. In: Proceedings of ICASSP, pp. 269–272 (2005)
7. Tokuda, K., Masuko, T., Miyazaki, N., Kobayashi, T.: Multi-space probability distribution HMM. Inst. Electron. Inform. Commun. Eng. (IEICE) Trans. Inform. Syst. **85**(3), 455–464 (2002)
8. Sadat Tehrani, N.: The Intonational Grammar of Persian. Ph.D. thesis, The University of Manitoba (2007)
9. Praat: doing phonetics by computer, http://www.fon.hum.uva.nl/praat/
10. Bahaadini, S., Sameti, H., Khorram, S.: Implementation and evaluation of statistical parametric speech synthesis for Persian language. In: Proceedings of Machine Learning Signal Processing (MLSP) (2011)
11. Bijankhan, M., Sheikhzadegan, J., Bahrani, M., Ghayoomi, M.: Lessons from creation of Persian written corpus: Peykare. Lang. Resour. Eval. J. **45**(2), 143–164 (2010). Springer, Netherlands

Word-Level Confidence Estimation for Statistical Machine Translation Using IBM-1 Model

Mohammad Mahdi Mahsuli$^{(\boxtimes)}$ and Shahram Khadivi

Human Language Technology Lab, Department of Computer Engineering
and Information Technology, Amirkabir University of Technology
(Tehran Polytechnic), Tehran, Iran
{mahsuli,khadivi}@aut.ac.ir

Abstract. New confidence measures for machine translation using lexical translation models are presented. Confidence estimation for machine translation is a method for labeling each word as "correct" or "incorrect" in the output of a machine translation system. Compared to the existing measures, the measures proposed in this paper, offer the advantage of not relying on the system output, such as N-best lists or word graphs. As a result, these confidence measures are applicable to all types of machine translation systems. Experiments have been carried out on the translation of news lines in English-Farsi language pair. The result indicates the superior performance of the new confidence measures to similar existing ones. Finally, a method of tagging unlabeled training samples is introduced. This method - which has given promising results in the evaluation of machine translation, but not yet used in confidence estimation - is called translation error rate.

Keywords: Confidence estimation · Confidence measure · Machine translation · Natural Language Processing · Lexical translation model · Translation error rate

1   Introduction

Many free and commercial machine translation (MT) systems are available for both online and desktop use. However, errors are common in such translations. There are several sources of error, such as syntax mismatch between the source and the target languages, ambiguity in selecting the proper translation, and different choices for reordering of words. Nonetheless, the advantage of using MT systems justifies their vast usage, such as saving time and effort of human translators through translation hypotheses suggestions for post-editing, instead of translating from scratch. This suggestion process must yield a shorter post-editing time than what is required to carry out the traditional translation. To this end, there is a need to predict whether the machine-translated text is good enough to be used in post-editing. The research area addressing this problem is referred to as Confidence Estimation (CE) [1].

© Springer International Publishing Switzerland 2014
A. Movaghar et al. (Eds.): AISP 2013, CCIS 427, pp. 241–249, 2014.
DOI: 10.1007/978-3-319-10849-0_25

1.1   A Brief Overview of Statistical Machine Translation Principle

Let $\mathbf{f} = f_1,\ldots,f_J$ be the source sentence, which is to be translated by a Statistical Machine Translation (SMT) system. Also, let $\hat{\mathbf{e}} = e_1,\ldots,e_I$ be the target sentence that is generated by the system. $\hat{\mathbf{e}}$ must be the most probable sentence given $\mathbf{f}$:

$$\hat{\mathbf{e}} = \underset{\mathbf{e}}{\operatorname{argmax}}\ P(\mathbf{e}|\mathbf{f}) \tag{1}$$

By employing the Bayes rule, Eq. 1 is re-written as:

$$\hat{\mathbf{e}} = \underset{\mathbf{e}}{\operatorname{argmax}}\ P(\mathbf{e})P(\mathbf{f}|\mathbf{e}) \tag{2}$$

In Eq. 2, $P(\mathbf{e})$ is computed from a monolingual language model and estimates the correctness of the destination sentence. The term, $P(\mathbf{f}|\mathbf{e})$ is computed from a bilingual translation model and estimates the accuracy of translating $\mathbf{e}$ to $\mathbf{f}$. SMT systems can make mistakes that stem from several sources, such as insufficient training data. The latter leads to imprecise estimation of language and translation models. It is important to detect these mistakes and, confidence measures provide an effective means for this purpose.

2   Literature Review

2.1   Motivation and Principle of Confidence Estimation

Consider a generic application that for any given input $x \in X$ of a fixed input domain, X returns a corresponding output value $y \in Y$ of a fixed output domain Y. Moreover, suppose that this application is based on an imperfect technology, in the sense that the output values y can be "correct" or "incorrect" (with respect to some well-defined evaluation procedure). Formally, we can associate a binary tag $C \in \{0,1\}$, 0 for incorrect and 1 for correct, to each output y, given its corresponding input x. In machine translation, x is a sequence of words in a given source language and y is the equivalent sequence of words in a different target language [2].

CE has been extensively studied for speech recognition, but it is less known in other research areas like machine translation. This task can be applied in sentence, phrase, or word level. By the level of CE, we consider which segment of the SMT system's output the CE system should judge its correctness. Through post-edition, even a sentence which has some erroneous words may be usable. Therefore, word-level CE can be helpful for highlighting the incorrect words and reducing the time needed for post-editing.

Another possibility is to apply confidence measures in an interactive translation environment where a system proposes translations of the input text and a human translator can either accept or correct them. The system then adapts its proposals according to the modifications by the human translator. In such an environment, the system would only output those words that have a high confidence, and discard the others. Thus, it would spare the human translator time and effort for reading and correcting bad output. This approach to computer assisted translation is pursued for example in the European project TransType2.

The third and most challenging application of word-level confidence estimation is the scenario in which search criteria is based on confidence estimates. The translation hypotheses proposed by the system (represented e.g. in a word graph or an N-best list) can be recombined in order to find a better translation than the one preferred by the translation system [1].

Since we wanted to use CE in a post-edition application, word-level CE was focused on. To estimate the confidence of a word e_i produced from an SMT system (i.e. the i-th word of sentence $\mathbf{e}$), one could use the probability that generating the word e in the i-th position of the destination sentence, given the source sentence $\mathbf{f}$ leads to a correct translation [3].

$$\text{word confidence} = P(correct|i, e_i, \mathbf{f}) \qquad (3)$$

However, since the concept of correctness is not clear enough in word-level CE, this probability is difficult to be estimated directly and accurately. Therefore, researchers in the research area have proposed different measures to reflect the correctness (or a score depending on it) of each word in SMT system's output sentence.

2.2   Related Work

Blatz et al. [1] have proposed a variety of features at word level which can be categorized as below:

- Target language based features: These include semantic features which take advantage of WordNet's semantic similarity and polysemy (lexical ambiguity) count, basic syntax check for mismatching parentheses, and/or quotation marks.
- Word posterior probabilities and related measures: These include relative frequencies, rank-weighted frequencies and word posterior probabilities.
- IBM-1 model [4]: For a given target word e, this feature is just e's contribution to the total target probability:

$$C_{IBM-1\_f\_avg}(e) = P(e|\mathbf{f}) = \sum_{j=0}^{J} P(e|f_j)/(J+1). \qquad (4)$$

In Eq. 4, $\mathbf{f} = f_1, \ldots, f_J$ is the source sentence, and f_0 is the empty source word.
- SMT model based features: These features are based directly on the *Alignment Template* MT model. In this model, The SMT system segments the source and the target sentences into bilingual phrases called alignment templates.

Ueffing et al. [5] have also presented several confidence measures for statistical machine translation:

- Word posterior probabilities calculated on both word graphs and N-best lists: The word posterior probability can be determined by summing up the posterior probabilities of all sentences which contain this specific word in position i or aligned to the corresponding source positions. These confidence measures only exploit the information contained in the output of an SMT system.

- Relative frequency: For each word $\hat{e}_i$ in the best target sentence, the number of sentences in the N-best list containing this word in a position aligned to i is defined. Then, the relative frequency of word $\hat{e}_i$ in the N-best list with respect to the Levenshtein alignment is taken directly as a confidence measure:

$$C_{rel}(\hat{e}_i) = \frac{1}{N} \sum_{n=1}^{N} \delta(\hat{e}_i, \mathcal{L}_i(\hat{e}_1^I, w_1^{I_n})). \tag{5}$$

- Rank sum: This feature is simply the sum of the ranks of those target sentences containing word $\hat{e}_i$ as $\mathcal{L}_i(\hat{e}_1^I, w_1^{I_n})$ (normalized by the total rank sum):

$$C_{rank}(\hat{e}_i) = \frac{\sum_{n=1}^{N} (N-n).\delta(\hat{e}_i, \mathcal{L}_i(\hat{e}_1^I, w_1^{I_n}))}{\frac{N}{2}(N+1)}. \tag{6}$$

In Eq. 6, since we want ranks near to the top of the list to be scored better, we sum N-n instead of the rank n.

Furthermore, Ueffing & Ney [6] have proposed another confidence measure based on IBM-1 model. They modified the confidence measure defined in Eq. 4 by Blatz et al. [1], in order to prevent the average lexicon probability from being dominated by the maximum. In other words, the maximal translation probability of the target word e over the source sentence words can be defined as:

$$C_{IBM-1\_f\_max}(e) = \max_{j=0,...,J} P(e|f_j), \tag{7}$$

where f_0 is the empty source word.

3 Our Approach to Confidence Estimation

As introduced in [6], confidence measures based on IBM-1 model do not rely on system output and are thus applicable to all types of machine translation systems. Therefore, we have used four different confidence measures based on IBM-1 model:

- Forward average word posterior probability as defined in Eq. 4 by Blatz et al. [1].
- Forward maximal word posterior probability as defined in Eq. 7 by Ueffing & Ney [5].
- *Backward average estimation of word posterior probability:

$$C_{IBM-1\_b\_avg}(e) = P(\mathbf{f}|e) = \sum_{j=0}^{J} P(f_j|e)/(J+1). \tag{8}$$

- *Backward maximal estimation of word posterior probability:

$$C_{IBM-1\_b\_max}(e) = \max_{j=0,...,J} P(f_j|e). \tag{9}$$

Features marked with '*' have not been used before. To compute these values, we used lexicon probability tables (lex.e2f and lex.f2e) given by GIZA++ [7]. In the cases where no entry was available in the lexicon probability table, we used zero probability. Since the lexicon probability tables have been learnt previously at training process of SMT, the process of computing these four confidence measures becomes as easy as a search for specific entries in a table and putting their average or maximal value. This leads to very low cost in terms of time and computation.

Since most applications of CE (specifically our focused application, Interactive Computer-Assisted Translation) use binary decisions, we decided to directly use classifiers (instead of performing regression and applying thresholds). However, there's no conflict between these two approaches and we can use the probabilities given by classifiers (if needed in the future). We think that these probabilities can reflect the confidence of samples.

4 Experimental Setting

4.1 Corpora

The experiments were performed on the news part of the AFEC English-Farsi corpus [8]. This corpus contains parallel sentences in news domain. The corpus statistics are given in Table 1. We used the well-known SMT tool – Moses [9] – for phrase-based English to Farsi translation. Translation quality of our SMT system is given in Table 2.

Table 1. Statistics of the training, development and test corpora

		English	Farsi
Train	Sentences	282,227	
	Running Words	6,993,837	7,544,447
	Vocabulary	135,365	126,511
Dev	Sentences	400	
	Running Words	11,705	13,692
	OOVs	994	165
Test	Sentences	418	
	Running Words	11,870	13,945
	OOVs	1,113	181

4.2 Baseline Systems

We have dedicated two baseline models in our experiments. For the first baseline system (denoted by "Baseline1"), we have used three confidence measures which are reported to give promising results in [5]. These features are the word posterior probabilities, relative frequency, and rank sum. Since the word posterior probabilities calculated on the N-best list gives us better results than calculating them on the word graph [6], we decided to calculate this feature on the N-best list with N = 100.

Table 2. Translation quality [%] of the utilized SMT system on the test corpus described in Table 1

	English→Farsi
WER	38.3
PER	26.2
TER	20.6
BLEU	29.7

The second baseline system (denoted by "Baseline2") consists of two features based on IBM-1 model: the target word's contribution to the total target probability (Eq. 4) [1], and the maximal translation probability of the target word over the source sentence words (Eq. 7) [6].

4.3   Word Error Measures

In machine translation, it is not intuitively clear how to classify the output words of a system as "correct" or "incorrect" when comparing to one or more reference translations. On the other hand, tagging the output words using human judgment requires spending much time and money. Therefore, a number of word error metrics have been applied to tag the training instances of the CE system. Common word error measures are:

- Pos: This error measure considers a word as correct if it occurs in exactly this target position in one of the reference translations.
- WER (Word Error Rate): A word is counted as correct if it is Levenshtein-aligned to itself in one of the references.
- PER (Position-independent word Error Rate): A word is tagged as correct if it occurs in one of the reference translations. Here, the reference is regarded as a bag of words, i.e. the number of occurrences per word is taken into account.
- Set: In this error measure, the number of occurrences per word is not considered, i.e. a word occurring in the translation three times is tagged as correct every time, even if the reference contains it only once or twice. This is a less strict variant of PER.
- n-gram: This metric considers the word as well as its $n-1$ predecessors in the hypothesis and labels only those words as "correct" that occur in the references together with this history. n is chosen to be 2, 3, and 4.

In addition to the word error measures above, we used a measure which has been widely used in the evaluation process of machine translation and gives correlated results with human judgment, but has not been used in CE yet. This error measure is Translation Error Rate (TER) [10] and can be defined as below:

Through TER, words in a hypothesis can be added, deleted, and substituted (as in WER), in order to adapt the hypothesis into a reference. In addition, words in the hypothesis can be shifted. If a word in the hypothesis is aligned to a reference word according to TER, we consider the word to be correct.

All error metrics except for n-gram exist in two variants: First, each translation hypothesis is compared to the pool of all references (i.e. four different reference translations for our corpus). Second, we determine the reference that has the minimum distance to the hypothesis according to the metric under consideration and classify the words as "correct" or "incorrect" with respect to this reference. That is, under the metric PER for example, the pooled variant labels all those words which occur in any of the references, as "correct"; whereas the second variant considers only those words correct that are contained in the nearest reference [1]. In our experiments, we have used WER, PER, and TER as word error measures. These error measures are used with the pooled variant in order to tag the labels as "correct" in a more relaxed manner.

4.4   Evaluation Metric

After computing the confidence measures, we give their values to the desired machine learning method in addition to the tag that is computed using WER, PER, or TER. After training the model, we can now compute the confidence measures on the new test samples and get their estimated tags as "correct" or "incorrect". Afterwards, the performance of the CE system is evaluated using Classification Error Rate (CER). This is defined as the number of incorrectly[1] classified tags divided by the total number of generated words in the translated sentences.

5   Experiments

Table 3 shows the performance of four different sets of confidence measures on the hypotheses generated from our phrase-based SMT system. All experiments were performed using 10-fold cross validation. We see that in all settings, CE systems which use lexical translation models outperform "Baseline1". In addition, by comparing results from "Baseline2" with "IBM-1", we can see that adding the two proposed confidence measures decreases CER in comparison to using only forward features.

Finally, adding "IBM-1" to "Baseline1" leads to the best results when using WER or TER as word error measure. It is a valuable point that in all cases, our proposed features based on lexical translation models take part in the best CE system.

In most cases, J48 method gives us the best result. This machine learning method has benefits such as simplicity of implementation, high speed and low memory usage.

Moreover, overall performance is best reported when using TER as the word error measure. The fact that PER and TER are more relaxed than WER is well-known. It seems that TER has a higher correlation with human judgment in comparison to WER and PER. This can be studied by tagging the SMT's output words by a human translator and calculating correlation between each of these tag sets and human judgment.

---

[1] Not to be confused with "correct" and "incorrect" tags.

Table 3. CER[%] for different sets of confidence measures on the English→Farsi test set, references based on WER, PER, and TER. Hypotheses from phrase-based system. The best overal value is printed in bold. The best value for each CE system is marked with '*'.

CE System	ML Method	CER[%] on English→Farsi		
		WER	PER	TER
Baseline1	Naïve Bayes	*35.2	27.5	22.7
	MLP	*35.2	26.6	20.8
	RBF	*35.2	26.5	20.8
	J48	35.5	*26.4	*20.6
Baseline2	Naïve Bayes	35.8	26.3	25.8
	MLP	33.1	25.4	*19.5
	RBF	33.0	26.4	20.6
	J48	*32.8	*24.4	19.6
IBM-1 ($f_{avg}+f_{max}+b_{avg}+b_{max}$)	Naïve Bayes	37.8	31.5	31.3
	MLP	33.2	26.2	*19.6
	RBF	34.0	26.5	20.7
	J48	*32.5	**23.6**	19.7
Baseline1 + IBM-1	Naïve Bayes	32.5	27.2	22.4
	MLP	32.1	26.0	**19.4**
	RBF	33.3	26.3	20.8
	J48	**31.4**	*23.9	19.7

6   Conclusion and Outlook

Two new word-level confidence measures are presented with the advantage of independence from the MT system. In other words, contrary to other confidence measures, these measures do not rely on the system output, such as N-best lists or word graphs. They also have a very low computational cost because their input values are computed *a priori*. These confidence measures are hence applicable to all types of MT systems. Experiments are carried out on the translation of news lines in English-Farsi language pair. It is shown that the new confidence measures outperform similar existing measures.

Next, a method of tagging unlabeled training samples, called Translation Error Rate is introduced. This method - which has given promising results in the evaluation of MT, but not yet used in CE – is more relaxed than WER and PER methods and seems to have a higher correlation with human judgment when compared to them.

The future research direction is first to propose confidence measures based on different aspects of translation and next, to perform experiments using Probabilistic Graphical Models. The latter is a machine learning approach that employs label sequences to tag a sample's label. In the next stage, experiments will be performed on other corpora. Finally, correlation of TER with human judgment will be compared to WER and PER and its suitability for use in the field of confidence estimation will be tested.

Acknowledgement. The authors would like to thank Ms. Marzieh Salehi Shahraki for implementing the "Baseline1" system.

References

1. Blatz, J., Fitzgerald, E., Foster, G., Gandrabur, S., Goutte, C., Kulesza, A., Sanchis, A., Ueffing, N.: Confidence estimation for machine translation. Technical report, JHU/CLSP Summer Workshop (2003)
2. Gandrabur, S., Foster, G., Lapalme, G.: Confidence estimation for NLP applications. ACM Trans. Speech Lang. Process. **3**(3), 1–29 (2006)
3. Raybaud, S., Lavecchia, C., Langlois, D., Smaïli, K.: New confidence measures for statistical machine translation. In: Proceedings of the International Conference on Agents and Artificial Intelligence, pp. 61–68, Porto, Portugal (2009)
4. Brown, P.F., Pietra, V.J.D., Pietra, S.A.D., Mercer, R.L.: The mathematics of statistical machine translation: Parameter estimation. Comput. Linguist. **19**, 263–311 (1993)
5. Ueffing, N., Macherey, K., Ney, H.: Confidence measures for statistical machine translation. In: Proceedings of MT Summit IX. Citeseer (2003)
6. Ueffing, N., Ney, H.: Word-level confidence estimation for machine translation using phrase-based translation models. In: Proceedings of the Conference on Human Language Technology and Empirical Methods in Natural Language Processing, pp. 763–770. Association for Computational Linguistics (2005)
7. Och, F.J., Ney, H.: Giza++: Training of statistical translation models. Technical report, RWTH Aachen, University of Technology (2000)
8. Jabbari, F., Bakhshaei, S., Mohammadzadeh Ziabary, S.M.: Developing an Open-domain English-Farsi Translation System Using AFEC: Amirkabir Bilingual Farsi-English Corpus. In: The Fourth Workshop on Computational Approaches to Arabic Script-based Languages, p. 17 (2012)
9. Koehn, P., Hoang, H., Birch, A., Callison-Burch, C., Federico, M., Bertoldi, N., Cowan, B., Shen, W., Moran, C., Zens, R.: Moses: open source toolkit for statistical machine translation. In: Proceedings of the 45th Annual Meeting of the ACL on Interactive Poster and Demonstration Sessions, pp. 177–180. Association for Computational Linguistics (2007)
10. Snover, M., Dorr, B., Schwartz, R., Micciulla, L., Makhoul, J.: A study of translation edit rate with targeted human annotation. In: Proceedings of association for machine translation in the Americas, pp. 223–231 (2006)

ACUT: An Associative Classifier Approach to Unknown Word POS Tagging

Mohammad Hossein Elahimanesh[1]([✉]), Behrouz Minaei-Bidgoli[2], and Fateme Kermani[1]

[1] Computer Research Center of Islamic Science, Qom, Iran
elahimanesh@noornet.net, kermani_f@yahoo.com
[2] Iran University of Science and Technology, Tehran, Iran
b_minaei@iust.ca.ir

Abstract. The focus of this article is unknown word Part-of-Speech (POS) tagging. POS tagging which is one the fundamental requirements for intelligent text processing based on texts language. Therefore, this article firstly aims to provide a POS tagger with high accuracy for Persian language. The technique which is proposed by this article for handling unknown words is using a combination of a type of associative classifier along with a Hidden Markov Models (HMM) algorithm. Associative classification is a new classification approach integrating association mining and classification. The associative classifier used in this study is a type of associative classifiers that is innovated by this research. This kind of classifier not only uses sequence probability but also uses the CBA classifier. CBA first generates all the association rules with certain support and confidence thresholds as candidate rules. It then selects a small set of rules from them to form a classifier. When predicting the class label for an example, the best rule whose body is satisfied by the example is chosen for prediction. Based on the experimental results, the proposed algorithm can increase the accuracy of Persian unknown word POS tagging to 81.8 %. The total accuracy of proposed tagger is 98 % and its sentence accuracy is 63.1 %.

Keywords: Part-of-Speech tagging · Associative classifier · Hidden Markov Model · Unknown words

1 Introduction

In recent years the Natural Language Processing (NLP) has become an obsession for researchers in the area of computer and linguistics. Using computer and intelligent equipment has caused to do the tasks related to text with considerable accuracy and speed; moreover, it has made it possible to enter the areas which were unimaginable.

For instance we can mention Machine Translation (MT), semantic searches, intelligent text summarizing and so forth in this field. On the other hand each language alone can be the subject of all of the NLP applications. Alongside with that and in this article one of the NLP challenges which is called unknown words POS tagging has been addressed and put on the spotlight.

An Unknown word is a word that its occurrence is lower than a specific threshold in a unit of teaching of statistical methods, and rule-based engines are not capable of

© Springer International Publishing Switzerland 2014
A. Movaghar et al. (Eds.): AISP 2013, CCIS 427, pp. 250–263, 2014.
DOI: 10.1007/978-3-319-10849-0_26

handling it. So there are no specific tags for these words in the previous tagging. In the past research, these thresholds have values between 0 to 10 [1, 21]. Unknown word is also called unseen or out of the vocabulary words.

Taking into account the ability of natural language to produce new words, the problem of unknown words has always been a problem in natural language processing tasks. Hence, much research has already been done in the past. A series of works such as unknown word identification [8], unknown word syntactic processing [6], unknown word meaning [18] and the unknown word sense detection [7].

Unknown words can cause many problems for NLP tasks. For example, if the POS tag of a word in sentence is not set correctly. Then, it will be difficult to parsing and translation the sentence of this word. Furthermore, many of these words are not possible to analysis via rule base approaches. Thus, this paper presents an approach to deal with this problem using statistical features of unknown words. This approach uses one of the best classifier that called CBA classifier [10].

The rest of this article consists of five sections. In Sect. 2, the POS tagging is presented. Section 3 presents the works which have been done before. Proposed algorithm is presented in Sect. 4. Section 5 explains the results of the tests and experiments. Conclusion and future work are presented in Sect. 6.

2 Part of Speech Tagging (POS Tagging)

In computational linguistics, POS tagging of words in a text is the process of tagging each word with an appropriate POS tag. Given a string of words (for example: $W = w_1 w_2 \ldots w_n$), POS tagging of the words in this string can be shown with the Eq. (1):

$$POST(W) = T \tag{1}$$

Where T is series of POS tags like $t_1 t_2 \ldots t_n$, For example, suppose the following tagset is available (Table 1).

Equivalent tags of the words in the Persian phrase "گذشت/passed عمر/life من/my, اما/ but تو/you NULL/are در/in منی/my خیال/mind" will be as follows (Table 2).

Table 1. A simple POS tagset.

Part of Speech tag	Abbrevation
V	Verb
N	Noun
PRO	Pronoun
CONJ	Conjunction
P	Preposition
PUNC	Punctuation

Table 2. An example of POS tagged sentence.

8	7	6	5	4	3	2	1
منی	خیال	در	تو	اما	من	عمر	گذشت
V	N	P	PRO	CONJ	PRO	N	V

3 Related Works

Recently, many works have been done for Persian POS tagging. Also, many types of POS tagging algorithms have been applied in these works. For example, Hidden Markov Model (HMM) algorithm is one of the most popular tagging techniques that have been used in these researches [4, 14, 17]. Another type of POS taggers is Memory Based taggers (MBT) which has been used by Raja et al. [15] for Persian texts.

In addition to the above methods, the hybrid methods have been used for tagging as well. For example Fadaei et al. [9], using a combination of linguistic rules with bigram tagger, have tried for tagging Persian texts with a high accuracy rate.

In many of the previous studies the issue of tagging of unknown words is examined and evaluated. For example, Behmanesh [4] in his research has showed TNT algorithm [3] is capable of corrects tagging of Persian unknown words with 77 %. This algorithm is applied a type of HMM algorithms which is used for analyzing unknown words using their suffixes. This technique of solving the problem of unknown words has previously been studied by Samuelsson [16]. Fadaei et al. [9] has demonstrated that, assuming a 12 % coverage rate for Persian unknown words, the words can be tagged with an accuracy of 88 %. In the results section, some other previous studies of tagging for Persian unknown words are introduced.

4 Proposed Algorithm

As noted above, HMM tagger is one of the best POS taggers. Our proposed algorithm is a special kind of above HMM tagger which makes use of the famous data mining technique which is called mining association rules to solve the problem of unknown words.

In fact, the words which are detected as unknown word are analyzed by proposed algorithm. In this research, TNT algorithm [3] that is a type of HMM algorithms is used as a basis for the proposed algorithm. But the solution of unknown word POS tagging problem was replaced by our innovated associative classifier.

Associative classification is a new classification approach integrating association mining and classification [19].

If you are going to take a closer look at how the proposed algorithms works, we should know how many pre-processing steps have been used before a word tagged.

During pre-processing, the input text is broken into its constituent sentences. Separating the input text and splitting it into its constituent sentences.

In next step, a window of five words is taken into account for each word (see below) that the word is in middle of it. If the word is w_i, the corresponding window contains the words w_{i-1} and w_{i-2} of the words before and the words w_{i+1} and w_{i+2} of the words after (see Fig. 1). In fact, the usage of this window is to consider the impact of the words before and after the word under the discussion of its POS tagging.

Fig. 1. A sequence of 5 sequential words

We can show that the radius of two words adjacent to a word is the best radius it term of processing time and tagging accuracy. This radius is used in many previous papers. For example, Toutanova and his colleagues have used the same window to make the features of their learning engine [20]. Toutanova and his colleagues algorithm which is known by the name of Stanford University log linear POS tagger, has obtained the best results for English texts POS tagging. Recent developments of this tagger performed by Manning [12].

In this study, an unknown word is analysed in two steps. In the first step, try to analyse the word with ACUT procedure. The abbreviation ACUT stands for Associative Classifier Unknown-word Tagger and refers to our proposed approach in this paper. Finally, considering the inability of the previous step, the word is tagged with label N that is the most probable tag for unknown words in our testing environment. This tag stands for the Name. In the following we explained ACUT as the main above mentioned steps.

4.1   ACUT

ACUT consists of four parts. These four parts together make a powerful solution for Persian unknown word POS tagging. These four parts are: First, A few simple and efficient rules. Second, using of CBA associative classifier as a main part. Third, the use of other CBA classifier answers. And fourth, normalization as a post-processing. These four components are described below.

A Few Simple Heuristic Method. The first part explained in this section. In fact, a large number of unknown words follow simple patterns. For example, we can mention the numbers. Words in form of numbers include the characters 0 to 9, with a decimal separator characters (.). In this test in this research numbers are tagged by the name of NUM. It is possible to recognize words by a regular expression.

In addition to the numbers, there are other types of words which are made partly from numbers and partly from Persian characters. These kinds of words are often tagged ADJ which stands for adjective. For example, the word "22-part" or "22-episode" can be named. Recognizing these types of words is possible by regular expressions as well.

The third type was developed for the English words. These words are labeled RES which means miscellaneous. These are the words of the English alphabet with numbers in which at least one of the English alphabets exists. To detect this kind of words, regular expressions are used again.

Based on above heuristic and practical ways we can obtain 99.1 % accuracy for tagging the NUMs as well as ADJ with the same accuracy and that of RES with accuracy of 81.1 %.

In this study, an unknown word is analyzed in two steps. In the first stage, some simple and heuristic methods are used for detecting the tag of unknown word. The second stage processes the words that are not analyzed at the first place. Finally, considering the inability of the previous two steps, the word is tagged with label N that is the most probable tag for unknown words. This tag stands for the Name. In the following we explain the second and most important steps in detail.

Making Associative Classifier. A suitable associative classifier for tagging unknown words includes five steps. Among these steps, the construction of association rules, evaluation of production rules, using these extracted rules to make a CBA classifier [10], combining this classifier with sequential probabilities and as a final step, the normalization. Each of the aforementioned steps is studied in detail. It is the second stage.

Mining Association Rules. As it is mentioned above the second stage of unknown words analysis is using the association rules. With the assumption that each word along with its features in the training data can be assumed as the antecedent of an association rule and the corresponding tag of that word be the consequent of the rule. So, we can produce rules whose condition part of which is the features of that word and the result part is the word tag. Each word and its adjacent words can be illustrated under a directed graph (Fig. 2).

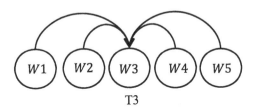

T3

Fig. 2. Effect of context feature on POS of word W3 in a directed graph

The above graph shows the word W3 and two adjacent words on its left as well as two adjacent words in the right. In this graph, the word W3 is marked with T3. As noted above, the best case is regarding the effect of 2 neighbor words for the discussed word. Table 3 contains a set of rules that are the result of the tag word W3 (T3) and the condition can be obtained from the above graph.

To generate the Table 3, the 4 words surrounding W3 are used. Any word in condition section can be either in the presence state or absence state. The absence of words such as W1 is marked by symbol (-).

For example, given word "اما/but" from Table 2, the sixth rule (W1-W4- → T3) is:

$$\text{تو - عمر - } \rightarrow CONJ$$

Table 3. Association rules that created from previous graph (Fig. 2)

Number	If part	Then part
1	W1W2W4W5	T3
2	W1W2W4-	T3
3	W1W2-W5	T3
4	W1W2–	T3
5	W1-W4W5	T3
6	W1-W4-	T3
7	W1–W5	T3
8	W1—	T3
9	-W2W4W5	T3
10	-W2W4-	T3
11	-W2-W5	T3
12	-W2–	T3
13	–W4W5	T3
14	–W4-	T3
15	—W5	T3
16	——	T3

Another type of association rules can be achieved by the word W3 itself (regardless of background characteristics of the word). If we assume that n is equal to W3 word length, the word can be found as:

$$W3 = w_{3,1}w_{3,2}...w_{3,n-1}w_{3,n} \tag{2}$$

In the above equation, each $w_{3,i}$ shows a character of W3. Given that the greatest suffix of W3 starts from $w_{3,2}$ and continues to $w_{3,n}$, the total number of possible extensions of this word is equal to n − 1. In this assumption, the linguistic suffixes of W3 are not considered and the end of the word as a sequence of several characters in as suffix is spotted. With this type of production, W3 can have the longest and largest suffix, the largest prefix and also the largest infix. The following figure (Fig. 3) shows the largest possible affixes for W3 word which are produced by our method.

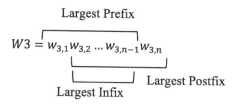

Fig. 3. Largest affixes of word W3

Having both the largest infixes and the way to compute these infixes, all prefixes, infixes and suffixes of word W3 can be produced. Table 4 shows the possible number of prefixes, suffixes and infixes that can be generated by this method.

Table 4. Number of affixes that created in this project for a word with length n

Type of affix	Count
Prefix	n − 1
Infix	$\frac{(n-2)(n-1)}{2}$
Postfix	n − 1

In order to make association rules, for each word in the training corpus, we calculate a set of rules which are taken from the context and those of the word itself. Number of produced rules for each word is calculated as follows:

$$|R_{w3}| = \frac{1}{2} * (n^2 + n) + 16 \tag{3}$$

For example, this amount for a word with length of 5 has 31 rules. Number of rules generated and the different distributions of these rules are provided in test results. Four rule sets which are accordingly called rules set of background, suffix rules set, a set of infix rules and a set of prefix rules are resulted from the process of making association rules.

Evaluation of Association Rules. Two criteria are used to assess association rules, support measure and confidence measure. Given a rule R as follows:

$$R : A \rightarrow B \tag{4}$$

Supports standard rules of R is equal to the number of transactions in Section A to the total number of transactions. If we consider S to be the set of all transactions, the rate of this measure which is shown with sup(R) can be calculated as follows:

$$sup(R) = \frac{|(s \in S; s \ contain \ A \ \& \ B)|}{|S|} \tag{5}$$

In the above equation, |S| is equal to the number of elements in set S. The benchmark of confidence rule of R is equal to the recurrence ratio of B in transactions involving A to the number of transactions involving A. The amount that is shown by conf (R) is calculated as follows:

$$conf(R) = \frac{|(s \in S; s \ contain \ A \ \& \ B)|}{|(s \in S; s \ contain \ A)|} \tag{6}$$

Other criteria such as Interest, Jaccard and Coefficient are used to evaluate the association rules whose usage results for tagging unknown Persian words can be seen in [5]. For more information about these criteria you can refer to [19].

Evaluating association rules generated from the last section comprises the training corpus is done. And each one of the words from the training corpus is considered to be a transaction.

Using Association Rules. The rules, which are made out of association rules after being evaluated, and filtered, turn into our rules set. This rules set forms the basis of the analysis of the proposed algorithm of unknown words. Words, which are recognized as Unknown during the tagging process are not detected as unknown words by the first stage of the analysis, can be analyzed by the using these rules.

To do this, first a list of all the Condition sections of the association rules that can be gained from an unknown word is generated. However, all rules are made out of ones which are included in the condition section of the above list. The resulting list is considered as a list of enabled or active rules for the unknown word. This list is specified by the symbol L in our research.

Although the list L possesses different solutions for tagging an unknown word, the results need to be sorted according to priority. To do this, the list L is arranged in terms of confidence and support respectively. Given the fact that this sort of prioritizing views confidence and support as two significant criteria, the results would be more promising in comparison with the use of confidence or support single pose. The sorted list above is called SL whose first response can be used as the tag name. For example, if you search for the word "انسانگر/humanist", some items in the beginning of the list SL are equal to:

As Table 5 shows, the first rule tags, the word "humanist" as an ADJ. The correct tag for this word is ADJ which proves the correct diagnosis or detection.

Another example of the application of association rules for the word "محسوسش/ appreciable" is some basic elements of corresponding word which are included in the following table:

As Table 6 shows, the first rule tags, the word "محسوسش" as an N. The word is correctly labeled as ADJ so it is a mistake to rule 1. This error can be corrected in two ways. The first way is to use better techniques for sorting rules. The second way that is used by this algorithm is to use all the answers in different phases or Fuzzy logic for all

Table 5. The first seven rules that fired for word "انسانگر/humanist" (sample 1)

Sample N.	N.	Rule type	If part	Then Part	Support count	Confidence
1	1	Postfix	ن گرا	ADJ	22	1
1	2	Postfix	ان گرا	ADJ	9	1
1	3	Infix	نسان گر	N	7	1
1	4	Postfix	سان گر	N	7	1
1	5	Postfix	انسان گر	N	7	1
1	6	Postfix	گرا	ADJ	7	0.96
1	7	Postfix	گرا	ADJ	217	0.94

Table 6. The first seven rules that fired for word "محسوسش/appreciable" (sample 2)

Sample N.	N.	Rule type	If part	Then part	Support count	Confidence
2	1	Postfix	وسش	N	5	1
2	2	Infix	حسو	ADJ	1,350	0.98
2	3	Prefix	محسو	ADJ	1,342	0.98
2	4	Postfix	سش	N	569	0.97
2	5	Infix	سوس	N	587	0.84
2	6	Postfix	ش	N	97,206	0.8
2	7	Infix	حسوس	ADJ	50	0.79

the answers. Answers rated higher have a closer connection with or attachment to the result section of those words for tagging unknown word. The obtained Fuzzy solutions from this method are clarified by tagging.

Sequential Associative Classifier (SAC). As it was shown in the previous example, it is highly likely that after sorting the list of active rules, the correct answer is not in the front of the SL. Thus, designing a mechanism by which the other answers can be utilized is an explicit focus of this research and is taken into consideration.

Using all the answers of association rules in a meaningful and balanced way as well as clarifying the relation among them with the help of Hidden Markov Model is the proposed approach or solution of this study by exploiting or making use of next or other answers, and the classification which results from that is called SAC.

Hidden Markov Model Tagging requires a probability table for each tag so that each row in the table specifies is the probability of each word with part of speech tagging (P(W|T)). Computing this table for unknown words is not possible since they do not exist in training corpus. Our proposed solution to compute the probabilities is the following relationship. Following equation shows the way the fuzzy amount of attachment of estimated word T for unknown word ($W_{unknown}$) is calculated.

$$P(W_{unknown}|T) = \frac{1}{1 + \alpha * \beta}(1 - P(T)) \tag{7}$$

In the above equation, P(T) is the prior probability of the tag T. It is equal to the number of occurrences of that tag in train corpus to all the words in this corpus. The value of α shows the rank of tag T in the list of fired rules. The β variable is a simple coefficient that tuned between 1 and 20 in experiments. In fact, classifier SAC is using the above equation to calculate the needed probabilities of the hidden Markov model algorithm for unknown samples. These probabilities cannot calculate by using the training data set directly.

In fact, SAC classification is a technique that provides more power for analyzing unknown words in combination with HMM and CBA algorithms. This technique can be used in many usages like, Machine Translation (MT), Name Entity Recognition (NER) and also Name Phrase Chunking (NP Chunking).

Managing the Impact of Word Count on Association Rules. There are some delicate points in making rules that can improve the quality of which when they are given heed. One of these points is the effect of occurrence of the different words in train corpus. Many words such as کشور/country, ایران/Iran and اسلامی/Islamic are the most repeated words in this corpus, and also the rules that created from this words have a high rating on support count. Also, when these words are not ambiguous (each word has one and only one possible POS tag), the confidences of created rules are very high. The following table (Table 7) shows the three words along with words whose prefixes are similar and take different label.

Table 7. Three group of words that have similar prefix but different POS Tags

Group Id	Word	POS Tag	Count
1	کشور	N	23,261
1	کشته	V	1,058
1	کشمیری	AJ	30
1	کشان کشان	ADV	12
2	اسلامی	AJ	18,361
2	اسلام	N	5,071
2	اسلامی اند	V	4
3	ایران	N	21,687
3	ایرانی	AJ	2,758
3	ایرانی ام	V	3

If we evaluate a rule like R: Prefix "کش" → N support count would equal to 23,261 and confidence of 95.5 %. While a rule like R: Prefix "کش" → V has support count of 1,058 and with a confidence of about 4.3 %, which is considered a very low accuracy. This type of construction of rules creates an optimism towards the rules that created from the mostly repeated words and consequently weakens the chances of rules that create from less repeated words. This issue can be solved by balancing the number of times a word is repeated so that the impact of the number of repetition is preserved and also that greedy manner is dismissed. The impact of this normalization is presented in the chapter concerned with tests and experiments.

5   Experimental Results

Experiments for this study have been performed on 10 million words Bijankhan corpus [2]. This corpus also called Peykare. The words in this corpus are tagged in two levels, from one hand there are just 14 main tags and on the other hand there are about 606 partial tags.

This version of Bijankhan corpus is the newest version of this corpus. During testing process in this article 90 % of the corpus is used for training data and the rest for the test data. In this research, first-level labels of this corpus have been used. Repetition

Table 8. Percent of known and unknown word in the corpus

Word type	Count	Coverage percent
Known	977,447	99.20 %
Unknown	7,546	0.80 %

rate of known and unknown words in this test is shown in Table 8. The calculated values in the following table are given by assumed ambiguity threshold of 0.

To prepare four rule sets for unknown words, the training data are used. After generating all possible rules from training data set, the rules of prefixes, suffixes and Infixes with confidence of less than 0.6 have been removed. Rules of the context words are huge. In our study, more than 50 million of these rules have been found. These rules are first filtered based on the support count of less than 5 and then refiltered based on confidence rate of less than 0.6. Table 9 indicates each rule set with number of rules remained.

Table 9. Created rule sets in this project

Rule set	Count of rules
Prefix rules	228,757
Infix rules	391,532
Postfix rules	250,155
Context rules	1,136,905
Total rules	2,007,349

Table 10 shows the results of utilizing the resolving phases for problems of unknown words in this study. In the Basic level, each unknown word tagged with tag N that is the most likely tag for these types of words. As the Table 10 shows, method number 6 includes the best results for Persian unknown word POS tagging. With the

Table 10. Result of proposed algorithms on Peykare

Id	Approach	Sentence accuracy	Known accuracy	Unknown accuracy	Total accuracy
1	Basic	61.3 %	98.1 %	59.4 %	97.8 %
2	TNT	61.8 %	98.1 %	65.1 %	97.9 %
3	Heuristic approach	61.8 %%	98.1 %	66.2 %	97.9 %
4	Heuristic approach + CBA	62.9°%	98.1 %	79.6 %	98 %
5	Heuristic approach + CBA + SAC	63 %	98.1 %	81.2 %	98 %
6	**ACUT** (Heuristic approach + CBA + SAC + Normalization)	**63.1 %**	**98.1 %**	**81.8 %**	**98 %**

improving 21.8 % compared to the Basic approach, it represents the accuracy of 81.8 % for unknown words POS tagging. In this method, the value of 14 for β in Eq. (7) is chosen. Normalizing range of 0 to 1000 has been used.

Since different rates of unknown words in previous researches have been applied, in order to compare the proposed method with previous researches, we have chosen the same amount of unknown words repetition rate. To do this the words in the training data are sorted based on the number of occurrences of that word in the corpus in an ascending list. Then the first element of the list considered as unknown word and fetched to reach the desired level of repetition rate. Comparison results are shown in the Table 11.

Table 11. Comparison between ACUT and most popular Persian POS Tagger

Approach	Unknown percent	Unknown accuracy	Total accuracy	ACUT unknown accuracy
A1	2 %	73.50 %	95.90 %	87.60 %
A2	12 %	88 %	90.90 %	90 %
A3	1.80 %	79.44 %	96.94 %	87.30 %
A4	2 %	69.35 %	96.07 %	87.60 %

In Table 11, the A1 algorithm is given by Mohseni and Minaei-Bidgoli [13]. The corpus used in A1 is the same we have used here. We have divided the corpus into two separating parts, part one 80 % as training data and part two 20 % as the test data. The rate of occurrence of unknown words of this study is different from the results we obtained.

Approach A2 shows the proposed method by Fadaei and Shamsfard [9]. Given that his research showed the highest accuracy in all of previous researches, the comparison of the proposed algorithm on his corpus is required. But with all the effort, the corpus used by Fadaei and Shamsfard was not available, so we have compared only through this type of comparison.

A3 is another research which is done by Raja and his colleagues in the past [15]. The rate of unknown words in this study is about 1.8 %. The final method of comparing is A4, this approach has been used by Behmanesh [4]. The repetition rate of unknown words in this research is about 2 %.

Finally, we note the fact that association rules have a very high capability to detect the tags of unknown words. In our research and for complex words, 18 rules fired in average. Considering the sorting method that we have used in this research, the probability of the correct answer in the first answer is 79 %, and 92 % in the first two answers, and 95 % in one of the first three answers.

6   Conclusion and Future Work

In this research a method for tagging Persian unknown words has been offered. This method can be used along with any other tagging methods. Also several tests for evaluating this method combined which TNT tagging algorithm was done. The results at the best state shows 8.18 % accuracy for tagging unknown words and 98.1 % accuracy for tagging known words. The proposed method of this research which is known as ACUT (Associative Classifier Unknown Tagger) is a combination of some simple heuristic rules, CBA classification SAC classifier and a type of normalization. SAC classification is a technique that provides more power for analyzing unknown words in combination with HMM and CBA algorithms.

Also, for the first time, we have provided a Persian sentence boundary detection. The results of experiments in this research for the best state showed 63.1 % sentence detection accuracy. This accuracy is better than best English sentence POS tagger [12]. As an improvement for proposed algorithm, other associative classifiers like CMAR [11] and CPAR [22] can be offered. Also it is offered to use classifiers like SVM for choosing correct answer among SL list.

Acknowledgments. The authors would like to thank Noor Text Mining Research group of Computer Research Center of Islamic Sciences (www.noorsoft.org) for supporting this work.

References

1. Attia, M., Foster, J., Hogan, D., Roux, J.L., Tounsi, L., van Genabith, J.: Handling unknown words in statistical latent-variable parsing models for Arabic, English and French. In: SPMRL 2010, pp. 67–75 (2010)
2. Bijankhan, M., Sheykhzadegan, J., Bahrani, M., Ghayoomi, M.: Lessons from building a Persian written corpus: Peykare. Lang. Resour. Eval. **45**(2), 143–164 (2011)
3. Brants, T.: TnT: a statistical part of speech tagger. In: Proceedings of the 6th Conference on Applied Natural Language Processing, 29 April–04 May, Association for Computational Linguistics Morris-town, USA (2000)
4. Behmanesh, A.A., Pilevar, A.H.: Statistical part of speech tagger for Persian words. In: JeTou 2011 (2011)
5. Elahimanesh, M.H., Minaei-Bidgoli, B.: Making part of speech taggers robust to unknown words, pp. 45–47. M.Sc. thesis, Islamic Azad University, Qazvin branch (2012, in Persian)
6. Erbach, G.: Syntactic processing of unknown words. IWBS report 131, IBM, Stuttgart (1990)
7. Erk, K.: Unknown word sense detection as outlier detection. In: Proceedings of NAACL 2006, New York, NY (2006)
8. Fu, G., Luke, K.-K.: Chinese unknown word identification using class-based LM. In: Su, K.-Y., Tsujii, J., Lee, J.-H., Kwong, O.Y. (eds.) IJCNLP 2004. LNCS (LNAI), vol. 3248, pp. 704–713. Springer, Heidelberg (2005)
9. Fadaei, H., Shamsfard M..: Persian POS tagging using probabilistic morphological analysis. Int. J. Comput. Appl. Technol. 264–273 (2010)
10. Liu, B., Hsu, W., Ma, Y.: Integrating classification and association rule mining. In: KDD'98, New York, NY, August 1998
11. Li, W., Han, J., Pei, J.: CMAR: accurate and efficient classification based on multiple class-association rules. In: proceedings of ICDM, pp. 369–376 (2001)
12. Manning, C.D.: Part-of-Speech tagging from 97% to 100%: is it time for some linguistics? In: Gelbukh, A.F. (ed.) CICLing 2011, Part I. LNCS, vol. 6608, pp. 171–189. Springer, Heidelberg (2011)

13. Mohseni, M., Minaei-Bidgoli, B.: A system for Persian text corpora POS Tagging and disambiguation. B.E. dissertation, 78 pp. Iran University of Science and Technology, Tehran (2008, in Persian)
14. Okhovvat, M., Minaei-Bidgoli, B.: A hidden Markov model for Persian part-of-speech tagging. In: Proceedings of Procedia CS, pp. 977–981 (2011)
15. Raja, F., Tasharofi, S., Oroumchian F.: Statistical POS tagging experiments on Persian text. In: Second Workshop on Computational Approaches to Arabic Script-Based Languages, 21–22 July 2007, Stanford, California (2007)
16. Samuelsson, C.: Morphological tagging based entirely on Bayesian inference. In: 9th Nordic Conference on Computational Linguistic NODALIDA-93, Stockholm University, Stockholm, Sweden (1993)
17. Seraji, M.: A statistical part-of-speech tagger for Persian. In: Proceedings of the 18th Nordic Conference of Computational Linguistics NODALIDA 2011. NEALT Proceedings Series, pp. 340–343 (2011)
18. Taylor, J.M., Raskin, V., Hempelmann, C.F.: Towards computational guessing of unknown word meanings: the ontological se-mantic approach. In: Cognitive Science Conference, Boston, MA (2011)
19. Tan, P.N., Steinbach, M., Kumar, V.: Introduction to Data Mining. Addison-Wesley, Boston (2005)
20. Toutanova, K., Klein, D., Manning, C.D., Singer, Y.: Feature-rich part-of-speech tagging with a cyclic dependency network. In: HLT-NAACL (2003)
21. Umansky-Pesin, S., Reichart, R., Rappoport, A.: A multi-domain web-based algorithm for POS tagging of unknown words. In: Coling 2010, pp. 1274–1282 (2010)
22. Yin, X., Han, J.: CPAR: classification based on Predictive Association Rules. In: proceedings of SIAM International Conference on Data Mining, San Fransisco, CA, pp. 331–335 (2003)

Systems and AI Applications

Adaptive Parameter Selection in Comprehensive Learning Particle Swarm Optimizer

Mohammad Hasanzadeh[✉], Mohammad Reza Meybodi,
and Mohammad Mehdi Ebadzadeh

Computer Engineering and Information Technology Department,
Amirkabir University of Technology (Tehran Polytechnic), Tehran, Iran
{mdhassanzd, mmeybodi, ebadzadeh}@aut.ac.ir

Abstract. The widespread usage of optimization heuristics such as Particle Swarm Optimizer (PSO) imposes huge challenges on parameter adaption. One variant of PSO is Comprehensive Learning Particle Swarm Optimizer (CLPSO), which uses all individuals' best information to update their velocity. The novel strategy of CLPSO enables population to read from exemplars for specified generations which is called refreshing gap m. In this paper, we develop two classes of Learning Automata (LA) in order to study the learning ability of automata for CLPSO refreshing gap tuning. In the first class, a learning automaton is assigned to the population and in the second one each particle has its own personal automaton. We also compare the proposed algorithm with CLPSO and CPSO-H algorithms. Simulation results show that our algorithms outperform their counterpart algorithms in term of performance, robustness and convergence speed.

Keywords: Particle Swarm Optimizer (PSO) · Comprehensive Learning Particle Swarm Optimizer (CLPSO) · Learning Automata (LA) · Parameter adaption

1 Introduction

Particle Swarm Optimization (PSO) [1, 2] is an iterative optimization approach that optimizes a problem by producing new feasible solutions in the problem space. In each generation of the PSO a new population produces and evaluates through a fitness function. Since the introduction of PSO, many researchers have developed the original framework of PSO. Having a well-known standard algorithm, Bratton and Kennedy defined a straightforward extension of the PSO algorithm in [3]. Comprehensive Learning Particle Swarm Optimizer (CLPSO) [4] is a PSO variant, which uses a new velocity update strategy based on historical best information of all particles. CLPSO preserves the diversity of the swarm and avoids premature convergence.

Learning Automata (LA) [5] are adaptive decision-making machines operating on unknown environment. Recently, many researchers explore the applications of LA in diverse fields such as: Evolutionary Algorithms (EAs) [6], Grid computing and Cloud computing [7, 8], Wireless Sensor Network (WSN) [9] and image processing [10].

© Springer International Publishing Switzerland 2014
A. Movaghar et al. (Eds.): AISP 2013, CCIS 427, pp. 267–276, 2014.
DOI: 10.1007/978-3-319-10849-0_27

LA has been successfully applied to various classes of EAs which consist of: PSO, Genetic Algorithm (GA), Differential Evolution (DE), Ant colony Optimization (ACO), Artificial Bee colony (ABC), Artificial Immune System (AIS), Firefly Algorithm (FA) and Imperialist Competitive Algorithm (ICA).

Standard PSO [3] easily get trapped in local minima when solving complex problems. A lot of research has been done on hybridizing PSO and LA so far. Adjusting the PSO parameters [11], controlling PSO population [12] and incorporating Cooperative PSO (CPSO) [13] mechanism into the standard PSO via the usage of a learning automaton [14] were among them. There is a key parameter in CLPSO [4] named the refreshing gap m, which allows a particle to learn from its exemplar for certain number of generations. In this paper, we have proposed learning automata based algorithms for adaptive parameter selection in CLPSO. Two categories of CLPSO parameter adaption are proposed. In the first category the refreshing gap is set for whole population while in the second category, each particle adjust its refreshing gap individually. The new CLPSOs with adaptive refreshing gap are tested on several benchmark functions. The experimental results show that the novel learning strategy has been improved the CLPSO's performance.

The rest of this paper is composed as follow: Sect. 2 reviews CLPSO and standard PSO. Section 3 gives an introduction to LA and a brief note of its applications. Section 4 describes the proposed algorithms based on LA. Section 5 gives the simulation results and performance analysis. And finally, Sect. 6 concludes the paper.

2 Comprehensive Learning Particle Swarm Optimizer (CLPSO) Versus Standard PSO

Premature convergence on multimodal functions and trapping in local minima are two problems of standard PSO [3]. Comprehensive Learning (CL) strategy of CLPSO [4] is aimed to avoid these phenomena by maintaining the population diversity. In the following we introduce the CLPSO algorithms in term of its differences toward standard PSO: (1) In standard PSO each particle simultaneously learns from its best personal position (*pbest*) and best global position of the swarm (*gbest*). While in CLPSO, an exemplar function is used for each particle of the population in which each dimension of particles learns from its corresponding *pbest* or another particle's *pbest* in that dimension. (2) As $f(x) = f([x^1, x^2, ..., x^D])$, the fitness value of a particle in standard PSO is determined with D variables. While in CLPSO the $f_i = [f_i(1), f_i(2), ..., f_i(D)]$ function specifies that each dimension of particle learns from which particle's *pbest*. 3) The velocity update equations of the standard PSO and the new CL strategy of CLPSO are different from each other.

3 Learning Automata (LA) Representation

Reinforcement Learning (RL) is the combination of dynamic programming and supervised learning. Learning automaton [5] is an stochastic optimization machine which is one of the branches of Reinforcement Learning (RL) algorithms. An automaton is composed of an action set and a probability vector. After enough interactions with the unknown environment, the optimal action will emerge which has the highest probability. The detailed formulation of Learning Automaton is reported in [5]. Moreover, Fig. 1 sketches how automaton interacts with its corresponding environment and receives reward and penalty signals.

Fig. 1. The interaction between learning automata and environment

Parameter adaption [11] is one of the most sophisticated tasks of EAs. As there are sensitive parameters in PSO, it needs a mechanism to synthesize and analysis them during the evaluation trend. Using LA as the movement engines of the PSO particles is another PSO variant [12]. In this model a learning automaton is designated to each particle and controlled the velocity of the particle. Cooperative PSO [13] is a new version of PSO which assigns an independent swarm to each component of solution vector and optimizes the problem cooperatively. A Hybrid CPSO (CPSO-H) [13] is an algorithm that combines the CPSO algorithm with the PSO [3]. Given that a learning automaton has the ability to learn the structure of benchmark function and that the CPSO-H and PSO algorithms have interleaved execution, it would be ideal to have an adaptive switching mechanism that could exploit both beneficial properties of these two algorithms adaptively. This adaptive approach is called Cooperative PSO – LA (CPSOLA) and is introduced in [14].

4 Proposed Algorithms

4.1 Naïve Tuning of CLPSO's Refreshing Gap

After executing exemplar function of CLPSO algorithm [4], the particles have specific number of generations to learn from their designated exemplar. This counter is refreshing gap m which is set to seven for all the benchmark functions. So, this parameter could not scale well with unimodal or multimodal problems. Also, the structure of the objective function may have influence in determining the exact value of this parameter. Figure 2 shows the refreshing gap changes and its related eligibility. This experiment conducted on Rosenbrock, Quadric, Ackley and Rastrigin benchmark functions with 10 dimensions and 10 particles. All the functions are optimization problems which the lower their fitness values, the better their performance are.

From Fig. 2, we can observe that m has a direct impact on problem results. For Rosenbrock, Quadric, Ackley and Rastrigin better results were reached when m is around 9, 3, 6 and 2 respectively. But, in CLPSO experiments [4], the refreshing gap m is set at seven for all benchmark functions which is a simple choice for this parameter.

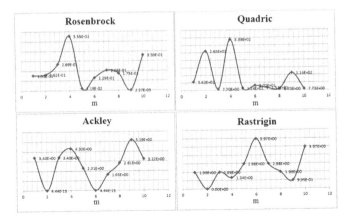

Fig. 2. CLPSO results on four test functions with different refreshing gap

Considering the CLPSO's refreshing gap [4] as a constant in all experiments is a prototype implementation which fades the significance of it. In order to have a reliable vision toward the problem space, we should adaptively adjust this parameter. Figure 3 depicts that CLPSO's population learn *m* times from exemplar function. In each generation of CLPSO algorithm all particles learn from their exemplar function for seven times. The following scenarios show the low flexibility of CLPSO's refreshing gap.

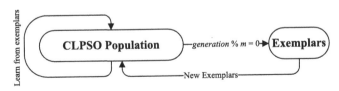

Fig. 3. In every *m* generations new exemplars are reassigned to particles

Scenario 1: In order to perform global search at the early generations of the CLPSO [4], we may consider refreshing gap *m* as a small value. Also while exploiting from local minima, we need larger refreshing gap *m* to perform local search. After exploiting from local minima, a realtime change in diversity is crucial to continue population search path toward global minima (again small *m* value is needed).

Scenario 2: The structure of existing benchmark functions such as unimodal and multimodal problems are coherent to their mathematical equations. For solving these problems, we may need an algorithm which dynamically optimizes the problems. In CLSPO [4] an adaptive mechanism could tune the refreshing gap *m* while solving different benchmark functions instead of considering it as a constant for all problems.

Scenario 3: One could adjust the refreshing gap *m* in the population and particle level. The regulation of this parameter in population level will promise similar explore and exploit abilities for all particles. This uniform refreshing gap m solved unimodal problems efficiently, but in order to optimize the multimodal problems more efficiently we will need proper diversity for this parameter. By adjusting this parameter in particles level, we could have proportional refreshing gap m for different particles.

4.2   Macroscopic Adaptive CLPSO (MaPSO)

In Macroscopic Adaptive CLPSO (MaPSO) a learning automaton is attached to the whole population. The automaton has the rule of adjusting refreshing gap m and has three actions: *increases*, *decreases* and *halts* the m value. Each time the automaton chooses an action and set the refreshing gap value, the particles of population will learn from their exemplars for m generations. The schematic view of MaPSO is depicted in Fig. 4.

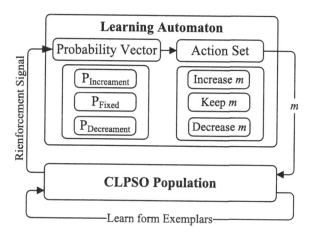

Fig. 4.   Structure of the MaPSO

We should define a suitable feedback from CLPSO population for selected action of the automaton. The MaPSO's reinforcement signal is calculated through (1), which i is the current generation number. In every m generations the *gbest* calculated and compared by previous *gbest* position of population. If the *gbest* fitness improved, then the selected action will get the reward otherwise it will be punished. Adjusting the value of refreshing gap m, The MaPSO has tried to balance the global and local search. Also this algorithm could have different search strategies toward solving different objective functions.

$$\beta = \begin{cases} 0 & \textit{if fitness}(gbest_i < gbest_{i-1}) \\ 1 & \textit{Otherwise} \end{cases} \tag{1}$$

4.3 Microscopic Adaptive CLPSO (MiPSO)

The CLPSO individuals exemplars are updated each $m = 7$ iterations, which is not a flexible mechanism for function optimization. The mentioned MaPSO algorithm adjusted the refreshing gap parameter in population level in which all particles read from a common refreshing gap m. In multimodal problems where population is scattered on multiple local minima, depending on the position of particles, each particle need a different m value to read from its exemplar. Previously in Sect. 4.1, we discussed the necessity of the adaptive refreshing gap m.

The Microscopic Adaptive CLPSO (MiPSO) is a variant of CLPSO, which a learning automaton is mounted on each individual. In MiPSO a set of LA is determine the value of refreshing gap for particles. The LA interact to the environment and receive their reinforcement signal from individuals' *pbest*. In multimodal test functions, while the population spread in the problem space, this mechanism will diversify the refreshing gap value. This diversity will be beneficial while trying to optimize complex multimodal problems. The internal structure of MiPSO employing CLPSO is given in Fig. 5.

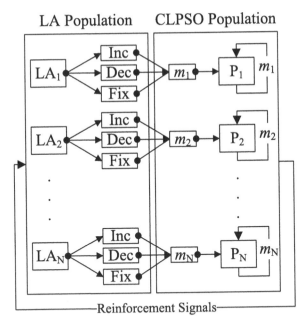

Fig. 5. Structure of the MiPSO where N is the population size

In MiPSO each particle learns from its exemplar for m generations. If the reminder of division of the current generation number and the particles refreshing gap is equal to zero, then the associating learning automaton will select an action and increase, keep or decrease the value of the refreshing gap m. The reward and penalty signals of each automaton are defined based on its associating *pbest*. If the *pbest* of the particle is improved, then the selected action will get the reward otherwise it will be punished. The reinforcement signal is calculating based on (2), which i and j are representing the current generation and current individual, respectively.

$$\beta = \begin{cases} 0 & \text{if fitness}\left(pbest_i^j < pbest_{i-1}^j\right) \\ 1 & \text{Otherwise} \end{cases} \qquad (2)$$

While giving flexibility to individuals, MiPSO gave different particles flexible exploration and exploitation powers. Population diversity in term of refreshing gap can completely cover the problem space in multimodal problems. In MiPSO each particle could have special exploration and exploitation attributes based on its refreshing gap m.

5   Numerical Simulation

The experiments are conducted on TEC 2006 benchmark functions [4] which are proposed to test CLPSO algorithm. Simulations were organized to compare MaPSO and MiPSO with 2 PSO algorithms including CPSO-H [13] and CLPSO [4] on 16 test problems with 10 and 30 dimensions. For 10 dimensional problems, the population size is set at 10 and the maximum number of function evaluations is set at 30000. For the 30 dimensional problems, the population size is set at 40 and the maximum number of function evaluations is set at 200000. For all experiments, 30 independent runs of the MaPSO and MiPSO and the other two algorithms were executed to obtain the average and standard deviation of the results. The results of these simulations are shown in Tables 1 and 2.

The MaPSO and MiPSO are tested on various kinds of learning algorithms and finally we selected the $L_{R\text{-}P}$ (Linear Reward-Penalty) learning schema with learning parameters $alpha = beta = 0.1$. Each automaton corresponding to MaPSO or MiPSO algorithms has an action set which varies the value of refreshing gap. The variation of refreshing gap m is in the range of $[1,20]$ and the initial value of refreshing gap is set to 1, for all automata.

5.1   10-Dimensional Problems

Table 1 shows the averages and standard deviations of the 30 runs of CPSO-H, CLPSO, MaPSO and MiPSO on 16 benchmark functions with 10 variables. The best results are bolded. From the results in Table 1, we can perceive that in Sphere problem (f_1), the MiPSO outperforms the other PSOs. The sphere problem is a simple and convex problem that MiPSO can optimize it faster than other PSOs. In Rosenbrock problem (f_2) the proposed algorithms are got trapped in local minima and the automata couldn't utilize the refreshing gap value properly. Also in unrotated multimodal problems $(f_3\text{-}f_8)$, MaPSO and MiPSO couldn't manage the global and local searches simultaneously and the algorithms performance is worse than their rival algorithms. In rotated multimodal problems $(f_9\text{-}f_{14})$, the algorithms that see the problem dimensions independently are failed to optimize these kinds of problems. The MaPSO optimizes 2 out of 6 of rotated problems. Finally in Composition problems CLPSO is the best choice.

Table 1. 10-dimensional results after 30000 function evaluations

F	CPSO-H [13]	CLPSO [4]	MaPSO	MiPSO
f_1	4.98E-45 ± 1.00E-44	5.15E-29 ± 2.16E-28	7.48E-75 ± 3.08E-74	**2.86E-116 ± 1.57E-115**
f_2	**1.53E + 00 ± 1.70E + 00**	2.46E + 00 ± 1.70E + 00	3.69E + 00 ± 1.56E + 00	3.56E + 00 ± 2.14E + 00
f_3	**1.49E-14 ± 6.97E-15**	4.32E-14 ± 2.55E-14	1.74E + 00 ± 1.37E + 00	1.64E + 00 ± 1.23E + 00
f_4	4.06E-02 ± 2.80E-02	**4.53E-03 ± 4.81E + 03**	1.72E-02 ± 2.12E-02	3.01E-02 ± 5.03E-02
f_5	1.07E-15 ± 1.67E-15	**0.00E + 00 ± 0.00E + 00**	6.45E-02 ± 1.74E-01	8.54E-02 ± 2.52E-01
f_6	**0.00E + 00 ± 0.00E + 00**	**0.00E + 00 ± 0.00E + 00**	1.03E + 00 ± 1.12E + 00	1.29E + 00 ± 1.61E + 00
f_7	2.00E-01 ± 4.10E-01	**0.00E + 00 ± 0.00E + 00**	1.57E + 00 ± 1.19E + 00	1.30E + 00 ± 1.06E + 00
f_8	2.13E + 02 ± 1.41E + 02	**0.00E + 00 ± 0.00E + 00**	4.56E + 02 ± 2.34E + 02	4.88E + 02 ± 2.27E + 02
f_9	1.36E + 00 ± 8.85E-01	**3.56E-05 ± 1.57E-04**	9.78E-01 ± 1.08E + 00	8.45E-01 ± 1.14E + 00
f_{10}	1.20E-01 ± 8.07E-02	4.50E-02 ± 3.08E-02	**3.23E-02 ± 2.60E-02**	5.01E-02 ± 8.24E-02
f_{11}	4.35E + 00 ± 1.35E + 00	**3.72E-01 ± 4.40E-01**	8.22E-01 ± 6.44E-01	5.64E-01 ± 5.47E-01
f_{12}	2.67E + 01 ± 1.06E + 01	**5.97E + 00 ± 2.88E + 00**	6.43E + 00 ± 2.34E + 00	6.50E + 00 ± 3.04E + 00
f_{13}	1.90E + 01 ± 9.05E + 00	5.44E + 00 ± 1.39E + 00	**4.93E + 00 ± 2.03E + 00**	4.51E + 00 ± 1.65E + 00
f_{14}	9.67E + 02 ± 3.67E + 02	**1.14E + 02 ± 1.28E + 02**	9.41E + 02 ± 2.48E + 02	1.02E + 03 ± 3.02E + 02
f_{15}	1.65E + 02 ± 1.42E + 02	**1.64E + 01 ± 3.63E + 01**	2.42E + 01 ± 4.06E + 01	3.62E + 01 ± 5.52E + 01
f_{16}	2.46E + 02 ± 2.18E + 02	**1.98E + 01 ± 2.93E + 01**	3.94E + 02 ± 7.67E + 01	4.11E + 02 ± 7.26E + 01

Table 2. 30-dimensional results after 200000 function evaluations

F	CPSO-H [13]	CLPSO [4]	MaPSO	MiPSO
f_1	**1.16E-113 ± 2.92E-113**	4.46E-14 ± 1.73E-14	2.78E-53 ± 1.19E-52	2.30E-64 ± 1.03E-63
f_2	**7.08E + 00 ± 8.01E + 00**	2.10E + 01 ± 2.98E + 00	2.31E + 01 ± 1.83E + 00	2.37E + 01 ± 1.17E + 00
f_3	4.93E-14 ± 9.17E-14	**0.00E + 00 ± 0.00E + 00**	1.10E-14 ± 3.00E-15	1.27E-14 ± 2.59E-15
f_4	3.63E-02 ± 3.60E-02	3.14E-10 ± 4.64E-10	**0.00E + 00 ± 0.00E + 00**	**0.00E + 00 ± 0.00E + 00**
f_5	7.82E-15 ± 8.50E-15	3.45E-07 ± 1.94E-07	**0.00E + 00 ± 0.00E + 00**	**0.00E + 00 ± 0.00E + 00**
f_6	**0.00E + 00 ± 0.00E + 00**	4.85E-10 ± 3.63E-10	3.32E-02 ± 1.82E-01	**0.00E + 00 ± 0.00E + 00**
f_7	1.00E-01 ± 3.16E-01	**4.36E-10 ± 2.44E-10**	3.33E-02 ± 1.83E-01	1.00E-01 ± 3.05E-01
f_8	1.83E + 03 ± 2.59E + 02	**1.27E-12 ± 8.79E-13**	2.40E + 02 ± 1.74E + 02	1.53E + 02 ± 1.43E + 02
f_9	2.10E + 00 ± 3.84E-01	3.43E-04 ± 1.91E-04	**1.07E-14 ± 3.49E-15**	1.28E-14 ± 2.57E-15
f_{10}	5.54E-02 ± 3.97E-02	**7.04E-10 ± 1.25E-11**	1.08E-08 ± 5.89E-08	1.40E-09 ± 4.78E-09
f_{11}	1.43E + 01 ± 3.53E + 00	3.07E + 00 ± 1.61E + 00	9.46E-01 ± 6.52E-01	**7.19E-01 ± 5.42E-01**
f_{12}	1.01E + 02 ± 3.53E + 00	3.46E + 01 ± 1.61E + 00	2.97E + 01 ± 1.21E + 01	**2.87E + 01 ± 6.87E + 00**
f_{13}	8.80E + 01 ± 2.59E + 01	3.77E + 01 ± 5.56E + 00	2.52E + 01 ± 6.36E + 00	**2.47E + 01 ± 8.93E + 00**
f_{14}	3.64E + 03 ± 7.41E + 02	**1.70E + 03 ± 1.86E + 02**	3.04E + 03 ± 4.04E + 02	3.16E + 03 ± 4.05E + 02
f_{15}	1.30E + 02 ± 1.64E + 02	7.50E-05 ± 1.85E-04	6.50E-04 ± 3.10E-03	**5.01E-07 ± 2.58E-06**
f_{16}	7.83E + 01 ± 1.60E + 02	**7.86E + 00 ± 3.64E + 00**	5.21E + 02 ± 8.12E + 01	5.54E + 02 ± 9.90E + 01

5.2   30-Dimensional Problems

The same experiments as 10 dimensional problems are performed on 30 dimensional problems and the results showed in Table 2. MaPSO and MiPSO are collectively suppress CPSO-H and CLPSO algorithms on $f_4, f_5, f_6, f_9, f_{11}, f_{12}, f_{13}, f_{15}$ and especially significantly improve the performance on f_4, f_5. The Group A problems are simple unimodal problems which require a simple iterative heuristic to optimize them. Although the number of functions evaluations increased from 30000 to 200000, the proposed algorithms couldn't maintain their performance on simple unimodal problems with respect to 10 dimensional problems. MiPSO algorithm optimizes the f_4, f_5, f_6 better than CLPSO and CPSO-H. Since CPSO-H and CLPSO are considered the variables of problem space independently, in rotated multimodal problems (f_9-f_{14}), because of the fully rotated nature of the problems the performance of CPSO-H and CLPSO drop off and the performance of MiPSO significantly improved. In the two composition problems (f_{15}-f_{16}) with randomly distributed local and global optima, MiPSO significantly improves the results on f_{15}. The set of learning automata associating with refreshing gaps of each particle of MiPSO population could balance the exploration and exploitation attributes of this heuristic. Finally CLPSO performs the best on f_{16}, because of its diverse solutions.

From the results of Tables 1 and 2, MaPSO and MiPSO are not the best choices for optimizing unimodal and simple multimodal problems and either they are not solving the 10 dimensional problems efficiently. Since there are many variables which are involved in real world problems and these problems are like multimodal optimization problems with high dimensions, it is reasonable to use an algorithm which performs well on multimodal and high dimensional problems.

6   Conclusion

In this paper we present two variants of Comprehensive Learning PSO (CLPSO) with adaptive learning strategy where learning automata regulate the refreshing gap of CLPSO. Two branches of intelligent algorithms are proposed. In the first category, the same refreshing gap is set for whole swarm while in the other category each particle has its own automaton which adjusts the refreshing gap individually.

According to the results of MaPSO and MiPSO on both 10 dimensional and 30 dimensional problems, we can conclude that the proposed algorithms do not act the best for low dimensional problems. There is a cost for tuning the refreshing gap in order to attain better results in high dimensional problems, and the cost is the slow convergence of the proposed algorithms in 10 dimensional problems. The MaPSO and MiPSO are achieved the best results in three, 10 dimensional problems. However they perform better on rotated multimodal problems where the problem dimensions are correlated together. Also in 30 dimensional problems the proposed algorithms perform the best in 7 out of 16 benchmark functions. From the clear difference of 10 and 30 dimensional problems, we observe that the proposed adaptive strategy enable the MaPSO and MiPSO to make use of the learning ability of the learning automata to optimize the problems more accurately than CPSO-H and CLPSO algorithms.

As long as the surface of 10 dimensional problems is plain, there is no need for extensive search to optimize the problems efficiently. The MaPSO outperforms MiPSO in 10 dimensional problems because of its simple one automaton structure. But in 30 dimensional problems where the problem space is complicated and in some cases the problem space is rotated, the distributed behavior of MiPSO's set of learning automata could appropriately adjust the value of refreshing gap by active feedbacks from the problem's landscape.

References

1. Kennedy, J., Eberhart, R.: Particle swarm optimization. In: IEEE International Conference on Neural Networks, pp. 1942–1948 (1995)
2. Eberhart, R., Kennedy, J.: A new optimizer using particle swarm theory. In: 6th International Symposium on Micro Machine and Human Science, pp. 39–43 (1995)
3. Bratton, D., Kennedy, J.: Defining a standard for particle swarm optimization. In: IEEE Swarm Intelligence Symposium, pp. 120–127 (2007)
4. Liang, J., Qin, A., Suganthan, P.N., Baskar, S.: Comprehensive learning particle swarm optimizer for global optimization of multimodal functions. IEEE Trans. Evol. Comput. **10**(3), 281–295 (2006)
7. Najim, K., Poznyak, A.S.: Learning Automata: Theory and Applications. Pergamon Press, Oxford (1994)
6. Hasanzadeh, M., Meybodi, M.R., Ebadzadeh, M.M.: Adaptive cooperative particle swarm optimizer. Appl. Intell. **39**(2), 397–420 (2013)
7. Hasanzadeh, M., Meybodi, M.R.: Grid resource discovery based on distributed learning automata. Computing **96**(9), 909–922 (2014)
8. Hasanzadeh, M., Meybodi, M.R.: Deployment of gLite middleware: an E-Science grid infrastructure. In: 21st IEEE Iranian Conference on Electrical Engineering, pp. 1–6 (2013)
9. Esnaashari, M., Meybodi, M.R.: A cellular learning automata-based deployment strategy for mobile wireless sensor networks. J. Parallel Distrib. Comput. **71**(7), 988–1001 (2011)
10. Abin, A.A., Fotouhi, M., Kasaei, S.: A new dynamic cellular learning automata-based skin detector. Multimedia Syst. **15**(5), 309–323 (2009)
11. Hashemi, A.B., Meybodi, M.R.: A note on the learning automata based algorithms for adaptive parameter selection in PSO. Appl. Soft Comput. **11**(1), 689–705 (2011)
12. Hasanzadeh, M., Meybodi, M.R., Shiry, S.: Improving learning automata based particle swarm: an optimization algorithm. In: 12th IEEE International Symposium on Computational Intelligence and Informatics, pp. 291–296 (2011)
13. Van den Bergh, F., Engelbrecht, A.P.: A cooperative approach to particle swarm optimization. IEEE Trans. Evol. Comput. **8**(3), 225–239 (2004)
14. Hasanzadeh, M., Meybodi, M.R.: A robust heuristic algorithm for cooperative particle swarm optimizer: a learning automata approach. In: 20th IEEE Iranian Conference on Electrical Engineering, pp. 656–661 (2012)

A Biologically Inspired Solution for Fuzzy Travelling Salesman Problem

Elham Pezhhan[(⊠)] and Eghbal Mansoori

Computer Science and Engineering Department, Shiraz University, Shiraz, Iran
pejhan@cse.shirazu.ac.ir, mansoori@shirazu.ac.ir

Abstract. Recently, biologically inspired methods have been proposed for solving combinatorial optimization problems like the travelling salesman problem (TSP). This is a well-known combinatorial optimization problem which belongs to NP-hard class. It is desired to find a minimum-cost tour while visiting each city once. This paper presents a variant of the TSP in which the traveling cost between each pair of cities is represented by fuzzy numbers instead of a deterministic value. To solve this fuzzy TSP, a bio-inspired algorithm based on physarum polycephalum model is used. This organism can find the shortest route through a maze by trying to locate the food sources placed at the exits. It also can attract the maximum amount of nutrients in the shortest possible time. Our algorithm is capable of finding an optimal solution for graphs with both crisp and fuzzy numbers as their cost of edges. Numerical examples of some networks are used to illustrate the efficiency of the proposed method.

Keywords: Combinatorial optimization · Fuzzy travelling salesman problem · Physarum polycephalum · Fuzzy numbers

1 Introduction

The TSP is a representative of a large class of problems known as combinatorial optimization problems well-studied in computer science, operation research and mathematics. The objective of this problem is to find the closed route of the shortest length through a given set of cities where each city is visited just once. This is an NP-hard problem [1], so it cannot be solved in polynomial time. Robot control, mobile computing, vehicle routing, automated guided vehicles scheduling and integrated circuits design are some practical applications of TSP [2]. A TSP is defined by providing its data consists of weights assigned to the edges of a finite complete graph. Commonly, the weight of each edge, which represents time or cost, is assumed to be crisp, but in practical applications, it is difficult for decision makers to determine the weights. A typical way to handle uncertainties in edge weights is to use fuzzy set theory [3–5]. The TSP in a graph with fuzzy edge weights is known as fuzzy TSP. Generally, neural network approaches, genetic algorithms [6], simulated annealing methods [7], ant colony optimization [8] and particle swarm optimization [9] are common bio-inspired algorithms for TSP [10].

Living organisms are systems which are adapted to effectively perform specific tasks that are necessary for their survival. For example, the large unicellular amoeba-like true slime mould physarum polycephalum can find the shortest route through a

© Springer International Publishing Switzerland 2014
A. Movaghar et al. (Eds.): AISP 2013, CCIS 427, pp. 277–287, 2014.
DOI: 10.1007/978-3-319-10849-0_28

maze by trying to locate the food sources placed at the exits, and to attract the maximum amount of nutrients in the shortest possible time. The physarum polycephalum plasmodium is an aggregate of protoplasm with tubular elements that can form a dynamic tubular network within the discovered food sources [11]. By extracting the physiological mechanism of its path finding ability, a path finding mathematical model was constructed [12]. Furthermore, it is capable of solving many graph theoretical problems [13–15].

In this paper, we are motivated to develop an algorithm for fuzzy TSP using physarum polycephalum. This paper is arranged as follows. In Sect. 2, some basic concepts and theories are reviewed. Section 3 briefly explains the physarum model. Section 4 describes the proposed algorithm for solving the fuzzy TSP. Experiments are presented in Sect. 5 where our algorithm is applied to solve some problem instances including a tourist problem for graph with crisp and fuzzy weights. Finally, concluding remarks are given in Sect. 6.

2   Definition

In this section, some basic definitions including fuzzy numbers and fuzzy distance [3, 16] are briefly explained.

2.1   Fuzzy Numbers

Definition 1. A fuzzy set $\tilde{A}$ in a universe of discourse X is characterized by a membership function $\mu_{\tilde{A}}(x)$ which associates with each element x in X a real number in the interval [0, 1]. The function value $\mu_{\tilde{A}}(x)$ is termed as the grade of membership of x in $\tilde{A}$.

$$\tilde{A} = \left\{ \langle x, \mu_{\tilde{A}}(x) \rangle | x \in X \right\} \tag{1}$$

Definition 2. A fuzzy set $\tilde{A}$ on X is normal iff $sup_{x \in X} \mu_{\tilde{A}}(x) = 1$ where sup means supremum (least upper bound) of a universe.

Definition 3. A fuzzy set $\tilde{A}$ on X is convex iff $\mu_{\tilde{A}}(\lambda x + (1 - \lambda)y) \geq (\mu_{\tilde{A}}(x) \wedge \mu_{\tilde{A}}(y))$, $\forall x, y \in X, \forall \lambda \in [0, 1]$, where $\wedge$ denotes the minimum operator.

Definition 4. A fuzzy set $\tilde{A}$ is a fuzzy number iff $\tilde{A}$ is normal and convex on X.

Definition 5. A triangular fuzzy number $\tilde{A}$ is fuzzy number that can be defined by a triplet (a, b, c), where the piecewise linear membership function can be determined as follows:

$$\mu_{\tilde{A}}(x) = \begin{cases} 0, & x < a \\ \frac{x-a}{b-a}, & a \leq x \leq b \\ \frac{c-x}{c-b}, & b \leq x \leq c \\ 0, & x > c \end{cases} \tag{2}$$

A triangular fuzzy number $\tilde{A}$ in the universe set X that conforms to this definition shown in Fig. 1.

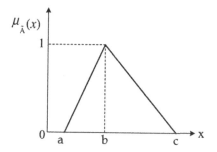

Fig. 1. A triangular fuzzy number $\tilde{A} = (a, b, c)$

Definition 6. Assuming both $\tilde{A} = (a_1, a_2, a_3), \tilde{B} = (b_1, b_2, b_3)$ are triangular numbers, then the basic fuzzy operations are:

$$\tilde{A} \oplus \tilde{B} = (a_1 + b_1, a_2 + b_2, a_3 + b_3), \text{for addition} \tag{3}$$

$$\tilde{A} \ominus \tilde{B} = (a_1 - b_1, a_2 - b_2, a_3 - b_3), \text{for subtraction} \tag{4}$$

$$\tilde{A} \otimes \tilde{B} = (a_1 \times b_1, a_2 \times b_2, a_3 \times b_3), \text{for multipulation} \tag{5}$$

$$\tilde{A} \o \tilde{B} = (a_1/b_3, a_2/b_2, a_3/b_1), \text{for division} \tag{6}$$

2.2 Fuzzy Distance

The fuzzy distance indexed by parameters $1 < p < \infty$ and $0 < q < 1$ between two fuzzy numbers $\tilde{A}$ and $\tilde{B}$ is a nonnegative function given by [3, 16]:

$$D_{p,q}(\tilde{A}, \tilde{B}) = \begin{cases} \left[(1-q) \int_0^1 |A_\alpha^- - B_\alpha^-|^p d\alpha + q \int_0^1 |A_\alpha^+ - B_\alpha^+|^p d\alpha \right]^{1/p} & , p < \infty \\ (1-q) \sup_{0 < \alpha \leq 1} \left(|A_\alpha^- - B_\alpha^-| \right) + q \inf_{0 < \alpha \leq 1} \left(|A_\alpha^+ - B_\alpha^+| \right), p = \infty \end{cases} \tag{7}$$

Where *inf* means infimum (greatest lower bound) of a universe. Since the significance of the end points of the support of the fuzzy numbers is assumed to be the same, $q = (1/2)$ and $p = 2$ in [3] are also adopted in this paper.

For triangular fuzzy numbers $\tilde{A} = (a_1, a_2, a_3)$ *and* $\tilde{B} = (b_1, b_2, b_3)$ the above distance is then calculated to [16]:

$$D_{2,(1/2)}\left(\tilde{A},\tilde{B}\right) = \sqrt{\frac{1}{6}\left[\sum_{i=1}^{3}(b_i - a_i)^2 + (b_2 - a_2)^2 + \sum_{i=1}^{2}(b_i - a_i)(b_{i+1} - a_{i+1})\right]}$$

(8)

3   Physarum Model

In this section, the Physarum Model is explained briefly [3, 17]:

Suppose that the shape of physarum can be represented as an undirected fuzzy weighted network. Starting and ending nodes are considered as two food sources, which are marked as N_1 and N_2 and other nodes are denoted by N_i. Q_{ij} denotes the flux through the edge between nodes N_i and N_j. According to the Hagen Poiseuille, the flux through the tube can be described by [3]:

$$Q_{ij} = \frac{D_{ij}}{\tilde{L}_{ij}}(\tilde{P}_i - \tilde{P}_j)$$

(9)

Where $\tilde{P}_i$ is the pressure at node N_i, $\tilde{L}_{ij}$ is the length of edge e_{ij} as a fuzzy number and D_{ij} is the conductivity of e_{ij}. Without loss of generality, Q_{ij} is initially set to crisp number 0 and D_{ij} to crisp number 1.

Since the inflow and outflow must be balanced, we have $\sum_i Q_{ij} = 0, (j \neq 1, 2)$. For the nodes that represent food sources, we have $\sum_i Q_{i1} + I_0 = 0, \sum_i Q_{i2} - I_0 = 0$, where I_0 is the flux from the source node which is set as a constant in the model. Using the above equations, the network's Poisson equation for the pressure with fuzzy number is derived as:

$$\sum_i \frac{D_{ij}}{\tilde{L}_{ij}}(\tilde{P}_i - \tilde{P}_j) = \begin{cases} -1, & \text{for } j = 1 \\ +1, & \text{for } j = 2 \\ 0, & \text{otherwise} \end{cases}$$

(10)

By initializing the pressure at source node to 0, the pressure at other nodes would be calculated. By using the triangular fuzzy numbers, the length of each edge and pressure at each node are represented as $\tilde{L}_{ij} = (\tilde{L}_{ij}^1, \tilde{L}_{ij}^2, \tilde{L}_{ij}^3)$ and $\tilde{P}_i = (\tilde{P}_i^1, \tilde{P}_i^2, \tilde{P}_i^3)$. By adopting fuzzy distance, Eq (9) can be reconsidered as follows:

$$Q_{ij} = D_{ij} \times \propto \times \sqrt{\frac{1}{6}\left[\sum_{k=1}^{3}\left(\frac{\tilde{P}_j^k}{\tilde{L}_{ij}^{4-k}} - \frac{\tilde{P}_i^k}{\tilde{L}_{ij}^{4-k}}\right)^2 + \left(\frac{\tilde{P}_j^2}{\tilde{L}_{ij}^2} - \frac{\tilde{P}_i^2}{\tilde{L}_{ij}^2}\right)^2 + \sum_{k=1}^{2}\left(\frac{\tilde{P}_j^k}{\tilde{L}_{ij}^{4-k}} - \frac{\tilde{P}_i^k}{\tilde{L}_{ij}^{4-k}}\right)\left(\frac{\tilde{P}_j^{k+1}}{\tilde{L}_{ij}^{3-k}} - \frac{\tilde{P}_i^{k+1}}{\tilde{L}_{ij}^{3-k}}\right)\right]}$$

(11)

Where $\propto$ is an adjustment coefficient which is needed since we are using the fuzzy distance measure instead of the fuzzy subtraction operation.

According to the relation between the flux and tube thickness, the variation of conductivity D_{ij} can be described using the following formula:

$$\frac{d}{dt}D_{ij} = f\left(\left|Q_{ij}\right|\right) - \gamma D_{ij} \tag{12}$$

where γ is decay rate of the tube and f is an increasing function with $f(0) = 0$.

Algorithm 1 illustrates the physarum model used for solving fuzzy shortest path problem.

Algorithm 1. Using physarum model to solve the fuzzy shortest path problem

---

```
D_ij ← 1    (∀ i,j = 1,2,...,n ∧ i ≠ j)
Q_ij ← 0    (∀ i,j = 1,2,...,n)
P̃_i  ← 0̃    (∀ i = 1,2,...,n)
count ← 0
repeat
      P̃_2 ← 0̃    // pressure at ending node
      Calculate the pressure of each node using (10)
      for i=1 to n-1
         for j=i+1 to n
         Calculate Q_ij using (11)
         end
      end
      Adopting D_ij using (12)
   count ← count + 1
until a termination condition is met
```

The algorithm will stop when all the conductivity values remain unchanged. The final result contains the tubes, whose conductivity values are near 1. These tubes will comprise the shortest path.

4   Our Proposed Method

For an n-city TSP, there is $(n-1)!/2$ possible tours. Obviously, for large values of n, generating all potential candidate tours is computationally intractable. This intractability has led to development of a number of heuristic approaches which can produce relatively short tours, though these tours are not guaranteed to be minimal [10].

Through observations and experiments on the plasmodium of slime mold physarum polycephalum and the physiological mechanism of tube formation, a mathematical model has been constructed. In this plasmodium, the tubes of network grow thicker in a given direction when shuttle streaming of the protoplasm persists in that direction for a certain time [15]. Based on this operation of physarum which can be employed to solve combinatorial optimization problems, its model is used in this paper to solve TSP as an NP-hard problem.

Since in TSP we should find a Hamilton cycle, this problem is considered as several constitutive shortest path problems which can be solved by physarum model. For this purpose, the cities in TSP are grouped into some clusters based on their geographical locations [18, 19]. Next, the two adjacent clusters are linked together via their two nearest cities. Then, the physarum model is run in each cluster to find the shortest path between its cities, provided two specific cities are predefined as start and end nodes of the path. These nodes are determined when a shortest link between two clusters is designated.

The detail of our proposed algorithm is explained in three steps:

4.1   Clustering the Cities

Many clustering algorithms can be used for grouping the cities according to their positions in the plane. K-means algorithm as one of the simplest unsupervised learning methods is used in our scheme. Its procedure follows a simple and easy way to classify a given data set through a certain number of clusters (i.e., k clusters). Since the results of algorithm depend on the value of k and there is no general theoretical solution to find the optimal number of clusters for any given data set, different values of k is tried.

Algorithm starts with k = n/3 clusters and then progressively decrements it in order to find the optimum number of clusters. Since the time complexity of our algorithm increases by reducing k, this reduction is terminated when k reaches n/8. The output of this phase would be k clusters C1, …, Ck.

4.2   Linking Clusters to Each Other

In order to link two adjacent clusters Ci and Cj, the connecting edges between each two cities of these clusters are ranked according to their weights. Then the shortest edge is selected as the connection between these two clusters. This process of connecting two adjacent clusters continues until all clusters have connections to their two nearest clusters. After connecting all clusters, the two marginal cities in each cluster are designated as start and end nodes. These cities are used in the next phase to find the shortest path among cities in each cluster.

4.3   Finding Shortest Path in Clusters

Providing the start and end nodes of each cluster, the cities in this cluster are given to *Algorithm 1* which uses the fuzzy physarum model. This algorithm finds the shortest path between cities. For fuzzy TSP with fuzzy weights on edges, the fuzzy distance is used in the algorithm. Fuzzy distance is adopted to measure the difference between two fuzzy numbers. Using fuzzy distance, our method can be applied on both triangular and trapezoidal fuzzy numbers as well as crisp numbers.

Figure 2 illustrates the details of our proposed method that are described in previous sub-sections in a flowchart form.

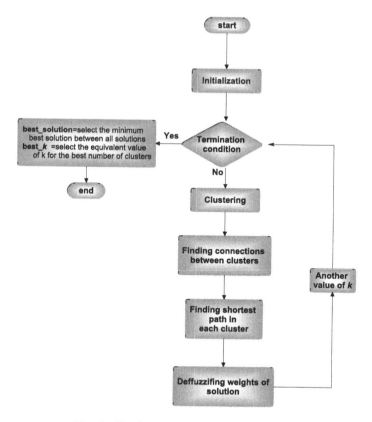

Fig. 2. The flowchart of our proposed method

5 Experimental Results

In this section some graphs are considered to demonstrate the consequence of the proposed algorithm. In the first subsection, the results of our method is shown for a classical TSP that is taken from TSPLIB [20] with crisp numbers between nodes, and in the second, fuzzy TSP is tested.

5.1 Classical TSP

The algorithm is checked for TSP benchmark problem "*Burma*14" that have exact solution. To perform the first step of method, K-means clustering is used to group cities and then the algorithm is executed for variant values of k. Figure 3 shows the position of cities for this problem and one of the consequences of clustering with $k = 3$.

On the second step, the shortest paths between clusters is found and start and end nodes are determined for each cluster (Fig. 4). After specifying these nodes, Algorithm 1 is used to find the shortest path in each cluster. The results of this step is depicted in Fig. 5. The optimal solution for this example by using proposed method is equal to

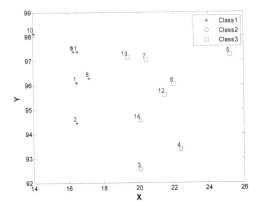

Fig. 3. Grouping cities into three clusters

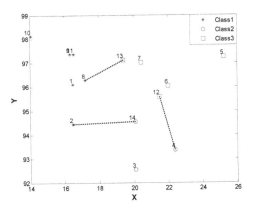

Fig. 4. Linking $k = 3$ clusters of "*Burma*14" to each other

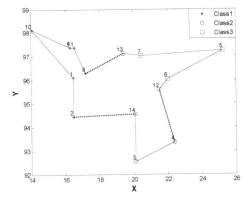

Fig. 5. Optimal tour of "*Burma*14" with crisp numbers

31.4536 and sequence of nodes is in the following form "2, 1, 10, 9, 11, 8, 13, 7, 5, 6, 12, 4, 3, 14, 2" that is as an optimal known sequence [20].

5.2   Fuzzy TSP

To illustrate our results for fuzzy graphs, crisp weights of three examples from TSPLIB [20] are transformed to triangular fuzzy numbers. To accomplish this, peak values are kept from crisp matrix, and two other elements resulted by adding and subtracting a constant value to the peak number. After finding the sequence of traveling cities, the fuzzy numbers are defuzzified by the Center Of Gravity (COG) method, which is simply the arithmetic mean of the three characteristic points of the fuzzy number, and then these crisp numbers are summed up providing the total distance of the tour [21].

An example that is tested in previous section ("*Burma*14"), is checked here with fuzzy numbers. Equation (13) is used as a constant value for constructing fuzzy numbers:

$$c = \frac{Maximum\ value\ of\ costs - Minimum\ value\ of\ costs}{Number\ of\ nodes} \tag{13}$$

After fulfilling the defuzzification, the total cost of the optimal tour for the "*Burma*14" problem with $k = 3$ clusters, would be equal to 34.8335 and sequence of nodes is "2, 1, 10, 9, 11, 8, 13, 7, 5, 6, 12, 4, 3, 14, 2".

"*ulysses*22" is another example from TSLIB, with 22 nodes and 231 edges. According to the proposed algorithm, the optimal sequence of the nodes for this graph with fuzzy triangular numbers and $k = 5$ clusters is shown in Fig. 6.

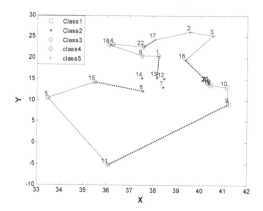

Fig. 6. Optimal tour of "*ulysses*22" with fuzzy numbers

Figure 7 shows the distribution of 29 cities of *bayg*29 and the optimal result obtained by the proposed algorithm with 7 clusters. The best solution found is the same as optimal known solution [20].

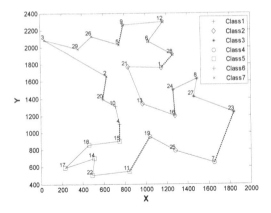

Fig. 7. Optimal tour of "*bayg*29" with fuzzy numbers

6   Conclusion

This paper proposed a bio-inspired solution for solving classical TSP d fuzzy TSP problems. Solutions in the literature are devoted to the classical problem, so after redefining the TSP and transforming it to fuzzy TSP a novel approach is proposed. In the fuzzy TSP, the costs between the nodes are represented by fuzzy numbers.

For finding the solution of problems, our proposed method combines the fuzzy theories (including fuzzy numbers and fuzzy distance) with a path finding model inspired by an amoeboid organism, physarum polycephalum.

Our method was tested first by classical TSP benchmark problem "*Burma*14". Then for inspecting of new algorithm, we transformed TSP problems, "*Burma*14", "*ulysses*22" and "*bayg*29" to the fuzzy graphs and show the results of them.

References

1. Chen, S.M., Chien, C.Y.: Solving the traveling salesman problem based on the genetic simulated annealing ant colony system with particle swarm optimization techniques. J. Expert Syst. Appl. **38**, 14439–14450 (2011)
2. Majumdar, J., Bhunia, A.K.: Genetic algorithm for asymmetric traveling salesman problem with imprecise travel times. J. Comput. Appl. Math. **235**, 3063–3078 (2011)
3. Zhang, Y., Zhang, Z., Deng, Y., Mahadevan, S.: A biologically inspired solution for fuzzy shortest path problems. J. Appl. Soft Comput. **13**, 2356–2363 (2013)
4. Tseng, M.L., Divinagracia, L., Divinagracia, R.: Evaluating firm's sustainable production indicators in uncertainty. J. Comput. Ind. Eng. **57**, 1393–1403 (2009)
5. Zade, L.A.: Fuzzy sets. J. Inf. Control **8**, 338–353 (1965)
6. Liao, Y.F., Yau, D.H., Chen, C.L.: Evolutionary algorithm to traveling salesman problems. J. Comput. Math. Appl. **64**(5), 788–797 (2012)
7. Geng, X., Chen, Z., Yang, W., Shi, D., Zhao, K.: Solving the traveling salesman problem based on an adaptive simulated annealing algorithm with greedy search. J. Appl. Soft Comput. **11**(4), 3680–3689 (2011)

8. Dorigo, M., Gambardella, L.M.: Ant colonies for the travelling salesman problem. BioSystems **43**(2), 73–81 (1997)
9. Wang, K.P., Huang, L., Zhou, C.G., Pang, W.: Particle swarm optimization for traveling salesman problem. In: International Conference Machine Learning and Cybernetics, vol. 3, pp. 1583–1585 (2003)
10. Jones, J., Adamatzky, A.: Computation of the Travelling Salesman Problem by a Shrinking Blob, arXiv preprint, arXiv:1303.4969 (2013)
11. Nakagaki, T., Kobayashi, R., Nishiura, Y., Ueda, T.: Obtaining multiple separate food sources: behavioural intelligence in the Physarum plasmodium. Proc. R. Soc. Lond. Ser. B-Biol. Sci. **271**, 2305–2310 (2004)
12. Tero, A., Kobayashi, R., Nakagaki, T.: A mathematical model for adaptive transport network in path finding by true slime mold. J. Theoret. Biol. **244**, 553–564 (2007)
13. Nakagaki, T., Yamada, H., Hara, M.: Smart network solutions in an amoeboid organism. J. Biophys. Chem. **107**, 1–5 (2004)
14. Zhou, H., Zhang, Z., Wu, Y., Qian, T.: Bio-inspired dynamic composition and reconfiguration of service-oriented internetware systems. In: Tan, Y., Shi, Y., Chai, Y., Wang, G. (eds.) ICSI 2011, Part I. LNCS, vol. 6728, pp. 364–373. Springer, Heidelberg (2011)
15. Zhang, Y., Zhang, Z., Deng, Y.: An improved maze solving algorithm based on an amoeboid organism. In: The 23rd Chinese Control and Decision Conference, pp. 1440–1443 (2011)
16. Mahdavi, I., Nourifar, R., Heidarzade, A., Amiri, N.M.: A dynamic programming approach for finding shortest chains in a fuzzy network. J. Appl. Soft Comput. **9**, 503–511 (2009)
17. Wang, Q., Zhang, Z., Zhang, Y., Deng, Y.: Fuzzy shortest path problem based on biological method. J. Inf. Comput. Sci. **9**(5), 1365–1371 (2011)
18. Jebari, K., El moujahid, A., Bouroumi, A., Ettouhami, A.: Unsupervised fuzzy clustering-based genetic algorithms to Traveling Salesman Problem. In: International Conference Multimedia Computing and Systems (ICMCS), Tangier, pp. 1013–1015 (2012)
19. Yoon, J.W., Cho, S.B.: An efficient genetic algorithm with fuzzy c-means clustering for traveling salesman problem. In: IEEE Congress Evolutionary Computation (CEC), New Orleans, pp. 1452–1456 (2011)
20. http://www.iwr.uni-heidelberg.de/groups/comopt/software/TSPLIB95/tsp/
21. Földesi, P., Botzheim, J., Kóczy, L.T.: Eugenic bacterial memetic algorithm for fuzzy road transport traveling salesman problem. Int. J. Innov. Comput. Inf. Control **7**(5), 2775–2798 (2009)

Extracting Parallel Fragments
from Comparable Documents
Using a Feature-Based Method

Zeinab Rahimi[1(✉)], Mohammad Hossein Samani[2],
and Shahram Khadivi[3]

[1] Department of Speech and Natural Language Processing,
Research Center of Intelligent Signal Processing (RCISP), Tehran, Iran
rahimi@rcisp.com
[2] Department of Secure Infrastructures, Research Center of Intelligent
Signal Processing (RCISP), Tehran, Iran
samani@rcisp.com
[3] Department of Computer Engineering, Amirkabir University of Technology,
Hafez Avenue, Tehran, Iran
khadivi@aut.ac.ir

Abstract. Here, a novel method for extracting parallel sub-sentential fragments from comparable corpora is presented. The proposed method aims to extract bilingual sentence fragments from noisy sentence pairs. We define a similarity measure between bilingual sentence fragments which is actually a linear combination of some new features. The features used are fragment length, LLR score, alignment path specifications in the block and translation coverage fraction. This method enables us to extract useful machine translation training data from comparable corpora that contain no parallel sentence pairs. Evaluations indicate that proposed method is very efficient and not only outperforms the existing similar systems in the measure of precision and recall; it also helps to improve the performance of a statistical machine translation system.

Keywords: Comparable corpora · Parallel fragments · Machine translation

1 Introduction

Data used for training statistical machine translation method are usually prepared from three resources: parallel, non-parallel and comparable text corpora. Parallel corpora are ideal resources for translation but due to lack of these kind of texts, non-parallel and comparable corpora are used.

Comparable corpora are consist of documents having similar subjects written in two different languages. Due to fast development of public communications, these documents are available in large amount. Tens of thousands of words of news describing the same events are produced daily, so comparable corpora exist in large scale and the ability to exploit them for parallel data acquisition is highly beneficial for the SMT field.

© Springer International Publishing Switzerland 2014
A. Movaghar et al. (Eds.): AISP 2013, CCIS 427, pp. 288–298, 2014.
DOI: 10.1007/978-3-319-10849-0_29

Most of existing methods for exploiting comparable corpora look for parallel data at sentence level. However, we believe that very non-parallel corpora have none or few good sentence pairs; most of their parallel data exists at the sub-sentential level.

Our proposed system is implemented based on extracting fragment blocks from input related sentences using score calculated from special features such as fragment length, LLR score, alignment path specifications in the block and translation coverage percentage.

The systems which our system is compared to, are fragment extraction system designed by Munteanu and Marcu (2006) as base system and an improved version of that, which are both implemented in C#. Base system has a problem about assigning alignments that is considering alignments greedily. It means that the best translation for each word is chosen as corresponding translation and is omitted from other words candidate sets. This is a defect for languages having multiple alignments like Farsi.

In improved version, some changes applied to base system such as considering multiple alignments instead of greedy alignments, optimized candidate detection phase, using length filter, normalizing LLR scores according to how comparable the input text is and changing some parameters for better adaptation for Farsi language.

2   Related Works

Most of the papers involving comparable corpora has focused on extracting word translations (Fung and Yee 1998; Rapp 1999; Diab and Finch 2000; Koehn and Knight 2000; Gaussier et al. 2004; Shao and Ng 2004; Shinyama and Sekine 2004). Another related research effort is that of Resnik and Smith (2003), whose system is designed to discover parallel document pairs on the Web.

Our work lies between these two directions; we attempt to discover parallelism at the level of fragments, which are longer than one word but usually shorter than a sentence. Thus, the previous research most relevant to this paper is that aimed at mining comparable corpora for parallel sentences.

The earliest efforts in this direction are those of Zhao and Vogel (2002) and Utiyama and Isahara (2003). Both methods extend algorithms designed to perform sentence alignment of parallel texts: they use dynamic programming to do sentence alignment of documents hypothesized to be similar. These approaches are only applicable to corpora which are at most "noisy-parallel", i.e. contain documents which are fairly similar, both in content and in sentence ordering.

Munteanu and Marcu (2005) analyze sentence pairs in isolation from their context, and classify them as parallel or non-parallel. They match each source document with several target ones, and classify all possible sentence pairs from each document pair. This enables them to find sentences from fairly dissimilar documents, and to handle any amount of reordering, which makes the method applicable to truly comparable corpora. The research reported by Fung and Cheung (2004a, b), Cheung and Fung (2004) and Wu and Fung (2005) is aimed explicitly at "very non-parallel corpora". They also pair each source document with several target ones and examine all possible sentence pairs; but the list of document pairs is not fixed. After one round of sentence extraction, the list is enriched with additional documents, and the system iterates. Thus, they include in the search document pairs which are dissimilar. One limitation of all these methods is that they are designed to find only full sentences. Our methodology is aimed at detecting sub-sentential correspondences. This is a difficult task, requiring the ability to recognize translationally equivalent fragments even in non-parallel sentence pairs.

There are not many mentionable works in the field of extracting parallel fragments. The main work done in the fragment extraction field is the system designed by Manteanu and Marcu (2006) that by analyzing potentially similar sentence pairs using a signal processing inspired approach, detect which segments of the source sentence are translated into segments in the target sentence, and which are not.

The work of Deng et al. (2006) also deals with sub-sentential fragments. However, they obtain parallel fragments from parallel sentence pairs (by chunking them and aligning the chunks appropriately), while we obtain them from comparable or non-parallel sentence pairs.

3   Extracting Parallel Fragments

The proposed method as previously mentioned, is a method for extracting parallel fragments from comparable corpora. In this section the details of proposed system is explained.

3.1   Document Alignment

For some documents such as "khameneii.ir" corpus, which source and target documents are not aligned together, document alignment is required. For this problem we addressed document alignment in comparable documents as an assignment problem of bipartite graph matching and intended to find the sub graphs having the maximum weight. This problem is an combinational optimization problem with known mathematical solutions which Here, Murker's assignment algorithm (Hungarian) was selected to solve the problem. Length and translation relevance of words considered as features.

3.2   Algorithm Procedure

In proposed method we use two different lexicon table similar to the base system. The first one is a simple dictionary for indicating candidate sentences and the second one is a lexicon based on LLR score which is used in fragment detection. The LLR based lexicon is obtained from the same way in Munteanu and Marcu (2006) which is based on the LLR computation formula in Moore (2004).

In proposed method, we use a score matrix for considering different alignments forms. In such a way that corresponding words LLR score matrix is created for each candidate sentence pair. Then in a descending order, the point having the highest score is chosen as starting point of fragment extraction and highlighted points (having highest scores) are processed for fragment extraction one after another.

The threshold value is obtained empirically. Lowering the threshold leads to a decrease in quality of fragments. So we decrease the threshold until the time that desired quality of fragments is not affected. Indeed, for each highlighted point clustering process is done and each cluster represents a fragment.

The procedure of finding fragment for each highlighted point is as below:

- The score of the fragment is computed according the features and patterns. Patterns are chosen considering languages type using the algorithm (currently English-Farsi) and common structures of fragments in these languages. Patterns are learned from a training corpus. For example diagonal structure with slope of +1 or −1 is one of the most common structures in English and Farsi fragments. Which means that consecutive words obeying diagonal structured usually are aligned together. Features will be explained in next section.
- Fragment's neighborhood is searched (first time the fragment is just a point and 8 adjacent points form its neighborhood) and total score of the fragment is computed. Then the points which leads to the highest score is chosen and will be added to the path.

  The chosen word will be connected to its parent (the word with minimum distance of x or y) in order to preserve fragment structure.
- The score is updated.

Figure 1 shows the algorithm block diagram. If block score is less than a certain threshold, the search is terminated. Also if a fragment is picked, its words are not used for next fragments (fragments do not overlap). Figure 1 shows an example of applying algorithm to a sentence pair and expanding path block around a highlighted point.

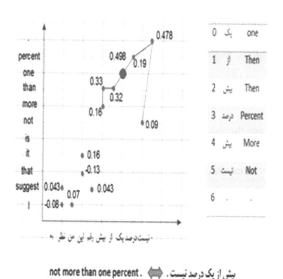

Fig. 1. Example of applying proposed method

3.3 Features

The following features used in proposed method:

1. Fragment length: longer fragments are preferred and scores are normalized considering length ratio. This feature's value is considered as path length which refers number of assignments.
2. Mean of LLR score: LLR score is initial factor and refers to translation feature, so the higher the LLR score, the better the fragment.

$$\text{Mean of LLR score} = \frac{\sum_{i=1}^{N} LLR_i}{N} \qquad (1)$$

3. Translation coverage: the number of words having translation in the range of maximum and minimum indices picked from matrix is important. More translation equivalents lead to higher score.

$$\text{Translation Coverage} = \frac{I}{X} \qquad (2)$$

Where I denotes the number of assignments, and X is the maximum length between the source and the destination sentences.

4. The slope of the fragment skeleton in a block: In the language pairs with nearly monotone word orders, the slope is close to one (diagonal form). The feature refers to total slope of block (Fig. 2).
5. Standard deviation of the slopes of the lines forming the fragment block: Checks fracture of the path. More than one fracture usually does not lead to good fragments. This feature is correlated with distribution of slope value of lines forming the fragment path.
6. Proximity of fragment block ribs length: it means that if length of equivalent source and target fragment are close, the block is more square-shaped. This feature is not correlated with block slope, just consider the fragments length of sentence pair.

$$\text{Proximity} = \left| \frac{(maxx - maxy)}{(maxy - miny)} \right| \qquad (3)$$

Which x and y are the coordinates of chosen points.

These scores are scaled between 0 and 10 and total score is obtained as linear combination of these features values and their weights.

$$Score = \frac{\sum_{i=1}^{6} w_i f_i}{\sum_{i=1}^{6} w_i} \qquad (4)$$

3.4 Features Weighting

To estimate the weights for the best performance, a golden corpus consists of 800 sentence pairs is randomly selected was built and 1630 reference fragments was

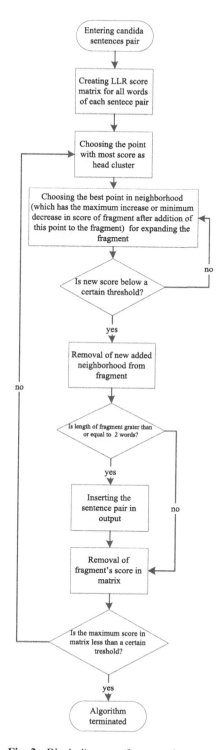

Fig. 2. Block diagram of proposed system

specified. According to this tuning corpus, features weights are estimated using the simulated annealing algorithm.

4   Experiments

4.1   Corpora and System Parameters

For initial system training and creating LLR lexicon table, probabilistic lexicon extracted form PEN corpus (Farajian 2011) was used which is a parallel news corpora (Table 1).

Table 1. parallel corpus and lexicon tables specification

Initial parallel corpora	30479 parallel sentence pairs
Simple lexicon	71090 entries
LLR lexicon	229747 entries

Precision, recall and F-measure are estimated on the word level. For the test phase, a human annotated corpus is used. The corpus is consisted of 1800 sentence pairs along with the correct reference fragments. Test corpus is consisted of text picked from four different comparable corpora having different domains, different styles and different quality of translation. The statistics of the test corpus are shown in Table 2.

Table 2. The statistics of test corpus

Reference fragments number	Quality of translation	Subject	Number of pairs	Corpus name
475	Bad-few common text	Political	500	Khameneii.ir
602	Average-comparable	Art-general	500	Tehran avenue
652	Good-semi parallel	News-political	500	Central Asia
278	Good-comparable	General	300	Books

In the evaluation phase, the experiments are conducted to answer the following two questions:

- How good are the extracted fragments?
- What is the impact of these extracted data on an SMT system?

The experiments are done using precision and recall measures which are calculated as below: (assuming X is candidate set and Y is reference set)

$$recall(Y|X) = \frac{|X \cap Y|}{X} \tag{5}$$

$$precision(Y|X) = \frac{|X \cap Y|}{Y} \tag{6}$$

$$F-measure = \frac{2 * precision * recall}{precision + recall} \tag{7}$$

4.2 Extracted Data Experiment

In this section, we want to evaluate how good the extracted fragments are.

Figure 3 shows proposed method total performance for different kinds of corpora. As is clear the most important factor for improving performance of algorithm is domain adaptation of test and train corpora for creating LLR lexicon which leads to more fragments and consequently improving recall. Also structure of input sentences affects algorithm precision, because the diagonal patterns which are used as feature, obtained from language structure. But clearly the precision of algorithm is very high and the reason is choosing appropriate features.

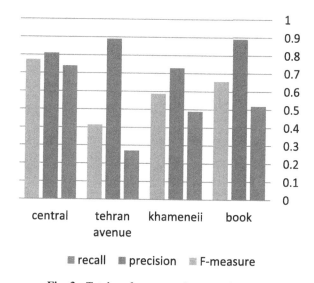

Fig. 3. Total performance of proposed system

4.3 SMT Performance Results

In this section we want to evaluate the effect of extracted data on SMT system. The proposed method is applied to "book", "khameneii.ir" and "Tehran avenue" comparable corpora which could not be used for system training because of low quality before. 9834 fragment (almost 26000 words each side) was extracted from them.

For evaluation, we trained SMT system once with PEN corpora and second extracted fragments are added to train set. For test process, once 1000 sentences from PEN (not used for training) were chosen and the other time 1000 sentences chosen from "khameneii.ir", "central Asia" and "Wikipedia" are used for test set. Result of BELU measurement of systems are as below:

As the Table 3 shows, adding extracted data to train set, has improved system BELU in both systems (Although extracted data compared to PEN corpora are small). In the first case which test set was picked from PEN, improvement is just 0.33 but in the second case, although system total BELU is decreased but BELU in second system has increased by 1.4 points compared to the baseline system. This increase appeared because data extracted from "khameneii.ir" was in second system train set and helped in translation process. Also the reason for total decrease of system BELU is that train data is insufficient for test set and test set text was mainly speech and hard to translate.

Table 3. Evaluation of extracted data effect on SMT system

System with added data	Base system	
18.46	18.16	**Test set 1**
15.75	14.36	**Test set 2**

4.4   Comparing Proposed System to Other Implemented Systems

As Fig. 4 indicates, proposed method has better results in both recall and precision criterions in comparison to base system and improved base system.

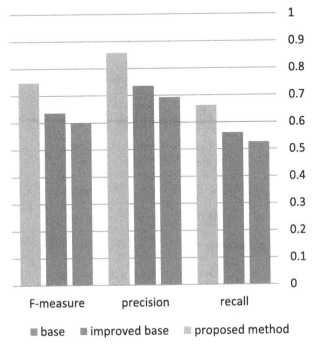

Fig. 4. Comparison of proposed system and two other systems

These better results is obtained because of choosing more precise features and considering proper patterns for fragment extraction.

The results of improved base system is also better than base system which is because of not using greedy alignment and using multiple alignments which is more appropriate for nature of Farsi language.

As Fig. 4 shows, recall is lower than precision and f-measure criterions that is because of some reasons such as difference of test and train domain and conversational sentences in test set which are not obeying language structures and make it hard to detect equivalent translation.

5 Conclusion

In this paper a novel system was introduced which is implemented based on extracting fragment blocks from source and target candidate sentence pairs using score calculated from special features. These features set consists of fragment length, LLR score, gradient value of fragment skeleton in block, distribution of gradient values of lines forming the fragment block, proximity of fragment block ribs and translation coverage percentage. This method is used to extract useful machine translation training data from comparable and non-parallel corpora, which contain no parallel sentence pairs. Evaluations showed that proposed method is very precise and not only outperforms the existing similar systems from precision and recall viewpoints, but also its extracted data improves the performance of a base statistical machine translation system from 0.33 up to 1.4 BELU points according to different test set.

References

Cheung, P., Fung, P.: Sentence alignment in parallel, comparable, and quasi-comparable corpora. In: LREC2004 Workshop (2004)

Deng, Y., Kumar, S., Byrne, W.: Segmentation and alignment of parallel text for statistical machine translation. J. Nat. Lang. Eng. **12**, 235–326 (2006)

Diab, M., Finch, S.: A statistical word-level translation model for comparable corpora. In: RIAO2000 (2000)

Farajian, M.A.: PEN: parallel english-persian news corpus. In: Proceedings of 2011 International Conference on Artificial Intelligence (ICAI'11), Nevada, USA (2011)

Fung, P., Cheung, P.: Mining very non-parallel corpora: parallel sentence and lexicon extraction vie bootstrapping and EM. In: EMNLP 2004, pp. 57–63 (2004a)

Fung, P., Cheung, P.: Multi-level bootstrapping for extracting parallel sentences from a quasi-comparable corpus. In: COLING 2004, pp. 1051–1057 (2004b)

Fung, P., Yee, L.Y.: An IR approach for translating new words from nonparallel, comparable texts. In: ACL 1998, pp. 414–420 (1998)

Gaussier, E., Renders, J.-M., Matveeva, I., Goutte, C., Dejean, H.: A geometric view on bilingual lexicon extraction from comparable corpora. In: ACL 2004, pp. 527–534 (2004)

Koehn, P., Knight, K.: Estimating word translation probabilities from unrelated mono-lingual corpora using the EM algorithm. In: National Conference on Artificial Intelligence, pp. 711–715 (2000)

Moore, R.C.: Improving IBM word-alignment model 1. In: ACL 2004, pp. 519–526 (2004)

Munteanu, D.S., Marcu, D.: Improving machine translation performance by exploiting non-parallel corpora. Comput. Ling. **31**(4), 477–504 (2005)

Munteanu, D.S., Marcu, D.: Extracting parallel sub-sentential fragments from comparable corpora. In: Proceedings of ACL 2006, pp. 81–88 (2006)

Rapp, R.: Automatic identification of word translations from unrelated English and German corpora. In: ACL 1999, pp. 519–526 (1999)

Resnik, P., Smith, N.A.: The web as a parallel corpus. Comput. Ling. **29**(3), 349–380 (2003)

Utiyama, M., Isahara, H.: Reliable measures for aligning Japanese-English news articles and sentences. In: ACL 2003, pp. 72–79 (2003)

Vogel, S.: Using noisy bilingual data for statistical machine translation. In: EACL 2003, pp. 175–178 (2003)

Wu, D., Fung, P.: Inversion transduction grammar constraints for mining parallel sentences from quasi-comparable corpora. In: Dale, R., Wong, K.-F., Su, J., Kwong, O.Y. (eds.) IJCNLP 2005. LNCS (LNAI), vol. 3651, pp. 257–268. Springer, Heidelberg (2005)

Zhao, B., Vogel, S.: Adaptive parallel sentences mining from web bilingual news col-lection. In: 2002 IEEE International Conference on Data Mining, pp. 745–748 (2002)

Robotics

Modified TangentBug Navigation Algorithm with Application to Car-Like Robots

Navid Hoseini Izadi$^{(\boxtimes)}$ and Maziar Palhang

Artificial Intelligence Laboratory,
Electrical and Computer Engineering Department,
Isfahan University of Technology, Isfahan, Iran
navid.hoseini@ec.iut.ac.ir, palhang@cc.iut.ac.ir

Abstract. Autonomous navigation in unknown environments is a challenging task. Several sensor-based methods like the Bug algorithms have been proposed to tackle the problem. But most Bug-type algorithms neglect practical implementation issues like robot dimensions and maneuver limitations. This paper presents a modified version of TangentBug algorithm especially designed for car-like robots. The method proposes a revised heuristic distance for more stable robot motion-to-goal behavior. Also the boundary following is modified to suit the limited steering of car-like robots. Simulation results show that the modified TangentBug is applicable to car-like robots with acceptable performance.

Keywords: Sensor-based · Autonomous navigation · Unknown environment · Obstacle avoidance

1 Introduction

Today one of the most active fields of research in robotics is autonomous navigation of mobile robots. Several projects have been reported in the literature ranging from autonomous navigation in completely known indoor environments to completely unknown outdoor environments.

Crucial to every autonomous mobile robot is the ability to detect and avoid the obstacles that may appear on the robot path to the goal. In scenarios where the environment is known in advance, the robot can make use of the map to compute a feasible and optimal path to the goal and with the aid of a good localization method it can reach the goal (if it is reachable). But as the environment gets bigger more memory and processing power is needed to maintain its map. Besides it is not always possible to build a map of the environment in advance. That is why navigation methods that assume no prior knowledge of the environment and only rely on available data provided by robot onboard sensors (sensor-based methods) are attractive. Using these methods the robots can navigate through the unknown environments and reach the goal without colliding with any obstacle [1].

The family of sensor-based Bug-type navigation algorithms is famous for their simplicity. They assume local knowledge of the environment but try to reach the global goal. One of the first algorithms of this family is Bug1 [2] which is followed by Bug2 [2] and Bug2+ [3]. A flavor of Bug-type algorithm is RoverBug [1] which is an

© Springer International Publishing Switzerland 2014
A. Movaghar et al. (Eds.): AISP 2013, CCIS 427, pp. 301–310, 2014.
DOI: 10.1007/978-3-319-10849-0_30

extended version of WedgeBug [1]. WedgeBug is especially designed and optimized for operation under severe resource constraints e.g. power consumption, and memory usage. Instead of range sensors it uses stereo vision to detect and bypass obstacles. Another interesting algorithm which utilizes Bug2+ algorithm is ABug [4]. It uses Bug2+ to generate multiple paths to goal and then performs A* search on the tree of generated paths to obtain the optimal path.

Most of the Bug-type algorithms assume that robot can perform perfect localization and sensor readings are flawless. However that is not the case in a real world scenario. Yet another extension of Bug algorithm that has tried to tackle the problem of inaccurate localization and sensor data is IBug [5]. This algorithm assumes the robot is unable to obtain accurate data from its sensors and so unable to localize itself accurately. The only sensor on the robot which provides real values is the one which measures the strength of a signal emanating from the goal position [5]. The robot can also check whether it is facing the goal or not using the alignment sensor.

TangentBug [6] is perhaps one of the most important Bug algorithms to date. It is especially designed to work with range sensors instead of tactile ones used in Bug1 and Bug2. This algorithm tries to shorten the path traveled by utilizing range data. Since TangentBug does not consider robot dimensions and its maneuver limitations, it is not possible to readily use it as navigation algorithm on car-like robots. This paper addresses practical implementation issues of TangentBug with application to car-like robots.

The rest of this paper is as follows: Sect. 2 gives an overview of TangentBug algorithm. Section 3 describes the changes made to TangentBug. Section 4 presents simulation results. Section 5 concludes the paper.

2 TangnetBug Algorithm Overview

TangentBug, like other Bug-type algorithms has two modes of operations (behaviors) that are motion-to-goal and boundary-following and assumes no prior knowledge of the environment. The algorithm starts with motion-to-goal behavior. At each time step local tangent graph (LTG) is built based on range sensor data. Then the robot moves directly toward the goal point if the direct path to it is clear according to LTG. But if the path is blocked by an obstacle then the endpoints of the obstacle named O_i's are found and the one which maximally reduces a heuristic distance is chosen and the robot moves toward it. This heuristic distance may be defined as [7]:

$$heuristic\_distance(x, T) = d(x, O_i) + d(O_i, T) \qquad (1)$$

where x is the robot position, O_i is the obstacle endpoint position, T is the goal position and d(a, b) denotes Euclidean distance between a and b points.

The robot stays in motion-to-goal behavior and tries to decrease the heuristic distance until (1) the goal is reached or (2) the heuristic distance starts to increase. In the first case, the algorithm halts with success. In the second case, the robot will switch to boundary following mode. In this mode, the robot follows the boundary of the nearest obstacle (also referred to as followed obstacle) in the same direction selected by the most recent motion-to-goal behavior step. The robot continues to follow the boundary of the followed obstacle until (1) goal is reached or (2) it completes a cycle around the followed obstacle or (3) leaving condition is met. In the first case the algorithm halts with success. In the second case the goal is unreachable and the algorithm halts with failure. In the third case the algorithm switches to motion-to-goal behavior since the following leaving condition is met. Let $d_{min}(T)$ be the shortest distance to the goal observed so far, along the followed obstacle boundary. Now the leaving condition is satisfied if there is a node V_{Leave} in the current LTG s.t.: $d(V_{Leave}, T) < d_{min}(T)$ [6].

3 The Proposed Method

TangentBug algorithm is not directly applicable to a real robot especially to a car-like one because it assumes the robot to be a point. But a real robot has specific dimensions. So the robot always needs to keep its distance from the obstacles for its safety. TangentBug also assumes that the robot is capable of moving directly toward any chosen point (on a straight line from robot position to the chosen point) regardless of the amount of difference between robot heading and target vector (vector from robot position to the chosen point). But a car-like robot has nonholonomic constraints i.e. it cannot move freely to any direction. Also, the minimum turning radius of the robot which is a function of steering angle and robot wheelbase (provided that robot speed is slow) is nonzero which causes the robot to always move on an arc. So to make TangentBug suitable for a car-like robot, some changes must be done.

3.1 Changes Made to the Original TangentBug

As mentioned before the method proposed here is based on TangentBug and is designed with application to car-like robots in mind. To make TangentBug applicable to a real car-like robot, some modifications have been applied.

Changes Made to LTG. Since the robot dimensions are nonzero i.e. the robot is not a point, in LTG construction phase, any pair of adjacent obstacles that the free space between them is not enough for the robot to pass through safely, must be considered as a single obstacle in order to prevent the robot from colliding with them. To this end, assume the range sensor scan direction is clockwise and the first point of any sensed obstacle i (in clockwise direction) is called SO_i and the last point of it is called EO_i. Also assume the robot shape is estimated by its bounding circle with radius R_b. Now construction of LTG is performed in two phases. In the first phase, LTG is built based on sensed obstacles as stated before in [6]. In the second phase, any pair of adjacent obstacles like (SO_i, EO_i) and (SO_{i+1}, EO_{i+1}) that satisfy Eq. (2) will be merged and considered as one obstacle namely (SO_i, EO_{i+1}).

$$d(EO_i, SO_{i+1}) < R_b + s \tag{2}$$

where s is a tuning parameter which is used to make sure that the robot keeps a minimum safe distance from the obstacles when moving between them. So, to consider adjacent obstacles as separate ones, the free space between them must be greater than $R_b + s$. In Fig. 1, a sample environment is shown in which three obstacles with red (labeled with R), green (labeled with G) and blue (labeled with B) colors surround the robot. In Fig. 2 the small circle with a needle attached to it shows the robot position and heading, respectively. The red circle which only three fourth (270°) of it is drawn shows the region scanned by the range sensor (mounted on the robot). As can be seen in Fig. 2(a), red (SO_r, EO_r), green (SO_g, EO_g) and blue (SO_b, EO_b) obstacles are considered separately but the robot cannot move through the free space between green and blue ones because it is not wide enough. Figure 2(b) shows the result of merging phase in LTG construction based on a predefined R_b and s. Blue and green obstacles are merged and considered as one obstacle (SO_{bg}, EO_{bg}). But obstacle (SO_{bg}, EO_{bg}) is not merged with (SO_r, EO_r) because the free space between them is enough for the robot to move through (according to Eq. (2)).

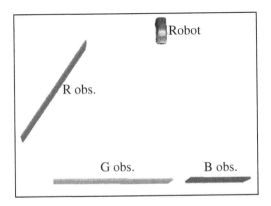

Fig. 1. Three obstacles surround the robot namely R, G and B. The free space between G and B is not enough for the robot to pass through safely. But the space between G and R is enough (Color figure online).

Changes Made to Heuristic Distance. In some scenarios the heuristic distance used by TangentBug causes the robot to repeatedly switch between the two endpoints of the blocking obstacle it is trying to bypass in motion-to-goal behavior. This switching in endpoint selection causes constant oscillation in robot heading while moving toward the chosen point which in turn causes robot collision with the obstacle eventually. As an example of this scenario assume robot is in motion-to-goal behavior and the path to the goal is blocked. So one of the two endpoints (SO and EO) of the blocking obstacle must be chosen to bypass the obstacle. Moreover assume the whole obstacle is not within the range sensor scan region. Also note that TangentBug has no memory of its past so it cannot remember anything about the real dimensions of the blocking obstacle and at each time step only the portion of the obstacle which is within the scan region is considered by TangentBug. In Fig. 3, x is the robot current position. s is the robot start position. T is the goal point. SO and EO are the endpoints of the blocking obstacle. The dotted line connecting any pair of points shows the Euclidean distance between them. The light gray trail between s and x shows the path traveled by the robot so far. Note that in each part of Fig. 3(a, b, c and d) the visible portion of the blocking obstacle is shown by thick black lines and the portion of it which is outside of scan region is shown by thinner black lines. Also note that in each part of Fig. 3, a point labeled as c is shown which is the safe point computed based on the chosen endpoint. It is computed because the robot cannot head toward the chosen endpoint directly or it will collide with the blocking obstacle [8]. Point c is computed in a way that the robot distance to the chosen endpoint is kept in both vertical and horizontal directions. In Fig. 3(b, c) d1 and d2 are the vertical and horizontal distance to EO (SO), respectively.

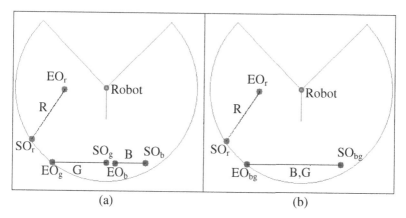

(a)   (b)

Fig. 2. (a) LTG constructed without merging phase: R, B and G obstacles are considered separately. (b) LTG merging phase result: B and G obstacles are merged as {B, G} (Color figure online).

As can be seen in Fig. 3(a), d(x, SO) + d(SO, T) is less than d(x, EO) + d(EO, T). So the chosen endpoint is SO. The more robot moves toward the computed safe point (c) based on SO, the more the blocking obstacle goes out of scan region. This causes the heuristic distance of the path through EO to decrease until at some point it becomes less than the heuristic distance of the path through SO and this is the case shown in Fig. 3(b). After switching the chosen endpoint to EO the new safe point is computed and the robot moves toward it. As a result, the portion of the blocking obstacle within the scan region starts to increase. This in turn causes a situation similar to that of Fig. 3 (a) and the chosen endpoint will be switched to SO again which is shown in Fig. 3(c). This switching process continues until the robot collides with the obstacle (Fig. 3(d)). This switching issue is independent of the robot platform type and it is indeed a drawback of the defined heuristic distance itself.

To solve the switching problem, a coefficient K is multiplied to the heuristic distance value. Given x, SO and EO in the global coordinate system, two vectors namely $\overrightarrow{xSO}$ and $\overrightarrow{xEO}$ are computed using Eq. (3). Let $\overrightarrow{H}$ be the robot heading vector with respect to the global coordinate system. Then sAngle and eAngle are computed

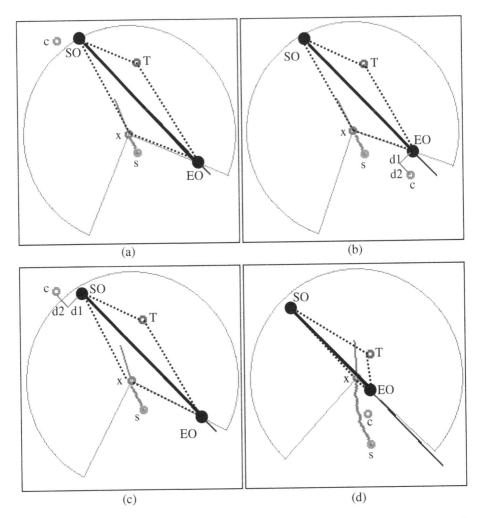

Fig. 3. Oscillation in blocking obstacle endpoint selection: (a) SO is the chosen endpoint. (b) EO is the chosen endpoint. (c) SO is the chosen endpoint. (d) Robot has collided with the obstacle due to repeated switching between SO and EO endpoints.

using Eq. (4) where $|\overrightarrow{H}|$ is the magnitude of $\overrightarrow{H}$, $|\overrightarrow{xSO}|$ is the magnitude of $\overrightarrow{xSO}$ and $\overrightarrow{H}.\overrightarrow{xSO}$ denotes the dot product between $\overrightarrow{H}$ and $\overrightarrow{xSO}$. The same holds for $\overrightarrow{H}$ and $\overrightarrow{xEO}$. Note that sAngle (eAngle) is the angle between $\overrightarrow{H}$ and $\overrightarrow{xSO}$ ($\overrightarrow{xEO}$).

Next sAngle and eAngle are normalized. Since the range of arccos is $[0, \pi]$, sAngle and eAngle are divided by π to become normalized. Let K_s be the normalized sAngle and let K_e be the normalized eAngle (Eq. (5)). Now the new heuristic distance for the path through SO (EO) endpoint is given by Eq. (6).

$$\overrightarrow{xSO} = SO - x, \quad \overrightarrow{xEO} = EO - x \tag{3}$$

$$\angle sAngle = \arccos\left(\frac{\overrightarrow{H}.\overrightarrow{xSO}}{|\overrightarrow{H}|\,|\overrightarrow{xSO}|}\right), \quad \angle eAngle = \arccos\left(\frac{\overrightarrow{H}.\overrightarrow{xEO}}{|\overrightarrow{H}|\,|\overrightarrow{xEO}|}\right) \tag{4}$$

$$K_s = sAngle/\pi, \quad K_e = eAngle/\pi, \quad (0 \le K_s, K_e \le 1) \tag{5}$$

$$\text{heuristic\_distance} = \begin{cases} K_s \times (d(x, SO) + d(SO, T)), & \text{for SO endpoint} \\ K_e \times (d(x, EO) + d(EO, T)), & \text{for EO endpoint} \end{cases} \tag{6}$$

K_s and K_e coefficients act as weighting factors. The more value of sAngle (eAngle) increases the more K_s (K_e) increases which in turn causes heuristic distance of the path through SO (EO) to increase. In other words, by using K_s and K_e in heuristic distance equations, TangentBug will be biased toward selecting the endpoint which causes less change in robot heading. This way in scenarios like Fig. 3 switching between obstacle endpoints will not occur anymore. For example, consider the situation in Fig. 3(b). TangentBug heuristic distance will choose EO endpoint. But note that moving toward SO causes less change in robot heading than moving toward EO so K_s will be less than K_e which in turn causes SO heuristic distance to be less than EO heuristic distance. So according to the revised heuristic distance (the proposed one), SO point will be chosen as the endpoint for obstacle avoidance and this way robot will continue its motion toward SO and no oscillation will occur. Figure 4 shows the result of using the revised heuristic distance. As can be seen, robot behavior during motion-to-goal mode is stable and no collision with the obstacle has occurred.

Changes Made to Boundary Following. To follow an obstacle boundary, robot can move on a path which is consistently orthogonal to the obstacle surface normal [7]. Assuming that the followed obstacle is locally flat, at each time step the obstacle surface normal can be determined using range sensor data. Let m be the global minimum of the range data and let x be the robot position. Now vector $\overrightarrow{mx}$ can be considered as the surface normal and the robot can move in the direction which is orthogonal to $\overrightarrow{mx}$ (parallel to the obstacle surface) for a short distance and this process repeats [7]. Note that this way the robot always follows the boundary of the obstacle which contains point m.

While the boundary following method described above is suitable for robots that have a minimum turning radius of zero such as differential drive ones, it is inappropriate for robots with nonzero minimum turning radius such as car-like ones. As an example, suppose l1 and l2 are two straight walls orthogonal to each other. Moreover, assume that a car-like robot is currently moving parallel to l1 (which means point m belongs to l1), and l2 intersects with both l1 and the robot path. Note that the robot always keeps a safe distance (W^*) from the followed wall. So the robot distance to the nearest point on l1 (m) is approximately equal to W^* [7]. The robot will keep following l1 until its distance to the nearest point on l2 becomes less than W^* i.e. l2 becomes the wall which has point m on its boundary. Now if the robot minimum turning radius (R_{min}) is greater or equal to W^*, the robot will collide with l2.

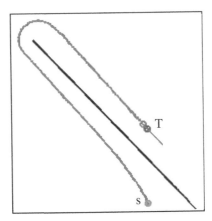

Fig. 4. Robot stable behavior as a result of using revised heuristic distance

One way to solve this issue is to choose W^* greater than R_{min}. But this causes W^* to be dependent on R_{min} which may not be desirable. An alternative approach is to revise the boundary following policy; instead of moving in the direction orthogonal to the obstacle surface normal, the robot moves toward a safe point computed based on one of the obstacle endpoints. The endpoint is selected among SO or EO based on the type of the one chosen by the most recent motion-to-goal behavior i.e. if in the last motion-to-goal behavior the type of the chosen endpoint was SO (EO) then SO (EO) endpoint of the obstacle is selected for safe point computation. By steering the robot according to the chosen endpoint of the obstacle, the robot has enough free space to align itself with the obstacle boundary provided that, R_{min} is less than total range of the range sensor which is a reasonable assumption if the range sensor is a laser scanner.

The revised boundary following has two advantages. First, the safe distance value is independent of R_{min} and second, the path length traveled by the robot in boundary following mode is reduced because the robot does not exactly follow the obstacle boundary but a smooth approximation of it.

4   Simulation Results

To test the proposed method, Autonomous Vehicle sample project of Webots simulator has been modified and used as the test environment. The simulation results show that our method is capable of navigating a car-like robot in unknown environments.

Figure 5(a) compares the result of TangentBug boundary following method with the proposed boundary following method. Robot starts from point s in motion-to-goal behavior. The motion-to-goal portion of the paths generated by TangentBug and proposed method are the same (the paths are overlapped). But when the robot switches to boundary following, the paths generated by original TangentBug and our method do not overlap anymore. As can be seen the proposed method does not exactly follow the curve of the boundary (the circle-shape part of the obstacle). Instead the endpoint of the boundary is followed which has caused a safe path for the robot (light gray path from s to x2). But the original boundary following method has caused robot collision with the obstacle (dark gray path from s to x1).

Figure 5(b) demonstrates the result of merging phase in LTG construction. As can be seen the obstacles between E and F points are merged and the robot has avoided them as if they were a single continuous obstacle.

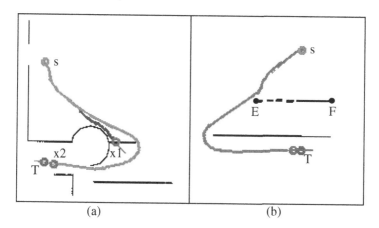

(a)   (b)

Fig. 5. Simulation results: (a) comparison of original TangentBug boundary following (dark gray path from s to x1) with the proposed one (light gray path from s to x2), (b) the obstacles between E and F points are merged and considered as one obstacle in LTG merging phase.

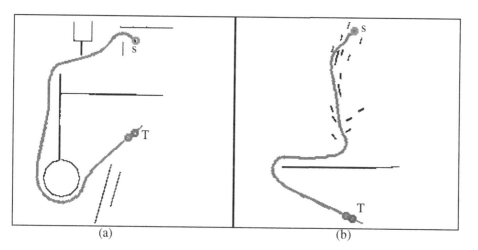

(a)   (b)

Fig. 6. Simulation results: (a) successful navigation to goal (b) robot has moved through many small obstacles successfully.

Figure 6(a) shows the successful obstacle avoidance performed by the robot. Figure 6(b) shows that the proposed method can handle dense environments which are filled with many small obstacles with small free spaces between them.

5 Conclusion

The original TangentBug algorithm is modified to be used as the navigation algorithm for a car-like robot. In LTG construction, any pair of adjacent obstacles without enough free space between them is considered as one obstacle. The heuristic distance is revised to make the motion-to-goal behaviors more stable. Plus, the boundary following implementation is changed to make the car-like robot, capable of following obstacle boundary without colliding with it. The simulation results show that our method is capable of guiding the robot through unknown environments while avoiding obstacles on the robot path. In addition to simulations, we have tested our method on a real robot. The results of our experiments will be published in a future paper.

References

1. Laubach, S.L., Burdick, J.W.: An autonomous sensor-based path planner for planetary microrovers. In: IEEE International Conference on Robotics and Automation, pp. 347–354. IEEE Press, New York (1999). doi:10.1109/ROBOT.1999.770003
2. Lumelsky, V.J., Stepanov, A.A.: Dynamic path planning for a mobile automaton with limited information on the environment. IEEE Trans. Autom. Control 31, 1058–1063 (1986). doi:10.1109/TAC.1986.1104175
3. Antich, J., Ortiz, A., Minguez, J.: Bug2+: details and formal proofs. Technical report A-1, University of the Balearic Islands (2009)
4. Antich, J., Ortiz, A., Minguez, J.: A bug-inspired algorithm for efficient anytime path planning. In: IEEE/RSJ International Conference on Intelligence Robots and Systems, pp. 5407–5413. IEEE Press, New York (2009). doi:10.1109/IROS.2009.5354182
5. Taylor, K., LaValle, S.M.: I-Bug: an intensity-based bug algorithm. In: IEEE International Conference on Robotics and Automation, pp. 3981–3986. IEEE Press, New York (2009). doi:10.1109/ROBOT.2009.5152728
6. Kamon, I., Rimon, E., Rivlin, E.: TangentBug: a range-sensor-based navigation algorithm. Int. J. Robot. Res. 17, 934–953 (1998). doi:10.1177/027836499801700903
7. Choset, H., Lynch, K., Hutchinson, S., Kantor, G., Brgard, W., Kavraki, L., Thurn, S.: Principles of Robot Motion, Theory, Algorithms and Implementation. MIT Press, London (2005)
8. Zhu, Y., Zhang, T., Song, J., Li, X.: A new bug-type navigation algorithm considering practical implementation issues for mobile robots. In: IEEE International Conference on Robotics and Biomimetics, pp. 531–536. IEEE Press, New York (2010). doi:10.1109/ROBIO.2010.5723382

Differential Evolution Optimization of Ferguson Splines for Soccer Robot Path Planning

Elahe Mansury[1], Alireza Nikookar[2], and Mostafa E. Salehi[3(✉)]

[1] Mechatronics Research Lab, Islamic Azad University,
Qazvin Branch, Qazvin, Iran
elahe.mansury@qiau.ac.ir
[2] Department of Computer Engineering, Islamic Azad University,
South Tehran Branch, Tehran, Iran
arn_nik@acm.org
[3] School of Electrical and Computer Engineering, Faculty of Engineering,
University of Tehran, 14395-515 Tehran, Iran
mersali@ut.ac.ir

Abstract. Moving over the best path across the game field is crucial for soccer robots, which makes path planning an important task for them. In this paper, we propose a solution for the problem of path planning by employing Differential Evolution (DE) algorithm and cubic Ferguson Splines. At first, a path for robot movement is described by Ferguson splines, and then we apply DE algorithm to optimize the parameters of the splines in order to find an optimal path between the beginning and the end points considering obstacles between them. The simulational results showed the performance improvements of the proposed solution in comparison with other intelligent algorithms.

Keywords: Path planning · Differential evolution (DE) · Ferguson splines · Humanoid soccer robot

1 Introduction

Path planning is a vital task in the soccer robot game environment, where a robot must find the best path between starting and end points without colliding with obstacles between them. To find such a path, the robot must consider different criteria, including distance, time, cost, etc. to overcome the issue, which makes it a kind of a constrained optimization problem [1, 2].

Differential Evolution grew out of Ken Price's attempts to solve the Chebychev Polynomial fitting problem that had been posed to him by Rainer Storn [3]. It is population-based algorithm and employs mutation, crossover and selection operations to obtain the best population at each generation until find the best solution to the problem. Unlike genetic algorithm that relies on crossover, DE relies on mutation besides selection to navigate the search toward the optimal solution. DE algorithm has been widely used to solve many optimization problems [4–6].

© Springer International Publishing Switzerland 2014
A. Movaghar et al. (Eds.): AISP 2013, CCIS 427, pp. 311–319, 2014.
DOI: 10.1007/978-3-319-10849-0_31

Many polynomials have been proposed to define the path of soccer robots. However, most of them have their cons such as complexity of computations, finding improper trajectory, etc. In [1, 3, 4] the cubic Ferguson Splines were employed to describe the path between the arbitrary points to overcome the problem of other polynomials.

In this paper, we introduce the application of Differential Evolution algorithm to find an optimal path for a humanoid soccer robot in a game field using cubic Ferguson splines. The rest of the paper is organized as follows: in Sect. 2, we describe the Ferguson splines, Differential Evolution algorithm, a fitness function that is used for optimization, and how parents are coded for finding optimum solution. Experimental results are presented in Sect. 3 to reflect the performance and advantages of Differential Evolution algorithm in finding optimal path in comparison to other algorithms including ABC, Clerk's PSO (CPSO) and PSO. Finally, the paper will be concluded in Sect. 4.

2 Methods

2.1 Cubic Ferguson Splines

To define a Ferguson spline considering two arbitrary points P0 and P1 of the spline and their corresponding tangent vector P'_0 and P'_1, we can use the following equation [11]:

$$X(t) = P_0 f_1(t) + P_1 f_2(t) + P'_0 f_3(t) + P'_1 f_4(t) \tag{1}$$

Where $t \in [0, 1]$ is parameter, Corresponding $f_1 - f_4$ are Ferguson multi-nomials which can be described by:

$$f_1(t) = 2t^3 - 3t^2 + 1 \tag{2}$$

$$f_2(t) = 2t^3 + 3t^2 \tag{3}$$

$$f_3(t) = t(t-1)^2 \tag{4}$$

$$f_4(t) = t^2(t-1) \tag{5}$$

Equations (1–5) implies that we can acquire both P0 and P1 points by $X(0)$ and $X(1)$. P'_0 and P'_1 is simply obtained by substitution of derivations.

$$f'_1(t) = 6t^2 - 6t \tag{6}$$

$$f'_2(t) = -6t^2 + 6t \tag{7}$$

$$f'_3(t) = 3t^2 - 4t + 1 \tag{8}$$

$$f'_4(t) = 3t^2 - 2t \tag{9}$$

Using Eqs. (1) and (6–9), we can conclude $P'_0 = X'(0)$ and $P'_1 = X'(1)$. If second Ferguson spline exists:

$$\bar{X}(t) = \bar{P}_0 f_1(t) + \bar{P}_1 f_2(t) + \bar{P}'_0 f_3(t) + \bar{P}'_1 f_4(t) \tag{10}$$

We can connect these two splines by rule Eq. (11) and simply describe a path by a string of Ferguson splines. The continuity of the first derivation is mandatory.

$$P_1 = \bar{P}'_0, P'_1 = \bar{P}'_0 \tag{11}$$

2.2 Differential Evolution

The Differential Evolution is a population-based algorithm, which is introduced by Ken Price and is widely used to overcome the optimization problem in many situations. Like other evolutionary algorithms, it tries to gain the best result by improving the solutions through generations. It employs mutation, crossover and selection to perform the improvement, much like genetic algorithm. However, DE mostly relies on mutation and selection to direct the searching process and non-uniform crossover is applied to shuffle information and provide better searching process [3, 7, 8].

To find the best solution for the problem, DE starts with a population of potential solutions and in each generation, it employs mutation as the main operator to produce trial vectors from each individual. These vectors will later be used by a crossover operator to produce offspring. To produce the trial vector, DE applies the following equation:

$$u_i(t) = x_{i1}(t) + \beta(x_{i2}(t) - x_{i3}(t)) \tag{12}$$

Where $x_i(t)$ represents an individual in the population and β is the scale factor. The crossover operator performs the recombination of trial vector, and the parent vector used in mutation step to produce the offspring. The general schema for Differential Evaluation algorithm is as follows:

```
1: Initialize Population
2: Evaluation
3: repeat
4:     Mutation
5:     Recombination
6:     Evaluation
7:     Selection
8: until requirements are met
```

2.3 Parents Coding and Fitness Function

In order to simplify the problem of path planning, we can show mathematical notation of Ferguson spline in 2d space as follows [9, 10]:

$$r(t) = (x(t), y(t)) = a_0 + a_1 t + a_2 t^2 + a_3 t^3 \tag{13}$$

where

$$\begin{cases} a_0 = 2P_0 - 2P_1 + P_0' + P_1' \\ a_1 = -3P_0 + 3P_1 - P_0' + P' \\ a_2 = P_0' \\ a_3 = P_0 \end{cases} \tag{14}$$

Each spline is defined solely by points P0 and P1 and vectors. According to Eq. (3), every two neighboring splines in the string share one of the terminal points and the corresponding vector. Total number of variables that defines the whole trajectory in 2D space is 4(n + 1), where n is the number of splines in the string. Structure of the parents for optimization is shown in Fig. 1.

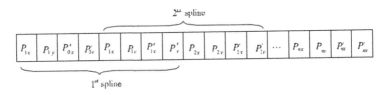

Fig. 1. Structure of a parent source.

An important part of an evolutionary algorithm is the selection of a good evaluation function as a fitness, which in this problem, global minimum of the function could correspond to smooth trajectory that is safe and short. As the fitness function, we choose the one introduced in [6]. The function consists of two parts that penalize the long distance of the trajectory (f_1) and the trajectories that causes collision with obstacles (f_2). The fitness function is as follows:

$$f = f_1 + \alpha f_2 \tag{15}$$

Where α is a weight factor that adjusts the prortion of the length and safety. f_1 is defined by the following equation:

$$f_1 = \frac{L}{L_{min}} \tag{16}$$

Where L is the length of trajectory and L_{min} is Euclidian distance between starting and end point. f_2 is defined by the following equation as well:

$$f_2 = \begin{cases} L, & d_{min} > d_{safe} \\ e^{\frac{D_{safe}+1}{d_{min}+1}+1} & d_{min} \leq d_{safe} \end{cases} \tag{17}$$

Where d_{safe} is a constant that determine the influence of that obstacles.

3   Experimental Results

We performed two simulations to evaluate and compare the behavior of our proposed model in finding an optimal path for a soccer robot on the game field. In each simulation, the goal for the robot is to find and travel an optimal path between two points located arbitrarily on different sides of the field without any collisions with three obstacles that were placed between the start and the end points randomly. Each simulation was designed in a way to compare the behavior of the model in different conditions in a soccer game.

In the following, first, we describe parameters of each algorithm used through the simulations and then we will show and compare the results and performance of our proposed solution with three other models introduced in the literature, including CPSO, PSO and ABC [9, 12] through two simulations to find an optimal path for a soccer robot to travel on the game field. For each simulation, the best path and the convergence curve as well as the process of finding an optimal path are shown.

3.1   Settings

In both simulations, values of common parameters such as population size and number of iterations were the same for all algorithms. For each model, some specific settings were needed to be considered given in Table 1. The population size, which indicates the number of potentially optimal paths between the starting and end points was chosen to be 25. Number of iterations considered for each run was 100, and each path between the designated points were constructed by two splines. According to Eq. (10), each spline needs eight parameters for interpolation (four parameters for beginning of the spline and four parameters for end point of it). Since the starting and end points were already known for each simulation and two splines were used for constructing the path, we only needed to find the essential parameters for the joint point of the two splines; therefore, the number of parameters for each population to be optimized is four. Safety parameter for collision avoiding was chosen as 0.6 to consider a safe distance between the path and obstacles.

Table 1. Configuration parameters of the algorithms.

ABC	CPSO	DE	PSO
Min and Max Value: 3, −3	Min and Max Value: 0, 5	Min and Max Value: 0, 2	Min and Max Value: 0, 3
The number of colony size: 50	c1 and c2: 1	weighting factor: 0.7	c1 and c2: 1
Limit: 100	X: 1	crossover constant: 0.3	

Simulation I. The robot must travel a path from an arbitrary point inside its own half-field toward another arbitrary point close to the opponent's goal (Fig. 2). On the subject of optimal path, DE, PSO and ABC found paths close to each other. However CPSO performance was better and it found a little shorter path rather than 3 other algorithms. Considering the convergence and time, CPSO converged in around 10th iteration, DE in 15th, ABC in 16th and PSO in 25th. Regardless of converging very fast, DE took longer total time for finding the optimal path than other algorithms and CPSO outperformed in the matter of timing. However, in terms of converging iteration, DE converged in a fewer iterations than PSO and ABC (Fig. 3).

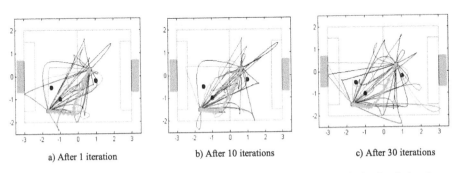

a) After 1 iteration   b) After 10 iterations   c) After 30 iterations

Fig. 2. The process of finding optimal path for a random situation in in simulation 1.

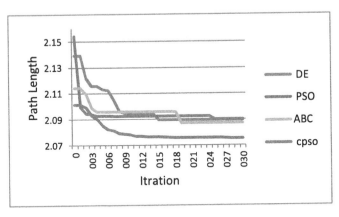

Fig. 3. The convergence steps of the four explored algorithms in 30 iterations for scenario 1.

Simulation II. The robot must travel a path from an arbitrary point inside its own half-field toward another arbitrary point inside the opponent's half-field but close to the starting point (Fig. 5). As depicted in Fig. 6, CPSO and DE executions resulted in finding the best outputs among all algorithms; PSO and ABC performed averagely. On the matter of convergence, DE, ABC and PSO approached their final results in around

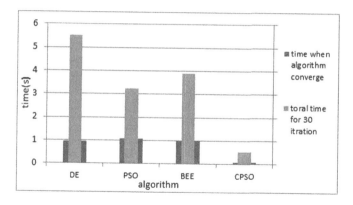

Fig. 4. The total and converging time for all algorithm in scenario 1.

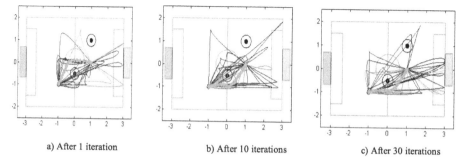

a) After 1 iteration   b) After 10 iterations   c) After 30 iterations

Fig. 5. The process of finding optimal path for a random situation in simulation 2.

26th iteration, while PSO converged in around 20th iteration. Over the timing issue, algorithms behaved nearly like scenario 1 with CPSO stays at top and DE is places at the bottom of the list with longer time to find the best path. However, in terms of converging time, DE finds its optimal path nearly in half of the time PSO and ABC have needed and stays after CPSO (Fig. 7).

Discussion. In order to evaluate the excellence of our model, we compared it with three other algorithms, including ABC [7], CPSO and PSO [9, 10]. We tested all the four models in two different situations and described the comparison results in this section. Considering the optimal path, as shown in Figs. 2 and 4, our model found the optimal paths closer or better than ABC and PSO in both scenarios, but in comparison with CPSO, the result in the second situation was only close, which indicates that DE is a good solution for finding the optimal path in short distances. Considering convergence as well as total execution time, simulations showed that DE did not perform much better than others, however, as illustrated in Figs. 4 and 7, DE converged to the best optimal path in shorter time than ABC and PSO.

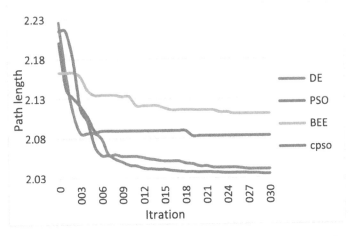

Fig. 6. The convergence steps of the four explored algorithms in 30 iterations for scenario 2.

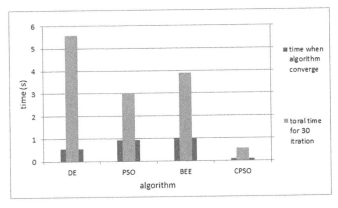

Fig. 7. The total and converging time for all algorithm in scenario 2.

4   Conclusion

In this paper, a solution for the problem of path planning is proposed using Differential Evolution algorithm and Ferguson Spines. The path between two arbitrary points in the game field was described by Ferguson splines and DE algorithm was applied to seek the desirable values of the splines' parameters, which were led to an optimal path avoiding the obstacles between the points. Two simulations were conducted considering situations in which a robot must travel on long and short paths. The simulation with the longer path showed that DE performed nearly the same as Artificial Bee Colony (ABC) and PSO in terms of path length, convergence and time; CPSO outperformed in this scenario. In the second simulation with the shorter path, our model performed better than ABC and PSO and closely equal to CPSO considering path length, convergence and time. However, CPSO performed very well over the timing issues. Using mutation as the main operator helped DE to overcome the local minima problem very fast. Considering the results of both simulations in terms of all criteria, DE provided a good solution for scenarios of short paths. For future work, improved version of DE can be applied to obtain better outcomes in comparison with CPSO, which is an improved version of PSO, and applications of other spline functions can be applied to gain better results with less complexity and more smoothness.

References

1. Raja, P., Pugazhenthi, S.: Optimal path planning of mobile robots: a review. Int. J. Phys. Sci. 7(9), 1314–1320 (2012)
2. Saska, M., Macas, M., Preucil, L.: Robot path planning using particle swarm optimization of Ferguson splines. In: Proceedings of the IEEE Symposium on Emerging Technologies and Factory Automation, pp. 833–839 (2006)
3. Engelbercht, A.P.: Computational Intelligence: An Introduction, 2nd edn. John Wiley and Sons, England (2007)
4. Musrrat, A., Siarry, P., Pant, M.: An efficient differential evolution based algorithm for solving multi-objective optimization problems. Eur. J. Oper. Res. 217(2), 404–416 (2012)
5. Fábio, F., Krohling, R.A.: A co-evolutionary differential evolution algorithm for solving min–max optimization problems implemented on GPU using C-CUDA. Expert Syst. Appl. 39(12), 10324–10333 (2012)
6. Piotrowski, A.P., Napiorkowski, J.J., Kiczko, A.: Differential evolution algorithm with separated groups for multi-dimensional optimization problems. Eur. J. Oper. Res. 216(1), 33–46 (2012)
7. Karaboga, D., Basturk, B.: A comparative study of artificial bee colony algorithm. J. Appl. Math. Comput. 214(1), 108–132 (2009)
8. Karaboga, D., Basturk, B.: On the performance of artificial bee colony (ABC) algorithm. Appl. Soft Comput. 8, 1 (2008)
9. Wu, X.X., Guo, B.L.: Mobile robot path planning algorithm based on particle swarm optimization of cubic splines. Int. J. Robot, 31(6), 556–560 (2009)
10. Xian, W., Yan, M., Juan, W.: An improved path planning approach based on Particle Swarm Optimization. In: 11th International Conference on Hybrid Intelligent Systems (HIS), pp. 157–161 (2011)
11. Ye, J., Qu, R.: Fairing of parametric cubic splines. Math. Comput. Model. 30(5/6), 121–131 (1999)
12. Mansury, E., Nikookar, A., Salehi, M.E.: Artificial bee colony optimization of ferguson splines for soccer robot path planning. In: First RSI/ISM International Conference on Robotics and Mechatronics (ICRoM), pp. 85–89, 13–15 Feb 2013, doi:10.1109/ICRoM. 2013.6510086

A Group Decision Support System (GDSS) Based on Naive Bayes Classifier for Roadway Lane Management

Rayehe MoienFar$^{(\boxtimes)}$, S. Mehdi Hashemi, and Mehdi Ghatee

Department of Computer Science, Amirkabir University of Technology,
Hafez Ave., Office 218, 15875-4413 Tehran, Iran
{mfar,hashemi,ghatee}@aut.ac.ir

Abstract. Artificial intelligence's objective is to replace human decision makers, while decision support system (DSS) has the aim of supporting rather than replacing. In a group DSS (GDSS) a number of managers need to be involved in the decision process. Roadway lane management can be implemented by different strategies whichever is appropriate for particular situation, based on the environment and individuals' behavior. Solving lane management problem requires setting weights for different management strategies by some experts based on standards on physical characteristics of the road and some other experts based on the individual's behavior. Finally, the planner(s) will choose the most appropriate strategy based on the current characteristics of the roadway and its users and also based on previous experience on that country. This article makes an environment which exerts experts' consult and for each roadway/society situation estimates fuzzy results based on this consult and previous implementation experience from knowledge base. A Naive Bayes classifier is the core of the proposed GDSS which handles the irrelevant attributes, and can get a good estimate of the probability and do not require a very large training set.

Keywords: DSS · GDSS · Fuzzy · Naive Bayes classifier · Lane management

1 Introduction

The term "managed lanes" includes different types of strategies that some of them have been applied on the roads. The goal of Lane Management is maximizing productivity of current road capacity by using operational tools. When HOV lanes are implemented, people tend to use high capacity vehicles [1]. The central concept of HOV lanes is to move more people rather than more cars. So, especial lanes of the way will be dedicated to high-occupant vehicles that carry the minimum number of people posted at the entrance signs. This strategy can be implemented in different ways, whichever is appropriate for particular situation, based on the environment and individuals' behavior.

Societal and public opinion regarding the implementation of a managed lanes strategy may be the single most important nonoperational factor in a facility's success or failure. Unfavorable public opinion can result in either the curtailment or

© Springer International Publishing Switzerland 2014
A. Movaghar et al. (Eds.): AISP 2013, CCIS 427, pp. 320–331, 2014.
DOI: 10.1007/978-3-319-10849-0_32

cancellation of projects or provide a preconceived notion of the effectiveness of a strategy that may affect future projects. Therefore, in addition to the physical characteristics some other properties must be checked to maximize the likelihood of success. As an illustration, if the rate of high-occupant cars is less than 30−45 vehicles per hour, then people will think HOV lane is inapplicable. Poorly thought out strategies combined with insufficient public education can lead to implementation problems. Therefore, the planner must consider two aspects in decision making. First is the power of analyzing physical constraints and second is considering nonoperational factors. Not only multiplicity of features and their different values in various strategies can be confusing, but also analyzing them and estimating with previous experience in one country is too puzzler.

When it is not desirable to delegate all decision making process steps to an automated system, a kind of information system called DSS is applied to assist decision making [4]. There are numerous applications of DSS for solving various problems in different industries due to their capacities in: (a) effectively addressing the needs of multiple decision maker [5], (b) adequately modeling the subjectiveness and imprecision of the human decision making process [6], and (c) greatly reducing cognitive demand on the decision makers in the decision making process [7]. If an individual manager is responsible to make the decision, a Personal DSS (PDSS) is used. But when a management team needs to get involved in the process, it is necessary to use a group support system (GSS) [8]. Solving lane management problem requires weighting different management strategies by some experts based on physical characteristics of the way and some other experts based on the individual's behavior. Finally, the planner(s) will choose the most appropriate strategy based on the current characteristics of the roadway and its users and also based on previous experience from knowledge-based. For this purpose, the planner uses the values of current road and users properties as input, and the processor based on experience of previous implementations from knowledge based and weighted strategies based on pre-defined standards by experts helps the planner to make the best decision.

In this study a Naive Bayes Classifier has proposed and used in the processor engine of the GSS. A Naive Bayes classifier is a supervised learning method which considering the class variable, presence (or absence) of different features are not dependent together. This classifier is particularly suited when the dimensionality of the inputs is high. There are theoretical reasons in the literature about implausible efficiency of Naive Bayes classifiers [9] which state that not only they have oversimplified assumptions and naive design, but also in comparison with other classification algorithms such as random forests or boosted trees, Bayes classification surpasses other approaches [10]. The power of Bayesian classifiers caused some researchers use it as the central computation engine in their decision support systems [11–13]. Naive Bayes classifiers are robust to noise data because such noise data are averaged out when estimating the conditional probabilities from all data set. Naive Bayes classifiers are also practical classifiers to handle the irrelevant attributes. Using Bayes Theorem, it can get a good estimate of the probability and do not require a very large training set.

In this study, a Naive Bayes classifier is adopted to identify the most likelihood hypothesis (strategy) when the planner assumes some properties take place. The following chapters are organized in this way. Section 2 addresses the problem precisely and presents the suggestion model and its variables. Section 3 discusses the prototype designed based on Bayesian learning to assist the HOV planner.

2 Numerical Model and Formulation

Suggestion Models provide processing support for a suggested decision in a relatively structured task. So, we first define a model for lane management problem.

In roadway lane management problem, there are 19 objectives available for the user to select and then set the appropriate strategy to enhance them:

1. Increase vehicle-carrying capacity.
2. Increase person-carrying capacity.
3. Increase goods-carrying capacity.
4. Maintain free flow speeds.
5. Maintain or improve the LOS.
6. Reduce travel time.
7. Increase trip reliability.
8. Provide travel alternatives.
9. Reduce peak-period vehicle trips.
10. Improve express bus service.
11. Provide transmodal connectivity and accessibility.
12. Minimize traffic crashes involving large trucks.
13. Improve air quality from mobile sources.
14. Address environmental justice concerns.
15. Encourage transit-oriented development.
16. Fund new transit and managed lanes improvements.
17. Produce enough revenue to cover O/M and enforcement.
18. Produce enough revenue to cover debt services.
19. Provide private investment return on investment.

Obviously, there is correlation between objectives and different managed lane strategies. In summary, Table 1 shows the various objectives (on the right) and how they can relate to the different strategies (on the left). By weighting objectives, the planner is able to determine which strategy fits requirements perfectly. In this study, based on the Tehran requirements, such as increase both vehicle and person-carrying capacity, reduce peak-period vehicle trips and etc. the focus is on HOV lanes. HOV lanes are not tolled for any types of vehicles and just High-occupancy vehicle, bus/BRT, LEV, Taxi/Shuttle, motorcycle and emergency vehicle are allowed to use them [2].

In this article 4 types of strategies are considered for HOV implementation: 1. Two-way HOV barrier separated (BRRHOV2), 2. Reversible HOV barrier separated (BRRHOV1), 3. Two-way HOV buffer separated (BFRHOV2), 4. Two-way concurrent HOV (CHOV). Differences in implementations are described in the following section.

Table 1. Objectives of managed lane strategies

Managed lane strategy	Objectives
Express Toll Lanes Separated lanes with limited access where all vehicles pay a toll	• Increase vehicle-carrying capacity • Reduce travel time • Provide travel alternatives • Fund new transit and managed lanes improvements • Produce enough revenue to cover O/M and enforcement • Produce enough revenue to cover debt service • Provide private investment profit
HOV Lanes Lanes that only allow vehicles that meet or exceed a required number of occupants	• Increase vehicle-carrying capacity • Increase person-carrying capacity • Reduce travel time • Increase trip reliability • Provide travel alternatives • Reduce peak-period vehicle trips • Improve express bus service • Improve air quality from mobile sources • Address environmental justice concerns • Encourage transit-oriented development
Express Lanes Separated lanes with limited access	• Increase vehicle-carrying capacity • Reduce travel time • Provide travel alternatives
Exclusive Transitways Lanes or roadways which are meant to exclusively serve buses	• Increase person-carrying capacity • Reduce travel time • Increase trip reliability • Provide travel alternatives • Reduce peak-period vehicle trips • Improve express bus service • Provide transmodal connectivity and accessibility • Improve air quality from mobile sources • Address environmental justice concerns Encourage transit-oriented development
Exclusive Truck Lanes Dedicated lanes in which only large trucks are permitted	• Increase vehicle-carrying capacity • Increase goods-carrying capacity • Maintain free-flow speed • Reduce travel time • Minimize traffic crashes involving large trucks

(Continued)

Table 1. *(Continued)*

Managed lane strategy	Objectives
Truck Restricted Lanes Lanes of the roadway in which large trucks are restricted	• Maintain free-flow speed • Maintain or improve LOS • Minimize traffic crashes involving large trucks
HOT Lanes HOV lanes that allow vehicles that do not meet the occupancy requirement to use the lanes for a fee or toll.	• Increase vehicle-carrying capacity • Increase person-carrying capacity • Maintain free-flow speed • Reduce travel time • Improve express bus service • Improve air quality from mobile sources • Address environmental justice concerns • Encourage transit-oriented development • Fund new transit and managed lanes improvements • Produce enough revenue to cover O/M and enforcement • Produce enough revenue to cover debt service • Provide private investment profit

2.1   Formulation the HOV Evaluation and Selection Problem

The central concept of HOV lanes is to move more people rather than more cars. So, especial lanes of the way will be dedicated to high-occupant vehicles that carry the determined minimum number of people. The separated HOV facility is physically separated from main lanes or general-purpose lanes of the freeway with either a concrete barrier or a wide painted buffer. The lanes may be either two-way or reversible. Two-way separated HOV lanes usually consist of one lane in each direction, often have limited access, and may have their own direct ingress and egress treatments [2]. A concurrent-flow HOV lane is a freeway lane that flows in the same direction as the rest of traffic and is not physically separated from the main lanes of the freeway. Either a buffer or distinctive paint striping may separate the HOV lane from other traffic lanes.

Regarding to HOV strategy, some physical constraints should be satisfied:

- Current level of service in the highway (CLS),
- The lane length (LL),
- Number of lanes (NL),
- The average number of high-occupant vehicles passing the highway per hour (HVPH),
- The width of the highway (LW),
- The average speed of vehicles passing the highway (speed),
- And the ratio of flow in two-direction of the road (VRate).

As it is demonstrated in Fig. 1, each HOV strategy has some criteria. Based on the level of these criteria satisfaction, the strategy is degreed between well-applicable or not.

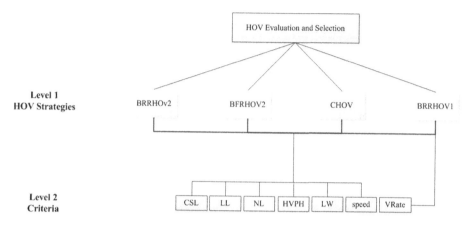

Fig. 1. The model of HOV selection problem

There are numerous articles present numerical calculations for HOV design based on previous experiences in HOV implementation. As an illustration, Figs. 2, 3 show the calculations for designing reversible barrier separated managed lanes regards to the highway width.

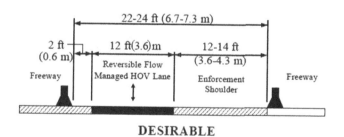

Fig. 2. Desirable measures for BRRHOV1 [3]

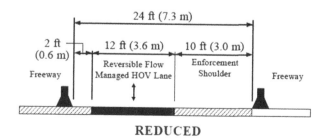

Fig. 3. Reduced measures for BRRHOV1 [3]

Desired measures are calculated generally, in literature. Experts in each country can calibrate them proportional to the physical characteristics of special vehicles and environment. Table 2 shows the minimum specifications of criteria.

Table 2. Desirable specifications for criteria

.	BRRHOV2	BFRHOV2	CHOV	BRRHOV1
CSL	>=D	>=D	>=D	>=D
LL	>=8 km	>=8 km	>=8 km	>=8 km
NL	>=3 lanes each direction	>=3 lanes each direction	>=3 lanes each direction	>=3 lanes each direction
HVPH	>=30	>=30	>=30	>=30
Speed	<=48 km/h	<=48 km/h	<=48 km/h	<=48 km/h
VRate	–	–	–	35–65 %
LW	>=16.2 + 2*3.6* NL	>=16.2 +2*3.6* NL	>=27	>=8.4 + 2*3.6* NL

2.2   Naive Bayes Classifier Formulation

In this section the Naive Bayes principles are described, briefly. The next section outlines how to use this classifier as the GSS processor. Consider a supervised learning problem in which we wish to approximate an unknown target function $f : X \rightarrow Y$, or equivalently $P(Y|X)$. To begin, we will assume Y is a Boolean-valued random variable, and X is a vector containing n Boolean attributes. In other words, $X = <X_1, X_2..., X_n >$, where X_i. is the Boolean random variable denoting the ith attribute of X [14].

Applying Bayes rule, we see that $P(Y = y_i|X)$ can be represented as:

$$P(Y = y_i|X = x_k) = \frac{P(X = x_k|Y = y_i)P(Y = y_i)}{\sum_j P(X = x_k|Y = y_j)P(Y = y_j)}$$

Where y_m denotes the *mth* possible value for Y, x_k denotes the *kth* possible vector value for X, and where the summation in the denominator is over all legal values of the random variable Y.

One way to learn $P(Y|X)$ is to use the training data to estimate $P(X|Y)$ and $P(Y)$. We can then use these estimates, together with Bayes rule above, to determine $P(Y = y_i|X = x_k)$ for any new instance x_k. The expression for the probability that Y will take on its *kth* possible value, according to Bayes rule, is:

$$P(Y = y_k|X_1...X_n) = \frac{P(Y = y_k)P(X_1...X_n|Y = y_k)}{\sum_j P(Y = y_j)P(X_1...X_n|Y = y_j)}$$

Where the sum is taken over all possible values y j of Y. When X contains n attributes which are conditionally independent of one another given Y, we have:

$$P(X_1...X_n|Y) = \prod_{i=1}^{n} P(X_i|Y) \tag{1}$$

Now, assuming the X_i are conditionally independent given Y, we can use Eq. (1) to rewrite this as:

$$P(Y = y_k|X_1...X_n) = \frac{P(Y = y_k) \prod_i P(X_i|Y = y_k)}{\sum_j P(Y = y_j) \prod_i P(X_i|Y = y_j)} \tag{2}$$

Equation (2) is the fundamental equation for the Naive Bayes classifier. Given a new instance $X^{new} = <X_1, X_2..., X_n>$, this equation shows how to calculate the probability that Y will take on any given value, given the observed attribute values of X^{new} and given the distributions P(Y). and $P(X_i|Y)$ estimated from the training data. If we are interested only in the most probable value of Y, then we have the Naive Bayes classification rule:

$$Y \leftarrow argmax_{y_k} \frac{P(Y = y_k) \prod_i P(X_i|Y = y_k)}{\sum_j P(Y = y_j) \prod_i P(X_i|Y = y_j)}$$

Which simplifies to the following (because the denominator does not depend on Y_k).

$$Y \leftarrow argmax_{y_k} P(Y = y_k) \prod_i P(X_i|Y = y_k) \tag{3}$$

2.3 Bayesian Classifier for HOV Selection

When the planner is going to decide which strategy is the most appropriate one, 4 hypotheses are possible to choose (BRRHOV2, BRRHOV1, BFRHOV2, and CHOV). The learning rule in Eq. 3 explains how to choose the most likely hypothesis, having information about previous successful projects properties. If the properties of each project be listed as $<X_1, X_2..., X_n>$ then we are looking for the most likely Y_k, k = 1...4.

Here, the value of n for BRRHOV2, BFRHOV2 and CHOV equals 6 and for BRRHOV1 equals 7. Tables 3, 4, 5, 6, 7, 8, 9, 10, 11, 12 present the values for probabilities $P(Y = y_i|X = x_k)$, for each y_i and x_k. These values as is described in Sect. 3, has set based on some standards from literature. Also, experts in each country can customize them a little, based on special physical environment and individual's behavior.

3 Prototype of GSS for Lane Management

A prototype of GSS for lane management is created in Microsoft Visual Studio with C#. This prototype is composed of three parts: 1-The knowledge-base, 2-The entrance gate for getting the values of current situation of a roadway, 3-The processor engine which is a Naive Bayes Classifier to evaluate the most likelihood answer.

As it is mentioned in Sect. 2, there are four strategies that the planner wants to choose the most likelihood answer among them. Some features got extracted from literature based on standards of HOV design. The most desirable and also reduced measures for HOV features are also available in literature. But, this measurement can get customized based on some variables in each country. The software presents the range of acceptable values and allows experts manipulate them. So, using Eq. 3 in Sect. 2.3, Y_k (four strategies) and $<X_1, X_2 \ldots, X_n>$ are known. From previous experience in implementation, experts set the values of $P(Y = y_i | X = x_k)$. As an illustration, suppose the possible ranges for HOV lane length as it is shown in the first column of Table 4, is less than 2 Km, between 2 to 3, 3 to 4, 4 to 6, 6 to 8 and longer than 8 Km. Then, $P(Y = BRRHOV2 | X = > 8)$. outlines that what percentage of successful HOV projects had HOV lanes longer than 8 Km. These probabilities will be set based on data sets using Eq. 2 in Sect. 2.3.

At the entrance gate, there are 7 inputs for our decision support system (CSS, NL, LL, HVPH, Speed, Vrate and LW) which are entered by the planner to define the current road situation. The properties set is allowed to be equal {v1, v2, v3, v4, v5, ∅, v7}. Note that since our system has been programmed in modular way, the number of inputsnd possible control measures can be extended easily.

The processor engine will load $<X_1, X_2 \ldots, X_n>$ sets for each $Y_k, k = 1, \ldots, 4$. from predefined data base and the planner input then applies Eq. 3 to find the most likelihood strategy. Probabilities are reported to planner as 4 numbers and also are described in detail. As an example, the result might show that the BRRHOV2 implementation is less likely to be successful. The application shows the reason of this decision to the planner. It might happen because of line length or line width or other properties. The application determines which properties did not get fit with experts' comments.

Appendix: Tables

Table 3. CLS probabilities

.	BRRHOV2	BRRHOV1	BFRHOV2	CHOV
F	30	30	30	30
E	30	30	30	30
D	30	30	30	30
C	10	10	10	10
B	1e-08	1e-08	1e-08	1e-08
A	1e-08	1e-08	1e-08	1e-08
Total	100	100	100	100

Table 4. LL probabilities

	BRRHOV2	BRRHOV1	BFRHOV2	CHOV
>8	80	80	70	65
6 << 8	15	15	25	25
4 << 6	5	5	5	10
3 << 4	1e-08	1e-08	1e-08	1e-08
2 << 3	1e-08	1e-08	1e-08	1e-08
<2	1e-08	1e-08	1e-08	1e-08
Total	100	100	100	100

Table 5. NL probabilities

	BRRHOV2	BRRHOV1	BFRHOV2	CHOV
>=5	50	98	95	90
4	27	98	95	90
3	23	90	85	80
2	1e-08	1e-08	1e-08	1e-08
Total	100	100	100	100

Table 6. HVPH probabilities

	BRRHOV2	BRRHOV1	BFRHOV2	CHOV
>60	23	23	23	23
50 << 60	23	23	23	23
40 << 50	22	22	22	22
35 << 40	22	22	22	22
30 < 35	10	10	10	10
<30	1e-08	1e-08	1e-08	1e-08
Total	100	100	100	100

Table 7. Speed probabilities

	BRRHOV2	BRRHOV1	BFRHOV2	CHOV
<30	50	50	50	50
30 << 48	40	40	40	40
48 << 65	10	10	10	10
65 << 80	1e-08	1e-08	1e-08	1e-08
80 << 100	1e-08	1e-08	1e-08	1e-08
100 << 120	1e-08	1e-08	1e-08	1e-08
Total	100	100	100	100

Table 8. Vrate probabilities

.	BRRHOV2	BRRHOV1	BFRHOV2	CHOV
<20->80	–	49	–	–
30–70	–	30	–	–
35–65	–	20	–	–
40–60	–	0.1	–	–
50–50	–	1e-08	–	–
Total	–	100	–	–

Table 9. LW probabilities: BRRHOV2

.	BRRHOV2
>=x + 16.2	35
x + 14 << x + 16.2	30
x + 11.5 << x + 14	25
x + 10.3 << x + 11.5	10
<x + 10.3	1e-08
Total	100

Table 10. LW probabilities: BRRHOV1

.	BRRHOV1
>=8.5 +x	40
8 + x$\ll$ 8.5 + x	35
7 + x$\ll$ 8.5 + x	25
<7 + x	1e-08
Total	100

Table 11. LW probabilities: BFRHOV2

.	BFRHOV2
>16.2	15
12.6 + x$\ll$ 16.2	40
10.2 + x$\ll$ 12.6 + x	45
<10.2 + x	1e-08
Total	100

Table 12. LW probabilities: CHOV

.	CHOV
>=27	80
22 << 27	20
<22	1e-08
Total	100

References

1. Louis G. Neudorff, P.E., Jeffrey E. Randall, P.E., Robert Reiss, P.E., Robert Gordon, P.E.: Freeway management and operations handbook. Office of Transportation Management Federal Highway Administration (2003)
2. Parsons Brinckerhoff Quade, Douglas, Inc., Rim Resources, Inc.: Report 414: HOV Systems Manual Texas Transportation Institute, Transportation Research Board, National Research Council, Washington, D.C. (1998)
3. Kuhn, B., et al.: Managed Lanes Handbook, Texas Transportation Institute, the Texas A&M University System College Station, Texas (2005)
4. Wibowo, S., Deng, H.: Intelligent decision support for effectively evaluating and selecting ships under uncertainty in marine transportation. Expert Syst. Appl. **39**, 6911–6920 (2012)
5. Yeh, C.H., Deng, H., Wibowo, S.: Multicriteria group decision for information systems project selection under uncertainty. Int. J. Fuzzy Syst. **12**, 170–179 (2010)

6. Zimmermann, H.J.: An application-oriented view of modeling uncertainty. Eur. J. Oper. Res. **122**, 190–198 (2000)
7. Wibowo, S., Deng, H.: A consensus support system for supplier selection in group decision making. J. Manage. Sci. Stat. Decis. **6**, 52–59 (2008)
8. Arnott, D., Pervan, G.: A critical analysis of Decision Support Systems research. J. Inf. Technol. **20**(2), 67–87 (2005)
9. Zhang, H.: The optimality of Naive bayes. In: Barr,V., Markov, Z. (eds.) Proceedings of the Seventeenth International Florida Artificial Intelligence Research Society Conference. AAAI Press, Miami Beach (2004)
10. Caruana, R., Niculescu-Mizil, A.: An empirical comparison of Supervised learning algorithms. In: Proceedings of ICML (2006)
11. Schurink, C.A., Visscher, S., Lucas, P.J., van Leeuwen, H.J., Buskens, E., Hoff, R.G., Hoepelman, A.I., Bonten, M.J.: A bayesian decision-support system for diagnosing ventilator-associated pneumonia. Intensive Care Med. **33**, 1379–1386 (2007)
12. Mortera, J., Vicard, P., Vergari, C.: Object-oriented Bayesian networks for a decision support system for antitrust enforcement. Ann. Appl. Stat. **7**, 714–738 (2013)
13. HelaLtifi, G., Ayed, M.B., Alimi, Adel M.: Dynamic decision support system based on bayesian networks application to fight against the nosocomial infections. Int. J. Adv. Res. Artif. Intell. (IJARAI) **1**(1), 22–29 (2012)
14. Mitchell, T.: Machine Learning. McGraw Hill, New York (1997). New added Chapters

A Novel Extracellular Spike Detection Approach for Noisy Neuronal Data

Hamed Azami[1(✉)], Morteza Saraf[2], Karim Mohammadi[3],
and Saeid Sanei[4]

[1] Department of Electrical Engineering,
Iran University of Science and Technology, Tehran, Iran
hamed_azami@ieee.org
[2] Institute for Research in Fundamental Sciences (IPM), Tehran, Iran
msaraf@ipm.ir
[3] Faculty of Electrical Engineering,
Iran University of Science and Technology, Tehran, Iran
mohammadi@iust.ac.ir
[4] Faculty of Engineering and Physical Sciences,
University of Surrey, Guildford, UK
s.sanei@surrey.ac.uk

Abstract. Neural action potential, named spike, plays an important role in comprehending the central nervous systems. Neuronal spike detection is a technical challenge due to the effect of strong noise and nonstationarity. There are two main problems for almost all conventional spike detection approaches. First, a filtering approach is often followed for pre-processing the data. Selection of the filter parameters is a time-consuming task. To overcome this problem we suggest utilizing empirical mode decomposition (EMD) and a filter whose parameters are selected automatically. The second problem is that the spike detection method is signal dependent and the performance changes considerably when the data changes. To tackle this problem, a novel approach which utilizes the data distribution is proposed. This method exploits the fuzzy set theory to combine a number of spike detectors to achieve a higher performance. The results demonstrate the superiority of the proposed method.

Keywords: Noisy neuronal data · Extracellular spike detection · Empirical mode decomposition · Singular value decomposition · Genetic algorithm

1 Introduction

Extracellular recordings of neural activity provide a noisy measurement of action potentials produced by a number of neurons adjacent to the recording electrode. Characterization of the neural action potentials (also known as nerve impulses or spikes) play an important role in understanding the central nervous system [1, 2]. Extracting useful information from these measurements depends on the ability to correctly detect the spikes from the measurements [3]. The environment and measurement noises in one hand and contribution of more than one neuron to each of the recorded spike signal on the other hand are two main problems in spike detection [4, 5].

© Springer International Publishing Switzerland 2014
A. Movaghar et al. (Eds.): AISP 2013, CCIS 427, pp. 332–343, 2014.
DOI: 10.1007/978-3-319-10849-0_33

There are three main approaches to detect spikes in neural data. The first type includes algorithms that can be implemented in hardware. Amplitude threshold detection is the simplest one of this category. When the signal amplitude exceeds a user-defined threshold, a spike can be discovered. However, this method has a major drawback: its performance is sensitive to the threshold, it is not capable to distinguish between spikes with different morphologies and similar amplitudes, and its performance degrades rapidly when there are many resource noises [6, 7].

Mtetwa and Smith proposed five spike detection techniques and three thresholding criteria for spike detection [3]. The best method between these methods is based on normalized cumulative energy difference (NCED). This method inspired by the fact that the energy in a spike should be greater than that in noise of the same length.

In [8] three methods based on the fractal dimension, smoothed nonlinear energy operator (SNEO), and standard deviation to detect the spikes of noisy neuronal data were proposed. To reduce the effect of noises, two pre-processing steps by using discrete wavelet transform (DWT) and Savitzky-Golay filter were employed [8].

There are 2 main drawbacks in the majority of conventional spike detection approaches: (1) Usually, choosing appropriate parameters for each noise reduction method is a time-consuming task, and (2) Generally, each spike detection approach is only suitable for a limited number of signal types and applications.

To overcome the first problem, we propose an adaptive approach to set appropriate filter parameters automatically by genetic algorithm (GA). Also, we suggest using empirical mode decomposition (EMD) method that there is not any parameter to set. EMD is a powerful and new method applied to decompose the data into a number of intrinsic mode functions (IMFs) and a residual signal from a complex time series [9]. Since each IMF has almost a specific frequency with mean value of zero, it can be considered as a noise signal originated from a special and unknown source. Thus, the residual signal is a filtered version of the original signal combined with a number of noise sources. In this paper, to achieve a much better performance compared with that can be achieved by the conventional neuronal data spike detection methods, we propose an approach based on the probability and fuzzy concepts.

The next section explains the proposed method. The performance evaluation of the proposed method and the conclusions are provided in Sects. 3 and 4 respectively.

2 Proposed Methods

First, in order to reduce the noise effect and increase the performance of the proposed method, EMD and intelligent singular spectrum analysis (SSA) are employed. In comparison with other conventional filters, the parameters of the proposed filters don't need to be adjusted.

As mentioned before, EMD decomposes the signals into their IMFs. This decomposition, so called sifting process, uses the mean of the upper and lower envelopes. The sifting process must be repeated until every component satisfies two conditions:

1. The number of extrema and the number of zero-crossings must either be equal or differ at most by one
2. At any point, the mean value of the two envelopes defined respectively by local maxima and local minima must be zero.

For an arbitrary time series $x(t)$, the sifting process can be summarized as follows:

1. Identify all the local extrema (maxima or minima) of signal $x(t)$, and then connect all the local maxima by a cubic spline line (upper envelope)
2. Repeat similarly for all the local minima (lower envelope).
3. The mean of the upper and lower envelopes is designated as $m(t)$. The difference between the data and $m(t)$ is the first component as follows:

$$h_1(t) = x(t) - m(t) \tag{1}$$

4. Consider $h_1(t)$ as the new original signal and repeat the above steps [9, 10].

Generally, this process must be repeated until the last $h_1(t)$ has at most one extrema or becomes constant. However, in many cases, it is not a suitable criterion. In this paper we use the criterion applied in [10].

SSA is a flexible and powerful tool used in many applications in which short and long, one-dimensional and multi-dimensional, stationary and non-stationary, almost deterministic and noisy time series are to be analyzed [11]. Moreover, the subspace selection and reconstruction process by SSA is much faster than many existing filters such as those based on DWT and has been used for spike detection recently [12]. However, this process, like almost all the filters, has an important short-coming, i.e. there are some parameters to be adjusted using a large number of trials. Sometimes we know the range or average of the signal-to-noise ratio (SNR). In this case, we propose a new method based on the GA. GA is a powerful search algorithm to find the approximate solutions in the defined space. The GA has many benefits, for example, its concept is easy to understand, it supports multi-objective optimization, it is good for noisy environments, and so on [13].

Assume a Gaussian noise with SNR = 2 dB is added to $x_1 = 5\sin(3\pi t)$. There are many ways for choosing the two parameters of SSA, i.e. window length (i.e. embedding dimension) l and m disjoint subsets $I = [I_1, \ldots, I_m]$ to reconstruct the time series. The filtering process for a particular signal is sensitive to selection of these parameters. When l and I are selected too large, some important information of the original signal is removed by this filter. For too small I and l, however, this filter cannot attenuate destructive noises sufficiently. Moreover, in many applications due to lack of information about a signal, selecting these parameters are very difficult. To overcome this problem, in this study, we propose to use the GA with the following fitness function:

$$H = \left| SNR - \overline{SNR} \right| = \left| 10. \log_{10}\left(\sum_{i=1}^{n} (x_f(i)^2 / \sum_{i=1}^{n} (x(i) - x_f(i))^2 \right) - \overline{SNR} \right| \tag{2}$$

where n, x, x_f, and $\overline{SNR}$ are length of the signal, noisy signal, filtered signal, and SNR average of a signal, respectively. $x - x_f$ is the noise. In other words, the GA tries to reduce H by changing l and I for the SSA. It should be mentioned that we use the proposed improved filter where the SNR average or at least the range of noise power is known. The GA employed here has 20 populations and the number of iterations is 30.

The results for three different sets of l and I are shown in Fig. 1. As can be seen in Fig. 1a, $l = 6$ and $I = [1]$ are not large enough for filtering the signal with an SNR = 2 dB. In Fig. 1b, $l = 30$ and $I = [1]$, where $[k]$ states that only k eigentriples are used, and in Fig. 1c $l = 30$ and $I = [2]$ are chosen. It is evident that in both figures the amplitudes decrease considerably for an original signal with amplitude 5. Figures 1b and c demonstrate irregularities in the first and the last time samples. Here, GA is used to select suitable sets of filter parameters primarily for SNR = 2 dB. The result of employing the proposed filter is shown in Fig. 2c.

After filtering the signal, two similar windows scroll along the signal. For each window, the standard deviation, FD with the katz's algorithm are computed. H and G functions for respectively standard deviation and FD are used to detect the signal spikes as follows:

$$H_a = |std_{a+1} - std_a|, \quad a = 1, 2, \ldots, m - 1 \tag{3}$$

$$G_a = |FD_{a+1} - FD_a|, \quad a = 1, 2, \ldots, m - 1 \tag{4}$$

where a and m are the number of analyzed window and the total number of analyzed windows, respectively. std_a and FD_a denote respectively the standard deviation and fractal dimension of a part of the signal which falls within the ath analyzed window.

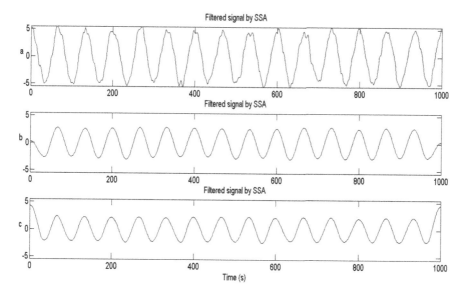

Fig. 1. Results of applying three different sets of l and I for the SSA; (a) $l = 6$ and $I = [1]$, (b) $l = 30$ and $I = [1]$, and (c) $l = 30$ and $I = [2]$.

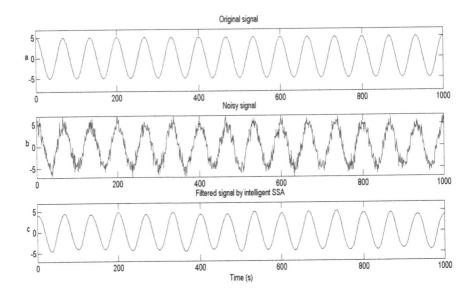

Fig. 2. Improved SSA by GA; (a) original signal, (b) noisy signal (SNR = 2 dB), and (c) optimal filtered signal.

If the local maximum is larger than the threshold, the mean value of H_a or G_a, the current time is selected as a spike of the signal. Also, the SNEO that is a powerful tool for spike detection is defined comprehensively in [8, 12].

As mentioned before, there are some suggested spike detection methods in the literature each with some advantages and disadvantages [1–8]. For example, as can be seen in Table 1, the standard deviation-based methods are the best ones when SNR is large and in case SNR is lower than 0 the method is unreliable. FD methods have different definitions to choose the threshold. The SNEO approaches are sensitive to noise as reported in [14].

In this paper we propose a technique to combine some of them based on the fuzzy and probability concepts to increase the accuracy of spike detections. For each sample, we consider:

$$HC = \frac{\lambda_1.SDA_1 + \lambda_2 SDA_2 + \ldots + \lambda_n SDA_n}{SDA_1 + SDA_2 + \ldots + SDA_n} \tag{5}$$

where if the spike of the ith spike detection method is detected $\lambda_i = 1$ else $\lambda_i = 0$. n is the number of considered spike detection methods and SDA_i is spike detection accuracy of ith considered method by using semi-real data. In fact, this technique is originated from the concept of existence or absence probability of a sample as a spike. Thus, if this probability is more than 0.5 we assume this signal sample is indeed a spike and vice versa. As it is clear, for semi-real data if SDA_m is larger than SDA_n, mth method is more reliable and trustworthy than nth method, so we show this effect on Eq. (5). Two different parameters, namely, the true positive (TP) and false positive (FP) ratios were used to evaluate the performance of the proposed and conventional methods. These parameters are defined as $TP = \left(N_t/N \right)$, and $FP = \left(N_f/N \right)$; where N_t, and N_f represent the number of true, and falsely detected spikes and N shows the actual number of spikes. It should be mentioned, since the false negative (*FN*) parameter used to assess the spike detection methods is dependent on *TP* (*TP* = 1-*FN*), in this paper we only consider TP and FP parameters. Considering FP is based on the inability detections, we define $SDA = \left(\frac{TP+(1-FP)}{2} \right)$.

As an example, we consider a part of a real signal of the CARMEN project managed by Prof. Leslie S. Smith. This part of the signal is shown in Fig. 3a. There are more or less probabilities for nine lines. There are some spike detection approaches for semi-real neuronal data in [8, 3]; in this paper we combine five of these methods to assess the real neuronal signal. Based on the *SDAs* of those methods provided in Table [1] and the real signal has about SNR equals to 0 dB we have:

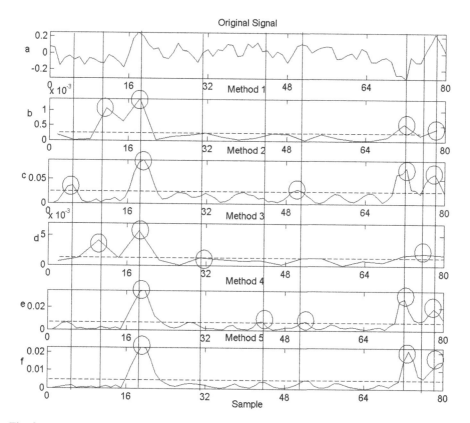

Fig. 3. The proposed method for combination four existing methods; (a) original signal, (b) FD with DWT, (c) FD with Savitzky-Golay, (d) SNEO with DWT, (e) standard deviation with DWT, and (f) SNEO with Savitzky-Golay filter.

$$SDA_1 = \left(\frac{0.98 + (1 - 0.18)}{2}\right) = 0.9, \ SDA_2 = \left(\frac{0.98 + (1 - 0.44)}{2}\right) = 0.87,$$

$$SDA_3 = \left(\frac{0.96 + (1 - 0.3)}{2}\right) = 0.83, \ SDA_4 = \left(\frac{1 + (1 - 0.22)}{2}\right) = 0.89,$$

$$\text{and } SDA_5 = \left(\frac{0.96 + (1 - 0.24)}{2}\right) = 0.86.$$

For the first line we have $HC(1) = \frac{0*0.9 + 1*0.87 + 0*0.83 + 0*0.89 + 0*0.86}{0.9 + 0.87 + 0.83 + 0.89 + 0.86} < 0.5$; thus, the sample of the first line cannot be considered as a spike. Considering $HC(2)$, $HC(4)$, $HC(5)$, $HC(6)$, or $HC(8)$ is less than 0.5, 2nd, 4th, 5th, 6th, or 8th lines are not a spike. Also, since $HC(3)$, $HC(7)$, or $HC(9) \geq 0.5$, 3rd, 7th, or 9th lines can be considered as spikes.

3 Data Simulation and Results

Because of the lack of ground truth data (i.e., spike timings for each neuron) spike detection methods are often difficult to evaluate. In [15] generation and transmission of intracellular signals from neurons to an extracellular electrode were modeled and a set of MATLAB functions based on this analysis provided. The codes were used here to generate a set of close-to-real synthetic data. They produce realistic signals from a set of nearby neurons including interference from more distant neurons and Gaussian noise. These data best resemble the output of deep mesio-temporal brain discharges observed at cortical electrodes. By following this synthesizing method, We have randomly generated 70 semi-real neuronal data each including Gaussian noise with SNR = −5, 0, 5, 10, 20 and 50 dBs. For each SNR level, each data contains 12 to 14 spikes. Therefore, we have about 70*6*13 = 5460 spikes to test. One of 70 signals that contains 13 spikes with SNR = 5 dB is randomly selected as the test signal.

In this paper we propose to employ EMD to reduce the noise. As stated before, the residual signal obtained by EMD can be considered as a filtered version of the signal extracted from an original signal combined with some noise sources with mean values of zero. In Fig. 4, we can see the result of decomposition performed by EMD of the filtered test signal. This figure illustrates that the first mode has a higher frequency than the second mode where modes are ordered from highest to lowest frequencies. Figures 5d, 6c, and 7c respectively show the outcomes of using EMD with FD, SNEO, and standard deviation for the test signal. As can be seen, all spikes can be detected by these methods and EMD as a pre-processing step. As mentioned before, the very important advantage of employing EMD is that unlike usual filters, the EMD parameters do not need to be adjusted.

Figures 8b, c, and d respectively show the outcomes of using SNEO with SSA, standard deviation based method with SSA, and FD with SSA for the test signal. It can be seen that all thirteen spikes can be accurately detected. It is worth mentioning that SSA was presented in [12], but in this paper an intelligent SSA by using GA is

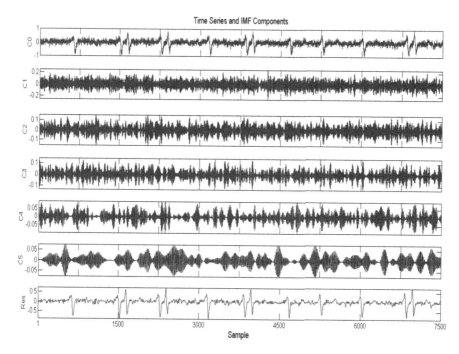

Fig. 4. Components of the restored semi-real signal by EMD. The first time series is the filtered signal. The decomposition yields 5 IMF and a residual. The IMFs are the time-frequency constituents or components of the semi-real neuronal signal.

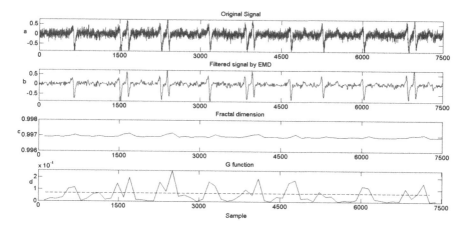

Fig. 5. Spike detection in test signal using FD and EMD; (a) original signal, (b) filtered signal by EMD, (c) output of FD, and (d) G function result.

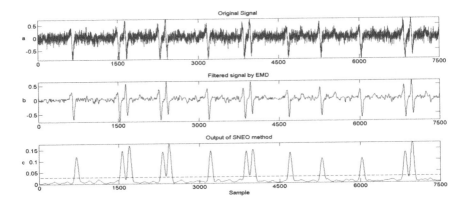

Fig. 6. Spike detection in test signal using the SNEO and EMD; (a) original signal, (b) filtered signal by EMD, and (c) output of SNEO method.

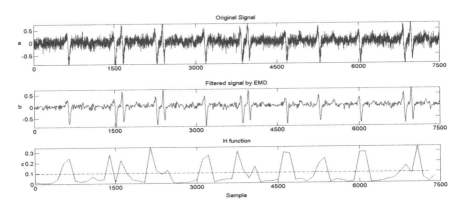

Fig. 7. Spike detection in test signal using standard deviation and EMD; (a) original signal, (b) decomposed signal after applying EMD, and (c) H function result.

proposed to automatically adjust the SSA parameters and ensure correct selection of the subspace of spikes.

In Table 1, the results of spike detection for the semi-real data are shown. As we can see in Table 1, when SNRs > 0, EMD performs best in terms of all the parameters. In addition, when SNRs < 0, SNEO with SSA is the best algorithm in terms of TPs among all the proposed methods. The intelligent SSA has better performance between all mentioned pre-processing algorithms among FD-based methods except EMD. Also, unless standard deviation-based methods, the performance of the intelligent SSA is better than DWT and Savitzky-Golay filter. The main difference between the basic SSA [12] and the intelligent one is their computational costs for adjusting the parameters and the intelligent SSA is much faster in adjusting them.

In Table 2, you can find the comparison between the spike detection rates for two best proposed methods, combination approach and NCED for a part of the real

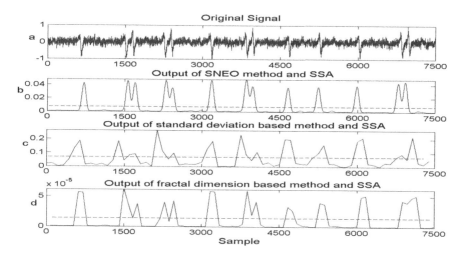

Fig. 8. Spike detection in test signal; (a) original signal, (b) output of SNEO method and SSA, (c) output of standard deviation based method and SSA and (d) output of fractal dimension based method and SSA. It can be seen that all thirteen spikes can be accurately detected.

neuronal data. The data is 900 seconds long and sampled at 20,000 samples/sec taken from the CARMEN database. From the table, except the combination approach by Eq. (5), the best methods in terms of TP and FP are improved SNEO by intelligent SSA and spike detection using FD and intelligent SSA, respectively. These methods are superior to NCED as the best method among various approaches suggested in [3].

Table 1. Results of these suggested and improved approaches on the semi-real neuronal data compared with corresponding conventional methods.

Method	Parameters	-5 dB	0 dB	5 dB	10 dB	20 dB	50 dB
Improved SNEO by DWT [8]	TP	96 %	**96 %**	100 %	100 %	100 %	100 %
	FP	48 %	**30 %**	0 %	0 %	0 %	0 %
Improved SNEO by Savitzky-Golay filter [8]	TP	96 %	**96 %**	100 %	100 %	100 %	100 %
	FP	53 %	**24 %**	2 %	0 %	0 %	0 %
Improved SNEO by intelligent SSA	TP	100 %	**100 %**	100 %	100 %	100 %	100 %
	FP	27 %	**8 %**	2 %	0 %	0 %	0 %
Improved SNEO by EMD	TP	79 %	**91 %**	100 %	100 %	100 %	100 %
	FP	81 %	**39 %**	0 %	0 %	0 %	0 %
Spike detection using FD and DWT [8]	TP	96 %	**98 %**	100 %	100 %	100 %	100 %
	FP	46 %	**18 %**	2 %	0 %	0 %	0 %
Spike detection using FD and Savitzky-Golay [8]	TP	96 %	**98 %**	100 %	100 %	100 %	100 %
	FP	68 %	**44 %**	39 %	25 %	32 %	25 %

(Continued)

Table 1. *(Continued)*

Method	Parameters	-5 dB	0 dB	5 dB	10 dB	20 dB	50 dB
Spike detection using FD and EMD	TP	82 %	**89 %**	100 %	100 %	100 %	100 %
	FP	86 %	**55 %**	12 %	10 %	3 %	2 %
Spike detection using standard deviation and DWT [8]	TP	100 %	**100 %**	100 %	100 %	100 %	100 %
	FP	43 %	**22 %**	10 %	14 %	17 %	11 %
Spike detection using standard deviation and Savitzky-Golay filter [8]	TP	98 %	**96 %**	100 %	100 %	100 %	100 %
	FP	68 %	**24 %**	30 %	14 %	19 %	18 %
Spike detection using standard deviation and intelligent SSA	TP	98 %	**100 %**	100 %	100 %	100 %	100 %
	FP	51 %	**22 %**	18 %	10 %	16 %	10 %
Spike detection using standard deviation and EMD	TP	80 %	**89 %**	100 %	100 %	100 %	100 %
	FP	82 %	**46 %**	18 %	14 %	13 %	8 %

Table 2. Comparison of spike detection rates for two best proposed methods, combination of them, and NCED method as one of the best spike detection mehod tesed in real neuronal data.

Parameter	The proposed combination method	Proposed improved SNEO by intelligent SSA	Spike detection using FD and intelligent SSA	NCED [3] method
TP	97 %	94 %	91 %	89 %
FP	8 %	17 %	12 %	21 %

4   Conclusions

The aim of this work is to investigate and demonstrate the ability of the intelligent SSA, EMD, and a hybrid of the existence methods in detecting the noisy neuronal data. Since conventional noise reduction algorithms such as SSA and Kalman filter have several parameters that must be adjusted by many trials, in this paper we have proposed the intelligent SSA and the residual signal obtained by EMD. It is worthy to mention that providing an intelligent method to reduce the effect of the noise resources based on the SSA and GA can be used in many noise reduction applications. Then, to increase the performance of the existing approaches, we have suggested a novel and powerful technique based on combination of the conventional spike detection methods. The results indicate superiority of the proposed method comparing with three well-known methods.

References

1. Nenadic, Z., Burdick, J.W.: Spike detection using the continuous wavelet transform. IEEE Tran. BioMed. Eng. **52**(1), 74–87 (2005)
2. Yuan, Y., Yang, C., Si, J.: An advanced spike detection and sorting system. In: International Joint Conference on Neural Networks, pp. 3477–3484 (2009)
3. Mtetwa, N., Smith, L.S.: Smoothing and thresholding in neuronal spike detection. Neurocomputing **69**(10–12), 1366–1370 (2006)
4. Yuan, Y., Yang, C., Si, J.: An advanced spike detection and sorting system. In: International Joint Conference on Neural Network, pp. 3477–3484 (2009)
5. Liu, X., Yang, X., Zheng, N.: Automatic extracellular spike detection with piecewise optimal. Neurocomputing **79**, 132–139 (2012)
6. Kim, S., Mcnames, J.: Automatic spike detection based on adaptive template matching for extracellular neural recordings. Neurosci. Methods **165**(2), 165–174 (2007)
7. Shahid, S., Walker, J., Smith, L.S.: A new spike detection algorithm for extracellular neural recordings. IEEE Trans. Biomed. Eng. **57**(4), 853–866 (2010)
8. Azami, H., Sanei, S.: Three novel spike detection approaches for noisy neuronal data. 2nd International eConference on Computer and Knowledge Engineering, pp. 44–49. IEEE Xplore (2012)
9. Xiaoming, N., Jian, Z., Xingwu, L.: Application of Hilbert-Huang transform to laser doppler velocimeter. Opt. Las. Tech. **44**(7), 2197–2201 (2012)
10. Battista, B.M., Knapp, C., McGee, T., Goebel, V.: Application of the empirical mode decomposition and Hilbert-Huang transform to seismic reflection data. Geophysics **72**(2), H29–H37 (2007)
11. Sanei, S., Lee, T.K.M., Abolghasemi, V.: A new adaptive line enhancer based on singular spectrum analysis. IEEE Trans. Bio. Eng. **59**(2), 428–434 (2012)
12. Azarbad, M., Azami, H., Sanei, S.: Spike detection approaches for noisy neuronal data using singular spectrum analysis. In: Iranian Conference on Electrical Engineering (2013)
13. Azami, H., Sanei, S., Mohammadi, K., Hassanpour, H.: A hybrid evolutionary approach to segmentation of non-stationary signals. Digit. Signal Proc. **23**(4), 1103–1114 (2013)
14. Calvagno, G., Ermani, M., Rinaldo, R., Sartoretto, F.: A multiresolution approach to spike detection in EEG. In: IEEE International Conference on Acoustic, Speech and Signal Processing, pp. 3582–3585 (2000)
15. Smith, L.S., Mtetwa, N.: A tool for synthesizing spike trains with realistic interference. Neurosci. Methods **159**(1), 170–180 (2007)

Author Index